GENDER AND NATIONALISM
IN COLONIAL CUBA

ADRIANA
MÉNDEZ
RODENAS

*G*ENDER AND *N*ATIONALISM IN COLONIAL CUBA

The Travels of
Santa Cruz y Montalvo,
Condesa de Merlin

VANDERBILT UNIVERSITY PRESS
NASHVILLE & LONDON

First edition 1998
98 99 00 01 02   5 4 3 2 1

This publication is made from recycled paper and meets the minimum requirements of
American National Standard for Information Sciences—Permanence of Paper for Printed
Library Materials ∞

Library of Congress Cataloging-in-Publication Data

   Mendez Rodenas, Adriana.
     Gender and nationalism in colonial Cuba : the travels of Santa
   Cruz y Montalvo, condesa de Merlin / by Adriana Mendez Rodenas. --
   1st ed.
         p. cm.
     Includes bibliographical references and index.
     ISBN 0-8265-1299-2 (alk. paper)
     1. Merlin, Maria de las Mercedes Santa Cruz y Montalvo, comtesse
   de, 1789-1852. Havane. 2. Havana (Cuba)--Description and travel.
   3. Cuba--Description and travel. 4. Cuba--History--1810-1899.
   5. Feminist criticism. I. Title.
   F1799.H3M4736 1997
   972.91'05--dc21   97-21193
                                                                 CIP

Manufactured in the United States of America

Para Juliana

CONTENTS

List of

Illustrations

PREFACE

This book could not have been written without the generous assistance of the University of Iowa Faculty Scholar Award, which gave me the necessary leave time to write this book and also supported a research trip to Havana during the fateful summer of 1989. The Faculty Scholar Award permitted a scholarly transition from the twentieth to the nineteenth century, which was not merely of an intellectual nature but implied a return to a mythical past akin to a Carpentierian "Journey Back to the Source." I am grateful to my friend Enrico Mario Santí, whose invitation to participate in Cornell University's 1985 Humanities Symposium "The Emergence of Cuban National Identity" stimulated the search for Mercedes Santa Cruz's "lost steps" in numerous archives and in our twin cities of Havana and Miami. My own "discovery" started during one of the numerous trips I took to Havana in the late 1970s, when I stumbled upon a copy of Salvador Bueno's edition of *Viaje a la Habana* in a Vedado district bookstore.

During my brief stay in Cuba in June 1989, I immersed myself in the fabulous Colección Cubana of the Biblioteca Nacional José Martí, a veritable treasury of documents, images, and collective memory from a remote past that the library staff helped bring to life for me. I owe a great debt of gratitude to Araceli García Carranza, head bibliographer, who was always ready to locate an arcane newspaper or manuscript source for me, and whose wide knowledge of Cuban literature and history helped me find the right document in the right place. The rest of the staff of the Colección Cubana stand out in my mind for their unfailing assistance and good humor; to Josefina García Carranza, Nancy Machado, Martica García Hernández, Obdulia Castillo, and Nilda Porto, my heartfelt thanks and deep appreciation for their essential Cubanness and female solidarity. They maintained a lively spark in the midst of scarcity, food shortages, and an oppressive political climate. Thanks are due also to Tomás Robaina and Zoila Lapique of the Biblioteca Nacional, who helped in my inquiries.

As my summer in Havana drew to a close, I consulted the library at the Instituto de Lingüística y Literatura of the Academia de Ciencias. I am indebted to my dear friend Yolanda Vidal Felipe for helping me locate sources from other nineteenth-century periodical publications, and for generously sending these articles to me. It was Nara Araújo, *mi otra yo* in terms of our similar intellectual pursuits, who first suggested that I probably had enough material to write an entire book on Merlin. Salvador Bueno, whom I visited in his Miramar home, eagerly shared with me his broad erudition on nineteenth-century Cuban literary culture over a cup of espresso. I acknowledge my debt to both of these important critics, who helped pave my way into the labyrinth of Merlin's life and works and of Creole culture in general.

My summer in Havana was memorable not only for academic reasons, but for political ones as well. While in the morning I exhausted the riches of the Colección Cubana, during the evening I stayed close to the television watching the Ochoa trials. It was then that I understood Merlin's travelogues in a different light, for they helped me realize that Cuba had reverted to a neocolonial condition, with a new Captain-General absorbing all powers and energies, much in the same way that la Comtesse described the institution of the Captain-Generalcy in the nineteenth century. My lifelong friends José Lorenzo Fuentes and Lida Rodríguez accompanied me during that fateful summer.

Roberto Fernández Retamar, head of Casa de las Américas, was influential in helping me obtain the visa that allowed me entry into Havana in June 1989. Esther Pérez and the entire staff of the Departamento Internacional of Casa de las Américas took care of many amenities during my stay in Havana, from safeguarding my laptop computer to making sure I had medical coverage during my pregnancy. I am most grateful to the generosity they showed me during my stay in Havana.

I spent part of the winter of 1992 in Miami to consult the Archives and Special Collections at the University of Miami's Otto E. Richter Library, a trip that was also funded by the University of Iowa Faculty Scholar award. Esperanza Varona located for me important archival sources pertaining to the slavery debate and gave me access to a series of uncatalogued prints. I am most grateful to her for providing the beautiful illustrations of colonial Havana that accompany this book. Gladys Ramos helped me find a number of antislavery pamphlets housed in the University of Miami archives. Special thanks are due to Jorge Yviricu for providing a photograph of Merlin's portrait from his own private collection. My friend Blanca Bastanzuri and her family provided much warmth and support while I consulted Harvard University Library.

This book has gone through various stages, and I want to thank the many people who have helped me along the way. In its later stages, I am grateful for the unflinching support provided for this project from Raúl Curto, an Argentine mathematician who chaired the Department of Spanish and Portuguese in recent years. Professor Curto supported my request for funds from the Graduate College to edit the manuscript, and also provided funds to translate the original French and Spanish quotes into English. I am grateful to Rosalva Bermúdez Bellón for her fine translation of these quotes and for her patient support of the entire project. My colleague Charles Hale read individual chapters and provided a valuable historian's insight, while both William Luis and Antonio Benítez Rojo contributed much to the chapter on slavery.

To my friend Lois Parkinson Zamora, I owe the luck and inspiration of finding an editor who helped me render the *vericuetos* of style into readable English prose. My great thanks go to Polly Koch, who did a masterful job of editing the the full manuscript and who quickly grasped not only what the book was about but also its broader ramifications. María Fitch of the University of Iowa Undergraduate Scholars Program did a superb job of polishing the manuscript. Jennifer Tanner, my research assistant during Fall 1995, helped locate sources and bring the manuscript into final form; at an earlier stage, Dean Makulini helped me compile the bibliography. I have benefited greatly from my stint as a scholar-in-residence at the University of Iowa's Obermann Center for Advanced Studies, where I wrote and rewrote many of the chapters and where I finally brought this book to light. This task was aided by the kind assistance of Lorna Olson and the Center's Director, Jay Semel, who protected the scholar's solitude at the same time that they provided vital collegial support. I am most grateful to Enrico Mario Santí, who was instrumental in bringing the book to publication, and to my readers—Antonio Benítez Rojo and Roberto Ignacio Díaz—for their insightful comments and suggestions. Finally, I wish to thank the director and staff of Vanderbilt University Press for their enthusiastic support, including Bard Young, the editor, for the care given the final edition, especially his attention to the book's multilingual format and to the original spellings and punctuation of my sources, and Polly Law, the marketing manager, for her untiring effort to place this book before the interested public. Thanks also go to Gregory McNamee, who did the copyediting, and to Mary Jane Frisby, who did the index.

May this book contribute, then, not only to the life and works of our exemplary ancestor, but also to the complex issues of Cuban identity and the exile experience for which La Condesa de Merlin serves as an emblem across the generations and the barrier of time. My choice of English as the language for this critical venture only reflects the labyrinth of solitude through which Mercedes, too, attempted to find her way. This book is warmly and lovingly dedicated to my daughter Juliana, who came into this world as it was being forged and who has illuminated these pages with her smile. Juliana's bright presence is, for me, the best proof that culture is carried in the genes; after all we have endured, we have not merely survived, but have indeed transcended.

GENDER AND NATIONALISM
IN COLONIAL CUBA

FROM THE MARGINS OF HISTORY

Gender and Nationalism in Spanish American Literature

Until very recently, the silencing of women has been dominant in the empirical, positivistic literary history that has traced the contours of Latin American culture. Particularly in the nineteenth century, women's contributions to the emerging discourse of national identity have all but been ignored. Latin American literary history attests to the fact that, as Joan Scott says, "women's history does not have a long-standing and definable historiographic tradition within which interpretations can be debated and revised."[1] Feminist scholars in the Latin American tradition have an urgent critical task to perform: to reappraise women writers relegated to the margins of history, to rediscover a lost literary tradition, to trace a lost matrix in time.[2] Here I use the word *matrix* first as a powerful metaphor to signify the legacy of women's writing, often unknown, often derided, that has to be dug up, virtually unearthed, from the predominantly male literary history of Latin America.[3] The term also connotes an alternative symbolic order, or order of significant relations, based not on the phallus but rather on the continuity of a female lineage, operative both at the psychoanalytical level, primarily in terms of the mother/daughter bond, and also at the cultural domain, as a particular kind of textuality.

3

For the most part, women have figured in the foundational discourse of Latin American identity and nationality primarily as a symbol. The nineteenth-century literary imagination established a poetic correspondence between nation and womanhood, so that the emerging sense of national cohesion was figured largely through a female protagonist, who came to embody the core values of the nation. Romantic novels like *Amalia* (1851–1855) and *María* (1867) express the symbolic equivalence between woman and nationhood that was prevalent in nineteenth century Latin American literature. Cirilo Villaverde's classic *Cecilia Valdés* (1892), read as a cornerstone of Cuban literature, became the veritable emblem of the process of miscegenation at the heart of Cuban culture. As Doris Sommer has showed, foundational claims to a colonized America by the Creole upper class were couched in terms of marriage, then fatherhood. Hence the frustrated plot of the family romance reveals a project of nation-building based on the hegemony of that Creole class.[4] The traditional association between woman and land, with man as patriarch, has resulted in women's roles being largely metaphorical.[5] Because the figuring of nation so dominated the Romantic literary imagination, woman is prohibited entry into the textual inscription of origins because, as a symbol, she cannot participate actively in the Symbolic process of *inventing* an identity.[6]

In nineteenth-century Latin America, then, historical agency has been relegated almost exclusively to the phallic realm, resulting in the "grand narrative" of Latin American historiography, a tradition marked by a predominance of male-authored texts. As Sylvia Molloy has shown, the Independence Wars created a separatist discourse of male political actors who used the genre of the autobiographical memoir to justify their ideological/political stance and to recount their exemplary lives.[7] Biography was also used for historiographical purposes, as educated Creoles of the emergent ruling class documented in biographies the lives of the native, autochthonous presence typified as the Other. The emblematic text in this tradition is Domingo Faustino Sarmiento's *Facundo* (1845), a biography of a gaucho from the Rioja province in Argentina who became a strong *caudillo* figure embodying a negative moral force.[8] In contrast, Sarmiento's self-portrait, *Recuerdos de provincia* (1850), reads as "a text endowed with historical and moral significance, an example for posterity and a national testimony."[9] In both cases, the male author adopts a heroic stance in which self becomes synonymous with homeland, presenting a paternalistic conception of nationhood; Sarmiento proudly figures himself as the "father of the country."[10] Following this paradigm, nineteenth-century Latin American history for the most part comprises "a pantheon of heroic, exemplary figures."[11]

This rhetoric of self-aggrandizement characterizes the bulk of nineteenth-century Latin American historical prose, shaping Latin American cultural identity and its sense of "historical uniqueness."[12] The equation of self with state is also indicative of another, more pervasive literary convention: "the naive conflation of male subjectivity and human identity," so that "male experience is identified as the normative human paradigm."[13] As a result, the heroic, paternalistic narrative is considered not only the most influential but also the only existing historiographical tradition in nineteenth-century Latin America.

Against this tradition emerges an alternative history that subverts and refutes the heroic stance of biographer-authors like Sarmiento in Argentina. From the margins of history, nineteenth-century Latin American women also left a record of their historical experience, expanding the concept of historiography to include private genres like letters, diaries, travelogues, or personal memoirs. Women's memoirs were as concerned with the affairs of state and the governing of the new countries as were the public texts of male political leaders. The difference lies, however, in their reception, for women's histories are excluded from most traditional accounts of Latin American nationalism. Whereas Sarmiento's *Facundo* has acquired the status of an authoritative history, a charting of Argentina's political and cultural destiny—his theory of "civilization and barbarism" has weighed heavily upon Latin American letters—women's memoirs are deemed to be a secondary, if not outright inferior, mode of discourse, one irrelevant for the most part to the construction of nation.

Latin American pronationalist movements, however, were not predominantly male. Particularly in the Southern Cone, a growing feminist criticism has highlighted the public role assumed by women in Latin American independence movements, a role sustained either in literary salons or in "minimalist" genres.[14] These critical essays are constructing an archeology of women's writing that, in turn, is prompting new periodizations and generic definitions within Latin American literary studies. Sara Castro Klarén clearly points out the need to dust off the traditional archive of Latin American literary history, for, "[a]s the search for woman legitimizes studies on topics previously thought unimportant, the tenets of autobiography, testimonial writing, and other forms of 'private' writing _ receive the scrutiny and thoughtfulness previously reserved only for 'important' texts."[15]

Part of this gesture of recovery of a women's literary tradition involves taking a second look at the genre of travel narrative. During the nineteenth century, travel accounts were important rhetorical vehicles enabling women to assert their status as historical subjects. This is particularly true in the case of European women's travel books, which are often structured as a series of private letters written to an anonymous interlocutor and only "unintentionally" published.[16] In my view, these autobiographical accounts definitely fall within the range of "women's history." The hidden texts of generations of female patriots in Latin America configure a trend that resists the heroic, protonationalist plot erected by educated Creoles such as Sarmiento, and offers a new window onto the often cataclysmic events of the early nationalist period in Latin America. European women travelers to nineteenth-century Spanish America prove, indeed, that "the private sphere is public creation."[17] A study of this corpus of writing, partially undertaken by Mary Louise Pratt, dissolves traditionally held oppositions between the public and the private spheres, for European women embark on their journeys from a secure place inside the self.[18]

This hidden tradition of women's histories in Latin America illustrates that "those absent from official accounts partook nevertheless in the making of history."[19] The memoirs of "Madame la Comtesse Merlin," neé María de las Mercedes Santa Cruz y Montalvo in colonial Havana, point to such a noticeable absence. Transforming herself by marriage into the French Comtesse de Merlin, a change that also implied a transition to authorship, Merlin's many years of residence in France prompted a return trip to Havana in 1840 to secure both her father's legacy and a lost sense of insular belonging. Originally written in French, Merlin's *La Havane* (1844), a three-volume account of the political, economic, and social organization of the Cuban colony, is also a travel book tracing the author's sentimental return to her native island.[20] Both *La Havane* and *Viaje a la Habana*, a shorter Spanish edition also published in 1844, represent a hybrid perspective provided by Merlin's privileged yet marginal status as both Frenchwoman and Creole.[21] This divided identity transforms Merlin's travelogues into both a vision from afar, understood in Cintio Vitier's terms of *lejanía*, and a vision from within, a more involved and genuine perspective than the detached view of the common European traveler.[22] Merlin's Cuban birth sets her apart from other European women travelers of the period, like Flora Tristan and Frances Calderón, and suggest a destabilizing view of the self that (en)genders an alternative history of the Cuban colony, and a difference in the project of nation-formation.

Despite their importance as foundational texts in Latin American literature, *La Havane* and *Viaje a la Habana* have suffered the same fate accorded other women's writing: exclusion both from the national canon of Cuban literature as well as from a broader account of Spanish American Romanticism. This study of the travel books and historical memoirs of la Condesa de Merlin attempts to reverse that fate. Stressing *La Havane*'s "pivotal role" in Spanish American Romanticism, Roberto Ignacio Díaz reads it "not as a foreign piece, but as an archetypal work of 19th-century Spanish American writing, and, indeed, as the invisible touchstone of much Cuban literature."[23] Moreover, I shall argue here that Merlin's place in Cuban literary history deserves to be that of the first woman writer seriously to assume the historian's task. Although Cuba, along with the rest of the Spanish Antilles, remained a colony of Spain until 1902, Merlin's memoirs are exemplary of women's contribution to the founding discourse of Latin American national identity established during the nineteenth century. Written within the colonialist period, Merlin's works nevertheless offer a substantially different account of the overseas colonies, one that provides an alternative model for an emerging Cuban nationalism.

This historical paradox, in a sense, captures the contradictions embodied in Merlin's own name. Who is she? Santa Cruz y Montalvo, the young Mercedes who left Cuba and returned in search of her past, or la Comtesse Merlin, the French visitor who viewed Cuba with a foreign "I"? In this study I refer to the author as "la Comtesse Merlin" to signal the adoption of her married name as stamp of authorship, and also as "la Condesa de Merlin," the name with which she has become known by generations of Cuban writers and critics, and the one that signals her (forgotten) place in literary history. To break this dichotomy between the French and Spanish names, I also add the author's given name, Mercedes Santa Cruz y Montalvo, the name obliterated by marriage, but one that becomes the veritable emblem of her search for origins, for an insular past, and for the need to be legitimated as a *criolla*.[24]

Throughout this study, I draw on previous feminist criticism that has filled in forgotten chapters of Latin American literary history and has enriched our understanding of the nineteenth century and the rise of Spanish American nationalism. My account of women's historiography in nineteenth-century Latin America follows what Joan W. Scott calls the "her-story" approach, which emphasizes "the exclusive focus on female agency, on the causal role played by women in their history, and on the qualities of women's experience that sharply distinguish it from men's experience."[25] According to Scott, the "her-story approach" corresponds to the first phase of feminist inquiry in historical studies, a critical method also pertinent to literary history.[26] From this perspective, women become "the focus of inquiry, the subject of the story and the agent of narrative."[27] Although Scott notes that North American feminist historians for the most part have abandoned this model in favor of studies that define gender as primarily a social construct, the "her-story approach" nevertheless remains pertinent to the Latin American literary tradition. Its emphasis on "the valuation of women's experience" as well as on women's separate roles as historical agents is much more attuned to Latin American feminism,[28] which posits difference rather than a "neutralizing" of gender as a basis of analysis. Though this topic merits further debate, in these pages I subscribe to a feminist viewpoint that embraces both nature and culture in the definition of gender.

The discovery of a "lost continent" of women's history in Latin America is linked to the reappraisal of travel narrative as a founding genre of Latin American literature. In his book *Myth and Archive: A Theory of Latin American Narrative* (1990), Roberto González Echevarría proposes that the nineteenth-century European travel book, especially the scientific account, provided Creole intellectuals with a vision of their own land.[29] The scientific travelogue offered not only a means to describe New World nature but also a way to account for the continent's "historical uniqueness."[30] By assimilating the vision of the European traveler, the American writer could explore the paradoxical sense of being different and yet the same, European and Creole, native and other. Travel accounts have been used to compose the social history of a country or region, as in Louis Pérez's *Slaves, Sugar, and Colonial Society: Travel Accounts of Cuba 1801–1899* (1992), an anthology that groups textual fragments under sociological categories in order to reflect a broad spectrum of Cuban social life.[31] Missing in the section dedicated to "Havana" is, precisely, *La Havane*, a text that enhances the picture of the colonial city through its unique perspective of presenting both an "inside" and an "outside" view.[32] Both trends to date in Latin American studies have failed for the most part to take into account the role played by women's travel narrative of the colonial and nationalist periods.

The notable exception is Nara Araújo, who in her introduction to the anthology *Viajeras al Caribe* defines women's travel narrative as a personal testimony rather than as a documentary source, while addressing the difficulties of assembling a lost corpus of women's writing.[33] Anthologies like *Viajeras al Caribe* point out the need to incorporate the texts of nineteenth-century European women travelers into the canon of Latin American literature. These writings represent a gendered history that encompasses difference while stressing an alternative view of the emerging countries of Spanish America.

Despite their importance, Merlin's travelogues have been hailed as polemical in Cuban literary history, and she herself has been unjustly labeled as a "colonialist" writer.[34] Critics in postrevolutionary Cuba have assumed a direct correlation between Merlin's views and those of the landed Creole aristocracy, reading her works as a sheer reflection of a classist ideology. Salvador Bueno has stated that "[c]uando habla de las costumbres de los habaneros, son los 'habaneros' de su propia clase y condición, cuando habla de sus 'compatriotas' se refiere a los compatriotas de su misma procedencia social" ("when she speaks of the customs and mores of Havana, she is referring to the habits of her own class and condition; when speaking of her 'compatriots,' she is referring to those of her own social extraction").[35] In the introduction to her fine edition of *Mis doce primeros años*, Nara Araújo more categorically claims that Merlin "[f]ue fiel exponente de los intereses de su clase" ("was a faithful proponent of her class interests"), characterizing her by a "dudosa condición nobiliaria y su vinculación con la burguesía esclavista cubana" ("uncertain noble status and connection to the slaveholding bourgeoisie").[36] Thus la Comtesse Merlin has been negatively portrayed in Cuban literary history on two counts: first, for propounding slavery and, second, for ostensibly denying the nationalist claim for autonomy. As Díaz correctly states, "[t]o this day, Merlin is officially seen as a representative of European colonialism."[37]

This charge, however, would have to be borne out by the judgment of history. During the 1840s, Creole intellectuals did not yet regard

independence to be a particularly viable alternative, but rather considered a wide spectrum of political choices: at one extreme, annexation
to the United States, and, at the other, a precarious autonomy predicated
on keeping the tie between Cuba and Spain intact. This option, which
at the time seemed to be the better alternative, favored a call for
reform of Spanish colonial administration to allow for more Creole participation. Coinciding with Merlin's visit to Havana in 1840, the first tensions were being felt between peninsular Spaniards and Creoles, tensions
that mounted and eventually erupted in the Ten Years' War (1868–1878),
the first failed independence war in Cuba. However, even the liberal
group headed by Domingo del Monte, who advocated resistance to colonial authority, did not break completely with the metropolis but strove
to negotiate much-needed reforms. At mid-nineteenth century, independence was conceived, at best, as a remote possibility, in the event that
the other political options were to fail.[38] Hence, the charge of Merlin's
exclusively procolonialist status clearly stems more from a gender bias
than from an accurate assessment of the political positions assumed by
the Creole ruling class.

This book refutes the bias against Merlin's colonialist views by
holding that, ultimately, the political argument in *La Havane* gives way
to "a feminine position of mediation" that attempts not only to bridge
the distance between Spain and Cuba but also to abate all traces of political conflict among the two countries.[39] This intermediary position stems
fundamentally from a gendered view of cultural origins that stresses
the continuity of tradition and language shared by both Spaniards and
Creoles. Transcending at times the political dimension, Merlin imagines the colonial condition in terms of a powerful female matrix where
the motherland embraces in its waters the "lost children" of the islands.
Such an Imaginary resists the radical separation and discontinuity implicit
in the notion of political independence.

Merlin's travelogues, though ostensibly in defense of the colony,
in fact present an alternative discourse of the nation during the period
of Creole cohesion that anteceded the break from Spain. *La Havane* in
particular transforms the protonationalist views typified in Domingo del
Monte's *tertulia*, primarily by rewriting the genre of *costumbrismo*. The
tensions and contradictions evident in Merlin's (re)writings suggest the
ambivalence that lies at the heart of colonialist discourse. Indeed, la
Comtesse can best be seen as an emblematic case of what Homi K. Bhabha

has termed the "colonial hybrid," a confluence of power and desire that nevertheless resists the absoluteness of colonial rule.[40] In the same light, Merlin's much-debated political position can be understood in terms of the radical ambivalence or "negative transparency" produced by a subject caught between the dominance of empire (her adherence to Spanish colonial rule) and a strong identification with the colony (Merlin's childhood identity as a Creole). This ambivalence explains why on one hand Merlin defends in her writing the now unpopular view that Cuba should remain a colony, while on the other hand she sharply critiques the abuses of Spanish colonial administration in the letters of *La Havane*. The fact that Merlin dedicated the pages of *La Havane* to both Captain-General Leopoldo O'Donnell and to her compatriots in the island attests to the same radical ambivalence. Not only does this double gesture show Merlin's own divided identity, but it also suggests the structuring of her memoirs as a "double writing." In Bhabha's terms, *La Havane* exemplifies the kind of "*double* vision which in disclosing the ambivalence of colonial discourse also disrupts its authority,"[41] a two-layered text caught in the interstices between Europe and America, Spain and the colony.

The notion of hybridity typifies the textual organization of Merlin's memoirs. Both *La Havane* and *Viaje a la Habana* form a collage, a set of intertextual echoes and references both to Cuban *costumbrista* literature and to source documents provided by members of Domingo del Monte's literary circle. As Díaz has pointed out, "[t]his hybrid nature expresses itself most clearly in the adoption of literary strategies associated with a diversity of genres, including not only romantic travel writing in the European tradition, but also the *crónicas de Indias*, the *cuadros* and narrative fiction of Cuban *costumbrismo*, and, perhaps more significantly, autobiographical writing."[42] In this regard, the eclectic organization of Merlin's memoirs might be said to resemble the hybridity of the colonial condition itself. According to Bhabha, "hybridity is the revaluation of the assumption of colonial identity through the repetition of discriminatory identity effects."[43] What this suggests is that Merlin's contradictions as a "colonial subject"—caught between her identification with France and Spain and with her native island—emerge at the textual level in the hybrid texture of the narrative; in its combination of many and varied sources.

At one level, then, Merlin's own double identity as both French and Creole conditions the hybrid nature of *La Havane* by the mere fact that it was written in French. This doubling of identities, in the Borgesian sense, is reflected, in turn, in the duplication and thematic break between the French and Spanish editions of the book—the gap between *La Havane* and *Viaje a la Habana*. Hence, Díaz argues that Merlin "interweav[es] a series of opposing pairs—Cuba and France, Spanish and French, native *costumbrismo* and European exoticism, memory and present"[44] into her memoirs. Coupling the notion of hybridity with Cixous's *écriture feminine*, I claim, however, that Merlin effectively cancels out such binary oppositions in favor of a "double writing" or ambivalent text that follows the contours of a more fluid, female "sexte."[45] This fluidity enables her to sustain the tension between her Old and New World identities. Merlin envisions the link between metropolis and colony by means of a maternal metaphor, a figurative mother-daughter bond, which is thematically represented by dedicating many letters of *La Havane* to her daughter, Madame Gentien de Dissay. This maternal metaphor resurfaces in the narrative structure of her travel books, particularly in *Souvenirs et Mémoires* (1838), an autobiographical account of Merlin's married years in France constructed in terms of a "mother-daughter plot."[46]

The exclusion of Merlin from Cuban literary history and, by extension, from the broad spectrum of Spanish-American Romanticism attests not only to a characteristic devaluing of female authorship in Latin American criticism, but also to the assumption that Latin American literary history pertains only to works written in Spanish or Portuguese. The choice of French as a literary language with which to speak of New World affairs is part of another hidden tradition that includes multilingual texts in the larger category of Spanish American literature.[47] Salvador Bueno's characterization of Merlin as "una escritora habanera de expresión francesa" ("a Havana writer of French expression") is emblematic of a critical attitude that considers a text written in a foreign language as an act of betrayal of Spanish American cultural origins. As Roberto Ignacio Díaz claims, "escribir en idioma extranjero se interpreta fácilmente como signo de deslealtad y desunión" ("to write in a foreign language is considered a sign of disloyalty and disaffection").[48] Díaz's work has shown us that multilingualism has been, for the most part, discounted in the formation of Spanish American national identity. Despite the fact that Salvador Bueno has played an invaluable role in recuperating Merlin from oblivion, it is telling that he chooses to classify her in regional rather than in national terms. His epithet thus emphasizes an exclusively masculinist concept of identity, one which was prevalent mostly in the last century, hence implicitly denying Merlin any claims to an "authentic" Cuban nationality.[49]

Debates surrounding the "literary nationality" of exceptional women writers have effectively blocked women from literary partnership, as the case of Gertrudis Gómez de Avellaneda dramatically shows.[50] But whereas Gómez de Avellaneda, Merlin's younger peer, has received a place in both the Cuban and the Spanish Romantic canons, Merlin has been granted, at best, a marginal position in nineteenth-century Cuban literature. It is not true, as Díaz claims, that "[e]n las historias de la literatura cubana, . . . no es la nacionalidad de la Condesa de Merlin lo que verdaderamente se cuestiona, sino la nacionalidad . . . de su escritura" ("histories of Cuban literature question not so much la Condesa de Merlin's nationality, but the nationality of her writing"),[51] for authoritative literary histories show a clear misappropriation, at best, or an else an outright exclusion, at worst, of this important precursor. A case in point is Max Henríquez Ureña's authoritative *Panorama histórico de la literatura cubana* (1963), where Merlin receives barely a passing mention, and is singled out only for daring to adapt Ramón de Palma's *Una Pascua en San Marcos* (1838) into the text of *La Havane*.[52] The most glaring omission is found in José Antonio Portuondo's *Bosquejo histórico de las letras cubanas* (1960), considered a basic reference book in postrevolutionary Cuba; Merlin does not even figure in this study.[53]

Clearly, the shadow cast on Merlin by patriarchal critics has not changed substantially since colonial times. Henríquez Ureña, for instance, basically follows the line of thought initiated by the vitriolic Félix Tanco, a member of the del Monte circle, who lambasted the French-Creole visitor for her allegedly blatant plagiarism of Cuban *costumbrista* writers. A change in critical attitude is marked by the publication of Salvador Bueno's essays, which genuinely recuperate the figure of Merlin in Cuban literary history. Still, Bueno's conclusion sidesteps the issue of Merlin's "literary nationality" in light of a more universal and hence diffused prominence: "Como escritora no podemos, por supuesto, compararla con su compatriota Gómez de Avellaneda, pero como personalidad humana poseía rasgos que la sitúan en lugar destacado entre las mujeres notables del siglo XIX" ("As a writer we cannot, of course, compare her to her compatriot Gómez de Avellaneda, but humanly she possessed personality traits that place her among the most notable women of the nineteenth century").[54] Even as sensitive a critic as Nara Araújo falls into the patriarchal trap when she classifies Merlin with the unflattering epithet *"mujer de armas tomar"* (roughly translated, a woman to be reckoned with), thus echoing a prejudice against the women writer also unjustly applied to Gómez de Avellaneda.

Resisting the way in which traditional literary history has depicted Merlin as merely a foreign intruder in Cuban letters, in chapter 2, "The Return of the Prodigal Daughter: The New World Discovery of La Condesa de Merlin," I provide a psychoanalytic account of Merlin's voyage as a means to inscribe her within Cuban literary history. The feminist contextualization of Merlin's life and works serves the double purpose of introducing a relatively unknown author to modern readers and of reinserting Merlin wholly within Spanish American Romanticism.

Chapter 3, "The View from the Harbor: Gender Subversion in the Literature of the Second Discovery," places *La Havane* within the literature of travel and exploration initiated by Columbus's *Diary of Navigation* (1530; 1825), a tradition continued in the texts of nineteenth-century scientific travelers, particularly Alexander von Humboldt's *Political Essay on the Island of Cuba* (1801; 1826). How do women's texts fit into the dominant (male) paradigm of conquest and discovery? Is there a difference in women's historical vision? In my judgment, the texts of women travelers subvert both the detached outlook of male scientific explorers like Humboldt and the titanic stance of nationalist heroes like Sarmiento. How does women's marginality affect the writing of history, that is, the type of historiography produced? These and other questions are explored within the trope of discovery and dominance assumed by the texts of male explorers.

In the next two chapters, I read *La Havane* within a specific nationalist context, that is, as part of the discourse of Cuban national identity that emerged during the latter half of the nineteenth century. In chapter 4, "A Nation Invented: Imagining Cuba in Merlin and the del Monte Circle," I argue that Merlin poses a challenge to the positivistic image of nationhood inaugurated by the del Monte circle. Merlin's strategy of appropriation, textual borrowing, and outright plagiarism anticipates a concept of nation as simulacrum rather than as originating source, a poststructuralist tenet later taken up by Severo Sarduy, Merlin's contemporary succesor in France. In chapter 5, "(In)Versions and (Re)Writings: *Viaje a la Habana* and the Origins of Cuban Literature," I detail Merlin's rewritings from Cuban *costumbrista* writers to show how parody transforms the Carpentierian "Journey to the Source" prefigured in Merlin's travelogues, thus suggesting an alternative route to arrive at the notion of self and identity.

Chapter 6, "Bound to the (Male) Book: Gender, Colonialism and Slavery in *La Havane*," analyzes the polemical "Lettre XX" of *La Havane*, which deals with the illegal slave trade, as well as other letters that probe the contradictions of Cuba's colonial society. Critics have relied on these letters to sustain the image of Merlin as either a pro-colonialist, "imperialist" writer, or else as an outspoken defender of slavery. Resisting this view, I argue for a more complex reading of the slavery letter based on Bhabha's theories of hybridity as the discourse produced within a colonial context. This discourse hinges on the notion of ambivalence, an ambivalence generated by the tensions between "traditional discourses on authority" and the subversion of that authority "founded on uncertainty."[55] As an emblematic case of the colonial hybrid, Merlin's assessment of the dilemmas generated by slavery evidences the ambiguities and shadings of a colonial discourse. Likewise, her ambivalent portrayal of Cuba's black population ranges from the desire to dominate to a terse acknowledgment of the slave as inescapable presence within the Creole family. Though Merlin projects onto the Other the fear of exclusion, in part stemming from her own marginalized condition as woman and exile, in other places within her text Merlin adopts a sympathetic view of the female slave, particularly those slaves that evoke for her the maternal archetype.

After tracing the continuities between the discourse of slavery and the discourse of nationhood in *La Havane*, this chapter then turns to the letters pertaining to Cuba's colonial condition. Whereas in the slavery letter Merlin reveals her debt to José Antonio Saco, thus highlighting the woman writer's terse relationship to the Male Book, in subsequent letters the autobiographical "I" of the travel book assumes a reformist stance that attempts to reconcile the conflicts between Spain and the colony. I argue here that Merlin consciously places herself in the role of arbiter or a "feminine position of mediation."[56] In short, Merlin's rhetoric of mediation transforms the paradigm evident in Latin American colonial literature of adhering to legal documents as a means to gain legitimacy and identity through the paternal line.[57]

Chapter 7, "Creole Women: The Other as Self," traces Merlin's idyllic picture of Creole women and family relations as well as her crit-

ical view of the strong matriarchal component in Creole society. It also
details the polemic carried in Cuban newspapers of the period sparked
by the publication of Merlin's letter to George Sand. The feminist debate,
as I call it, modifies in part the prevailing view of Merlin as both intruder
and welcomed guest portrayed in the colonial press of Havana, an ambivalence that both reflects and deflects Merlin's own split subjectivity.

The final chapter, "La Comtesse Stares Back: The Many Faces of
Merlin in Cuban Literature," traces the reception of Merlin's life and
works by generations of Cuban writers. Although Merlin has been notice-
ably absent from Cuban literary history, inasmuch as her works have not
properly figured in an insular "city of letters," she has also been notice-
ably present, particularly in the texts of contemporary exiled writers like
Guillermo Cabrera Infante, Severo Sarduy, and Reinaldo Arenas. By
means of different narrative strategies, all three master novelists evoke
the elegant nineteenth-century countess as a psychic projection for their
own tortured sense of marginality and exile, or their troubled gender
identities. Resisting the traditional exclusion of Merlin from literary history, this chapter is meant to write her back into the canon.

1. Paula Promenade lined with poplars. Frédéric Mialhe, *Viage pintoresco alrededor de la isla de Cuba dedicado al Señor Conde de Villanueva* (Havana: Litografia de Luis Marquier, ca. 1848). Archives and Special Collections, Otto G. Richter Library, University of Miami, Coral Gables, Florida.

2. Rear view of the Havana Bay, taken from the Roncali Promenade. Frédéric
Mialhe, *Viage pintoresco alrededor de la isla de Cuba dedicado al Señor Conde de Villanueva*
(Havana: Litografía de Luis Marquier, ca. 1840). Special Collections Department, Otto
G. Richter Library, University of Miami, Coral Gables, Florida.

THE RETURN OF THE PRODIGAL DAUGHTER

The New World Discovery of La Condesa de Merlin

As she glimpsed the shores of Cuba on a warm summer evening, María de las Mercedes Santa Cruz y Montalvo (1789–1852) recorded in her diary the sense of wonder evoked by the tropical landscape: "Dia 6 á las ocho de la tarde, á la vista de Cuba. Hace algunas horas que permanezco inmóvil, respirando á mas no poder el aire embalsamado que llega de aquella tierra bendecida de Dios" ("Day 6 at eight o'clock in the evening, at the sight of Cuba. For many hours now I have remained still, breathing the perfumed air that comes to me from that blessed land").[1] The beginning of June 1840, in which this diary entry is inserted, marked a hopeful moment separating Mercedes Merlin's thirty-eight years of exile in France from the present moment filled with nostalgic recognition of her origins. She next sighted the small port of Santa Cruz, "que recibió su nombre de mis antepasados, y que se adelanta graciosamente hácia la orilla" ("that got its name from my ancestors, and that graciously comes to view along the coastline") (6), which was closely joined to the town of Jaruco, named after her father's title of nobility. Yet she returned to Cuba not as María de las Mercedes, the daughter of parents well established in the Creole sugar aristocracy, but rather as "Madame la Comtesse

Merlin," widow of the late general Count Antoine Christophe Merlin
(1771–1839) and a famous belledame of the Parisian salons.

Merlin's two names indicated two concealed identities beneath the
sign of self. She was born into one of the founding families of the Cuban
sugar aristocracy, the first child of Don Joaquín Santa Cruz y Cárdenas
(1769–1807), third count of Jaruco, and Teresa Montalvo y O'Farrill
(1771–1812).[2] Though Salvador Bueno underlines the couple's extreme
youth, claiming that the count was fifteen and Teresa just over twelve
when they married,[3] Calcagno fixes the date of marriage as June 29, 1786,
which makes the count seventeen and Teresa Montalvo fifteen at the
time of marriage.[4] Mercedes was the only one of the four Santa Cruz y
Montalvo children born in Havana, the others having been born in Spain,
where her parents resided soon after her birth. In 1802, when she was
thirteen, the family emigrated for good to Madrid. Her childhood in
Havana was spent under the care of her maternal great-grandmother,
the venerable Luisa Herrera y Chacón, warmly evoked as "Mamita" in
Merlin's early memoirs.

While his eldest daughter grew up in Havana, Count Jaruco returned
for a time to Madrid, where he achieved distinction in the Spanish court,
in part with the aid of Francisco Arango y Parreño, who had obtained
approval from the king for commerce in black slaves.[5] The count also
relied on Manuel Godoy, under whose protection he managed to arrange
an important trade concession involving the right to exchange flour from
the United States for rum.[6] The count returned to Cuba in 1797 as subin-
spector of troops. He was in charge of a mission to explore and colonize
the area around Guantánamo, a scientific expedition that failed, which
may have prompted the Count's return to the luxury of Havana and a
reunion with Mercedes.[7]

After five busy years, during which he achieved an enviable position of commercial monopoly in colonial Havana, the count arranged
for his trip back to Spain "para informar sobre los resultados de su comisión
colonizadora y gestionar concesiones adicionales y el aplazamiento de
pago de sus deudas con la Hacienda Real" ("to report on the results of
his colonizing mission and to arrange additional concessions as well as
the delay of his debt payments to the Royal Treasury").[8] Looking into
his domestic affairs long enough to consider his daughter's education,
Santa Cruz decided that the only alternative to her great-grandmother's
leniency was to shut Mercedes inside a convent of Franciscan nuns.[9] Her

period of confinement at the Convento de Santa Clara had a great impact on Mercedes, as narrated in the moving pages of *Mes douze premières années* (1831), Merlin's first book of memoirs, which is dedicated almost in its entirety to her early years in Havana.[10] She also wrote *Histoire de la Soeur Inés* (1832), which tells the tale of the sorrowful nun who helped Mercedes escape from the convent. This later work is linked to the first set of memoirs by literary convention, for, during the final scene of *Mes douze premières années*, the nun's autobiography is delivered to the narrator in Madrid.[11]

According to the memoir, by far the most central event in Mercedes' life was her departure from the island in April of 1802, an event which "cleaves her life in two and marks a watershed in the text."[12] Sylvia Molloy's sensitive reading of Merlin's primitive autobiography renders it as a text of separations, "scattering a self in the making, disrupting any attempt at coherent self-composure."[13] Merlin nonetheless succeeds in possessing herself in her second set of memoirs, *Souvenirs et Mémoires* (1836), chronicling a time before the rupture of exile was manifest, when Mercedes embraced her newly found mother simultaneously with her arrival in Madrid.[14] In *Souvenirs et Mémoires*, Spain thus becomes a metonym for Teresa Montalvo, a veritable mother-country, later replaced by France as surrogate motherland.

The shift from colony to metropolis coincided almost exactly with Mercedes' transition from youth to adulthood. In Madrid the young Mercedes blossomed into adolescence, showing a heightened sensibility and a tendency toward melancholy: "Je ne tardai pas à retomber dans cet état de mélancholie et de découragement qui, se reproduisant sans cesse chez moi, finissait souvent par altérer ma santé. . . . J'avais beau faire, ma sécurité première était detruite sans retour" ("It didn't take me long to return to this state of melancholy and discouragement which kept happening in me and often ended up affecting my health. . . . I had done it well, my first security was destroyed with no return").[15] This propensity toward melancholy is inevitably linked to the childhood trauma of parental abandonment, which erupts in Merlin's early memoirs as a constant trace of loss and separation. The opening pages of *Souvenirs et Mémoires* marks this family history with a dream forewarning "Mamita's" loss, to be followed shortly afterward by news of the death of Count Jaruco, who had since returned to Havana in the hopes of dissolving his debt to the Crown.[16] Although Merlin charitably attributed her father's death to an "excess of vitality," historian Leví Marrero points to Count Jaruco's financial irresponsibility as the principal cause of his downfall.[17] According to Marrero, the count's commercial ventures and lust for material luxury finally caught up with him; though Joaquín Cárdenas earnestly sought to cancel his enormous debt in one lifetime, it eventually took two entire generations to liquidate it.[18]

Alone and plagued with money worries, Teresa Montalvo remained in Madrid, where she sought the protection of her uncle, General Gonzalo O'Farrill; his political influence would later prove to be especially advantageous during the French occupation.[19] During this period, Mercedes had a string of suitors, but her astute mother undid every match until José Bonaparte himself arranged the marriage of Teresa's eldest daughter to Antoine Christophe Merlin (1771–1839), a French count who distinguished himself as a general in Bonaparte's army.[20] Tied to her mother by the invisible strings resulting from her early abandonment, Mercedes surrendered to her mother's wishes with passive acquiescence: "Je me décidai donc à la laisser maîtresse de mon sort, si toutefois je n'éprovais pas de répugnance pour la personne qu'on me proposait pour mari" ("I made up my mind then and there to let her be mistress of my destiny, but only if I did not feel any repugnance for the person that they intended for me as a husband").[21] She consented to marry the handsome, Nordic, blue-eyed man who appeared to her as both daunting and dashing:

> Le soir, le général Merlin fut présenté à ma mère. Son extérieur me parut froid et sévère; il me sembla plus homme du nord que les autres Français . . . à mes yeux, peu habituée . . . aux teints blancs et aux yeux bleus: tout cela, sans me déplaire, m'en imposa d'abord. Du reste, Merlin était un beau militaire: il portait son uniforme de hussard . . . et il le portait à merveille.

> (That evening, General Merlin was introduced to my mother. His outward appearance struck me as cold and harsh; he looked to me more like a man from the North than a Frenchman . . . at least to my eyes, which were not acquainted . . . with people of such white complexion and blue eyes. All this, without displeasing me, caught my attention at first. For the rest, Merlin was a handsome military man: he wore his hussar uniform . . . marvelously.)[22]

Marriage meant another transformation, another parting, and even further geographical displacement. The family pattern of attachment and separation was paradoxically repeated when Merlin decided to blend her destiny with that of the Count. If before, "Cuba (with its synecdoche, Mamita) is synonymous with the abandonment of the parents," and "[c]onversely, reunion with the parents is synonymous with the abandonment of Cuba," then Merlin's marriage is synonymous with the loss of Madrid and its promise of attachment to the mother.[23] Though the marital bond did not wholly sever her connection to her mother, it did imply a distancing in time and place that was to mark Merlin's identity as an exile.[24] As her biographer Domingo Figarola Caneda claims, on her wedding day, October 31, 1809, "María de las Mercedes was no longer a Spaniard nor a Cuban; she became the French general's woman."[25] And also a Frenchwoman, for the Merlins were forced to leave Spain in 1812 after the defeat of Bonaparte, an episode dramatically narrated in her memoirs.[26]

Over the course of her marriage, from 1813 to 1839, the *criolla* Santa Cruz y Montalvo transformed herself into one of the leading *belles-dames* of the Parisian cultural establishment. Her salon at 40, Rue de Bondy, attracted many of the musical and literary personalities of her time; indeed, attending her salon was considered a must for aspiring musicians hoping to gain entry into exclusive artistic circles.[27] The notoriety of Merlin's salon as a fruitful meeting place for musicians and artists is documented in various nineteenth-century works that describe the vibrant social life of the Parisian salons; in these texts, Merlin is described as blending the best of two cultures: "A la grace poétique de l'espagnole, elle joignait l'esprit et la distinction de la française" ("To the Spaniard's poetic charm, she adds the French spirit and distinction").[28] In his biography of Merlin, Figarola Caneda documents the cycle of concerts and musical soirées that graced the Merlin household, and even includes a copy of Merlin's compositions and a picture of her in costume to sing in the opera *Norma*.[29] Many of these concerts were held as fundraising events for charitable and political ends; for example, benefit funds were used to help earthquake victims in Martinique, to support the Polish uprising of 1831, and to assist those injured by the Lyons flood.[30] This contradicts the traditional picture of Merlin as a demure aristocrat with no social concerns (past critics have described Merlin's musical interests as little more than a frivolous indulgence). The shining glamour of this Parisian period also allowed Merlin to bridge the literary and musical worlds with a biography of the singer Maria Malinbran, a frequent visitor to her salon.[31]

The alluring activity of Merlin's Parisian salon ended abruptly with her husband's death in 1839.[32] Merlin had borne him four children: her namesake, María de las Mercedes Josefa Teresa Ana (1812–1876), who would become the future Madame Gentien de Dissay alluded to in Merlin's travelogues; Francisco Dieudonné, (1814–1900), who followed in his father's footsteps to become a military officer; Gonzalo Cristóbal (1816–1887), the only one to die in Havana; and little Annette Elisabeth Joséphine (1818–1821), who died at the tender age of three.[33]

Alone and without resources, Merlin was motivated to return to Cuba in part by her wish to claim a share in the inheritance of her father's estate. This involved settling accounts with her brother, Don Francisco Javier, who had acquired the greater part of the family fortune, along with the father's title of Count of Jaruco.[34] While disputing the ownership of the sugar mill at Nazareno, Merlin took refuge in the Havana home of her uncle, the influential Juan Montalvo y O'Farrill. There she wrote the pages of her travel diary, *Viaje a la Habana* (1844), a poetic reminiscence of her journey back to the island, which is essentially a censored version of the longer work *La Havane* (1844). Because the sale of the Nazareno estate in her brother's favor left Merlin in a financially precarious situation, she returned to France, but she carried back her memories of Cuba and the ambitious plan to write an extensive analysis of the Spanish colony. Pinning all her hopes for regaining prosperity on the book's success, Merlin produced under hardship the three volumes of *La Havane*, an ambitious book that recorded the political, economic, and social organization of the island of Cuba.[35] Its most salient sections have to do with the history of the colony, the status of women in Creole society, and the pressing question of slavery.[36]

Though *La Havane* (1844) would not be the financial success Merlin hoped for, this was due perhaps to her association with the French *philosophe* Philarète Chasles, the man who dominated her emotional life during the vulnerable period when she found herself aging and alone, and lacking financial security. Though Merlin considered him an intellectual peer and a partner in the ambitious enterprise of publishing what she thought to be her major work, Chasles proved himself to be not only a treacherous lover but also a ruthless exploiter of her limited resources. After many bitter exchanges with Chasles over questions of money and his presumed responsibilities in editing *La Havane*, Merlin finally mustered up the courage to leave him.[37] Merlin apparently never recovered from this heartbreak and died on March 31, 1852, as alone and melancholy as when her parents left her behind in infancy. Discovering the family crypt tucked away in a Parisian cemetery, Figarola Caneda wryly noted that her tomb "has no epitaph."[38]

Though Merlin's place in literary history is primarily as a travel writer, she also engaged in literary endeavors, publishing several novels including *Les lionnes de Paris* (1845), signed with the pseudonym "Feu le Prince de ***" ("The Prince of Fire") because it was based on the intrigues of Parisian high society; *Lola et Maria* (1845), partially reproduced in the *Faro Industrial de la Habana*; and the posthumous *Le Duc d'Athens* (1852) which at first was erroneously attributed to an obscure "marquis de Foudras" who only happened to write the prologue.[39]

Voyage as Autobiography: *La Havane* as Mother/Daughter Text

In his study of European travel narrative, critic Dennis Porter has pointed out its psychoanalytic underpinnings, locating in the father/son relationship one of the principal motivations for discovering and exploring foreign territory.[40] According to Porter, the connection between geographical displacement and the satisfaction of basic instincts is best seen in the grand tour, where a rebellious son goes in search of adventure and to stake out an identity separate from a strict father's dictates of love and duty.[41] Such a conceptual scheme would be inapplicable to the woman writer, particularly during the nineteenth century, when women were confined for the most part to home and hearth.[42] Indeed, by reversing the traditional Western paradigm of the son's rebellion against the father by seeking out adventures in strange lands, Merlin's texts clearly suggest that the psychological motivation for women's travel narrative lies elsewhere: in the daughter's need to recapture the lost "fatherland" and attempt to define a self in relation to the Name of the Father.

The oedipal knot in Merlin's case is the exclusive bond forged between the child Mercedes and her father, the dashing young count who returned to Havana in 1797. As if to make up for lost time, once he was reunited with his long-lost daughter, the count set up house with her and showered her with excessive affection, to which the young Mercedes added her own sentimental response. Merlin recasts her relationship with her father in this way:

Me establecí en casa de mi padre, no como una niña, sino lo mismo que lo hubiera sido mi madre. Todo estaba sometido a mis caprichos, todo cedía a mi voluntad. . . . Mi padre me amaba con una ternura extremada, y parecía querer indemnizarme de su pasada indiferencia, dispensándome con profusión todos los gustos que mi edad me permitía gozar.

(I took up residence at my father's house, not as a child would, but just as my mother would have done. Everything was subordinated to my whims, everything gave in to my will. . . . My father loved me with extreme tenderness, and he seemed to want to free me from his past indifference, generously allowing me all of the pleasures that my age permitted me to enjoy.)[43]

Merlin's need to recuperate the intimacy of the oedipal bond is quite pronounced in the two travelogues centered on Cuba, where Count Jaruco's presence is evoked both inside the parental house, which Merlin revisited, and in the father-surrogate represented by her maternal uncle, the powerful Count of Montalvo, with whom she lived during her stay in Havana.[44] Merlin's yearning to recover the lost world enclosed within the paternal mansion anticipates many a text in modern Latin American literature; echoes of Juan Rulfo's *Pedro Páramo* (1955) and Elena Garro's *La casa junto al río* (1983) are heard in Merlin's tremulous entry into her father's chamber:

[A]penas entré en el zaguan, el corazon me empezó a latir; me pareció reconocer aquella casa, y en efecto no me quedó la menor duda. Yo la habia habitado, yo habia atravesado mil veces aquellas puertas, habia jugado en aquellos escalones de mármol, habia subido y bajado mas de cien veces aquella escalera. . . . No, no me engañaba, era la casa de mi padre. Todo estaba en el mismo sitio: . . . [a]quí, delante de esta mesa, era donde mi padre me ponia en sus rodillas, y me enseñaba su árbol genealógico. ¡Ah! ¿dónde está mi padre? Yo no hallo mas que un monton de piedras sin vida, y un recuerdo eterno.

(As soon as I crossed the entrance hall, my heart began to throb; I seemed to recognize the house, and sure enough, there was no doubt about it. I had lived here, I had walked through those doors a thousand times, I had played on those marble stairs, I had gone up and down the staircase more than a hundred times. . . . No, I was not deceiving myself, this was my father's house. Everything remained in the same place: . . . here in front of this table, was the spot where my father would sit me on his lap and show me his family tree. Oh, where is my father? I find only a pile of dead stones, and an eternal memory.)[45]

Though Merlin's voyage was motivated ostensibly by financial need, it was inevitably overtaken by a powerful sentimental urge, to retrace her "lost steps" and so renew a broken family bond. She wrote her own "personal narrative" of discovery while seeking to restore a symbolic bond within the patrimony of name and land.

The acute desire to reencounter the father is also evident in Merlin's appeal to the law as the organizing principle of an otherwise chaotic social order. Merlin's faith in the law as sole arbiter in resolving the problem of slavery demonstrates how a psychological complex can find a natural ally in the political philosophy of reform. By positing the law as the one cohesive force for the entire fabric of colonial society, Merlin attempted to compensate with an external authority for the paternal presence she sought and found missing in her own life.

In addition to the strong oedipal resonances in Merlin's texts, the Cuban travelogues also weave a "mother/daughter plot." Merlin inscribes herself in them as both mother and daughter, constructing a bivocal "female text" that reverses the patriarchal ordering of history and nationhood.[46] In such a text, "imagination is fueled not by loss but by longing to reexperience the symbiotic union with the mother."[47] This desire is sublimely articulated in a passage from Merlin's *Souvenirs et Mémoires*: "moi, de qui les actions, les paroles, la vie entière était employée á me faire aimer d'elle, á mériter sa confiance; moi, qui mettais dans cette conduite tout l'enthousiasme et l'exagération de la jeunesse" ("I, whose actions, whose words, whose entire life had no other end but to make myself be loved by her, to deserve her confidence, I, whose behavior had all the enthusiasm and exaggeration of youth").[48] In Merlin's case, the trauma of abandonment was compounded by her mother's expressed preference for her sister, born in Madrid not only at a more favorable period in the family history but after Teresa had gained greater maturity. Merlin writes:

Ma mère m'amait; néanmois, de lègéres circonstances, qui se renouvelaient á chaque instant, venaient m'avertir que son attachement pour moi était l'effet de ma bonne conduite et de mes soins pour elle; tandis que le tendre abandon et la faiblaisse d'une mère étaient réservés á ma soeur.

(My mother loved me; nevertheless, certain small signs, which repeated
themselves continually, would come to warn me that her attachment to
me was the result of my good behavior and of my attentions to her;
meanwhile, a mother's tender abandonment and foibles were reserved
only for my sister.)[49]

Merlin's family romance represents a classic case of the narcissis-
tic wounding described by Swiss psychoanalyst Alice Miller in *The Drama
of the Gifted Child*.[50] Reversing Freudian notions about infantile sexuality, Miller traces the roots of childhood trauma to the parents' own experience of loss or abuse when they were children. In Miller's account, the
mother's impaired self-esteem causes her to see the child not as a separate individual but as an extension of her own self; the child's actions must
then compensate for the mother's perceived feelings of inadequacy.
According to Miller, the expectations placed on a child caught in this
predicament far exceed his or her capacities; instead of developing his or
her true self, the child suffers from an impaired self-image and consequent loss of self-esteem. Likewise, the mother's rejection of the
child's core self leads to a compensatory compulsion to excel, in which
the child tries to live up to the expectations thrust on him or her in
exchange for some degree of acceptance or love.[51]

This psychological drama is neatly duplicated in *Souvenirs et Mémoires*,
where the compulsion to excel is translated into Mercedes's constant
desire to please her mother, even after she becomes an adult. As in all
cases of childhood abandonment, the loss of her parents triggered in
Merlin a desperate need for love. Deeply affected by her mother's early,
primal rejection, the young Mercedes tried to conform to her mother's
wishes by marrying the man she chose for him, in an attempt to secure
a place for herself within the family structure, ruptured as it was by the
experience of exile and the father's absence.[52] Writing, with its incessant
obsession and re-creation of the past, offered Mercedes a means to further compensate for the loss of her true self.[53]

Later passages of the memoirs (written while she was still living in
Madrid) reveal how the continuity of the mother/daughter bond was
secured with Merlin's own pregnancy. Mercedes's ardent wish for a daughter whom she would name after Teresa underscores a deeper psychological need: the gift of a granddaughter would thus substitute symbolically
for her own mother and cancel out Teresa's perceived indifference. Mercedes even wished that her mother's beauty would be imprinted onto her
own unborn daughter:

[J]e voulais une fille: je l'avais devinée. Alors, j'imaginais que mon amour extréme pour ma mère devait, par une secrète sympathie, transmettre sa beauté à mon enfant. J'étais conquette déjà, pour ma Teresa; je la voulais belle, mais de la beauté de ma mère.

(I wanted a daughter: I had already imagined her. I fancied that my extreme love for my mother would, by a secret sympathy, transmit her beauty to my child. I was already won over by my Teresa; I wanted her to be beautiful but with the beauty of my mother.)[54]

This passage exemplifies the two movements implied in Hirsch's notion of a mother/daughter plot: the glance back to discover the mother's life story, followed by a break in tradition when the "feminist daughter becomes a feminist mother who can tell her feminist daughter about that process of becoming."[55] Placing herself precisely in the position of the "feminist daughter," Merlin retells her mother's life's story at the same time that she lovingly intertwines her own autobiography with the budding life of her newborn child.

Present in the text of *Souvenirs et Mémoires*, then, is "the story of female development . . . in the voice of the mothers as well as in that of the daughters."[56] In Merlin's case, the continuity of roles implied in this process of female development worked to arrest her growth to full psychic maturity, for it was not until Teresa's final illness that Merlin received the ultimate gift: "l'estime de ma mère" ("my mother's esteem"), the crucial emotional factor that would help her attain her own authentic sense of self.[57] This fierce attachment to the mother was ciphered in the body: as Mercedes's womb swelled in pregnancy, Teresa's body diminished in size as a consequence of a lingering illness. Repeating the pattern ingrained since early childhood and attempting to restore the broken bond with her mother, Merlin made lavish preparations for Teresa's convalescence in her own household. Significantly, one room was decorated with a painting of tropical scenery, as if to facilitate a merging of mother and daughter in a mutual reminiscence of their origins:

J'avais fait prendre le salon à fresque. . . . Il représentait un paysage de l'île de Cuba . . . des palmiers mêles aux papayers chargés des fruits, des groups de tamarins étreints par des lianes vivaces . . .; cà et là, des zinzontes, des guacamayos, et d'autres oiseaux aux plumages brillans; puis, un ciel bleu, transparent . . . , de l'air, mais un air chaud, pur, l'air du pays.

(I had the living room made over with frescoes. . . . It represented a
scene of the Island of Cuba . . . of palm trees blended with papaya trees
full of fruit, groups of tamarind trees hugging each other with sprightly
lianas. . . . Here and there zinzontes [hummingbirds], macaws, and
other birds of radiant plumage; next, a blue and transparent sky . . . air,
but hot and pure air, the air of my country.)[58]

Not only are mother and daughter fused in this image of the land, but
they also share a similar destiny of exiles, a detachment from the source,
as if the distance in time and place were proportional to the intensity of
their memory: "Il est vrai qu'elle était partie bien jeune de la Havane;
mais, plus le temps nous éloigne des premières impressions, plus le
souvenir nous en rapproche" ("It was true that she had left Havana at a
very young age; but the more time distances us from our early impressions, the more memory brings us closer to them").[59] Overlapping her
mother's life story with her own autobiographical account provided partial impetus for Merlin's future journey. The voyage to Cuba in 1840
would be simultaneously an incursion into the past and a venture into a
preoedipal realm of female genealogies whose generative source or matrix
lay in "Mamita."[60]

　　Documenting her "lost" history in her travelogues offered Merlin
a way of recuperating the origin through writing.[61] Prefiguring that gesture, Merlin described in her memoirs the agonizing moments of her
mother's death in an effort to sustain somehow the flow of time and to
seal in ink her sense of belonging to a generation of women bonded in
the primal experiences of birth and death.[62] Indeed, the text of *Souvenirs et Mémoires* dramatically juxtaposes the psychological drives of Eros
and Thanatos: shortly after finding her mother asleep forever in her bier,
Merlin goes into labor, an affirmation of the life force.[63] Leaving her
mother only for the imminent birth of her own daughter, Merlin declared
to the end her unswerving fidelity to the mother bond: "[m]a tendresse
pour elle absorbait alors tout ma vie: je ne voyais rien au delà des parois
de sa chambre" ("my tenderness for her took up my whole life then: I did
not wonder beyond the walls of her chamber.")[64]

　　By describing in vivid detail her first experiences of motherhood,
including a painful and protracted labor and, later, her extreme disappointment at being unable to lactate, Merlin's autobiography seals the
narrator's subjectivity in terms of mothering.[65] The link between mother
and daughter was further strengthened when Merlin named her new-

born after Teresa and herself. In this way the "female family romance" resists the classic psychoanalytic account based on separation from the mother.[66] Not only does the experience of childbirth touch the deepest emotional chords, but it also solidifies the mother/daughter bond in a mutual process that both connects with and recognizes a separate existence. Merlin described the paradox of mothering with its bittersweet mixture of pain and joy:

> Sensation douce et enivrante! . . . première jouissance d'un coeur maternel! C'était le premier signe de vie de mon enfant! Ce fut un cri de douleur . . . mais c'était la vie, c'était une existence toute à lui, indépendante de la mienne! . . . [S]i je ne sentais plus sa douce chaleur, j'étais inquiète, une sensation pénible et presque douloureuse s'emparait de moi, comme si mon enfant eût fait encore partie de moi-même.

> (Sweet and intoxicating sensation! . . . the first pleasures of a maternal heart! This was the first sign of my infant's life! That was a cry of pain . . . but this was life, this was an existence in and of itself, independent of mine! . . . If I could not feel her sweet warmth, I was restless, for a distressing sensation, almost a painful one, would take over me, as if my child had again been a part of myself.)[67]

Merlin celebrated the endurance of the mother/daughter bond in which two separate selves remain fused within the intimate unit formed by infant and mother. Her writing in the pages of *Souvenirs et Mémoires* suggests a recognition of the mother's subjectivity, both in her own right and as the source for the daughter's identity, a reciprocal mirroring that curtails the domineering phallic eye/I in favor of an embracing glance at the next generation.[68]

One of the most poignant passages in the autobiography describes Merlin's inability to nourish her newborn at her breast, to the point that she was forced to hire a wet nurse to save her daughter's life.[69] This forced displacement of her maternal function unsettled Mercedes' budding identity. Aware of her sense of failure, the doctor who procured the wet nurse tried to console Merlin by pointing to her infant happily sucking. In the pages of her memoir Merlin cries out her deep frustration and points out that the doctor's gesture was founded on patriarchal values that diminished the importance of nursing as a distinctively female experience: "Mais vous ne voyez donc pas que vous m'arrachez le coeur? . . . que vous

m'assassinez?" ("But can't you see that you are tearing my heart apart
. . . that you are killing me?") Gender difference is forcibly conveyed in
this contrast between paternal acquiescence and maternal fervor. In
response to the doctor's reasoned "Mais, mon enfant, je suis père
aussi" ("But, my child, I am a father also"), Merlin asserts her mother
rights: "Mais, qu'importe, vous n'êtes pas mère!" ("But, never mind, you
are not a mother!")[70] Throughout the rest of the text, the autobiographical
narrator asserts the fragility of the lifeline between mother and daughter, made more acute by the family's precarious external circumstances; at this time, they were forced to flee from Madrid, crossing of
La Mancha, a desertlike terrain where the lack of water threatened the
daughter's life anew.[71] By Merlin's own account, it was the concern for
her daughter's survival under such precarious circumstances that enabled
her to resist the countering pull of the death wish, and that eventually
restored her wounded sense of self. Merlin herself describes the partial
resolution of her own "drama of the gifted child" in this way:

> Le fond de mélancolie que j'ai éprouve à toutes les époques de ma vie,
> cette impuisance à satisfaire les forces de mon ame . . . m'a rendue peu
> soucieuse à l'idée de la mort. . . . Mais, j'avais ma fille dans mes bras,
> qui dormait d'un sommeil tranquille . . . et moi, je ne pouvais rien pour
> elle!

> (The backdrop of melancholy that impaired me throughout life, this
> inability to satisfy the needs of my soul . . . has made me a little anxious
> about death. . . . But I had my daughter in my arms, who sleeps a
> peaceful sleep . . . and I would do anything for her!)[72]

Merlin's life story formulates the exile experience not only as a
double rupture but associates it more deeply to the trauma of parental
loss and abandonment.[73] Painful as it was, the initial break from Cuba
during childhood only anticipated the flight from Spain as an adult woman,
which coincided with the loss of the mother. Merlin assumed an identity as an expatriate only after her mother's death and subsequent emi-
gration to France. While in Madrid, she had merged into the mother-country,
repeating the mechanism of psychic compensation her mother Teresa
Montalvo had taught her. Hence Merlin's memoirs inscribe not a radical distancing from Cuba but rather a curious juxtaposition between insular scenery and peninsular territory, admirably phrased in the following

passage: "Née entre les tropiques, je raconte ce que j'ai éprouvé sous le ciel de Madrid" ("Born amidst the tropics, I relate what I experienced under the Madrid sky").[74] Replaying the scene of departure from Cuba depicted earlier in *Mes douze premières années*, Merlin describes in her later memoir the anguished moment when she had to sever herself from the literal and symbolic ground represented by the Spanish peninsula:

> Je souffrais toutes les angoisses de la séparation, sans que l'idée du retour vint se présenter un instant à ma pensée. Un secret pressentiment, plus puissant que la raison, s'était emparé de moi, et me répétait tout bas: Pour toujours, loin de la patrie! et, comme la génie du mal, il me suivait partout, et me répétait sans relâche: Pour toujours, loin de la patrie!
>
> (I suffered the anguish of separation, without allowing the idea of return to present itself in my mind. A secret premonition stronger than reason took hold of me, and repeated to me quietly: Forever, away from the homeland! and, like a spirit of evil, it followed me everywhere, and repeated to me without respite: Forever, away from home!)[75]

Rebelling against both the imposed destiny of the expatriate and her marital ties, Merlin wished that some unforeseen circumstance could keep her and her daughter in Spain.[76] In a double pull emblematic of the female experience, the closer she came to crossing the Pyrenees, the more ardent her budding nationalism grew, as in the exalted passages that hailed the heroic exploits of the Spanish resistance at Zaragoza.[77] When after an arduous flight through desert and mountains Merlin finally glimpsed the borders of her new country, her husband's native France, she aptly described her sense of geographic and metaphysical estrangement: "[l]à, étrangère a tout, livrée à une solitude presque absolue, je m'abandonnais à une melancholie profonde" ("there, a stranger to everything, surrendered to almost complete solitude, I gave myself up to a deep melancholy").[78] For Merlin, the loss of country was tied to the image of the mother and apprehension for her absent husband, still fighting on the French lines. Only at the end of her memoirs was she able to reconcile herself to the double loss, not only of her past homelands but also of her mother tongue. This reconciliation was due in part to a feminine need for connection. Merlin replaced the abstract category of homeland and the broken continuity of origins, ever the obsession of a male imagination, with the metaphoric association she created between a European and an American space, each representing a particular affection. Addressing France as her "belle patrie adoptive" ("beautiful adopted homeland") Merlin staked out a place for herself that conferred on her a new identity forged in the vividness of the past as well as in a deep rootedness to the present: "Réchauffée à la douce chaleur de ta bienveillante hospitalité, j'ai pris racine sur ton sol et depuis bien long-temps j'ai fini par me croire sous le soleil de la Havane" ("Comforting myself in the sweet warmth of your benevolent hospitality, I took root under your sun and for a long time now I have come to believe that I am under the Havana sun").[79]

In the Cuban travelogues, this feminine consciousness is asserted in the moving passages describing Merlin's first sight of Havana (quoted at the beginning of the chapter). Lovingly dedicated to her daughter, these entries testify to the strong attachment that is guaranteed by the female lineage. To remember her daughter, who had now become Madame Gentien de Dissay, in these pages was a way for Merlin both to evoke her during her voyage and at the same time to be symbolically present, thus compensating for her own motherly absence. This is why the daughter's presence grows stronger as the ship approaches harbor and the island/mother is sighted. In *La Havane* the connection between mother and daughter is elevated to a category of symbol-formation and imagination, subverting the phallic notion of the Symbolic for a powerful maternal metaphor.[80] Eloquent in this regard is the fact that Merlin finished the book while staying at the Château de Dissay, her daughter's mansion, suggesting a kind of writing predicated on a maternal Symbolic.[81]

La Havane is also a "daughterly" text because Merlin, in writing her travelogue, clearly inscribed her desire to belong to the Creole community from which she was cut off at the age of twelve; in depicting her return to Cuba, Merlin wrote as her father's daughter and as heiress to a city. By describing herself as "créole endourcie," Merlin sided with her insular past, yet by dedicating the most poignant sections of her travelogue to her daughter, she also intensified her connection to France, the country where her daughter lived and which she had adopted as a mother-surrogate to Spain, Teresa Montalvo's extended homeland. A helix is formed, in which Merlin was as absent and present to her daughter as the waters surrounding Cuba were to her. Although the journey to Cuba also conjured her own mother's childhood, the tale thus unwinds in a cyclical, spiraling process of encounter and renewal, rupture and reparation.

The implications of this complex web of relationships go beyond the sphere of insular history or even of Latin American history, for Merlin's double marginality—as a woman and as an exile—is tied also to the marginalized figure of the mother, whose power and symbolism has all but been erased from the Western tradition.[82] The unrepresentability of motherhood as experience theorized in Marianne Hirsch's account reenacts, at another level, the unspeakability of the exile condition. Although Merlin has a place in the Cuban imagination as the archetypal mother—Plácido's verses written upon Merlin's departure from Havana are the most eloquent in this regard—little has been done to uncover Merlin's gendered position as woman, mother, and exile.[83] It is this locus of desire as both absent mother and as a lost child adrift from the coast that Merlin represents in the Cuban Imaginary. Contemporary writers like Reinaldo Arenas, Severo Sarduy, and Guillermo Cabrera Infante have riveted their own severed selves onto the image of la Comtesse Merlin in a gesture of symbolic and psychological projection.[84]

In Hirsch's terms, the double helix of the "female family romance" enacts a break in tradition, particularly in the male-gendered narrativity that is sustained by separation from the mother and by logo-centered chronological time frames.[85] Traces of the "*continued opposition, interruption and contradiction*" characteristic of the mother/daughter plot are first visible in the rambling structure of *Mes douze premières années* and *Souvenirs et Mémoires*, only to reappear in the "oscillation," repetitions, and editorial breaks that occur between *La Havane* and *Viaje a la Habana*.[86]

La Havane: The Double Reading

Merlin's Cuban travelogues duplicate the author's inner division between her Creole and French identities. Characterized by a both a thematic and rhetorical duplicity, *La Havane* and *Viaje a la Habana* reveal the source of that duplicity to be Merlin's divided self, acutely described in a passage of *Souvenirs et Mémoires*:

> [J]'ai deux moi, qui luttent constamment, mais c'est le *fort*, le superbe, que j'encourage toujours; c'est ne pas parce qu'il est le *plus fort* que je lui donne la préférence, mais parce qu'il est le plus malheureux: il ne réussit à rien.

> (I have two selves, which are constantly fighting, but it is the strong, the superb one, that I always encourage; it is not because it is the

strongest that I give it my preference, but because it is the most unfortunate: it does not succeed at anything.)[87]

These "two selves" underline the curious editorial decision that resulted
in two different versions of the Cuban travelogue: the three-volume
French original and the Spanish edition of *Viaje a la Habana*, published
in Madrid in 1844 with a prologue by Gertrudis Gómez de Avellaneda.
The "strong," masculine-identified self produced the political and historical analyses dominant in *La Havane*, whereas the "softer," more feminine self created the poetic, literary narration of *Viaje a la Habana*.[88]
Merlin herself underlined the gender division at the core of her travelogue when she classified parts of *La Havane* into "severe" or political letters and "entertaining" or literary ones; in her correspondence with
Philarète Chasles, she indicated that the French edition would contain
"las cartas más severas" ("the most severe letters"), and asks him, "¿Has
suprimido algunas cartas de la edición inglesa, para no dejar más que la
parte *divertida*?" ("Have you taken out some of the letters from the English edition, so as only to leave the most entertaining?").[89] Salvador Bueno
uses the same terminology to analyze the letters of *La Havane* as either
"political" or "literary."[90]

The rhetorical structure of *La Havane* also generates, in effect, two
texts in one—and partly accounts for the double edition. Organized as a
series of letters dedicated either to influential personalities in Europe or
to Merlin's family members (primarily to her daughter), the epistolary
format created a specific pact between the autobiographical first person and the addressee. A prime example of this form of rhetorical address
is Merlin's use of political argument. She hoped by means of these letters to gain support for a project of reform inducing Spain to improve
colonial institutions and safeguard the prosperity of the island. Hence,
if the addressee was a political opponent, Merlin tried to convince him
of the letter's argument, as was the case with her slavery letter, dedicated
to a noted French abolitionist. If, on the other hand, the addressee was
sympathetic or influential (or both), the letter was designed to involve
him in promoting the cause of Cuba's reform.

La Havane was directed not only to the French nobility and to
Spanish officials but also to implied readers like José de la Luz y Caballero
and José Antonio Saco; these Creole leaders, who were exiled in Europe
at the time, collaborated with Merlin by providing valuable manuscript
sources and statistical accounts of insular prosperity.[91] The real and hypo-

thetical audience of *La Havane* was thus presented with detailed accounts of the colony's military and judicial administration, economic and agricultural affairs, and social mores, in a way that guaranteed the readers' tacit participation in colonial reform. In effect, *La Havane* reads both as a manifesto of reformist goals and as a vehicle of nation-building.

The work's political engagement is clear from the opening pages; *La Havane* is doubly dedicated to the Spanish Captain-General Leopoldo O'Donnell and to the author's compatriots in the island—yet another sign of Merlin's ideological and existential split.[92] Cuban critics today tirelessly point out that Merlin's impassioned dedication to O'Donnell placed her in a politically sensitive position: O'Donnell figures in Cuban history as one of the most repressive of colonial officials.[93] He gained his reputation by spearheading the (in)famous Conspiración de la Escalera, or Ladder Conspiracy, a repression of blacks carried out by the Matanzas Military Commission in 1844 and clearly intended to wipe out the emerging class of freed blacks and mulattos.[94] Named after the torture tactics of the Commission, the Conspiracy of la Escalera remains an enigma in Cuban historiography; conflicting theories exist as to its causes and effects. British historian Hugh Thomas offers what has come down as the most accepted version of this cruel episode:

> In early 1844, about 4,000 people (in Matanzas) were suddenly arrested, including over 2,000 Negroes, over 1,000 slaves and at least seventy whites. Negroes believed to be guilty of plotting were tied to ladders and whipped to confess—the name La Escalera thus becoming notorious. . . . The period of acute repression continued for half a year. Among those shot was the mulatto poet "Plácido," the musician Román and other of the more brilliant and attractive free Negroes.[95]

After analyzing the role played by British abolitionists, Spanish colonial authorities, and the Creole planters, historian Robert Paquette concludes that the conspiracy was not a single event, but that it "existed as several conspiracies, each having distinct cores of whites, *pardos*, *morenos* or slaves, each overlapping . . . at particular times between 1841 and 1844."[96] Whether Merlin wrote her dedication before or after these events is difficult to say. Earlier critics, like Emilio Bacardí Moreau, have suggested that the dedication could have been an astute maneuver on Merlin's part to curry favor from the man close to the top of the pyramid of colonial power:

> La Condesa de Merlin, ansiosa de conquistar para su patria nativa la
> libertad que le es negada por la metrópoli española, comienza por
> poner su libro *La Havane* bajo la protección del entonces Capitán
> General de la Isla de Cuba, Leopoldo O'Donnell, en el año 1846 [*sic*], y
> [cree], conforme a su propia grandeza moral, que podría conseguir algo
> de un militar de hierro.

> (Anxious to obtain for her native land the freedom denied it by the
> Spanish metropolis, Countess Merlin begins by placing her book
> *Havana* under the protection of Leopoldo O'Donnell, then Captain-
> General of the Island of Cuba, in 1846 [*sic*], for, according to her own
> moral greatness, [she believed] that she might be able to get something
> out of a strong-as-steel military man.)[97]

What might have been intended as a patriotic gesture on Merlin's part
has been interpreted, then, as unabashed complicity with colonial rule.

Following Bacardí Moreau's interpretation, I argue, instead, that
the dedication to O'Donnell stemmed from Merlin's hope to play a mediating role between Spain and the colony, a role attuned to the "feminine
position of mediation" followed by other Latin American women during the struggle for independence.[98] Moreover, although O'Donnell certainly typifies the epitome of colonial power, Merlin's choice must be
seen not in isolation but rather in conjunction with the second dedication—to her peers on the island. Both sets of inscriptions together form
a powerful rhetorical strategy by which Merlin attempted to gain legitimacy as a Creole in the midst of family members and other influential
circles in Cuba, thus securing her active involvement in the island's political destiny.

Merlin's tactic also represents a significant departure from the
model that had been operative in Latin American colonial letters since
Garcilaso de la Vega's *Comentarios reales*, where a Creole son sought legitimation by writing a letter to a central authority in the form of a petition, following the rhetorical formula of the legal document or *relación*.[99]
To begin with, instead of entreating the Captain-General for a personal
favor, Merlin begs him instead to embrace the Creole cause by *becoming* a Creole rather than a Spaniard: "soyez havanais, général" ("General,
be a true *habanero*").[100] This was a radical request indeed if understood in
the context of the period, where only *peninsulares* had the right to hold
political office and where the position of the Captain-General repre-

sented an extension of the powers of the absolute monarchy. More significantly, the appeal to O'Donnell affirmed a heightened sense of regional
identity that was coalescing in such *criollo* claims to the crown as the right
to political representation that was argued in the Spanish Cortes in 1837.[101]
Also, if the O'Donnell dedication is seen in the context of the work as a
whole, which is structured as a series of letters to multiple addressees,
then the central authority of the Captain-General as privileged recipient is amply diffused as this power is distributed among a series of key
readers. In the last analysis, Merlin chose not to comply with existing
rhetorical molds but devised instead an effective strategy that acknowledged O'Donnell's influence while maintaining her own autonomy.

In contrast to *La Havane*, a historical text that chronicles the state
of the Cuban colony in 1840, *Viaje a la Habana* reads as a personal memoir devoted to the lyrical reconstruction of origins; the truncated text
of *Viaje a la Habana* emerges as essentially a poetic variant of the French
original. Of the thirty-six letters that compose *La Havane*, only ten were
included in the Spanish volume. Censored were the "severe" letters that
analyze the Cuban colony from a sociological and economic perspective,
as well as those passages that reveal the work's stated political agenda.
Gone too are the companion pieces in support of Merlin's argument
against abolition, the "Pièces Justificatives" ("Documentary Evidence")
that give *La Havane* a sense of definitive closure.[102] While *Viaje a la Habana*
opens with the arrival scene at the shores of the island, leaving the date
intentionally imprecise, *La Havane* begins in Europe with a description
of the ship's departure from the port of Bristol on April 15, 1840, continues with Merlin's experiences in New York, and recounts her subsequent sailing on the *Christophe-Colomb* bound for Havana.[103] The thematic
and editorial break between *La Havane* and *Viaje a la Habana* stems not
only from Merlin's political program but also from the vagaries of women's
literary vocation, as it stills remain a mystery who exactly was responsible for both the editing and translation of the Spanish version. Was it
the treacherous Philarète Chasles, who hoped to profit from Mercedes'
dependence on him? Or did la Comtesse herself supervise the Spanish
edition and translation, breaking the original text in two as an effect of
her own splintered self?

Unable to resolve this enigma of authorship, however, I do resist
the dichotomy that has persisted to this day in criticism of Merlin, and
hold that the literary and political dimensions of *La Havane* merge to

create an alternate historiography. The fusion of discourses inside the folds of the text permitted Merlin to blend her double identity and to forge a bridge between the Old World and the New. Likewise, Merlin's desire to be recognized as "hija de la Habana" by her peers in the island reveals a profound feeling of insular belonging, which I call the archeological strata of Cuban nationality (*pertenencia* or belonging). This is also inscribed in the "subjective" letters, which register Merlin's encounters with the core of her family relations and eventually document the various forms of social interaction among the Cuban Creoles. These letters attest to a particular sensibility that Merlin, though an out(in)sider, appropriated as her own. Included within these poetic passages are letters that describe colonial Havana in minute detail (details that become paramount in *Viaje a la Habana*), from its architecture to its topographical contours to social rituals such as the afternoon outing in the *volanta*, a horse-drawn carriage typically characterized by its giant wheels and immortalized in Frédéric Miahle's prints. This poetic dimension includes as well scenes of rural characters and mores in which the epistolary format becomes a vehicle for intertextual drafting.

As Bueno has noted, the letters centered on *guajiro* themes borrow from the pages of those *costumbrista* authors who were Merlin's contemporaries in Havana.[104] Indeed, because of her penchant for plagiarism, the members of Domingo del Monte's *tertulia*, specifically Félix Tanco y Bosmeniel, severely accused Merlin of this and so tarnished her reputation in the press of the period.[105] It is ironic that her contemporaries labeled Merlin's vision of the colony a "foreign view," in that they had access in most cases only to the Spanish version of the travelogue, which emphasized literary re-creation over historical fact.[106] It is in this sense that Roberto Ignacio Díaz notes "the transformation of *Viaje a la Habana* into just *la Habana*, as if to signal that Merlin will not be regarded now as a mere traveler."[107]

The split between the political and the poetic perspectives on the island colony appears to be duplicated in the divided self of the first-person narrator of the travelogues. The letters of *La Havane* present a "créole endurcie" ("ardent creole") who not only shares the interests of the sugar aristocracy but also argues on behalf of the ruling elite. Although writing under her acquired name of "la Comtesse Merlin," the lyrical voice of María de las Mercedes Santa Cruz y Montalvo emerges under the signature of authorship, asserting a sense of *pertenencia* and so guaranteeing the continuity of class and family origin. Merlin's desire was to play a leading role in the conversion of insular territory into *patria*, and her best means of doing so was writing the documentary script of *La Havane*. Yet just as powerful as her poetic Creole voice was the parallel presence of a European perspective, measured by a sense of detachment and an incisive, critical attitude toward island affairs. This is most prominent in the letters examining family codes and gender arrangements, where Merlin showed a definite European bias that moderated, in part, her impassioned defense of *criollo* cohesion. Such paradoxes are partly explained by the mechanisms of autobiographical narration: writing the self as Other tends to reproduce exactly the author's bicultural dilemma. In *La Havane*, the literary portions of the travelogue accentuate the acquired self of authorship, because the autobiographical voice recreates—and fictionalizes to a degree—the submerged Creole identity evoked in the lyrical first person of *Mes douze premières années* and *Souvenirs et Mémoires*. The voyage to *La Havane* is one of discovery, but it is a text written in the acquired language of rationality. Linguistic difference provides a filter of distance or *lejanía*, as the perspective on the colony shifts between the self that was and the self that writes. Where *Viaje a la Habana* traces a nostalgic recovery, the gesture of return to the mother tongue, in a manner anticipating Alejo Carpentier's "Viaje a la semilla" (1944), Merlin's vision is one of *cercanía*, as the autobiographical first person seems to fuse with the *criolla* self revived through the memoirs.

3. View of Havana taken from the entry of the seaport, no. 1. Frédéric Mialhe, *Viage pintoresco alrededor de la isla de Cuba dedicado al Señor Conde de Villanueva* (Havana: Litografía de Luis Marquier, ca. 1840). Special Collections Department, Otto G. Richter Library, University of Miami, Coral Gables, Florida.

3

THE VIEW FROM THE HARBOR

*Gender Subversion in the Literature of the
Second Discovery*

As her ship, aptly named the *Christophe-Colomb*, anchored overnight in the harbor, Madame la Comtesse Merlin used ecstatic language to describe the moonlit bay of Havana:

> Je suis dans le ravissement! Depuis ce matin je respire cet aire tiède et amoureux des tropiques, cet air de vie et d'enthousiasme rempli de molles et douces voluptés! Le soleil, les étoiles, la voûte éthérée, tout me paraît plus grand, plus diaphane, plus splendide!"
>
> (I am in ecstasy! Since this morning I breathe the warm and amorous breeze of the tropics, that lively and enthusiastic air, full of soft and sweet voluptousness. The sun, the stars, the celestial sphere, everything appears bigger, diaphanous, and splendid!)[1]

Her poetic response summons up *la noche insular*, Cintio Vitier's term for the experience of nightfall in a tranquil Caribbean setting, echoing as well José Lezama Lima's image conjoining night and sea: "Unía la caída de la noche con la única extensión del mar" ("Nightfall united with the vast expanse of sea").[2]

Her metaphorical approach contrasts with that of another traveler also newly arrived in the Havana bay:

> The view of Havana from the entrance to the port is one of the most picturesque and pleasing on the northern equinoctial shores of America. This view, so justly celebrated by travelers of all nations, does not possess the luxury of vegetation that adorned the banks of the Guayaquil, nor the wild majesty of the rocky coasts of Rio de Janeiro . . . but the beauty that in our climate adorns the scenes of cultivated nature, unites here with the majesty of vegetable creation, and with the organic vigor that characterizes the torrid zone.[3]

These two passages, the first from Merlin's *La Havane* (1844), and the second from Alexander von Humboldt's *The Island of Cuba* (1826), suggest a gender difference at the scene of the discovery. Whereas Merlin adapted a sentimental perspective to describe the American landscape, Humboldt has been seen as emblematic of the scientific approach. These attitudes have, in turn, conditioned the classification of the European travel book into the sentimental and scientific genres[4]; according to Pratt, "[i]n travel literature . . . science and sentiment code the imperial frontier in the two eternally clashing and complementary languages of bourgeois subjectivity."[5] Yet, rather than form a strict dichotomy between the two types of travel account, the comparison between Merlin's and Humboldt's appropriation of New World nature yields varying markers of gender. Whereas the sentimental voyage has traditionally pictured the traveler-as-protagonist, the scientific account assumes, instead, a position of mastery and detached observation.[6] However, in Merlin's and Humboldt's Cuban travelogues, gender difference surfaces as a gap between Humboldt's minute descriptions of the contours of the island, and the loving embrace of landscape represented by the French-Creole countess, what I call a position of *pertenencia*.

Despite these differences, certain textual and autobiographical connections link the work of Merlin and Humboldt as well. Humboldt reached Havana in the late 1700 following a journey of exploration in South America with the French botanist Aimé Bonpland. They were to stay in Cuba until mid March of the following year, using the time to sort and categorize the specimens of minerals and plants they had collected. Besides measuring the geographic contours of the port of Havana, Humboldt also undertook a series of side trips around the city and to the valley of Güines and the area surrounding the port of Trinidad. It was none other than the Count of Jaruco, Merlin's father, who served as Humboldt's host at the Rio Blanco estate near Trinidad, the site of his final departure. For Humboldt sailed from Trinidad back to South America to resume his scientific voyage, later recounted in his famous *Personal Narrative of Travels to the Equinoctial Regions of the New Continent During the Years 1799–1804* (Paris: 1807). Humboldt's *Essai politique sur la île de Cuba*, which originally formed part of the longer work, appeared as a separate volume in 1826, to be followed a year after by the Spanish translation.[7] Although Humboldt's editions are not substantially different, the proliferation of his works resemble the division within Merlin's own travelogues.

Humboldt's travelogues stand out from countless other European travel books as the paradigm of scientific explorations of the New World.[8] More than any other traveler, Humboldt has been dubbed "a new Columbus," not only because of the depth and breadth of his explorations, but also for his bold conquering of America for science.[9] Merlin, too, has been seen as adapting a pose similar to Columbus in her vision of insular landscape and particularly in her understanding of Cuba as "a space devoid of history;" thus "Columbus' writings is a clear model" for the rediscovery of the island implied in the poetic passages of *La Havane* exalting New World nature.[10]

Humboldt adopts what Mary Louise Pratt calls "'the face of the country'" approach in his description of the Havana bay, a method followed throughout his travel writing in his portrayals of New World nature.[11] This method consists of conveying a panoramic view that compresses in one discursive sweep the complex range of a landscape, through comparative descriptions based on the salient features of varying terrains.[12] In this case, not only did Humboldt describe the bay of Havana as less grand than Guayaquil or Rio, but he also compared the extremes of American landscape to the more temperate climate of Europe. This approach, geared to "familiarize the unfamiliar," presupposes an observer's gaze that apprehends the terrain from above; critic Scott Slovic has called this an other-worldly view similar to the mountaineer's perspective—a "summit survey."[13] Other critics, like Pratt, equate this vision with a "fantasy of dominance" in which "[t]he eye 'commands' what falls within its gaze," yet appears "powerless to act upon or interact with this landscape that offers itself."[14] According to Pratt, this rhetoric of "anti-conquest" implies a particular European gaze that, even though it displays itself as "uncontested," is nevertheless unable to transcend its own limited subject position; the viewer is denied that sense of radical Otherness predicated on an encounter with Nature.[15]

Humboldt's narrative technique of "detached surveyor of landscapes" represents the prototype of the scientific mind, which is predicated on the distance between self and other, subject and object. In her essay "Gender and Science," Evelyn Fox Keller defines the basis for the "genderization of science" or the association of scientific thought with masculinity as follows: "The relation specified between knower and known is one of distance and separation. It is that between a subject and object radically divided, which is to say, no worldly relation. Simply put, nature is objectified."[16] This objectification of nature is best exemplified in the following passage from an early history of scientific exploration to the New World:

> This is the story of *man's* conquest of the earth-mansions of South America.
>
> It is the story of *men*, all inspired by the spirit of creative curiosity and directed enthusiasm, who scrambled over the rock-hard Cordilleras; who fought through the voiceless regions of the South American jungles. . . .
>
> There are neither conquistadores nor pirates, fierce-eyed and blood-stained, in this conquest, nor steel-clad knights. . . . The most offensive weapons of these *men of conquest* are vasculums, sextants, and pincers, for its heroes are the naturalists, the scientists who *opened* South America. (Emphasis added).[17]

In the genre of scientific exploration, European travelers interposed the grid of classification and taxonomy as a means to maintain the distance between self and Other—a rhetorical device quite literally enacted by carrying into the jungle the instruments of science.[18] Yet as he "journeyed in search of the secrets of nature," the European traveler also underwent a process of self-discovery.[19] In the course of overcoming obstacles for the sake of knowledge, he found that "[t]he most arduous trial" consisted of retaining his sense of self and particularly his identity as a European; "[i]t was difficult to write with detachment in the midst of a world that threatened to unveil a secret that could conceivably jolt the traveler out of his identity."[20]

Merlin's memoirs, on the other hand, convey an experience of landscape that radically differs from Humboldt's detached stance. The scientist's reverie is transformed in her text into a contemplative yearning for a fusion with nature, not mastery of it.[21] Rather than impose a "civilizing mission," Merlin's project of discovery implied the desire for permanence and attachment to a particular setting.[22] Instead of detailing the geographical contours of the Havana bay, as in Humboldt, her travelogues traced the profile of the colonial city, imagined as an intimate space asleep by the bay. Where Humboldt leveled the natural exuberance of the New World by means of comparisons to other tropical settings, Merlin strove to represent the excess (the "voluptuousness") of tropical scenery in terms analogous to what poet Lezama Lima has called *la sobrenaturaleza*, a state of being conditioned by the poetic image as it symbolically summons the world of nature: "La penetración de la imagen en la naturaleza engendra la sobrenaturaleza" ("When the image pierces the realm of nature, it engenders the supernature").[23] In contrast to the all-seeing eye of the scientist and to his posture of detached observation, Merlin struggled to interiorize her reencounter with the tropics, all the while acknowledging the limitations of her senses. Her memoirs entail, then, a sentimental appropriation of landscape, what I earlier have called *pertenencia*.[24]

Both types of travel books produce a shift from nature writing to history, a move predicated on the fact that the scientific travel account established the continent's "historical uniqueness" precisely by providing descriptions of New World nature.[25] Indeed, "the European travelers brought an idea of history that would allow Latin American nature to provide the basis for an autonomous and distinct Latin American being."[26] Because the scientists classified and named New World flora and fauna, they were considered "second discoverers" of the continent; later in the nineteenth century, scientific discourse enabled the Creole's discovery of his own land.[27] This was the case with Domingo Sarmiento's *Facundo* (1845), a crucial text of Argentine nationality and an influential model for Latin American letters. Here, Sarmiento's vision of the *pampas* is mediated by the inclusion of Humboldt's comparison of the South American plains to Oriental steppes.[28]

In contrast to Sarmiento, who adopted the European travel book as a lens with which to view the vast Argentine *pampa*, Merlin structured her vision of Havana by means of an eclectic borrowing from various sources; among them, the texts of the *cronistas* but, more precisely, the *versions* of the early chronicles that appeared in periodical publications in Havana during the time of her journey.[29] This technique of textual borrowing enabled her, in turn, to maneuver effectively the contradictions stemming from her double identity as both European and Creole. Reversing to a certain extent the predicament of the European (male) scientific traveler, who in his travels sought to transcend yet at the same time remain fixed in his (gender) identity, Merlin's voyage to the New World became an introspective journey. Rather than preserve a singular sense of self, as was the case with Humboldt, Merlin's "journey back to the source" attempted to dissolve a divided self-identity. Travelers like Merlin "wind up being both subject and object of their gaze, and the language they use detaches them artificially from who and what they are in the same way that scientific discourse presumably establishes a distance between naturalists and the world they study."[30] Merlin needed a language with which to ground herself as a subject, and so to recuperate by writing her past self as María de las Mercedes Santa Cruz y Montalvo. By choosing French as a literary language, Merlin became an "other" to herself, inasmuch as she was striving to recuperate a lost Creole identity while framing the discovery of her island in terms derived from European culture. Instead of turning New World nature into an object of inquiry,[31] Merlin established an intimate connection with the island landscape, a bonding with the literal source of her history as well as with the symbolic space of the origins. Not only did she aspire to a position of involvement rather than detachment, but she also confronted the necessity of speaking from a gendered position—that is, of developing a consciousness of being "other with respect to man."[32]

If the account of Humboldt's voyage is considered the paradigm of scientific exploration in the New World, how do Merlin's memoirs compare to the master-text of the discovery? What influence, if any, did the literature of the second discovery, like Humboldt's works, have in shaping her reencounter with America and her view of the other? The differences between Merlin's *La Havane* and Humboldt's *The Island of Cuba* (1826),[33] both in terms of their relationship to the New World and their respective narrative strategies, show that, though Humboldt's text acquired the status of master narrative, *La Havane*, by representing an alternative tradition (albeit from the margins) broke free of certain textual restrictions and so pointed to a new historiography. Because women have been traditionally excluded from historical discourse, which has been defined as authentic only when written by men, Merlin embedded earlier historical accounts by male authors into her memoirs as a means to legitimate her own text. The result is a hybrid construction that represents a third and different genre, analogous to what Alejo Carpentier has called, in the context of the Latin American baroque, "un *tercer estilo*" ("a third style").[34]

My comparison of Humboldt's *The Island of Cuba* and Merlin's *La Havane* as historical discourse will focus on their respective treatments of a scene from the conquest and early settlement of Cuba in the sixteenth century: the conflict between Diego Velázquez and Hernán Cortés that led to the latter's invasion of Mexico and subsequent conquest of the Aztec empire. Not only is literary mediation at work in these two writers' memoirs through their reliance on previous sources, particularly on the texts of colonial historiography to describe the historical moment, but the way in which such texts were appropriated also shape the authors' "historical comprehension"—that is, the historian's use of narrative in order to "[think] together in a single act . . . the complicated parts experienced as *seriatim*."[35] Once the differences between Humboldt's and Merlin's methods of historical representation are established, particularly their manner of imaginatively constructing a narrative or "story,"[36] a comparison of their accounts of the Velázquez/Cortés episode can turn on questions of narrative relevance. How does each author choose to represent the colonial past?[37] What episodes are selected or filtered out?

Here I resist the heavily ideological reading that Pratt proposes in her book on travel narrative about Africa and the New World. According to Pratt, the criterion of relevance for the genre of scientific exploration is that of an all-scanning "I/eye" that looks at the land as future prospects for European expansion.[38] She claims that "Alexander von Humboldt reinvented South America first and foremost as nature," as "a spectacle capable of overwhelming human knowledge and understanding," and as an empty expanse of land inhabited not by historical subjects but by the silent presence of "the hypothetical traveler-seer"—that is, Humboldt himself and the European explorers that would follow.[39] Pratt distinguishes Humboldt's *Political Essay on the Kingdom of New Spain* (1811–1814) and *The Island of Cuba* from both the *Personal Narrative* and *Views of Nature* (1850; 1896), in terms of their mythologizing of New World nature, and goes on to claim that the first two works are characterized by "ahistoricity and the absence of culture."[40] Contrary to Pratt, my reading of Humboldt reveals, rather, his involvement with both landscape *and* history in a way that problematizes such a static reduction of genre to mere ideological motive.

Likewise, Roberto Ignacio Díaz has argued that Merlin's "disregard for Cuban history seems even more apparent in other sections of *La Havane*,"[41] yet those chapters that recreate colonial historiography clearly demonstrate Merlin's concern for history. Not only does *La Havane* manifest an implied act of judgment on Cuba's colonial past, but it also embellishes that past as the period that shaped Cuba's present condition as a colony. This act of judgment gives coherence to a multilayered narrative which purports to account for all the visible dimensions of Havana: as a port, as a colonial city, as the site for an emerging Creole intellectual culture, including an incisive analysis of the administrative and judicial systems. For Louis Mink such a sweeping judgment constitutes both the aim of historical writing and the end result of "historical understanding," an understanding that conveys a sense of the *meaning* of historical events within a "grammar" of history that yields resemblances between events but also conveys their uniqueness.[42] The historian arrives at this final "synoptic judgment," as Mink calls it, by means of "ingredient conclusions," conclusions that are "represented by the narrative order itself," *exhibited* rather than *demonstrated*.[43]

A close reading of Merlin's and Humboldt's texts reveals historical judgments that hinge on the selections of previous texts and also on the conclusions construed in the narrative. In both Humboldt's and Merlin's memoirs, the rhetoric of colonial historiography ultimately serves a political argument, what I call the political mediation implied in both their works. In the last analysis, the introduction of a political argument by recourse to the colonial past effects a shift in the two main paradigms of European travel writing ostensibly represented by Merlin's and Humboldt's texts—the sentimental and scientific journeys. This shift eventually makes the two travelogues converge in their respective visions of the future of Cuba.

In his treatment of historical events in *The Island of Cuba*, Humboldt used the comparative method he had adopted for landscape description, subordinating such events to his primary goal of observing and categorizing physical phenomena. Comparison, in this case, entailed the juxtaposition of factual discourse—statistical tables, measurements, latitude and temperature charts—with narrative "capsules" that compressed historical time either in one bold statement or in more expansive causal explanations.[44] The "capsules" are analogous to his famed landscape descriptions. It is the longer narrative passages that constitute the historiographical dimension of Humboldt's text. These passages are related to the "manners-and-customs descriptions" typical of the European travelogue, which, according to Pratt, represent a normalizing discourse geared to the "stable fixing of subjects and systems of differences."[45] However, this categorization does not totally apply in Humboldt's case. In one notable passage from *The Island of Cuba* that contains a comparative view of the racial composition of the Americas as well as a capsule account of the slave trade in the Antilles and Brazil, this "eye of the historian" approach leads up to an energetic statement against slavery that, rather than "fix" the black in a stable position, is sympathetic to his plight.[46] Given the external constraints on the configuration of his narrative (i.e., the fact that his voyage was financed by the Spanish authorities), Humboldt did indeed stretch the limits of a scientific discourse to include anticolonialist statements. There is no better proof of this than the fact that his text was banned by the city of Havana in 1827 for its abolitionist passages and implicit criticism of colonial authority.

Besides this comparative perspective, Humboldt employed throughout the text of *The Island of Cuba* a random method of historical observation, one that I call a "spot-check" approach. It consists primarily of inserting casual references to historical events among scientific descriptions and statistical tables. This method results in a particular type of hybridization: a discursive shift from literary to scientific description, from factual observation to social and political commentary, without any apparent stylistic transition.[47]

In Merlin's memoirs, hybridization is the result of the method of composition itself and not merely a stylistic effect created by the "shifting" of discourses; it is one of the many "discriminatory identity effects" resulting from her double condition as cultural hybrid and woman.[48] Though she included in her narrative a number of statistical and population tables, these fragments were never original; moreover, they are copied in her text with conscious errors. This "margin of error" (or error at the margins, for these objectifying discourses are always subservient to the dominant historical mode), shows Merlin to have been consciously deriving her work from a number of apparently unrelated and quite diverse

genres that include the travelogue, political treatise, and poetic reverie.
Yet *La Havane* unfolds as a uniform text, an effect achieved through
the technique of textual grafting; this may range from the simple quotation and revision of original sources to the rewriting of entire literary
works.[49] By placing different fragments of texts together on the same discursive level, Merlin constructed what I call a hybrid historiography, one
that lays claim to legitimacy by incorporating previous sources.

   If Humboldt with his comparative descriptions sought to recreate
the traveler's emotional response to a particular setting, Merlin sought
to faithfully reproduce the tracks in the historian's mind: "on est ravi
d'ouvrir . . . un de ces bon vieux chroniqueurs sans fard et sans artifice,
main qui possèdent le premier art de l'écrivain, celui de rendre exacte-
ment leurs souvenirs et leurs impressions" ("it is delightful to open . . .
those good and old chroniclers who, without artifice, possess the writer's
most important art, that of narrating exactly his memories and impressions").[50] Hence there was in Merlin an (un)conscious identification with
the historian's craft, an identification that stemmed back to adolescence when, witnessing the effects of the French occupation in Madrid,
she opted to "read" great men rather than novels.[51] Nevertheless, despite
her avowed dedication to history, Merlin also claimed in the opening
pages of her work that she, too, "[j]'ai écrit ces lettres sans art, sans préten-
sions d'auteur, ne pensant qu'à reproduire avec fidélité les impresions,
les sentiments et les ideés qui naissaient de mes voyages" ("I wrote these
letters without art, without authorial pretensions, thinking only to faithfully reproduce the impressions, feelings and ideas that were born from
my travels").[52] This posture of literary naïveté is, of course, a powerful
strategy in the hands of a woman author. It allowed Merlin to identify
and at the same time select which type of source document she would
exploit in her account. Adopting the same tone of innocence, Merlin conveyed how "avec un joie d'enfant et dans un long recueillement" ("with
a little girl's happiness and a long concentration") she dusted off the
ancient documents ("j'ai consulté nos anciennes chroniques") in order
to "leur demandant tous les détails possibles sur les faits et les noms historiques qui touches de près ou de loin à mon île maternelle" ("inquire
in them for all possible details pertaining to the events and historical
names that directly or indirectly bear on my maternal Isle").[53] Unlike
Humboldt, who took great care to reproduce comprehensive, exact data,
Merlin strove rather to *select* only those historical passages that served

her purpose, which was, for the most part, the sentimental appropriation of landscape and country, of a sense of *pertenencia*.

Both writers described in their memoirs a scene from the settlement of the island by Velázquez in the early sixteenth century, a period lost in the denseness of time before Cuba was articulated either as a national boundary or as a sociocultural entity. The two travel accounts construct an archeology, a textual re-creation that defines the island in the scripture of the world (in historiography). The method of appropriation of colonial discourse selected by each writer determined, in part, the scope and breadth of each historical vision. Whereas Humboldt diffused historical commentary by combining it with a poetics of landscape and scientific observation, Merlin limited herself to accounts of the colonial past alone in order to better illustrate her analysis of the political present.

Humboldt's record of his sea voyage around the Jardines and Jardinillos (Gardens and Little Gardens), an archipelago of islands that spread from the southern coast of the Camagüey province to the larger Isle of Pines, anticipates, or more precisely corroborates, Lezama Lima's theories of the poetic image as an index of the condensed potential hidden in history. Indeed, Humboldt's account verifies how the New World landscape was a generative source of cultural meaning, in a manner similar to the engendering of the poetic image described in Lezama's *Las eras imaginarias* (1971) as "el *potens*, la posibilidad infinita" ("the *potens*, infinite possibility") embodying both the temporal conditioning and the perpetual transmutations of the historical process.[54] The site of the Jardinillos is notable not only for its surreal beauty but also for its historical "density," inasmuch as it was the point from which the rest of the island was first explored.[55] Whereas statistical tables and graphs dominate the narrative of *The Island of Cuba*, the last section, endowed with the poetic title of "Voyage to the Valley of Güines, to Batabanó and the Port of Trinidad, and to the Gardens and Little Gardens of the King and Queen," reduces Humboldt's scientific stance to cryptic measurements of latitudes and temperatures, and to descriptions of coral formations, rocks, and the manatees of fable.[56] The resulting poetic aura of Humboldt's narration sharply contrasts with his detached outlook; indeed, Humboldt interwove literary and scientific discourses to such an extent that the narrative appears to converge, or rather merge, in a textual fusion that harmonizes the opposing pull between detachment and involvement, at times tending more toward the latter extreme. This results in a different kind of hybridization than the one represented in the rest of *The Island of Cuba*, where the tone of mastery and control is maintained. If the expression of wonder at New World nature was a rhetorical device that helped the traveler persevere in his European identity,[57] here Humboldt surrendered, like a woman traveler, to the mystery enveloping him, as in the following description of a mirage effect in the surface of the islets:

> And in truth a portion of these misnamed gardens is very beautiful, for the voyager varies the scene momently, and the verdure of some of the islets borrows a new splendor from the contrast with others that present to the eye only white and arid sands. The surface of these, heated by the rays of the sun, seems to undulate as though it were water, and by the contact with the strata of air of unequal temperature, produces from ten in the morning until four in the afternoon, all the varied phenomena of a mirage.[58]

In the Jardinillos passages the tone is often one of enthrallment or exalted captivity, a rhetorical effect enacted quite literally by the events described, for Humboldt's expedition had no choice but to navigate slowly through the keys, impeded as they were by rocky shores and jutting coral reefs: "Three days passed before we could emerge from the labyrinth of the Jardines and Jardinillos" ("No pudimos salir sino pasados tres días de aquel laberinto de *Jardines* y *Jardinillos*").[59]

Whereas, sailing through the Jardinillos, Humboldt had deferred his scientific outlook to the experience of landscape, upon approaching the Isle of Pines he shifted the emphasis from nature to history; that is, history displaces both nature and science as a form of explanatory discourse. Notice, for example, this sentence that appears to anticipate a spectacular natural site but reveals instead the historical image possessed by (contained in) the landscape, as Lezama Lima's poetics suggest: "[t]hese regions possess a charm that is wanting in the greater part of the New World, for they recall to the mind memories which cluster around the greatest names of the Spanish monarchy: Columbus and Cortés."[60] In this poignant passage, the historical imagination takes over Humboldt's detached stance as observer of purely natural phenomena; rather, the natural world becomes endowed with meaning, for the geographical sites themselves bear historical import, as in the legendary actions invoked by the names of Don Cristóbal Channel and Cortés Bay. Consciously donning the mask of "second discoverer" at this point in the journey, Humboldt retraced the steps which the original discoverer made during his second journey while quoting extensively from Columbus's *Diary*. When the crew anchored at the Don Cristóbal Channel, Humboldt admired the splendid night of the Caribbean, evoking it in a hyperbole reminiscent of the First Discoverer's *Diary*.[61] In the same passage Humboldt quoted from accounts of Columbus's second and fourth voyages, alluding to his "ardent imagination" on thinking that he had arrived at the empire of Gran Khan while at the Little Gardens.[62]

Immediately following the evocation of Columbus is the Cortés episode which concerns us here. To document this episode, Humboldt referred to Antonio de Herrera y Tordesillas's *Historia general de los hechos de los castellanos, en las islas y tierra firme de el [sic] Mar Océano* (1601–1615).[63] Although Herrera's name first appears in Humboldt's account as a casual reference to explain the name of the Havana port, Humboldt used Herrera here to describe one of the most important historical episodes in the colonial history of the Caribbean: Cortés's departure from the Isle of Pines in order to free himself from his superior, Spanish Governor Velázquez, whom he had served as secretary. For Humboldt the area around the Isle of Pines not only was important to the settlement of the island of Cuba but held further historical treasures in its association with Cortés's subsequent conquest of Mexico. Hence, Humboldt's appropriation of the discourse of the *cronistas* fit his descriptive purpose of vastly expanding the historical field, much in the same way that he surveyed "a vast space of country" from the mountaintops of South America.[64] Cortés's exploits—his near shipwreck on the reefs of the Jardinillos, the gathering of his fleet near Cape San Antonio, and his clandestine flight from Velázquez's authority—are narrated not in story form but rather as a summary listing.[65] The strict attention to detail effaces any kind of sympathetic treatment of Cortés, reinforcing rather the impersonal mask of "historian of America" that Humboldt had unabashedly assumed elsewhere in *The Island*.[66]

Navigating with Humboldt up to this point, the reader is then astonished to discover that this listing of events has led up to the following "ingredient conclusion":

> Strange vicissitudes of human affairs! A handful of men, landing from the extreme west of Cuba upon the coast of Yucatán, tore down the empire of Montezuma; and in our time, three centuries later, this same Yucatán, which is part of the confederation of independent Mexican States, has almost menaced a conquest of the western shores of Cuba.[67]

As with his landscape descriptions, Humboldt has compressed here vast chapters of time into one brief episode; the rhetorical structure of parallel reversal allows him to condense into a single, breathless phrase three centuries of Latin American colonial history. Moreover, the super-imposition of Cortés as future conqueror of Mexico onto the return of the *criollos* to the site from which they were "discovered" has a hidden political implication, for Humboldt also referred here to the "The Black Eagle" society, a group of liberal Creoles in exile in Mexico who staged an "[i]ll-fated conspiracy in favor of independence in the early 1820s."[68] Organized as a Junta Patriótica (Patriotic Front) on July 4, 1825, the group sought recognition from Mexican president Guadalupe Victoria and the powerful General Santa Anna, but it received little official sup-port. Members then established links with Cuba and organized a con-spiracy that was led in Mexico by a former priest known as "Aguila Negra" (Simón de Chávez) and in Cuba by two Creole leaders (José Julián Solís and Manuel Rojo); the latter were joined by many other prominent Cubans. This early plot in favor of independence in Cuba was soon discovered and suppressed by Captain General Dionisio Vives, who arrested most of its leaders and sentenced them to jail. By means of this oblique reference, Humboldt signaled his leanings in favor of the island's independence, an opinion he would otherwise have had to suppress.[69]

Humboldt's narrative method also suggests that the significance of Cortés's expedition lies in that it both foreshadows and dramatizes Cuba's colonial predicament—a moral lesson gained through historical reversal and the superimposition of destinies. The broadening of the his-torical field in the Cortés passage masks Humboldt's hidden involvement with the present, an involvement that challenges his supposed stance as "detached surveyor of landscapes."[70] In his voyage through the submerged islets, Humboldt inserted himself, however indirectly, in the destinies of the New World which he was "discovering" for science.

In contrast to Humboldt, who for the remainder of *The Island of Cuba* subsumes history to physical science, Merlin consciously structured *La Havane* as a historical text, alluding in many places to the conquest and early settlement of the island. Though Merlin was, indeed, "a pas-sionate reader of the *crónicas de Indias*," the historical passages of *La Havane* are not drawn directly from these sources, as Roberto Ignacio Díaz claims,[71] but are lifted rather from secondary sources; mainly, the set of historical sketches on the discovery and conquest of the island written by Cuban *costumbristas* for the pages of *El Plantel*. Indeed, the Velázquez/Cortés episode included in the letter which opens the second volume of *La Havane* (XVIII) is unabashedly borrowed from two sketches published in *El Plantel* summarizing the exploits of both *conquistadores*.[72] In her version, Merlin resisted writing about Columbus, for he had already been "agrandi par son audace" ("aggrandized by his daring") in world history, and her preference was clearly for Velázquez, whom she considers "le vrai fondateur de la civilisation espagnole de Cuba" ("the true founder of Hispanic civilization in Cuba").[73] If in the first volume of *La Havane* "the literary figure that she prefers is Columbus,"[74] in the second volume the Admiral is displaced by Velázquez, who comes to represent the Hispanic legacy in the constitution of Cuban national identity. This choice merely reflects the fact that Merlin remained faithful to the interpretation of Cuban colonial history given by the anonymous Creole authors of the *El Plantel* sketches.

Such an interpretation clearly served a political purpose, for it staked out a claim of Cuba's colonial past that insured the continuity of cultural origins with Spain. Not only was an emerging sense of Cuban nationality posited on a shared Spanish inheritance, according to the leading Creole intellectual, José Antonio Saco, but a heightened sense of Hispanism offered also the only resistance to the alternative argument of annexation to the United States.[75] In her attempt to recuperate a lost Creole identity, Merlin emphasized the cultural bond tying the island to the peninsula, thus echoing the prevailing belief that the Creoles in Cuba constituted a hybrid race of "españoles-habaneros" ("Havana Spaniards"). *La Havane* illustrates precisely Cuban historian Jorge Ibarra's definition of a regional identity, which at that time prevailed over a more inclusive awareness of nationhood.[76]

Merlin's choice of Velázquez over Columbus was also a consequence of her method of historical inquiry, for her narrative includes what other historians left out. On the one hand, she rejected official interpretations of the Spanish conquest, such as Herrera y Tordesilla's *Historia general*, in its depiction of heroic exploits, and instead began where Herrera left off in his account of early colonization (thus rescuing from oblivion the figure of Velázquez). On the other hand, she based her interpretation not on original sources—the texts of the *cronistas* and especially Herrera y Tordesilla's *Decalogues*, which are privileged in Humboldt's account—but rather on *copies* of those texts as refashioned by contemporary Cuban authors like José Antonio Echeverría for nineteenth-century periodical publications. In this way Merlin dismissed the value of the original while privileging the secondary or supplementary version, which she in turn embellished with her own perspective on the past. Moreover, she mixed together those secondary texts with her own writing, choosing supplementary fragments at random wherever they fit her own discourse, and reinterpreting events to conform to her own historical logic, one in which nobility of intention took precedence over heroism. The result is an involved, female perspective characterized by a schematic account of events and by a focus on individual destinies. Whereas Humboldt's work tends toward a broad historical sweep, Merlin placed attention on the human drama—in particular on the conflict arising from the strong personalities of Velázquez and Cortés—revealed through personal interludes that, taken cumulatively, compose the written record of history.

Hence, Merlin's account of the early colonial period may be construed as a narrative in which events unfold as larger-than-life personalities act in tune with their innermost passions, a typically Romantic attitude that is nevertheless projected back onto the early history of the island. Although she derived the basic information on Velázquez from the sketch in *El Plantel*, Merlin recast the story of insular settlement in terms of an insoluble conflict between Velázquez and his headstrong secretary: "Dès que nous voyons dans le histoire ces deux hommes en face l'un de l'autre, leur secrète et ardente inimitié nous apparaît" ("From the moment these two men stand one in front of the other in history, their secret and ardent rivalry appears").[77] Whereas Echeverría merely recounted the episodes of Velázquez's life, following closely Herrera's *Decalogues* and even imitating the work's rambling style, Merlin wrote as an empathic witness to history. Resisting the detached tone of Echeverría's colorless tale, she sided with Velázquez over the perfidious Cortés, preferring the first for his elevated, noble stature and censuring the second for betraying the elder man's trust. If Humboldt specifically related Cortés's departure to a broader historical context, Merlin focused instead on narrative detail to highlight the human drama involved in the clash of historical agents. Though lifted directly from Echeverría's version, the scene of departure in Merlin's text is converted into a climactic drama to effectively convey an emotional effect:

[M]ais Cortez n'était pas homme à se laisser jouer: le 18 de novembre 1518 au matin, Velasquez promenait son indécision sur la plage, lorqu'il aperçut une chaloupe qui portait des armes, des bagages et Cortez lui-même.

"Quoi! compère, cria le gouverneur, c'est ainsi que vous vous en allez! Belle manière de prendre congé de moi!"

"Que votre seigneurie me pardonne, répondit Cortez debout dans la chaloupe, les affaires comme celles-ci ont besoin d'être faites avant d'être dites. Votre seigneurie a-t-elle quelque chose à m'ordonner?"

La chaloupe aborda la navire; le vent enfla les voiles de l'escadre; Velasquez resta sur la rive, et Cortez alla conquérir le Mexique.

(But Cortés was a man to be reckoned with, and so the morning of November 18, 1518, when Velázquez displayed his indecision on the beach [to give Cortés the order to sail], he saw a small ship that bore arms, equipment and the very same Cortés.

"Well, how, *compadre*, you go just like that! That's a fine way of saying good-by!"

"Forgive me, Sir, because these and other like things are better done than said!' replied Cortés, already aboard the boat. 'Does your Highness have any orders for me?"

The small boat reached the ship, the wind hoisted the sails of the fleet; Velázquez remained on shore and Cortés went off to conquer Mexico).[78]

In rewriting this scene Merlin was careful to suppress the mediating function of Echeverría's sketch and instead positioned herself on the same discursive level as Herrera y Tordesillas, constructing her tale from both the Velázquez and the Cortés sketches but making the result appear as an embellishment of the colonial historiographer. Thus her narrative departs from Herrera y Tordesilla's account when the latter "eliminates" Velázquez from his text in favor of the warrior exploits of Cortés and Pánfilo de Narvaez.

Merlin's appropriated nineteenth-century historical sketches serve a quite different purpose than that of the (derived) originals. Instead of introducing the reader to historical topics, her intention was to diminish the stature of Cortés's heroic exploits, thereby drawing attention to Velázquez's moral rectitude. The anti-heroic stance continues in her critique of Cortés's "sang-froid," ironically ridiculed as demanding "de persévérance et de fermeté que celle d'Alexandre et de César" ("the perseverance and harshness of Alexander and Caesar both").[79] Not only did Merlin restructure the Cuban *costumbristas'* appropriation of Herrera's original, but in doing so she also departed from the established narrative of conquest. In brief, she left Cortés at the footsteps of Tenochtitlán, thus frustrating the reader's expectations for a repeated staging of his victory over Montezuma. In addition, Merlin included an ironic meta-commentary on the historian's function, pointing out in no uncertain terms the deficiencies of existing histories: "La plupart des historiens de Cortez ont effacé ou diminué les grandes actions de son maître, comme si ces deux personnages n'étaient pas grands encore dans la rivali-té énergique de leurs passions, comme s'il fallait éteindre une gloire pour faire éclater l'autre!" ("The majority of historians of Cortés have effaced or diminished the role played by his master, as if the two char-acters were not great even in the energetic rivalry of their passions, as if it were necessary to stamp out the glory of one in order to make the other shine!").[80] As the only oblique reference to her hidden sources in *El Plantel*, this statement affirms Merlin's gendered subversion of existing histories. Reversing the trend of both colonial historiography and its *criollo* imitators to highlight Cortés, by taking the opposite path of tracing Velázquez's tale to the end of his career, Merlin valued the loser's moral virtues over the winner's physical prowess and pose of colonial mastery.

Merlin's "ingredient conclusion" reduces, then, the inflated hero-ism of the *conquistador* as depicted in the historiography of the con-quest and beyond in its *costumbrista* epigones. Likewise, her narrative seasons Echeverría's conventional interpretation of Velázquez's down-fall with an impassioned understanding of the governor's ethical and his-torical worth. Echeverría simply mentioned Velázquez's obscurity and drew a pathetic picture of his burial crypt reduced to ruins in a street cor-ner in Santiago, an apt emblem of the hero's fall from grace:

> ¡Triste emblema por cierto de la vida de Velázquez!. . . Mármol de buena veta, sacólo Dios de la oscuridad, é infundiéndole vida lo colocó en escelso [*sic*] puesto; pero su alma desvanecida con la altura, no pudo mantenerse en ella: y bajando de repente, vino á servir de escabel á otro mortal mas atrevido y de mas injenio, que supo adquirirse fama impere-cedera, y llenar con su nombre el mundo.

> (Truly a sad emblem of Velazquez' life!. . . Like a marble of rich vein, God took him out of the darkness, and after infusing him with life, he stationed him in a lofty place; but his soul fainted with the altitude, and consequently couldn't stay there: falling suddenly, he came to serve as a

footstool to another mortal who through daring and cleverness was able to acquire for himself immortal fame, and was able to spread his name throughout the world.)[81]

In contrast, Merlin transformed this anecdote into an important historical lesson, noting that any passerby wandering on these ruins would discover a fragment of Latin prose attesting to Velázquez's grandeur.[82] Instead of ending her account, like Echeverría, by again siding with Cortés, Merlin concluded the episode with epigrammatic irony, bringing the focus back to Cortés only to draw a picture of his last days as a broken, impoverished man. In picturing Cortés as "profondément blessé, découragé, presque désespéré" ("deeply hurt, discouraged [and] desperate"), Merlin leveled the heroic heights of male historiographical discourse and canceled out the gap between conquered and conqueror by pointing out their common disenfranchised fate.[83] Hence the judgment of history derived from her text is a moral lesson on waning power and the deaggrandizement of all heroes in a final, shared destiny.

Parallel to the demystifying thrust of her narrative is a concern for the role of women in history. Merlin attempted to recuperate the legendary figure of Marina—Cortés's interpreter and mistress—in Latin American history working from only a passing mention in the *El Plantel* sketch.[84] Although Merlin followed the lead of the semi-anonymous author J. M. de A. in trying to reverse "les falsifications historiques ou dramatiques" ("the dramatic, historical falsifications") to which Marina has been subject, their technique clearly differed. J. M. de A. presumably was citing a passage from Bernal Díaz del Castillo when he described Marina as "fidelísima intérprete de Hernán Cortés" ("a very faithful interpreter of Hernan Cortés"); although Merlin veered away from this conventional picture, she anachronistically cast the same passage as an "eyewitness" report.[85] As a matter of fact, Merlin could not portray Marina in her account as a fully developed historical agent because it was at this point that J. M. de A. took up an apology for Cortés, forcing Merlin to abruptly abandon Marina's narrative.[86] Frustrated in her attempts to fill this historiographical vacuum, Merlin transgressed the apologists' version of Cortés and so marked her distance from a male historiography.

In reverse movement to Humboldt, for whom the Cortés episode served to mask events in the historical present, Merlin privileged the past and the historian's subjective impressions, substantiating her account with Romantic/realistic interpretations of colonial history.[87] In similar fashion to Humboldt, however, Merlin also duplicated his gesture of writing himself into the present when at the conclusion of the Cortés/Velázquez episode she addressed the foundational figure of Francisco Arango.

Arango's crucial role in the early history of the colony was due to the fact that he nearly single-handedly promoted modern methods of cultivating sugarcane in Cuba and negotiated with Spain the lifting of trade restrictions. Like her earlier appropriation of the Cortés/Velázquez episode, Merlin's treatment of Arango's role in Cuban history closely followed Ramón de Palma's published sketch in the 1838 volume of *El Plantel*.[88] Echoing Palma's grandiloquent gesture of typifying Arango as a figure of his age, Merlin drew a portrait of Arango as both the originator of the Cuban trade in African slaves as well as the first proponent of abolition on the island.[89] Comparable in his civilizing role to the Argentine Sarmiento, Arango was caught in a similar paradoxical relationship to the non-European: whereas Sarmiento moved away from his culture by "reading" it in the texts of the European scientific explorers, Arango instigated a research trip to Europe "pour recueillir et appliquer aux besoins de notre île les documents relatifs aux progrès industriels" ("to collect and apply to the needs of our island documents relative to industrial progress").[90] Accompanying Arango on his voyage back to Europe was none other than the Count of Montalvo, Merlin's maternal uncle, whose name figures in the *Relacion del viage que hizò el señor de Arango, con el conde de Casa Montalvo*, a precursor text of the Creole's interior voyage. Arango is also linked to Merlin's own father, a protégé of Arango's at court who used Arango's influence to win a trade concession from the crown for introducing wheat into island commerce.[91] Arango and Montalvo brought back to the island the first specimens of Otahiti sugarcane, mentioned in Humboldt's account as a type of cane that produced one-fourth more juice than other types, given its thicker and richer stalk.[92] The introduction of this more productive species of sugarcane propelled Cuba's transition from the elementary economy of the *factoría* to the complex industry of the *plantación*, a shift which also occurred on the cultural sphere with the beginnings of Cuban national culture by Montalvo's generation, later intensified by the efforts of del Monte's literary circle.[93]

Arango figures in Merlin's text as a present-day analogue to Velázquez, both of them symbols of the Hispanic legacy in the constitution of Cuban nationalism. Hence, Arango also functions as an emblem for Merlin's self-proclaimed role as a mediator between Spain and the colony.[94] What appears at first to be an apology to her interlocutor, the Count de Saint-Aulaire, for extending herself on behalf of a Creole nobleman little known in Europe ends as an exhortation to the Spanish regime to grant Creoles the right to hold public office (a 1837 decision in the Spanish Cortes denied this right to native-born citizens of the "provincias de ultra mar").[95] Thus, in a manner similar to Humboldt, Merlin used the historical past as a pretext for inserting herself into the present. Not only did Arango serve as Merlin's literary precursor, but he also played a similar role for Alexander von Humboldt, who relied on Arango's pamphlets to write his chapter on island agriculture. One could even go so far as to say that Arango, in a very real sense, served as co-author of Humboldt's travelogue, for his extensive comments on island economy, the slave trade, and production quotas provided additional information that could not have been known by the famous European scientist.

Velázquez and Cortés were not the only ties between Merlin and Humboldt. For Merlin's and Humboldt's narrative fall together as well under the father's shadow, whose aid and hospitality enabled the Prussian to carry out his observations, along with Francisco Arango and Nicolás Calvo y O'Farrill, a member of the maternal branch of Merlin's family.[96] More than functioning as a literary model, then, Humboldt's text served Merlin, in part, as a means to recuperate the symbolic legacy of her father, for later on in her letter she would describe Arango as "father of the land." This intertextual echo suggests a recuperation of the father/daughter bond as literary legacy.

At one level, the contrast between Humboldt and Merlin hinges on the difference between a Romantic and a scientific sensibility; yet, at the level of literary affiliation, there is a sense in which both texts converge rather than diverge. In his introduction to the *Personal Narrative*, Humboldt explained that "the unity of composition [of a historical narrative] is observed when the traveller describes what has passed under his own eye, and when his attention is fixed less on scientific observations than on the manners of a people and the great phenomena of nature."[97] This is precisely the criteria operating in Merlin's *Viaje a la Habana*, the Spanish edition of the text that is devoid of historical analysis or political commentary. It is almost as if Humboldt would have liked to embark on a sentimental journey such as Merlin's, or to have written a text as eclectic as hers.

In assessing Merlin's method for the writing of history, one of her primary techniques is the shift of the documentary function to an impersonal historian. The formula "dit le chroniqueur," recurs throughout the chapters dealing with Cuba's colonial past, thus effacing Merlin's narrative persona. It is as if she were conscious that the task of the historian ran contrary to traditional expectations for women. However, this method also effectively eliminates all references to secondary sources, such as the articles in *El Plantel*, because all the quotes are leveled within a uniform rhetorical mold. This procedure, though analogous to Humboldt's shift of responsibility to a "historian of America," reveals Merlin's paradoxical relationship to a written tradition. By inserting into her narrative an internal historian, Merlin was participating in the founding archival fiction in Latin American literature that posits "[h]istory [as] a tissue of quotations."[98] However, she stands out from other Creole intellectuals, such as Sarmiento, who appropriated the texts of the scientific travelers in order to construct his own vision of the Argentine's *pampas*.[99] If Sarmiento ultimately fused with the "Other within" in his subconscious identification with the *gaucho*, Merlin fused instead with a symbolic grid of texts, at times replicating and at other times scissoring out various passages written by her Cuban contemporaries. This alteration/duplication of a secondary text also points back to the original—in particular, "the official story" represented by Herrera's expansive decalogues as court historian. Whereas in the case of *Facundo* "[t]he role of this web of texts . . . is to lend authority to Sarmiento's discourse, to serve as model and to give Sarmiento legitimacy as an author,"[100] in Merlin's case textual duplication authenticates her own account by means of parodic reversal. Thus, her absorption of literary models serves a quite different purpose than in Sarmiento's work, where "plagiarism count[s] for the most efficient originality by inverting the priority between model and revision" in an act tantamount to imaginary parricide.[101] Instead, in quintessentially feminine fashion, Merlin's text *hides*, in the sense of repressing, the debt to her precursors, thus aligning herself with figures like Arango who were responsible for the foundational enterprise. Merlin thus hoped to reclaim both the Name of the Father and its symbolic territory, the fatherland. Hence, in Merlin's work the strategy of appropriation stems from what Sandra Gilbert and Susan Gubar call the peculiar "anxiety of influence" suffered by a woman author: "a radical fear that she cannot create, that because she can never become a 'precursor,' the act of writing will isolate or destroy her."[102]

Does Merlin's almost naive method of representing the early colonial period reflect her supposedly "colonizing" view of the island, as Salvador Bueno claims?[103] On the contrary, I hold that Merlin's strategy of replicating historical sketches, which, in turn, are based on Herrera and other Spanish *cronistas*, is both a corollary of the colonial condition and an effect of the woman writer's paradoxical relationship to the master-text. In other words, if the colony was considered Spain's parodic double, then Merlin's derivative method merely reduplicated the discursive constraints which the peninsular empire placed on its overseas subjects and which dampened the expression of Creole national interests. By means of the technique of textual grafting, then, Merlin not only reenacted the colonial predicament, but this method served her as a powerful strategy of disavowal, in Bhabha's sense of resisting the submissiveness implied in the colonial condition.[104] Moreover, only by recourse to this "Pierre Menard" effect—copying the copy—could she hope to achieve a parallel status for her own text and so to insert herself into the writing of history. Because her gender prevented her from declaring herself a "historian of America," as Humboldt did,[105] Merlin claimed authenticity for her own text as a *reader* of history, a supplementary rather than an original presence.

This rhetorical choice not only modifies the detached stance of the male European explorer but also has broader implications for the writing of history. One of the remnants of universal history is "the idea that there is a determinate historical actuality, the complex referent for all our narratives of 'what actually happened,' the untold story to which narrative histories approximate."[106] By positing the reader as the source of that "determinate past," Merlin's memoirs suggest that "the significance of the past is determinate only by virtue of our own disciplined imagination," thus pointing to a more contemporary concept of history as imaginative reconstruction.[107]

Merlin's consciousness of writing from the margins heightened, rather than diminished, her political passion in arguing for the betterment of Cuba's colonial condition. Indeed, by virtue of its very marginality, *La Havane* founds an alternative tradition of European travel writing. In recent years, the view which holds that the literature of the scientific explorers was merely a monologic genre serving the interests of European capital expansion has gained in popularity.[108] The "literature of the imperial frontier" has been classified into two basic types—the scientific and the sentimental.[109] Merlin's account challenges both norms. In effect, *La Havane* constitutes a hybrid genre where history substitutes for science and where the sentimental is imbued with political passion, a reshuffling of paradigms that results from the dialogic nature of *La Havane* and *Viaje a la Habana*, evidenced in Merlin's conscious use of sources such as the Creole commentators in *El Plantel*. In comparison to Humboldt's *The Island of Cuba*, Merlin subverted the distanced outlook of the scientific travelers by her passionate desire to *belong* to the New World. It is telling that Humboldt, like Merlin, also harbored a secret longing to remain in the New World.[110] Neither the countess nor her venerable precursor was able to attain that dream.

4. Havana. Second view taken from Casablanca. Frédéric Mialhe, *Viage pintoresco alrededor de la isla de Cuba dedicado al Señor Conde de Villanueva* (Havana: Litografía de Luis Marquier, ca. 1848). Archives and Special Collections, Otto G. Richter Library, University of Miami, Coral Gables, Florida.

5. View of the Little Temple and part of the Plaza de Armas. Pierre Touissaint Frédéric Mialhe, *La Isla de Cuba Pintoresca* (Havana: Imprenta Litográfica de la Real Sociedad Patriótica, [1838?]) Special Collections Department, Otto G. Richter Library, University of Miami, Coral Gables, Florida.

CHAPTER 4

A NATION INVENTED

Imagining Cuba in Merlin and the del Monte Circle

Merlin's adult contact with her homeland spanned the beginning and end of a crucial period in Cuban history and culture, for her visit to Cuba in June 1840 came in the midst of the literary "boom" that erupted in Cuban letters between 1835 and 1844.[1] Critics have chronicled the outpouring of literary activity in mid-nineteenth-century Cuba as the direct result of Domingo del Monte's *tertulia*, or salon, founded in 1835.[2]

Although 1844 (the year of the Conspiración de la Escalera) marks the demise of the del Monte group, there is considerable disagreement as to the duration of the boom itself. Whereas William Luis declares that the group declined only in 1843, when del Monte was forced to leave the island, historian Larry Jensen situates the boom as spanning only 1838–1839, the year in which the bulk of *costumbrista* prose and antislavery novels appeared.[3] Likewise, Antonio Benítez Rojo considers 1838 as the initial year of the boom, for it marked the flowering of *costumbrista* tales by Ramón de Palma, Cirilo Villaverde, and Félix Tanco y Bosmeniel.[4] Whether "the first moment of splendor" in Cuban letters was "short-lived" or not, as Jensen claims, depends on which periodization is deemed to be the most accurate.[5] However, it is safe to say that the boom had lost

its momentum by the time Merlin arrived: "By 1840 [the year of Merlin's visit to Havana] the Cuban Parnassus was in shambles," Jensen writes.
"Although the nadir of creole expression would not come until the after-
math of the Escalera conspiracy in 1844, Cuban literati were dispersed,
disheartened, and so diverted by the pressures of earning a livelihood
that literature had receded to the status of a neglected avocation."[6] What
awaited Merlin when she arrived in Havana was a disenchanted generation, "a generation cut down in its literary prime, doomed to a series of
political and literary subterfuges that would eventually end in repression
and exile."[7] The publication of Merlin's memoirs in 1844 coincided with
the demise of the del Monte group, with the banishment and exile of
most of the members of the *tertulia* from the island, and with the end
of the project of the "imagined community."

Despite this waning of the moment of splendor in nineteenth-century Cuban letters, it is generally agreed that del Monte's salon articulated "a spirit of 'Cubanness,'" a discourse that prevails to this day in the
overarching view of Cuban culture as one dominated by the cycles of
sugar production.[8] Indeed, del Monte's *tertulia* set the basis for what
Benedict Anderson calls an "imagined community," an idea of the nation
stemming from a deep sense of bonding, that eventually led to a call
for sovereignty.[9] An emblematic case of Arnold's category of "creole pioneers," the del Monte group saw its self-proclaimed mission to be the
imagining of a country.[10] The del Monte group essentially carried out
what Octavio Paz has termed the foundational enterprise in Latin American literature: the "invention" of a nation and of a deep sense of identity
forged in the imaginary journey between Europe and America.[11] The del
Monte group, however, was also at the origin, in Paz's sense of the word,
for their aesthetic separation from the peninsula anticipated the political break that would culminate in the Cuban struggle for independence.

In this context, the appearance of a woman on the Havana literary scene was bound to cause a stir, especially if that woman came to claim
a share not only of her father's inheritance in the sale of the Nazareno
sugar mill, but also of the male literary tradition in Cuba. In this chapter, I trace Merlin's relationship to the del Monte circle and also explore
her reception among the members of the *tertulia* both before and after
her 1840 visit to Havana. At the crux of this relationship lies the often
conflicting nationalistic discourses espoused by both the del Monte group
and by Merlin herself. Whereas del Monte and members of his group

upheld what can be termed a "pedagogic" model for the construction of nation, Merlin, by contrast, put forth a performative model that ran counter to the positivistic ideas and the realist aesthetic promoted by del Monte.[12]

The del Monte Circle as "Creole Pioneers"

Most Spanish American literary histories highlight the inaugural role played by the del Monte group in the emergence of Cuban culture. Del Monte's exemplary standing is comparable to that of the Spanish American "creole pioneers" who, despite the fact that they "shared a common language and common descent with those against whom they fought," were nevertheless responsible for articulating national culture as distinct from the culture of the peninsula.[13] Anderson explains the rise of nationalism in South America as a result of colonial administrative units, which had served to delineate national boundaries.[14] Furthermore, even though at the service of the crown, the pilgrimage of Creole functionaries throughout their lands must have sparked early nationalist sentiment in Spanish America, for "on this cramped pilgrimage [they] found travelling-companions, who came to sense that their fellowship was based . . . on the shared fatality of a transatlantic birth."[15] Two clear examples of such "interior" voyages are the Count of Montalvo's trip with Francisco de Arango, narrated in the *Relacion del viage que hizò el señor de Arango, con el conde de Casa Montalvo,* and the Count of Mópox y Jaruco's failed expedition to Guantánamo. Inasmuch as these two men were Merlin's uncle and father respectively, they must have surely influenced the Creole countess's sense of embarking, herself, on a similar voyage during her return trip to Havana. This incipient Creole consciousness, in turn, gave rise to a sense of territoriality, which was gradually transformed into a full-fledged national identity, understood first of all as the *imagining* of a common symbolic space.[16] But in the case of Cuba, where the colonial government prohibited Creoles from performing administrative duties, the development of nationalist consciousness was not as clear-cut. Nor was the pioneering role of the del Monte circle to be sought in displacement and travel; rather it emerged in an inner vision, an invention, in Paz's terms, of the island as their own.[17]

How and in what circumstances did this vision come about? Enrique José Varona described colonial Cuba as a "pirámide tosca de servidumbres

superpuestas" ("a coarse pyramid of superimposed servitudes"), an apt
metaphor for the social, racial, and political strata composing Creole
society at that time.[18] In 1835 the island was governed by the Spanish
Captain-General Miguel Tacón, who imposed a tight control over all
administrative affairs in accordance with royal mandates from Spain.
Tacón was particularly known for his zealous defense of the crown and
of peninsular interests. Economically, the island of Cuba was shaped—
according to most interpretations—by the plantation system and
fueled by slave labor. As Manuel Moreno Fraginalls has shown in his
monumental study *The Sugar Mill*, by the 1820s the sugar plantation was
rapidly transforming itself from a rudimentary economy based upon manual labor to a semimechanized system of production based on the
steam engine or *máquina de vapor*.[19] This development led, in turn, to the
rise of the *factoría* or large mechanized sugar mill during the 1840s and
1850s, which not only caused the destruction of the island's forests but
also gradually took over as "a separate phenomenon" of rapid industrial expansion.[20] This industrialization process provoked a core contradiction in Cuban slave society. At the same time that the sugar mill
was requiring ever greater amounts of manual labor to keep up with its
spiraling production, the 1817 and 1835 treaties signed between Spain
and Britain had declared the slave trade illegal. Defying this legislation,
colonial authorities became ever more complicit with the now illegal slave
trade, supporting the efforts of both slave traders and slave owners, many
of whom were peninsular in origin.

As the sugar aristocracy strove to maintain its economic grip on
the island, it marked its social ascendancy by means of powerful institutions like the Sociedad Patriótica, or Patriotic Society, a civil society
created to serve its interests.[21] If one pole of colonial society was dominated by a constellation of power between the colonial authorities and
the sugar planters, a pole of resistance, or a counterdiscourse, gradually
emerged, primarily among educated, upper-class Creoles who comprised
the intellectual elite.[22] By the mid-nineteenth century these Creole intellectuals were reacting both to the strictures of colonial authority limiting their political participation and to the brutality of the slavery system.
Literature became the field where this battle was waged.

What most dramatically reveals this struggle is the Academia episode
staged in 1833. Its principal protagonists were José Antonio Saco, Domingo
del Monte, and José de la Luz y Caballero, three Creole intellectuals

gathered around the *Revista Bimestre Cubana*, a publication sponsored by the Comisión de Literatura of the Sociedad Patriótica.[23] This trio of Cuban intellectuals petitioned the Spanish government "to form an Academia de Literatura Cubana that would be independent from the Sociedad Patriótica," a petition that followed the timely birth of "Cuban literary discourse" one year earlier.[24] According to Benítez Rojo, the beginning of a nationalist discourse was marked by the publication of Saco's 1832 essay on Brazil, where he posed a direct challenge to "the slave traders and Spanish moneylenders."[25] With this move, Cuban intellectuals hoped to gain a foothold on power, using literature as "a weapon for expressing a national culture and changing society."[26] As could be expected, Captain-General Tacón rapidly dissolved the project. Spanish *peninsulares* represented by Juan Bernardo O'Gavan, director of the Sociedad Económica, and the Intendant Claudio Martínez de Pinillos also opposed the creation of a separate Academia, thus clashing with the emerging national sentiment.[27] Tacón eventually banished Saco to internal exile in the province of Trinidad, finally pushing him out of the country in September 1834.[28] This episode, which involved "the dissolution of the Academia, the termination of the *Revista* [*Bimestre Cubana*], and the exile of Saco," according to Benítez Rojo represents "the first organized effort by Cuban intellectuals to mount a common front of resistance against the power of the slave traders and the saccharocracy."[29] The tense situation was further compounded by a power shift within the Sociedad Patriótica. Whereas O'Gavan and his conservative faction won the crucial posts of censor and vice-censor in 1833, a Creole faction supported the election of Francisco Arango and Luz y Caballero as director and vice-director.[30] By overruling its effort to elect del Monte secretary of the Society, Tacón effectively suppressed the more progressive Creole faction and "intensified pressures already operating against creole expression."[31]

The Academia episode is related to another crucial event in Cuban colonial history that affected the course of nationalist discourse. In 1835 Tacón suppressed a liberal rebellion led by General Manuel Lorenzo, governor of Oriente province. Lorenzo had supported the reinstatement of the liberal constitution in Spain by trying to implement it in his province.[32] He had also backed the election of Creoles to the Spanish Cortes, among them Luz y Caballero, Saco and Juan Montalvo (Merlin's uncle).[33] Though the Creole candidates won in two consecutive elections, they were "prevented from carrying out their representation" by

events in Spain.[34] The denial of the Creoles' petition for representation
in the Spanish Cortes gutted the nationalist discourse; as Saco lamented,
"We do not have a country, no, we do not have one."[35] Both the suppression of the Lorenzo rebellion and the inability of Creoles to obtain
political representation sealed Cuba's fate as a colony and consequently "denied Cuban pretensions to equality within the Spanish nation."[36]

    Luis writes, "[t]he year 1835 appears to be pivotal for an overall
understanding of politics and literature in Cuba,"[37] and indeed, the articulation of a nationalist discourse in Cuba hinged on both politics and literature, evolving as it did from the contradictions and conflicts played
out in the colonial press as a result of societal tensions. In Anderson's
view, newspapers played a decisive role throughout Spanish America in
transforming a sense of territoriality into an "imagined community" or
cohesive national bond.[38] This is certainly true in the Cuban case, where,
according to Jensen, the colonial press "furnished elite Cuban creoles
with a vehicle to express, if not a sense of national identity, at least an
agenda of self interest—free trade, increased sugar production, and slave
imports."[39] Although the development of "print capitalism" in Cuba was
directly tied to the rise of nationalism, insofar as an elite group of Creoles was able to use the press to foster its own protonationalist program,
the colonial government also imposed severe content restrictions on the
press, which furthermore was controlled by the conservative factions of
the sugar aristocracy clustered around the Sociedad Patriótica.[40]

    Indeed, it was the Spanish crown's swing from constitutionalism
to liberalism that most affected the development of the colonial press,
which shifted from periods of severe external censorship to more moderate interludes.[41] According to Jensen, by 1835, "Tacón could boast that
as a result of his efforts, expressive license had been contained on the
island."[42] These events led to an "intellectual quarantine" that extended
to "opening suspicious packages and searching the luggage of passengers
docking in Havana."[43]

    At this juncture, seeing their efforts at authentic expression crushed,
Creole intellectuals turned inward, gathering at del Monte's salon in an
effort to salvage "the goals of the defunct academy."[44] One of their principal concerns was "the persistence of absolutist press standards" and
how the severe restrictions of colonial authority would affect their literary production.[45] Though Tacón's successor, Captain General Joaquín
de Ezpeleta, basically followed Tacón's policy of upholding strict censorship on all publications, he did permit a slight opening that allowed

a rise in the number of serial publications. The pages of *El Album, Aguinaldo Habanero, La Siempreviva, El Plantel,* and *La Cartera Cubana* thus were used by *costumbristas* and other authors associated with del Monte to inscribe a sense of emerging "Cubanness."[46] Despite the restrictions placed on them, members of the del Monte generation used literary imagination to fuel political discontent—giving another cast to the notion of "creole pioneers." That the energetic writers of the del Monte circle were able to forge a space of authentic expression proves that "[the] creative imagination was particularly appropriate for these young creoles, for imagination could not be shackled by political absolutism or monopolized by elite cultural institutions such as the Patriotic Society."[47]

As this capsule of historical events shows, del Monte's *tertulia* was forced into playing a subversive role in the establishment of Cuban culture. Its writers were attempting to shift the very definition of Cuban culture away from what Benítez Rojo calls *"Cuba grande"* ("Big Cuba"), the Cuba of the sugar mill and the slave compound, which had forged a culture "oriented toward the foreign sugar markets."[48] This was the Cuba imagined by the patriarchs or founding fathers of the island, including Francisco Arango y Parreño, who, though first to obtain permission from the Crown to engage in the traffic of African slaves, later recanted his position and denounced "tan asqueroso comercio" ("such distateful commerce").[49] Instead, the del Monte group evoked *Cuba Pequeña* ("Little Cuba"), which "looks inward, toward the land . . . its cultural poles . . . formed by the diverse elements of folklore and tradition."[50] These writers created a counterdiscourse that, by upholding local values and traditions, "directly challenged the colonial and slavery systems."[51] Hence, the del Monte group took on the task of building a tradition from the source, a tradition that would form *Cuba Pequeña* from the description of folkways and the revival of "indigenous cultural values."[52] This invention of *lo criollo* took the form of local color literature, or *costumbrismo,* a style consciously adopted by authors such as Palma and Villaverde to enhance the emerging sense of "Cubanness." In turn, this was the tradition that Merlin herself would deliberately imitate in her search for her own Creole identity, for it was *costumbrismo* that enabled the incorporation of "local idiom into Cuban prose."[53]

The del Monte group also developed another literary form that was more directly political: the antislavery novel. Del Monte commissioned two important antislavery works: the ex-slave Francisco Manzano's

Autobiografía (London edition, 1840) and Anselmo Suárez y Romero's novel *Francisco o las delicias del campo (Francisco or the delights of country life)* (1839; published 1880).[54] He also induced Tanco, future polemicist of Merlin, to write his *Escenas de la vida privada en la Isla de Cuba (Scenes of Private Life in the Island of Cuba)* (1838; published 1925), of which we have left only the story "Petrona y Rosalía." In promoting both the antislavery narrative and the *costumbrista* sketch, del Monte encouraged his disciples to follow Balzac and Walter Scott in their treatment of insular topics.[55] From this blend of European realism and Spanish *costumbrismo* emerged hybrid novels like Cirilo Villaverde's *Cecilia Valdés* (1882), which the proud author nevertheless placed under the realist rubric.[56]

Critics like Luis and Benítez Rojo have focused primarily on the achievements of del Monte's generation, but the conditions under which these works were forged are seldom examined. For example, literary critics make hardly any mention of the material circumstances limiting the exercise of a literary vocation in colonial Havana. Jensen's analysis of *El Plantel* shows how fledging Creole writers had to contend with greedy peninsular editors who often backed down on the original terms of their contract.[57] Constrained by both sets of restrictions—economic and political—Creole intellectuals felt their talent being blocked, and many even felt their dream of exercising a literary vocation rapidly vanishing.[58]

Notwithstanding the curtailment of their literary activities, the del Monte group is noted for its many achievements: the "boom" in Cuban letters produced both major and minor works that, taken as a whole, constitute the core of Cuban nineteenth-century narrative. This success must, however, be tempered by the fact that del Monte and his group dominated the entire spectrum of Cuban intellectual life at mid-nineteenth century. Again, it is Jensen who ponders what effect their dominant role may ultimately have had upon the development of Cuban culture. In his view, "this monopoly [of the press] froze the evolution of the medium and limited its impact upon Cuban society. It allowed a literary elite to define the acceptable boundaries of public expression and to suppress topics that might have attracted a larger readership."[59]

To what extent did these boundaries limit the presence of women like la Condesa de Merlin in the emerging Cuban culture? What kinds of conscious and unconscious repressions operated in the case of a woman writer? Furthermore, what role did the colonial press play in influenc-

ing Merlin's reception among the del Monte circle? In the next section, we will look more closely at the differences between del Monte and
Merlin's nationalist projects. Furthermore, can these differences account
for the ambivalent reception accorded the French-Creole woman during her stay in Havana?

Merlin / del Monte: Imagining Cuba across the Gender Divide

The insistence on a realist aesthetic as a means to promote the accurate
representation of national types situates del Monte's project close to what
Homi Bhabha has called a "pedagogic" model of nation formation.[60]
According to Bhabha, this type of nationalist discourse is rooted in a deep
sense of tradition; it implies a linear sense of history and, consequently,
of narrative. The pedagogic model constructs "the people" as a rhetorical strategy, an elevated rhetoric generating both "the objects of nationalist pedagogy" and the subjects of nationalist discourse.[61]

By recreating numerous types of local folklore, having the flavor
of popular language, feasts, and traditions, *costumbrista* sketches strove
precisely to construct "the Cuban people" as subjects of an "imagined"
insular community. In turn, these same "subjects" were represented—
that is, objectified—in the texts of the *costumbristas*. It is this double rep-
resentational movement that generated the traces of national identity.
Costumbrista writings also had a secondary, though equally important,
ethical function, as they were geared to affirm emerging national values and correct the wayward ways of erring Creole youth. Antislavery
narrative, on the other hand, performed its ethical function by raising
awareness of the many contradictions and injustices prevalent in
Cuban slave society. Hence, the positivistic, pedagogical thrust of the
tertulia is evident not only in the realist aesthetic promoted by del Monte,
but also in the types of literature the circle produced. For both *costumbrismo* and the antislavery novel are narrative genres fundamentally geared
toward an extraliterary goal, the imagining of country.

Given the dominant role played by the del Monte group as
"Creole pioneers," could la Condesa de Merlin effectively partake in the
emerging discourse of "Cubanness"? Merlin's dependence on *costumbrista* authors clearly demonstrates her desire to emulate the prevailing
discourse of the nation, and her attempt to insert herself, however

indirectly, into the text scripted by the foundational group. As was the case with her appropriation of historical vignettes from the colonial period, Merlin continued her practice of textual "borrowing" and other parodic strategies as a means to be counted among the members of the Cuban "imagined community," a topic dealt with in the next chapter. Here I trace the reviews and partial translations of Merlin's early autobiographical works, and particularly of *Mis doce primeros años* (1831), that appeared in the Havana press before and after her arrival in the island. My purpose in doing so is to show how the members of the del Monte circle appraised Merlin's works differently and on that basis proceeded to exclude her from the foundational enterprise.

At the heart of this exclusion lies not so much the author's status as a "foreigner," but a fundamental difference in Merlin's deployment of nationalistic discourse. In other words, Merlin's exclusion from Cuban literary history is not merely a consequence of the fact that her works were written in French, of her linguistic "extraterritoriality," as Díaz claims.[62] Rather, and perhaps more radically, it is also a sign of the Creole elite's deep-bred resistance against a woman ably fulfilling the roles of author and artist. The accusation of "foreignness" and other ambivalent responses to Merlin's presence made manifest in the periodical press during her stay in Havana cloaked a far deeper resistance against the very idea of female authorship.

Del Monte's reactions to the visitor from France are emblematic in this regard, but they also show another facet, which is how nineteenth-century literature stemmed from the political destinies of the island. The whole spectrum of his reactions to Merlin—from initial acceptance, to a later hesitant, even ambivalent reception, culminating in his final, unconditional avowal of Merlin's writing project—certainly respond, in part, to the repression by colonial authorities of the attempt to forge a Cuban "imagined community." For the *criollos'* initial rejection of Merlin was also linked to the fluctuations of colonial rule, to the cycles of censorship and expression permitted by Spanish colonial authority, and ultimately to the fate of the del Monte circle itself.[63]

Before her trip to Havana in 1840, Merlin enjoyed a reputation as the author of two books of memoirs, the early text of *Mes douze premières années* (1831) and the longer *Souvenirs et Mémoires* (1836). Proof that del Monte had access to the French editions of these works is present in an early review of Merlin's primitive autobiography, published in the *Revista*

Bimestre Cubana.[64] Indeed, both of Merlin's early memoirs must have circulated among members of the del Monte group, for Agustín de Palma, cousin to the novelist Ramón de Palma and hence affiliated with the *tertulia*, had translated the first work in its entirety in a Philadelphia edition of 1838.[65] Though Agustín de Palma's translation of the later work *Memorias y recuerdos*, was not published in its entirety in Havana until 1853, portions had appeared in the 1837 edition of *Aguinaldo Habanero* under the title "Recuerdos de una criolla," prefaced by none other than del Monte himself.[66] Yet a second series of fragments from *Memorias y recuerdos* was published two years later in the 1839 edition of *El Album*, this time with an introduction by the translator's cousin, Ramón de Palma.[67] In this second review, Palma gives proof that Merlin's early memoirs were indeed disseminated among the del Monte circle even before her trip. Cuban readers also knew about Merlin's biography of singer María Malinbran from an announcement made in the colonial press shortly before her 1840 visit.[68] Besides being familiar with her early works, Merlin's peers on the island were also aware of her cultural activities, for a review of one of her Parisian concerts was also reproduced in the *Diario de la Habana*.[69]

The contrast between del Monte's pedagogic model of nation-formation and Merlin as representative of the performative mode surfaces in these early reviews as a conflict between Romanticism and realism. One of the most eloquent statements in this regard was made by the commentator of Agustín de Palma's 1839 translation of *Mis doce primeros años*, which appeared that same year in the *Diario de la Habana*.[70] This anonymous critic is the first to notice Merlin alleged propensity for hyperbole and imagination, a point later stressed in del Monte and Ramón de Palma's reviews as well. Showing himself to be a faithful follower of the *tertulia*'s realist aesthetic, the reviewer patronizingly warns against the excesses of poetic rapture in relation to the truth-value of the memoirs:

> Vuelen pues estas flores de Navidad á las lindas manos de nuestras sensibles paisanitas, para que pasando por cima sus divinos ojos, se convenzan por ellos mismos [*sic*] . . . todavia, le falta á nuestro anuncio siquiera una chispa del alma que á todos ellos vivifica—la *exageración*: pudiendo con verdad estamparse al frente de mis Doce primeros años [*sic*], con no menos razon que al de las Memorias de la vida del insigne Goethe el lema caracteristico de *Poesia y verdad*.

(May these poinsettias fly into the pretty little hands of our sensitive female compatriots, so that when they cast their divine
eyes upon them, they might be convinced by themselves . . . however, our advertisement lacks that spark of the soul which enlivens
everybody—*exaggeration*: which could easily be stamped on the
front of my "Doce primeros años" [*sic*] with no lesser reason than
that for which the motto "Poetry and truth" was attached to the
Memoirs of the noted Goethe.)[71]

The charge of *exaggeration* directed against Merlin's depiction of Cuban
affairs will culminate in Félix Tanco's vitriolic *Refutacion al folleto intitulado Viage [sic] a la Habana, Publicado en El Diario* (1844), which first
appeared as a series of articles in the *Diario de la Habana* from April to
May 1844 under the pseudonym "Veráfilo."[72] Because of the importance
of Tanco's allegation—it was, indeed, the text that finally repudiated
Merlin's right to share in the discourse of the nation as woman and as
Creole—it will require a separate analysis. For the moment, I would like
to compare the initial 1839 review published in the *Diario* with another
anonymous piece, this time published in *La Cartera Cubana*, to show that
anti-Romantic sentiment was widespread among most Creole intellectuals.[73] Whereas the first critic ironically cites Goethe in order to highlight the Romantic tenor of Merlin's oeuvre, the second one simply stresses
imagination as the principal factor that enabled Merlin to link life and
literature in a vivid re-creation of past memories: "[S]e conoce que su
imaginacion se había desarrollado ya bajo el ardiente cielo de los trópi-
cos, pues de otro modo no es posible que conservase tan vivas reminis-
cencias de la naturaleza cubana y de las costumbres de aquel tiempo"
("One can see that her imagination developed under the fervent sky of
the tropics; otherwise she couldn't have kept so alive her memories of
Cuban nature and of the mores of the period").[74]

     Both of these critics, whose opinions have rightly remained anony-
mous, fade before the judgment that Domingo del Monte himself made
in his early 1831 *Revista Bimestre* article, which, despite its covert
patriarchal tone, remains one of the first attempts to seriously approach
Merlin's work in the colonial press. In this essay, del Monte pointedly
affirms that Merlin's memoirs are closer to the early Romantic tradition
in France and particularly to the confessional genre than to the realistic
norm with which Creole writers were striving to represent their intimate, insular world.[75] Moreover, del Monte clearly refutes Merlin's rep-

resentation of national types. The conflict between romanticism and realism surfaces here now in terms of the style of representation. Rather than appreciate Merlin's subversion of the dominant *costumbrista* paradigm by means of parodic reversal, del Monte offers a biting critique of a critical passage of *Mis doce primeros años*, one in which Merlin shows her penchant for imaginative portrayal of Creole norms and mores. The passage in question describes a young Creole who lingers all day in the luxury of a *butaca* (armchair), unconcerned with the mundane exploits of work or money (349). Though Merlin's description anticipates the portrait of Creole youth depicted in later Cuban novels—such as the image of a dissolute Leonardo in Cirilo Villaverde's *Cecilia Valdés*—del Monte severely criticizes this rather stereotypical portrait. In another sense, del Monte's critique implicitly recognizes a certain degree of validity in Merlin's exaggerated account, for he is forced to admit that the character defects noted in this description are an effect, not of individual psychology, but rather of the colonial condition itself; in his terms, a vestige in Cuban mores inherited from the Spanish administration (349). He contrasts this picture with one of enterprising young Creoles who help their fathers in the administration of money or in the study of science (349). In what can only be a veiled allusion to the failed attempt to found the Academia Cubana de Literatura, del Monte foresees the efforts of the Sociedad Patriótica in forming a series of groups where young men could dedicate themselves to promoting the nation's well-being and industry: "no vémos muy lejos la época en que, reuniéndose en sociedades literarias y científicas, contribuyan como *hombres*, como ricos y como instruidos á la ilustración y a la felicidad de su país" ("the day is not so far off in which, gathering in literary and scientific societies, rich and illustrious *men* will contribute to their country's enlightenment and happiness") (349).

Despite its progressive rhetoric, del Monte's review remains quite gender-bound and colors his subsequent appraisal of Merlin's style and content. Merlin's text is effectively dismissed as merely the memoirs of a young girl who, unlike her male counterpart, writes "con una delicadeza y un tino, peculiares solo á las personas de su sexo" ("with such delicacy and accuracy as are proper only to the persons of her sex") (355). Though he acknowledges his role as translator of the memoirs, del Monte remains skeptical as to their value, concluding that they could only be of interest to a local public (359).

Del Monte's review takes the conflict between Romanticism and realism a step further, for he first attributes certain stylistic traits to Merlin's gender, and then devalues the effect of her texts by circumscribing her reading public only to Havana. With this latter gesture, del Monte accomplishes two contradictory yet mutually contingent goals: on the one hand, he equates Merlin's text to those written by her compatriots in the island, the members of his circle interested in appealing only to a local audience, and yet he also simultaneously *devalues* her writing. This is established by a mechanism of unconscious control—possibly an effect of the kind of censorship experienced by del Monte and his group under Spanish colonial rule—which nevertheless operates at a more explicit, conscious level in the case of a woman writer.

Other critics echo del Monte's opinions in the colonial press of the period. The "friendly" critic of *La Cartera Cubana* makes the same point regarding the virtual readership of Merlin's memoirs with his patronizing assertion that her works can find no more avid reader than another *habanero*.[76] In an apparent move to unsettle his own position, the reviewer had at first considered the work in question to be of interest only to an European audience (100). He then resolves the contradiction, however, by noting the difference between a native and a non-native reader, a difference which hinges on the *effect* provoked in the reader by the text's obvious deployment of surprise and novelty (100). Whereas the European reader may be enthralled by Merlin's poetic reverie, the Creole reader, more intimately familiar with the island's exuberant landscape, will instead find pleasure in measuring Merlin's text against that reality: "[T]enemos la ventaja de juzgar con mas acierto de la veracidad de las pinturas, y en esto se encuentra un manantial tan profundo de placeres, que ninguno leerá Mis Doce Primeros Años [sic], con mas interés que un habanero" ("We have the advantage of judging more accurately the truthfulness of the paintings, and in this one can find such a hidden spring of pleasures that no one will read *Mis doce primeros años* with as much interest as an *habanero*").[77] Tanco's authorship is suspect here, for, of all the members of the del Monte circle, he was the one most emphatically concerned with upholding the criteria of verisimilitude. The opinion of either an apocryphal Tanco or his likely double that Merlin's memoirs have more appeal for an *habanero* than a foreign reader is an ironic remark geared to undermine the value of Merlin's writing as well as to downplay its contribution to the discourse of nationhood.

Hence, these and subsequent reviews serve to repudiate the woman author's claim to present herself and her views within the prevailing nationalist project.

Only Ramón de Palma, who was as yet unaware that the Creole countess would one day "steal" his best novel from him, dared to resist this prevailing opinion. In his preface to his cousin Agustín's translations of portions of *Souvenirs et Mémoires*, Ramón de Palma stated that the importance of this translation was that it made Merlin's work available to more readers than a few "curiosos."[78] By attempting to broaden the appeal of Merlin's memoirs to a wider public, Ramón de Palma thus implicitly acknowledged her contribution to an emerging discourse of nationalism. Palma's belief that Merlin should be considered a "famous writer" is particularly ironic in light of the fact that past and present Cuban critics have unjustly criticized Merlin for her appropriation of *costumbrista* authors, and particularly for her free adaptation of Palma's novella, *Una Pascua en San Marcos*.[79]

To the debates surrounding Merlin's literary personality and Romantic aesthetic must be added a second set of restrictive criteria. Not only did the critics associated with the del Monte circle question the relevancy of Merlin's early memoirs, but they even went so far as to limit her audience in terms of gender. The prevailing opinion, shared by critics from the influential del Monte to the less serious, anonymous commentators, was that, taken as a whole, Merlin's work was only pertinent to Creole women. In this way, Creole contemporaries consciously restricted the countess's contribution to an emerging sense of "Cubanness." Moreover, they also set the stage for the ensuing clash between the pedagogic and performative dimensions that took place during Merlin's visit to Havana. In attributing a pedagogic function to Merlin's oeuvre—to serve as example for Creole women or as a model to foster "native" female talent—the dominant group implicitly denied Merlin's own access to artistic language. Notice how the otherwise sympathetic reviewer of the *Diario de la Habana* had destined the pages of *Mis doce primeros años*, which he described as sweet "flores de Navidad" (poinsettias), to "las lindas manos de nuestras sensibles paisanitas" (the pretty little hands of our sensitive, female compatriots).[80] Likewise, in his role as translator of Merlin's early memoirs, Agustín de Palma attributed to himself the right to evaluate Merlin's work as one likely to stimulate dormant literary vocations among Creole women:

¿Qué habanera no sentirá en su corazon un placer indefinible al leer á 'Mis doce primeros años,'[sic] escritos en Paris por una *criolla*, en un estilo suelto elegante y afectuoso? Todas las cubanas deben apresurarse á adquirir esta preciosa obrita, que al propio tiempo de agradarles, servirá de estímulo para que algunas otras imiten á la ilustre condesa de Merlin.

(For what *habanera* wouldn't feel in her heart undefinable pleasure when reading 'Mis doce primeros años,' which was written in Paris by a *criolla* in a loose, elegant and gracious style? All Cuban women must hurry to get this precious little work, which besides being entertaining, will be able to serve as stimulus to some, so they too can imitate the illustrious Countess Merlin.)[81]

By setting Merlin up as an object of the pedagogic platform erected in the building of a nation, the del Monte circle not only objectified Merlin, but also generated the conditions for rejecting her when she finally appeared in their midst. Merlin's vibrant physical presence during her short visit to Havana in 1840 not only upset patriarchal notions attributed to the female gender, but it also countered the positivistic bent of the del Monte group.

In contrast to the elevated goals that nineteenth-century Creole intellectuals set up for themselves, Merlin operated within the performative mode in at least two dimensions: *textually*, by means of her (often radical) rewriting of the Cuban *costumbristas*, and *dramatically*, by her literal embodiment of what Severo Sarduy calls *lo sonoro* or resonant dimension in Cuban literature.[82] Merlin appears at the threshold of Cuban literature as a *voice*, in this way complementing Gómez de Avellaneda's act of imagining the island from afar in her famous sonnet "Al partir."[83] Remembered in her time as "la Malinbran cubana,"[84] Merlin has come down in Cuban literary history as a singer of operas, as a potent female power embodied in the sheer materiality of voice. It is precisely this image that will predominate in the writings of twentieth-century Cuban authors like Guillermo Cabrera Infante and Reinaldo Arenas, authors who simultaneously honor and mock Merlin for the wide range of feelings registered by her singing.[85] Understood within the performative dimension, Merlin's operatic voice is received by the Creole community as an excess, as an overabundance of femininity and female talent that threatened to unsettle not just accepted paradigms of female behavior but, most of all, the limits of creative expression allowed women within the tight circles of Creole society.

Merlin's dramatic effect as the literal representation of the performative mode is best seen in the famous Peñalver concert in which
Merlin played a starring role. In a letter to José Luis Alfonso dated from
Guanabacoa on July 10, 1840, written approximately one month after
Merlin's arrival, del Monte tells Alfonso about an important social event,
an evening concert celebrated two nights before, on July 8, at the
home of Nicolás Peñalver. This event clearly influenced how most of the
Havana elite subsequently reacted to the visitor from France. The Peñalver
concert revealed to the Havana "imagined community" the range of Merlin's beauty, voice, and exuberant femaleness, qualities which cast her
apart from the more "average" lot of Creole women.

A review of that same concert confirms that envy and national pride
conditioned the Creoles' reaction to the visitor from France. Under the
signature of "Un Concurrente," a pseudonym hiding the pen of José de
la Luz y Caballero, a long-time family friend of the Montalvos, the review
of the Peñalver concert appeared in the *Diario de la Habana* on July 12,
1840, just two days after del Monte's letter to Alfonso.[86] Luz y Caballero's
opinion clearly reveals Merlin's vibrant talent as the principal source of
antagonism among her Creole peers. Though this piece begins with praise
not only for Merlin's operatic voice but also for her "elegant and facile
pen," it gradually shifts to a regretful comparison between Merlin and
her less fortunate sisters on the island. Carried away by patriotic sentiment, Luz y Caballero bemoans the complex set of circumstances that
impede Creole women from realizing their full artistic potential:

> ¡Cuantas paisanas suyas, dotadas por la naturaleza con esas prendas
> brillantes de la imaginacion y de la sensibilidad orígen fecundo del ta-
> lento [*sic*], viven y mueren dolorosamente . . . en estado de crisálidas,
> sin hallar campo en que desplegar al sol sus lucidas alas! Fértil y rica
> semilla de Cuba, regada en un terreno no menos fértil y rico, ¿qué te
> ha faltado sino el rocio vivificante que te hiciera brotar y abrirse al sol
> el caliz perfumado de sus flores tropicales?

> (How many of her female compatriots, endowed by nature with the
> radiant jewels of imagination and sensibility which are the fertile origin
> of talent [*sic*], painfully live and die . . . enclosed as in a chrysalis, unable
> to open their wings to the sun! Fertile and rich Cuban seed sprinkled
> on a terrain no less fertile and rich, what have you been lacking but the
> life-giving dew that brings forth young shoots which open to the sun
> the perfumed calyx of its tropical flowers?)[87]

In comparison to her female peers on the island, then, Merlin is presented as a shining example of successful female talent.

Merlin's singing not only placed her wholly within the performative dimension, but also implicitly created a countercurrent of nationalist sentiment, another mode of affirming nationality that was in opposition to the pedagogical mode assumed by the del Monte group. Functioning still within this pedagogical mode, Luz y Caballero informs his reader that Merlin owed her operatic training to the García-Malinbran school.[88] After superlative praises of her voice, he faces the unenviable task of describing the performance of the other Creole women who also sang in this concert. Preserving to the last the unwritten code of Creole social hierarchy, he describes in descending order the singing of a gifted Señora Osorio on down to Teresa Peñalver, the host's daughter, to whom he owed at least a rhetorical homage. Luz y Caballero diplomatically suggests that "[la Srta. Martinez] parece haber olvidado los aplausos que tantas veces han acompañado y cubierto sus alegres y brillantes trinos de ruiseñor" ("[Miss Martinez] seems to have forgotten the applause heaped upon her happy and brilliant nightingale trills").[89]

Del Monte's second letter to Alfonso on July 30, 1840, mentions a second charity concert that Merlin gave shortly afterward at the Beneficiencia [Pública] (Public Welfare). Although in this letter del Monte attributes the Creoles' change of heart to Merlin's own "eccentricities,"[90] thus fulfilling the "madwoman in the attic" stereotype of the woman writer, the letter also makes clear that the superiority of Merlin's talent, which obviously diminished the efforts of local Creole women, rubbed the Creole elite the wrong way. As del Monte's letter shows, Merlin's stellar performance caused favored Creole singers like the popular Señorita Martínez to fall from grace, leaving them insecure, if not outright defensive, about their musical talent (or lack thereof). In his letter to Alfonso, del Monte describes the showdown between "native" and "foreign" talent in these amusing terms:

> [Merlin] tubo [*sic*] la bondad de prestarse á dar un concierto en el teatro de extramuros pª la Beneficiencia: convidaron á cantar en él a una muchacha Martínez que tiene una garganta privilegiada pº sin gusto ni expresion en su canto; —pues, porque se corrió que en los ensayos nunca la Merlin la quiso oir, y porque despues en el acto del concierto no sentaron a la dña. Martínez al lado de la Condesa y de Teresita Peñalver (que tambien cantó) por poco silvan a nstra amiga, pº ya que no lo hicieron, hubo una explo-

sion de aplausos desaforados al levantarse la Martínez pª cantar, que la otra conoció el busilis y quedó muy desazonada.

([Merlin] was so kind as to give a charity concert at the Extramuros Theater. They also invited the Martínez girl to sing; she has a privileged voice but no taste or expression in her singing; —well, gossip had it that at the rehearsals Merlin never wanted to hear her, and when after the concert they did not let D. Martinez sit beside the Countess and Teresita Peñalver (who also sang), they almost hissed at our friend. But, although they did not hiss, there was an explosion of disorderly applause when Martínez rose to sing, which hit the mark with the other one [Merlin], for it made her extremely anxious.)

The local public rose to Srta. Martínez's defense as a means to safeguard their own anxieties about women's creative potential. Tantamount in this response is the perception that Merlin had broken the norm of domesticity and of female behavior allowed Creole women at the time. Not only did Merlin break this norm, but she also *transgressed* the limit set by del Monte and other previous commentators on her work. Instead of serving as a model that Creole women could safely emulate in fostering their own hidden creative potential, Merlin's two performances countered this expectation by sharply superseding local musical talent.

The Outsider at the Door:
Merlin's Reception among the del Monte Circle

The differences between the pedagogic and the performative, phrased in terms of an opposition between realism and romanticism, help explain the ambivalent responses to which Merlin was subject to during her time in Havana. After considering the Creoles' resistance to Merlin's physical presence based on the superiority of her talent, I now turn to consider their reaction to her writing before and after her visit. Given the initial positive responses to her work which appeared in the colonial press, was Merlin recognized as author by her peers in the island? This question, in turn, opens up the dilemma as to whether gender was a possible category in the imagining of the Cuban nation. As a woman, could Merlin be an active agent in the representation of nation, or would she be relegated to serve only as a symbol?

Although Merlin, perhaps ingeniously, drew on the sources of *cos-tumbrista* writers to construct her portrait of colonial Havana and hence captured a deep sense of insular belonging, or Creole "imagined community," the members of this community, who initially welcomed her into their symbolic circle, shut the doors on her immediately after her visit. Many of the periodical publications acknowledged the sale of Merlin's works in Havana with brief reviews and editorial comments, and some even reported Merlin's arrival at the docks of the Havana bay, but later reviews depicted her as a "foreigner," often in scathing terms. How to account for this shift? What happened between the glad welcome announced in the pages of the *Diario de la Habana* and *La Cartera Cubana* and the more hostile reception of the del Monte circle after the countess had arrived on shore?

Merlin's notoriety, along with her aristocratic status and the fact of her Cuban birth, raised expectations for her imminent visit. The pages of the colonial press documented the journey of the *Christophe-Colomb*, noting Merlin's arrival in New York and later the ship's entry into the port of Havana.[91] After Merlin's arrival in Havana, the press continued to keep the Creole public informed, publishing a short summary of her experiences in the United States under the title "Novedades en Nueva York" in the June 17, 1840, edition of the *Diario de la Habana*.[92] This entry is significant, first because it suggests that Merlin was sending fragments of her travel diary to friends in Havana, hoping perhaps to create a positive environment for herself. More significant is that it shows the press initially greeting and accepting Merlin as a full-fledged Cuban writer: "Hace dias que tenemos entre nosotros á la ilustre escritora habanera que al cabo de mas de treinta años ha regresado y vive temporalmente en el seno de una de las familias mas conocidas y respetables" ("For days now we have had in our midst the illustrious *habanera* writer who has returned after thirty years and is temporarily living at the home of one of the most respected and well-known families").[93] It is as if her residence in the Montalvo home guaranteed Merlin's entry into the "imagined community." Hence, in these early news summaries and reviews, arrival becomes a trope for a broader gesture of insular belonging, a sentiment Merlin herself would try to recuperate through writing.

This initially enthusiastic reception had been conditioned, in part, by the favorable assessment of Merlin's works in the colonial press previous to her arrival. An anonymous editorial note published in the *Diario de la Habana* announcing the publication of *Mis doce primeros años* is typical of the positive valorization awarded Merlin years before she made her trip.[94] Important in this regard is the fact that the reviewer affirms Merlin's Cuban identity as a *symbol*. He casts an image of her as a source of nationalistic pride, an image predicated, paradoxically, on her exiled condition. Merlin thus becomes a symbol of Cuban nationality precisely because of her prolonged *absence* from the island. With this gesture, the reviewer dissolves the apparent contradiction of first hailing the appearance of the work as inherently Cuban, and then dismissing the charge of the author's literary "foreignness":

> Escrita la obra por una distinguida *habanera* . . . por una *criolla*, bajo cuya flexible pluma brotan las flores y los frutos con la misma franqueza y lozanía con que salen del seno de nuestra feraz tierra: . . . pluma que nos revela cifradas en feliz armonioso conjunto la sensibilidad cubana ataviada con las galas y gracias de la delicadeza parisiense (emphasis added).

> (The work was written by a distinguished *habanera* . . . by a *criolla* under whose flexible pen flowers and fruits bud forth with the same generosity and exuberance with which they bloom in the bosom of our fruitful land: . . . a pen that reveals to us the Cuban sensibility embellished as a harmonious, felicitous whole with the finery and graces of Parisian finesse.)[95]

In a similar fashion, all other commentaries on Merlin's early memoirs written before her trip to the island confirm her initial acceptance into the insular "imagined community," an acceptance predicated on her distance from the island. Eloquent in this regard is del Monte's 1831 review, which appeared in the *Revista Bimestre Cubana*, where he describes Merlin as "daughter of the land" and praises the nostalgic trace of patriotic sentiment which her work inspires. Del Monte's panegyric reveals that Merlin acquires symbolic status only because she is far away, a literal embodiment of the tradition of *lejanía*:

> El dulce sentimiento de cariño á la tierra patria, que respira esta obrita, y que nos consideramos como el primero y el mas puro de los afectos del alma . . . fuera ya de por sí recomendación suficiente para que fijasemos la atencion en ella.

> (The sweet love for the homeland which transpires in this little work, which we consider the first and purest sensation of the soul . . . this in and of itself would be sufficient reason for us to pay attention to it.)[96]

Del Monte's opinion, written during the high point of the *tertulia*, show that his group's willingness to include this French Creole within the Cuban "imagined community" was a factor of their idealization of distance.

The reception shifts once Merlin arrived on the island, for she presented the Creoles with the threat of becoming an active agent in the discourse-making process, in the project of imagining a nation. This shift can be traced in many of the reviews, written as early as 1831 and as late as 1839, as a clear repudiation of women's scriptural role. As many of these reviews show, Merlin's literary reputation as a writer for a female audience conditioned her later dismissal as merely a "foreign" writer. In other words, the subsequent ambivalence toward Merlin's dual nationality only cloaked a far deeper, earlier ambivalence—male resistance to a woman author.

Clearly the issues of authorship and reception that surfaced in the colonial press around the publication of Merlin's early memoirs show, on the one hand, the problematic issue of female authorship and, on the other, the contradictions, fissures, and gaps evident in the rhetoric of nationalism espoused by the del Monte group. At the intersection between gender and nationalism in nineteenth-century Cuba lies the curious "discursive ambivalence" that Merlin elicited from her Creole peers.[97] That ambivalence is, in turn, the site of emergence of the nation insofar as it dramatizes the various contradictory discourses giving rise to Cuban nationalism.

Again the key text here is del Monte's 1831 essay in the *Revista Bimestre Cubana*, a review structured according to what Bhabha calls a "double writing." Whereas Merlin figures in this review as symbol of the nation, there is obvious hesitancy on del Monte's part in approaching female authorship. What most clearly reveals del Monte's anxiety, not of influence but of gender, is his next rhetorical move, an apology for not revealing the name of the author:

> Sentimos sin embargo no poder hacer completa justicia á su mérito, mentando su nombre; pero oculto con el velo del anónimo, nosotros no le alzarémos descubriéndole: ningún habanero, por otra parte, necesitará de nuestra revelacion, al menos de los que hayan estado en París; pues siendo la casa de la autora el punto donde se reune como en su centro la flor de la hermosura, del ingenio y de la elegancia de aquella metrópoli, no podrá menos, al leer las púlidas páginas de este libro, de recordar en ellas el hidalgo trato y el modo apacible y suave de quien las escribió.

(We regret, however, not being able to do complete justice to her merit by mentioning her name; but hidden behind the veil of anonymity, we will not elevate her by revealing it. On the other hand, no *habanero* will feel the need of such disclosure, at least not those who have been in Paris, because the author's house is certainly the hub around which gather the cream of the crop, the talent and elegance of that metropolis. This reader, upon reading the polished pages of this book, will not be able but to remember the high-mannered treatment and the sweet and delicate style of the person who wrote them.)[98]

This passage serves as an ingenious means not only to excuse his own anonymity as a critic, but also to *evade* his own authorship.[99] Hence, the "double writing" or "negative transparency" (according to Bhabha, a kind of writing-in-reverse proper to the colonial subject) fulfills a double function: to downplay Merlin's literary worth and simultaneously to conceal del Monte's own identity as a critic.[100] That del Monte's reticence might have been tied to other reasons besides gender anxiety is a possibility. Yet the review appeared in 1831, one year before the publication of Saco's essay on Brazil, the event that provoked the conflict regarding the founding of the Academia in 1834.[101] Hence, there would have been no ostensible political factor to explain del Monte's hesitancy other than his discomfort regarding female authorship.

The same attitude is prevalent in del Monte's 1837 preface to "Recuerdos de una criolla" [*sic*] published in *Aguinaldo Habanero*.[102] After presenting his initial judgment that Merlin's works are representative of Romanticism, del Monte then cloaks his own views in the guise of a fictitious Parisian critic (71), thus evading any conclusive claim to an opinion on the virtue of Merlin's oeuvre. By displacing his negative appraisal of Merlin, del Monte thus absolves himself of any responsibility as a critic, repeating the same ambivalent move of his 1831 review. Hence, only by means of displacement can del Monte express his true judgment of Merlin, a mechanism that critics like Bhabha identify with the colonial condition.[103]

Along with his earlier review, del Monte's 1837 preface suggests that Merlin was accepted only when seen as the embodiment of quintessentially feminine virtues. Though he at first seems to acknowledge Merlin's literary nationality by claiming that he will dedicate this article to one of the "daughters of Cuba" who has most distinguished herself, in the last analysis it is not aesthetic virtue but rather the sociable characteristics attributed to the female sex that most attract his critical attention. Indeed, the determining factor in his favorable judgment of Merlin is her superb hospitality, for she consistently welcomed into her Parisian salon those unfortunate Creoles who had to leave the island (346). Del Monte's review thus echoes the predominant opinion of the time that a woman's worth is measured in terms of her conventional femininity: "no se sabe qué admirar más, si su maravilloso talento músico, y el timbre armonioso y penetrante de su voz, ó la viveza de su capacidad intelectual . . . ó el tesoro de sensibilidad y ternura que se le trasluce en las ráfagas brillantes y apasionadas de sus hermosos ojos" ("one knows not what to admire the most, whether her marvelous musical talent, or the harmonious and penetrating tone of her voice, or her lively intellect . . . or the treasure of tenderness and sensitivity which are transparent in the brilliant and passionate gleam of her beautiful eyes") (70–71). Furthermore, Merlin's femininity and her intellectual vocation are seen to be in tension. Thus, Merlin's works are deemed to be "less artful than her conversations," in that her intellectual style often falls short of the passionate tenor expected of her feminine nature (72). The model of femininity is then associated with the representation of Cuban traits, since, according to del Monte, Merlin's insular condition should have given her "un colorido brillante, cuyo secreto y magia ignoran los espíritus fríos de Europa" ("a radiant coloring, whose secret and magic are ignored by the cold spirits of Europe"), whereas her gender should have provided "espresiones seductoras, giros pintorescos y ocurrencias inesperadas" ("seductive expressions, picturesque figures of speech, and sudden witty remarks") (72).

The debates surrounding Merlin's role as writer in the Havana colonial press culminate in the 1839 *La Cartera Cubana* review, whose invisible authority effectively dismisses her legitimate claim to authorship:

> [S]us escritos [de la Condesa de Merlin] están muy lejos de igualarse todavía al hechizo y originalidad de sus conversaciones. Esta observación destruye la calumnia que han levantado algunos detractores del ingenio de la mujer, propalando que la Sra. Merlin se ha valido del auxilio de un hombre para escribir sus obras.

> (Her writings are by far less bewitching and original than her conversations. This fact destroys the slander raised by some detractors of

women's literary talent, who claim that Mrs. Merlin has relied on a man's help to write her works.)[104]

On the surface the *Cartera Cubana* critic attempts to defend the possibility of Merlin's authorship in light of further accusations against it; yet, through this ironical ploy, he ingeniously manages to raise doubt as to Merlin's ability to write her own works. Whether Tanco was, indeed, the hidden commentator of this piece is not as important as the fact that this review candidly preserves the symbolic agency as the exclusive domain of the male gender.

The *Cartera Cubana* review shows the limits of del Monte's project of the nation, which fundamentally relegated all women—and not only the visitor from France—to the position of outside observer. Merlin's oppositional aesthetic was compounded, then, by a more fundamental—and perhaps repressed—bias against the woman writer. The exclusion of women from the colonial literary scene was ensured by the del Monte group's adoption of markedly different aesthetic criteria according to the author's gender. In other words, whereas Merlin's works were read according to criteria specific to her sex, the works of other members of the *tertulia* were judged by a far more generous norm of acceptability and readability.

In this light, it is useful to consider Ramón de Palma's definitive article on Cirilo Villaverde that appeared in the 1838 edition of *El Album*.[105] Benítez Rojo considers this essay "a kind of preface to all the texts subsequently produced in the del Monte group"; its importance for Cuban literary history lies in the fact that it establishes "the criteria proposed by del Monte on the subject of what constitutes Cuban literature."[106] Simply put, Palma's essay promotes a realist aesthetic geared to the faithful depiction of national types. Rejecting the "con frecuencia inverosímiles y extravagantes" ("often unrealistic and extravagant") styles derived from European literature, Palma advocates a more detailed examination of Cuban reality, asserting that "hasta que no nos hayamos cansado de verla pintada tal cual es; no necesitaremos para encontrar novedad, que los escritores nos la pinten *como se les antoje*" ("as long as we do not tire of seeing her painted just as she is, we do not need, for novelty's sake, that writers depict her simply according to their whims").[107] Hence, Palma defines national literature as one based on originality rather than on imitation: "Nunca la verdadera literatura de una nación, se ha formado copiando la otra" ("Never has a nation's authentic literature been formed by copying another").[108]

However, in his prologue to Villaverde's *El espetón de oro*, also published in *El Album*, Palma questions originality in a work of art, particularly as it relates to plagiarism of previous works.[109] Here Palma appears more willing to consider the intertextuality of every work of art, given that "[e]s menester considerar que el hombre nada crea, ni ha creado, que el no hace mas que referir, y que las formas con que reviste los sucesos, son los que constituyen el distintivo de su ingenio" ("One must consider that man does not create anything nor has he ever done so; all he does is to refer, and the way in which he dresses up events is what constitutes the distinctiveness of his genius") (7). He further justifies his position by citing Shakespeare's comparison of a plagiarized work to "una linda muchacha que él sacaba de la mala sociedad para introducirla en la buena" ("a beautiful girl whom he pulled out of bad company in order to introduce her into a good one") (7). Bowing to Molière's assertion that when he took an idea from another book, it became his own by virtue of its more appropriate (re)presentation, Palma concedes that originality in and of itself does not guarantee literary value (7–8). With regard to Villaverde, then, he concludes that "aunque el argumento de *El espetón de oro* no sea en el fondo original, es una novela nueva en su género, y sobre todo muy cubana" ("though the argument of *El espetón de oro* may not be truly original, this is nevertheless a new novel in its genre, and above all, a very Cuban novel") (8). Although Palma himself and later Tanco were willing to admit literary borrowing on the part of other male authors of their group, they rejected Merlin precisely on those same grounds.

The whole range of responses elicited by Merlin among the del Monte circle—particularly the resistance against her daring attempt to portray Cuban themes in her writing—comes to a climax in Félix Tanco y Bosmeniel's articles, which appeared in serial form in the *Diario de la Habana* from April to May 1844.[110] Collected under the volume *Refutacion al folleto intitulado Viage a la Habana* (1844), these articles are an extensive critique of the Spanish edition of Merlin's travel diary.[111] The date is significant, for the articles come *after* the repression of the Conspiración de la Escalera and consequently after most Creole readers had *Viaje a la Habana* (1844) in their hands. Setting the tone for Merlin's subsequent negative treatment in Cuban literary history, Tanco levels against her the accusation of "foreignness": "La Sra. de Merlin, por decirlo de una vez, ha visto á la isla de Cuba con ojos parisienses, y no querido comprender que la Habana no es Paris" ("To say it once and for all, Mrs. Merlin has seen the island of Cuba with Parisian eyes, and has not quite understood that Havana is not Paris"). (55) For Tanco, the fact that Merlin was born in Havana and was raised there during her early years should have allowed her a privileged vision of the colonial context, but in his view she produced instead a "fantastic" version of the island and its inhabitants which distorted not only the existing social hierarchy but even basic data of topography and geography.[112] So, though a Creole by birth, Merlin sharply perverted her own "native" understanding of island customs and affairs to such an extent as to resemble a foreign spectator: "La señora de Merlin tiene un anteojo muy particular, cuyo uso recomendamos á los viageros curiosos y aficionados á transmitir *recuerdos é impresiones*" ("Mrs. Merlin has a very particular lens, whose use we recommend to the curious travelers who are interested in transmitting *recollections and impressions*") (7).

Tanco's position is based not only on linguistic grounds but also on national pride. Positioning himself as a spokesman for the emergent Creole culture, Tanco insisted on a realistic description of local scenes and types in accordance with del Monte's dominant aesthetic. As a self-styled arbiter of truth, Tanco faulted the flight of Merlin's imagination where it bore in on Cuba: "Fluidez, exactitud, brillantes imágenes, erudicion, todo resplandece aqui bajo el poder de una bella pluma, que por un raro contraste solo ha querido estraviarse cuando se ocupa de su propio pais" ("Fluency, accuracy, brilliant images, erudition, everything shines here under the power of a beautiful pen, which, by sharp contrast, tends to go astray only when she writes about her own country") (56). This straying from realistic description led Tanco to call into question Merlin's Creole identity, yet the contrast between realistic and nonrealistic discourse clearly points out another opposition: that of sexual difference and gender (9–10).

This is best seen in the closing pages of the *Refutacion*, where the author finally uncovers the hidden source of his resentment. According to Tanco, Merlin's travelogue, innocent as it may seem, introduces scenes of amorous conquest and seduction that are certain to upset righteous Creole women and, consequently, threaten the entire moral fabric of Creole society (58–59). Thus, the earlier accusation of literary transgression is framed now in moral terms as well; in taking up the pen, Merlin violated the chaste and demure role assigned to women in colonial society. As a last rhetorical ploy, the *Refutacion* ends with a scene where a group of indignant Creole matrons thrust into Tanco's hands a copy of Merlin's *Viaje*, urging him with dramatic gestures to write a treatise in defense of both honor and country:

> [Esta] impugnacion [*sic*] [la] emprendimos en defensa de las acusaciones hechas á nuestro pais, pero invitado tambien por el respetable sexo á quien mas se ataca en él. *Ellas* pusieron en nuestras manos el *Viage á la Habana de la Condesa de Merlin* y nos dijeron: "Si sois galan, si sois caballero, tomad á vuestro cargo nuestra defensa y la defensa de nuestro pais. . . ." (Emphasis in original)

> (We undertook this challenge in order to defend against the accusations that were made against our country, but also because we were encouraged by the fair sex who felt most attacked by it. *The ladies* placed into our hands the *Viaje a la Habana de la Condesa de Merlin* and told us: "If you are gallant and a gentleman, please take charge of our defense and the defense of our country. . . .") (59).

By masking himself as a self-proclaimed protector of female virtue, Tanco is merely cloaking the patriarchal assumption that women have no voice in the public domain.

Tanco's *Refutacion* marks the peak of the treatment of Merlin as the "outsider at the door" of nineteenth-century Cuban culture. In contrast to her earlier acceptance as "daughter of our land," Merlin was being denied the authority to represent Cuban culture because of her supposedly unrealistic descriptions of local color topics and alleged "foreign" status. Yet these charges only hide the del Monte circle's stubborn refusal to acknowledge female agency, understood as direct participation in the discourse of nationhood. Del Monte's letters to other members of the circle around the time of Merlin's visit to Havana prove, indeed, that Merlin's attempt to collaborate with them on a common project of nation-formation was a threat to their ascendancy both as male writers and as the dominant literary group in colonial Havana.

Besides visiting relatives, churches, and ruins, during the time of her visit Merlin actively pursued a literary exchange with del Monte and other members of his circle. Indeed, la Comtesse avidly sought out the *tertulia* leader's advice and even petitioned him for direct contributions to her book, which she described in an letter to del Monte as "un proyecto importante para nuestro país" ("an important project for our country.") In this letter, dated April 27, 1842, from Paris, Merlin tried to elicit del Monte's support by making him an integral part of a common nationalist project; her argument that "el proyecto es importantísimo, y no dudo que tenga gran influencia en *nuestros intereses* y en los progresos de ese país" ("the project is extremely important, and I don't doubt that it will have great influence on *our interests* and on the progress of that country") could not help but be persuasive.[113] Del Monte's response is evident in his July 30 letter to Alfonso, a document that sheds much light on the links between authorship, gender, and censorship operative in Cuba's slave society.[114] Although del Monte states that he willingly complied with Merlin's request for statistical notes on the state of the Cuban economy and society, it is clear that this compliance stemmed not so much from a desire to truly collaborate with her, but rather from his debt of friendship with Alfonso (addressed here as Pepe), who had initially recommended the visiting Creole to the leader of the *tertulia*. The letter begins:

> Mi querido Pepe:
> Con el *Havre* y *Guadalupe* no pude escribirte ni una letra porque hasta la ultª hora estuve escribiendo pª ntra amiga M.ᵐᵉ Merlin unos apuntes que me pidió sobre varios particulares de ntra Isla. Yo se los dí, tanto por ser persona recomendada tuya a quien deseaba obsequiar, cuanto por que supuse que ella había de publicar su Viaje a la Habana.

> (My dear Pepe: I wasn't able to send you a letter with the Havre and Guadalupe because up to the last minute I was writing to our friend Mme. Merlin, who had asked me for some notes regarding several matters about our Island. I did this willingly, first because you had recommended her to me and consequently I wanted to please, and second because I figured that she was going to publish her *Viaje a la Habana*.)

As the letter progresses, we sense once again the mounting mistrust of female authorship in del Monte's patronizing observation that "era mas conveniente que los datos en que apoyase sus observaciones fuesen exactos, que no fuera á escribir en el aire, o teniendo a la vista documentos y noticias *contrarios á la verdad y á nuestros intereses* [sic]" ("it was necessary that the data on which she based her observations be exact, so that she would not just be pulling facts out of the air, or have before her

documents and news which were *contrary to the truth and to our interests*")
(emphasis added). More significantly, del Monte sets himself apart from
the definition of "nuestros intereses," presumed by Merlin in her April
1842 letter to coincide with those of the *tertulia* leader. Hence, this letter
shows that del Monte anticipated a sharp divergence between his and Merlin's positions on an emerging discourse of Cuban nationalism.

Despite this initial hesitation, del Monte did, in fact, participate in
Merlin's writing project, precisely on the basis of "nuestros intereses" or
project for a Cuban imagined community. As the letter proceeds, del
Monte discloses the identity of those documents which he gave Merlin
in order to help her complete her work: "Le di tres mamotretos, uno
sobre la admnistracion de justicia, otro sobre el Comercio libre, y otro
sobre la poblacion blanca y de color en ntra Isla: le di ademas documentos oficiales en comprobacion de mi dicho: veremos qué partido saca
ella de esto" ("I gave her three hefty tomes, one about the administration of justice, another about free Commerce, and the last about white
and black population in our Island: I also gave her official documents
in support of my statements: in short, we shall see what she makes of
all this"). Then del Monte informs Alfonso that he encouraged Merlin
to ask the latter's help and to consult Saco's *Paralelo*, a work so popular
that it was not available in Havana at the time: "Le dije que si necesitaba
de algún otro dato te lo pidiera a ti, y muy particularmente el *Paralelo* de
Saco, que aqui no se encuentra" ("I told her that if she needed any other
data, she should ask you, especially for your copy of Saco's *Paralelo*, which
can't be found here"). Toward the end of the letter, del Monte asks Alfonso
to send him additional copies of Saco's *Paralelo*, given its high demand
in Havana, adding that he himself has given his last copy to foreign travelers.[115] Note here that though del Monte eagerly *disseminated* Saco's text,
endowing it with the representative authority of the pedagogic, he simultaneously dismissed Merlin's as yet unwritten manuscript in a patronizing display of superiority that downplayed her ability to write on Cuba's
social and political matters.

At one point in the letter del Monte asks Alfonso to consult
Merlin in Paris before returning to Havana in order to get a sense of how
she used the information given her:

> Bueno fuera, si vieras á esta Sra., antes de embarcarte para esta, que
> examinaras lo que haya escrito, ó al menos, las ideas que tenga pª hacer-
> lo; porque te advierto que aquí le pidió también noticias, ademas, a Pepe

de la Luz que no sé si se las dio, a Prudencio Hechevarría!!!, a Alvaro
López, y qué sé yo que mas!

(It would be good that if you get a chance to see this Lady before
returning here, examine what she has written, or at least the ideas which
she plans to use; because I warn you that here she also requested information from Pepe de la Luz, which I don't know whether he gave to
her, from Prudencio Hechevarria!!!, Alvaro Lopez, and from who knows
whom else!)

Hidden in del Monte's discourse is the fear of contention between Merlin and his circle on the crucial question of slavery and on the broader
issue of an emerging Cuban nationality. Hence, by asking Alfonso to
"check" on whether Merlin made proper use of the sources and information he provided, del Monte turns his initial mistrust into a form of
covert censorship, in a move destined to dismantle Merlin's narrative
authority. Del Monte's correspondence thus evidences both the nega-
tion of female authorship and discursive control over a woman's political writing, a dismissal that points to a "minus in the origin," a fissure in
the representation of nation by the liminal figure of woman.[116]

Four years later, indeed the same year that saw the publication of
Merlin's two travelogues, del Monte wrote to the American Alexander
H. Everett, delivering his final appraisal of the countess's endeavors. In
this letter, written from Paris on July 31, 1844, del Monte describes
the part played by Creole intellectuals in the final composition of *La
Havane* (1844):

> Dispuesta a escribir su "Viaje" solicitó de algunas personas en la Habana
> materiales sobre las rentas, el comercio, la legislación, etc. etc.; estos le
> fueron proporcionados con abundancia, los cuales unidos a los que después
> le dio Saco, en París, la pusieron en estado de escribir algunas cartas en
> muy buen sentido, y con datos bastante exactos sobre nuestras cosas públi-
> cas, salvo alguno que otro error o equivocación de la bella redactora, y
> *fácil de disculpar en una mujer que no entiende semejantes materias.*

> (Ready to write her "Viaje," she requested information from some peo-
> ple in Havana about incomes, commerce, legislation, etc; these statistics
> were given to her in abundance, and when it was compiled with the infor-
> mation which Saco later gave her in Paris, it enabled her to write some
> quite sensible letters, which contained pretty exact data about our pub-
> lic issues, with very few errors or oversights on the part of our beautiful

writer, *which would easily be forgiven in the case of a woman who does not understand such matters*.) (Emphasis added) [117]

This favorable response stemmed more from the changed circumstances
of the del Monte group after the Conspiracy of la Escalera than from an
actual reappraisal of Merlin's writing, as his last, patronizing comment
makes clear. It is obvious that del Monte was willing to grant validity to
Merlin's text only after the *tertulia* was disbanded and the project of a
Creole "imagined community" had been dispersed as a result of the 1844
repression by colonial authorities.

Del Monte's letter to Everett also reveals the reception of *Viaje a
la Habana* among Creole readers and what sort of impression Merlin left
behind once she returned to France. After commenting on Merlin's
reliance on *costumbrista* writers and discussing Gómez de Avellaneda's
prologue, del Monte goes on to describe the furor caused in Havana by
the countess's unique travel account:

> En la Habana han excitado estas cartas un *tollé tollé* contra la Condesa
> casi risible, porque le forman un proceso por cada inocente
> exageración, por cada fantástica pintura, por cada inevitable error
> geográfico, topográfico o cronológico, que no podía menos de cometer
> la ilustre "Peregrina en su patria."

> (In Havana, these letters have created such an outcry against the
> Countess that it's almost laughable, because they indict her for the
> slightest exaggeration, for each fantastic description, geographical,
> topographical, or chronological mistake, which the illustrious "Pilgrim
> at home" could not but help commit.)[118]

As if unconsciously revising his earlier ambivalent stance, del Monte then
comes rushing to Merlin's defense:

> Pero con todos estos defectos la obra de Mme. Merlin debe ser aprecia-
> da por los cubanos despreocupados y patriotas, porque en ella se
> encierran revelaciones y datos políticos de suma importancia para
> nosotros, se inculcan principios sanos de gobierno, se declama contra el
> comercio de negros, y se reclaman de la Metrópolis los derechos políti-
> cos de que nos ha despojado violentamente y por la fuerza desde 1837.

> (But, regardless of these defects, the work of Madame Merlin deserves
> to be appreciated by disinterested and patriotic Cubans, for it contains

revelations and political data of great importance for us; it proclaims healthy principles of government, it declares itself against the commerce of black people, and it demands from the metropolis the political rights which since 1837 have been violently taken from us.) [119]

At this point in Cuban history, after the apparent demise of the "imagined community," del Monte's vision of the nation and Merlin's strangely coincide. In this letter del Monte finally acknowledges the merit of Merlin's travelogues in presenting an alternative picture of Havana society and in its urgent call for the reform of colonial institutions. Perhaps the experience of exile had also tempered del Monte's views, forcing him to willingly suspend minor political differences for the more encompassing goal which both he and Merlin shared: inventing a nation.

Reading Merlin against the grain of the del Monte group reveals, then, two alternative and often contradictory images of a nation prevalent in nineteenth-century Cuba. The complicated debates in the colonial press of the period concerning both Merlin's personality and her works suggest that Cuban culture cannot be so neatly split into a strict dichotomy between "discourse" and "counterdiscourse," between the pro-sugar "*Cuba grande*" of the saccharocracy and the nativistic "*Cuba pequeña*" of the *costumbristas*, as both Luis and Benítez Rojo propose.[120] As a representative of the performative mode, Merlin disrupted this dualism in favor of a more celebratory attitude, almost a veneration, toward Creole culture. By the same token, though her tendency to affirm the cultural link between Spain and the colony set her apart from the potentially separatist leanings of del Monte and his group, this attitude was more in accord with a female-grounded vision centered on continuities rather than ruptures.

At some (un)conscious level, then, the people of Cuba must have appreciated and honored Merlin's voice, writing, and vibrant physical presence. That she herself elicited responses in the performative mode is proven by the many poems in praise of her voice and talent which appeared in the colonial press, particularly as the time of her departure grew near. In contrast to the brutal denigration of her person shown in Tanco's writings, these poems function as a kind of symbolic compensation which upsets the balance of the earlier derogatory treatment given Merlin in the colonial press and in Havana aristocratic circles. An anonymous poem acclaiming her as an "¡Admirable mujer!" and justifying her departure from Havana in terms of her maternal responsibilities can quite justly be read as an effect of a compensatory mechanism by which Merlin's maternal status is idealized in almost equal proportion to her earlier, debased status as a writer.[121] Another anonymous writer, boundless in praise, provides a different interpretation of the effect that Merlin's powerful voice inevitably had on the Havana public. It captivated the audience with its rich timbres and depth of feeling, and her operatic singing awoke an artistic sensibility that, for the most part, lay dormant in Creole circles: "Percibia que en estos cantos, tan repetidos en nuestros teatros, se ocultaba un manantial fecundo de sentimientos perdidos para nosotros hasta aquí, ó porque no se habian entendido, ó porque no se habian sabido esplotar [sic] y decir con el tino y maestría que adornan á la Sra. Merlin" ("I could see that in these songs, which were often performed in our theaters, lay a fertile spring of feelings which had thus far been lost to us, either because they had not been understood or because no one knew how to exploit them or talk about them with Mrs. Merlin's skill and mastery").[122] By actualizing a hidden reserve of creativity, Merlin revealed to her fellow Creoles what had been lost in the translation from a European cultural code to an American setting: a certain touch of the sublime, or the inspired grace of a true artist. This response not only counters the Creole elite's initial resistance to Merlin's operatic talent, but it also signals that perhaps, at a deeper, spiritual level, Merlin's performance was, indeed, acknowledged by the insular community as its own.

In these scattered poems written in her honor, Merlin's imminent departure from the island was seen as a loss both on a personal and on a collective level.[123] None other than the editor of the *Diario de la Habana* expressed this sentiment, when he anticipated Merlin's writing project in this way:

> Al anunciarse su venida esperabamos prolongase su permanencia en el pais, el tiempo suficiente para palpar el estado en nuestra sociedad [sic] sus adelantos en la educacion, en industria y en fin en los diversos ramos que tocados por su elegante pluma nos harian conocer de las personas ilustradas que se interesan en el progreso y mejora de los pueblos.

> (When her arrival was announced, we hoped that she could prolong her stay in the country long enough to sense the present state of our society, its advancements in education, industry, and various other branches, which, if they would be addressed in her elegant writing, would make us known to those illustrious people interested in the progress and improvement of nations.) [124]

Merlin left Cuba on July 25, 1844, in the hopes of meeting these expectations.

Though excluded from Cuban literary history both because of her alleged "foreign" status and because of her gender, Merlin remains both source and inspiration for the tradition of *lejanía*, as lovingly inscribed in her memoirs depicting her last gaze of longing for the island: "Nous longeons toujours l'île, et je reste toujours là immobile à la contempler jusqu'a ce qu'elle disparaisse" ("We skirted around the island, and I remained there forever motionless in order to contemplate all of her until she disappeared").[125] Leaving behind a poignant farewell that reads as a prose rendering of Gómez de Avellaneda's famous sonnet "Al partir," Merlin departed from the shores of Cuba, never to return.[126]

Despite their resistance to Merlin's presence among them, Creole readers did not completely forget her: the series *Lola* was published in the *Faro Industrial de la Habana* in 1845, and *Mis doce primeros años* and *Historia de Sor Inés* resurfaced again in 1902, at the dawn of the republic, as if to indicate that she had at least been partially included in the imagining of *patria*.[127] Not granted the status of *costumbrista* writers like Villaverde or Palma, who are recognized as "founding fathers" of the Cuban tradition, Merlin has remained at the margins of literary history. Yet it is her very marginality that permits a critical viewpoint for an emerging discourse on nationalism.

6. Cuban country dance (el zapateado). Frédéric Mialhe, *Viage pintoresco alrededor de la isla de Cuba dedicado al Señor Conde de Villanueva* (Havana: Litografía de Luis Marquier, ca. 1840). Special Collections Department, Otto G. Richter Library, University of Miami, Coral Gables, Florida.

(In)Versions and (Re)Writings

Viaje a la Habana and the Origins of Cuban Literature

For Merlin, the gesture of return to her native land implied embracing a past self and history that would somehow endow her with her true self, the girl Mercedes, lost in the years of separation and her gradual assimilation as a Frenchwoman. Becoming a subject was predicated on the recovery of the past and the forging of a (newly defined and discovered) Creole identity. Hence Merlin's writing project was marked by the desire to belong to the New World, a desire understood as *pertenencia*, the feeling of an inclusive insular identity that in mid-century Cuba expanded out of an already deep-seated regional consciousness.[1]

In this search for authenticity, Merlin's voyage to Havana structures itself as a journey back to a source, meaning not only the wish to rediscover her origins but also a conscious search for a language with which to inscribe the reality of the New World. By consciously parodying the local color sketches of the Cuban Romantics, the author Merlin was searching for a literary source or tradition in which to insert herself as a full-fledged *criolla*. In other words, for her to accurately describe the journey to the "natural" source—the island and native city—she desperately needed an artistic language into which she could translate her

experience. As Octavio Paz explains in his essay on a literature of foundations, Merlin needed a language to imitate, a literary source that would
imaginatively describe her Carpenterian "journey back to the source."[2]
In Merlin's case, this "original" language was afforded by the fledging
writers of del Monte's literary *tertulia*, who were experimenting with
Romanticism and early forms of realism in an effort to forge a distinctively national literature.

In the Latin American tradition, the concept of a national literature is inextricably bound to the notion of a unitary language; nationalism is conceived fundamentally as a monolingual project binding together
author, text, and reader in an organic, almost teleological, whole.[3] As
Roberto Ignacio Díaz has shown, this definition has led to the exclusion
of multilingual authors from the canon of Spanish-American literature,
given that "el recurrir a una lengua extranjera se interpreta como indi-
cio de antinacionalismo literario" ("the use of a foreign language is interpreted as a sign of literary antinationalism").[4] For this reason, Merlin's
choice of French as a literary language has caused her to figure as little
more than a "foreigner" in Cuban literary history. Indeed, the image cast
of her in most traditional literary histories is captured in Salvador Bueno's
ingenious epithet, "una escritora habanera de expresión francesa" ("a
Havana writer of French expression"), which not only limits Merlin's
contribution to the colonial city but also unequivocally classifies her as
a procolonialist writer.[5] Earlier in the Republic Gastón Baquero directed
an even more biting appraisal; in speaking of Merlin he unfairly charged
that "una cubana escritora no es siempre una escritora cubana" ("a Cuban
woman who is a writer is not necessarily a Cuban writer who is also a
woman").[6] Though Merlin has been subject to the prejudice that holds
that "escribir en idioma extranjero se interpreta fácilmente como signo
de deslealtad y desunión" ("to write in a foreign language is easily
interpreted as a sign of disloyalty and disaffection"),[7] it is no less true that
the accusation of linguistic "betrayal" is also due to another, perhaps even
more deep-seated prejudice, deriving from her gender. Hence, the issue
is not simply that past and present Cuban critics have questioned more
the "literary nationality" of Merlin's writing than her own literal nationality or cultural hybridity.[8] Rather, as was later the case with Gertrudis
Gómez de Avellaneda, not only were *both* dimensions of Merlin's nationality put into question, but, as we saw in the last chapter, the possibility
of partaking in the *discourse* of nationalism was also denied her.

The narrow definition of what constitutes national literature fails to consider the existential paradox captured in Juan Marinello's apt phrase: "*Somos* a través de un lenguaje que es nuestro siendo extranjero" ("*We are* through a language that is ours while being foreign").[9] To write in an adopted rather than a mother tongue is not only the veritable emblem of Merlin's cultural dilemma, but is also a literal performance (*puesta en escena*) of the paradox facing the Latin American writer. According to both Paz and Marinello, Latin American writers are caught between the need to affirm the continent's autochthonous races, considered the authentic "essence" of nationalism, and the historically forced assimilation of European language and tradition, what Marinello calls the "prison" of the inherited Spanish language.[10] But whereas this dilemma has been validated for the canonical male writer, the same does not hold for the woman writer, as Merlin's case so dramatically shows.

Part of this denial involved the accusation leveled against Merlin for committing "the perfect crime" of plagiarism, an accusation instigated by Félix Tanco in the nineteenth century and carried up to the present day. This accusation was mounted on two counts: one, Merlin had offended the del Monte group's sense of collective identity as the dominant literary circle in colonial Havana, a point clearly brought out in del Monte's correspondence; second, it was considered a supreme act of betrayal for a woman to dare to imitate her male precursors on the island.[11]

From another vantage point, Merlin's dependence on *costumbrista* authors suggests a conscious use of parody as the only possible means by which, as a woman writer, she could incorporate herself into the existing tradition, what in the text of *Viaje a la Habana* reads as a textual performance ranging from subtle displacement of the original text to more radical rewritings. In order to include in her account other sectors of this emerging national group—for example, rural types such as the *guajiros*—Merlin had to "borrow" from the *costumbrista* sketches of Cuban authors of the period, for, because her visit was confined to Havana, she had no opportunity for first-hand contact with rural areas and characters. In turn, many of these types had already been immortalized in the pages of *El Plantel*, *Aguinaldo Habanero*, and *El Album*, publications which set the stage for the origins of Cuban literature.[12] Hence, through the technique of textual "grafting," Merlin not only attempted to emulate the prevailing discourse of the nation but also tried to insert herself, however indirectly, into the text scripted by the *tertulia delmontina* in its function as "foundational" group.

This gesture of appropriation proves that Merlin desired to participate in Cuban literary circles not as a distanced European observer but rather as a "prodigal daughter" who returned home. Moreover, Merlin's "theft" of *costumbrista* authors constituted yet another instance of colonial misrepresentation. For Merlin was obviously playing by another set of rules, one by which imitation or repetition of "original" texts constituted both an acknowledgment of the cultural function played by *costumbrismo* in the constitution of Cuban nationality as well as a subversive strategy in its own right. For in her hands "wholesale plagiarism" is a mechanism with which to ransack the cultural memory in order to inscribe a trace not previously imagined—mainly, the presence and difference of woman.[13] Recasting in her own language the texts of the Cuban *costumbristas*, she was attempting to reconstruct "an image of a language"—*costumbrismo* as literary vernacular that conveyed an inherent sense of Cubanness—and deflect it back to a European audience that for the most part was not familiar with local authors.[14]

Though her parodic gesture paid homage to the authors of the 1838 literary boom, in another sense Merlin's (un)conscious ploy undermined del Monte's realistic aesthetic in favor of a sentimental vision whereby secondariness and imitation were exploited for the sake of projecting an alternative yet complementary vision of the nation. As a woman author, Merlin strove not to surreptitiously surpass the source, as in Sarmiento, but rather to merge with it in such a way that the fusion both flattened out her own authorial voice and at the same time showed its "minus in the origin," the hand that dared to tamper with the male original.[15] If, as Doris Sommer has shown, Sarmiento's was a case of literary insubordination, Merlin, in turn, was prone to gender-based insecurities that prevented her from fully assuming her literary vocation, except by adapting the role of meek imitator of the male tradition.[16] This dependence notwithstanding, Merlin's appropriative tactics do result in a different *reading*, a hermeneutic reshuffling of the foundational texts of Cuban literature that taken together compose a unity, as if the eclectic nature of *Viaje a la Habana* were meant to anticipate, in the condensed manner of a Lezamaesque image, the dream of national harmony and sovereignty.

Viaje a la Habana as Mimicry of the Other

Merlin's debt to Cuban *costumbrista* authors is verified not only in the pages of *La Havane*, but also in the "intimate correspondence" carried out with Philarète Chasles, the *philosophe* who served as editor and lover and who ultimately betrayed Merlin during the last years of her life. In a letter dated November 4, 1843, and written in Metz, Merlin repeatedly asks him to obtain for her the names of "two literary youth," presumably to ask their permission to quote directly from their works.[17] Either because Chasles failed to carry out his task or because she herself opted for the strategy of appropriation, most of Merlin's borrowings from Cuban *costumbristas* remain repressed in the fabric of her text, and can only be discovered by "detective" readers willing to investigate the secret signs of complicity with a larger literary tradition.[18] Such a reader may well consider the various strategies of appropriation employed by Merlin in crafting her *Viaje a la Habana* as an open door through which to (re)discover the imaginative contours of Merlin's Cuba. The essentially parodic connection established between Merlin and her male precursors also forces us to reconsider Bueno's charge of the author's procolonialist leanings.

The *motive* behind Merlin's appropriation becomes evident when we examine her takeoff on José Victoriano Betancourt's sketch "Velar un mondongo" in "Carta VIII" of *Viaje a la Habana*.[19] Betancourt's piece, which describes a pig roast as a ritual countryside feast, is strangely matched in the pages of *Viaje a la Habana* with another *costumbrista* scene: an anonymous piece called "El velorio," originally appearing in *La Cartera Cubana*.[20] Along with the remnants of Betancourt's tale, this surrealistic episode is transformed into an amusing vignette on funeral practices in the same "Carta VIII" of *Viaje a la Habana*. Why would Merlin chose to combine two such seemingly unrelated topics? The mystery is cleared when we trace the authorship of both vignettes, for Betancourt may very well have been the author of "El velorio," a supposition proven by the clear intertextual echo established between the two tales. In "Velar el mondongo," Betancourt resumes the *costumbristas'* principal aesthetic strategy of realistic mimesis, describing himself as primarily a portrait artist:

> [M]uy humilde es mi pretensión; pintar, aunque con tosco pincel y apagados colores algunas costumbres, bien rústicas, bien urbanas, á veces con el deseo de indicar alguna reforma, á veces con el de amenizar juntamente una página.

(My intention is quite humble: to paint, though with a coarse brush and in dull colors, some of the more rustic, more urbane, mores, sometimes to address the need to reform, and sometimes to simply write a charming page.) (363)

He makes a similar statement in the second piece, though in more apologetic tones: "*Aunque mi paleta no tiene colores*, aunque mi pincel es duro, y por último aunque no soy muy vivo de ingenio, me ha venido sin embargo el deseo de pintar un velorio con toda la verdad posible" ("*Though my palette has no colors*, and my brush is hard, and finally, though I am not very clever, I have nevertheless been overcome by the desire to paint a funeral wake with as much truth as possible") ("El velorio," 47). It is reasonable to conjecture that Merlin chose to weave together Betancourt's two tales into the fabric of her text inasmuch as they came from the same source, as if the singleness of authorship guaranteed a certain narrative consistency.

Betancourt's authorial confession also points out the nature of Merlin's parodic strategies, for her distance from the island causes her to change the relationship between text and audience. This is best seen in the French edition, where the same letter is dedicated to "la Vicomtesse de Walsh," though with a footnote lamenting her loss. The brief character sketch that follows hints that Walsh is a mirror image of the author herself, for she "réunissant à toutes les grâces féminines un courage et une volonté énergiques" ("combines with all the feminine graces a strong will-power and courage").[21] Though the Spanish edition suppresses this dedication, it nevertheless assigns the vice-countess as interlocutor of the letter by Merlin's initial invitation to join her in the sentimental journey home: ("Seguidme, querida vizcondesa") ("Follow me, dear vice-countess").[22] In contrast to Betancourt's avowed humility, which makes the *costumbrista* writer essentially a realist artist with a strong moralistic intent—the pedagogic model prescribed by the del Monte circle—Merlin claims for herself the role of "discoverer" of unknown mores (60). She invites her absent reader to witness "el espectáculo de unas costumbres que nunca han sido descritas, ni apenas observadas" ("the spectacle of some mores that have never been described, and hardly even observed") (60). This claim is made only after Merlin's visit to the Cathedral, narrated in the previous letter, which ended with her accidentally stumbling upon Columbus' tomb ("Carta VII," 58–59).[23] By extolling the virtues of the Spanish discoverer (58), Merlin thus rhetorically validates her own claim to authenticity, to her "hyperrealistic" depiction of the land beyond the borders of Havana. In contrast to Betancourt's pedagogical purpose—his declaration that "[l]as costumbres forman . . . la fisonomía moral de los pueblos" ("customs and mores constitute . . . the moral physiognomy of nations") ("Velar un mondongo," 363)—Merlin claims for herself the uncanny ability to *invent* new forms of social organization, to *envision* the country folk she never really knew. Merlin thus compensates for her lack of originality by overvaluing her alleged "discovery."

  This shift in perspective permits, furthermore, the representation of Creole cultural practices as exotic, for the "native" traits appear as "primitive" when compared with European ones (Merlin 60). Belying Félix Tanco's unjust allegations of her "fantastic" rendering of Cuban scenery, Merlin affirms a privileged vision that contrasts the sights and sounds of her surroundings with the remote landscape of her adopted France. Echoing the vision of the European traveler, she claims that "aquí todos los colores son vivos y exactos, y las costumbres estan impregnadas de una gracia natural y espontánea que no puede ser más extraña á nuestro modo habituado de vivir" ("here all the colors are bright and sharp, and the customs are impregnated with such a natural and spontaneous grace that it could not be stranger to our usual way of living") (60). By privileging insular culture all the while maintaining her "distanced" perspective as a European-bred Creole, Merlin effectively negotiates the autochthonous/"foreign" split of the Latin American writer. It is almost as if Betancourt, in his role as "original writer," lacked the distance of the external visitor, resulting in the dimmed lights or "apagados colores" of his brush. Merlin, by contrast, tries to forge a new reader for her texts in her appropriative strategy of (re)discovering the *costumbristas*.

  The overlapping of Betancourt's two tales into the fabric of *Viaje a la Habana* may have been due, in part, to a conscious exploration of the sonorous value of the verb *velar* (*velar un muerto/velar un mondongo*).[24] This poetic use of narrative suggests, however, what must have been Merlin's hidden authorial intention: to recreate, by means of parodic repetitions and substitutions, an image of the island beyond the confines of the colonial city. Hence, in her rewriting, Merlin sought to establish a series of links—between city and country, Spaniard and Creole, *guajiro* and slave—that contested the *costumbristas*' representation of similar topics. This is best seen in a curious dialogue that justifies the matching of two sets of customs, one from the country and the other from the city:

—¿[S]abeis lo que es un *velorio*? La velada de los muertos en la Habana?
—En verdad que debe ser una cosa muy divertida, le dije yo con ironía.
—Mucho mas que pensais; y cuando por fortuna me hallo en el campo,
y puedo formar parte de las reuniones que velan el *mondongo*, me
aprovecho con gusto de aquella circunstancia.
—Un *mondongo*! la velada de los muertos! Dos pasatiempos que creo
desde luego muy poco agradables.

(—Do you know what a funeral wake is? The soirée of the dead in
Havana?
—It must really be such an entertaining thing, I told him ironically.
—More than you might think; and when I'm fortunate enough to be out
in the country, and I can be part of the gatherings that keep watch over
the *mondongo*, I gladly take advantage of the opportunity.
—A *mondongo*! The soirée of the dead! Two pastimes I certainly consid-
er little less than agreeable.) (*Viaje a la Habana*, 60)

Rather than signal a rampant use of plagiarism for its own sake, the technique of appropriation fosters instead an inventive possibility—the imaginative joining together of two areas of the island that would otherwise
remain geographically and culturally separate. In this gesture, Merlin
tries to cancel out the country/city opposition in order to arrive at a more
inclusive picture of the nation. Let us look now at what other implications Merlin's absorption of Betancourt may have had for her construction of an insular "imagined community."

The first, rather colorless tale, *la velada de los muertos*, is a grotesque
combination of melodrama and macabre adolescent frolic amid a funeral
ritual. Though in itself the piece lacks literary value, what is suggestive
is the type of intertextual borrowing involved. Rather than "lift" an entire
piece onto the body of her text, as is the case with her "stealing" from
Villaverde and Ramón de Palma, Merlin here follows the technique
termed "radial reading" by incorporating traces of other texts into her
own, so that they read as oblique filaments or loose, disconnected fragments that are vaguely reminiscent of the original. In Betancourt's "El
velorio," the corpse is laid out by a picturesque character named "Picúo"
who, as he carries out the unenviable job of dressing the cadaver, provokes a comic conflict described in these humorous terms: "Mientras le
pegaba los ojos con cera derretida, hubo un buen altercado sobre si le
pondrían calzones de dril ó de paño; pero una tia de la viuda asomó su

rostro matusalénico por la cortina del cuarto y dijo que le pusieran cualquiera, porqué llevaba hábito franciscano" ("While he was shutting his eyes with melted wax, an argument ensued about whether they should put on the corpse drill or cloth breeches; but an aunt of the widow pushed her Methuselah face through the curtain and said that either one would be fine, because he was wearing a Franciscan habit") (48). This funny anecdote turns into deadpan dialogue in the *Viaje*:

> —¿Qué calzones ha de llevar el difunto?
> —Todavía no lo sabemos, respondió desde el interior otra voz tem-blona.
> —Los de cutí color de rosa, ó los de paño violeta? [*sic*]
> Entonces atravesó el corredor una vieja, pasó por delante de mí y levan-tó la cortina negra.
> —Nada de calzones, exclamó, llevará un hábito de San Francisco.
>
> (—What breeches should the deceased wear?
> —We still do not know, a shaky voice answered from inside.
> —The bed-ticking pink ones, or the violet cloth ones?
> Just then an old woman crossed the hall, walked in front of me and raised the black curtain.
> —No breeches, she said. He will wear a Saint Francis habit.) (61)

The same technique of radial reading is evident in the description of the dead man, which follows closely in both accounts (Betancourt 49; Merlin 62). However, from this point on, Merlin either absorbs another narrative or else invents her own, seeping in only the general outlines of Betancourt's sketch, such as an enamored youth's scandalous flirtations at the sight of death (Betancourt 50; Merlin 63). One interesting addition in the countess's (re)writing is the character of D. Saturnio, who appears as a downgraded version of the buffoon in an attempt to imbue the scene with a carnivalesque touch, almost as if to extend the reach of *costumbrismo* from the prosaic to the mythic mode.[25]

But by far the most striking difference between Betancourt and Merlin lies in the conclusions derived from the macabre episode. Tan-tamount for the first author is the philosophical import of the *velorio* scene, the dramatic contrast between youth and old age, light and dark, the waning and rejoicing of life; in short, the narrative dissonance between merrymaking versus melancholy moods:

> Al ver aquel contraste sublime, aquel cuadro donde aparecía el hombre y la existencia con cuanto tiene de hermoso y de horrible . . . donde se confundían todos los tintes desde el color de aurora hasta el negro de la noche, donde veía el mágico prisma de la juventud hecho pedazos ante el lúgubre aparato de la muerte . . . sentí mis cabellos erizarse, y conmovida mi alma traté de alejar de mí pensamientos tan profundos y meláncolicos.

> (Upon seeing that sublime contrast, that picture where man and existence appeared in all of its beauty and horror . . . where all the tints blurred, from the color of dawn to the blackness of night, where the magical prism of youth was torn to shreds before the lugubrious machinery of death . . . I felt my hair bristle, my soul moved, and I tried to distance myself from such deep and melancholy thoughts.) (Betancourt, 51)

For Merlin, however, the end of this contrived tale serves more a sociological purpose than a contemplative one. For she sets off not two contrasting attitudes toward life and death, but rather two opposing strata of Creole society. In her hands, the *velorio* scene serves to dramatize the widening gap between *peninsulares* and *criollos*:

> La gran etiqueta española en la sala del muerto; la indiferencia criolla en las demas habitaciones de la casa; un aturdimiento salvaje, unido al recuerdo de una civilizacion pomposamente religiosa, ¿no es este un conjunto único, compuesto de inesperados contrastes? Y ¿no sería un gran asunto para un cuadro especial de costumbres?

> (Spanish formality [reigned] in the room where the corpse was; Creole indifference in the rest of the rooms in the house; a wild bewilderment, coupled with the memory of a pompously religious civilization: Is not this a unique whole made up of unexpected contrasts? And wouldn't it be a great topic for a local color sketch?") (65)

Through the mouth of her narrator, an imaginary cousin that could very well have been modeled on a real blood relative, Merlin thus expresses her own wish-fulfillment, of becoming, herself, a *costumbrista* writer.

This desire is realized in the pages that follow with her tried-and-true recourse of appropriation, for the next tale is an adapted and slightly truncated version of Betancourt's "Velar el mondongo."[26] Gone from Merlin's account is Betancourt's theoretical introduction, which outlines the way in which *costumbrismo* functions as cultural text by taking a moral X-ray of a country (Betancourt 363). With this omission, Merlin positions herself not as a sympathetic witness of country mores but rather as a distant observer, overly conscious of the class differences that divide her from her object of study, yet also striving to record the peculiarities of the rural setting. In this sense, Merlin plays the role of the nativistic writer as "impassioned spectator," inasmuch as she is "both involved in and removed from the objects of [her] attention"[27]; yet a comparison between her text and the original shows that her spectatorship is twice removed vis-à-vis *costumbrista* narrative. Whereas here Merlin categorically stresses the town/country opposition as well as rigid class markers ("En vano buscarais en el interior de nuestras ciudades señales de esta costumbre; pertenece enteramente a la clase rústica") ("You would look in vain in the cities for any signs of this custom; it completely belongs to the peasant class") (65), Betancourt bridges spatial discontinuities by showing how cultural ritual serves similar functions in both city and country and by explaining this difference in economic terms ("La costumbre de velar mondongos huyó de la ciudad y se avencindó en nuestros campos, desempeñando en ellos la propia mision que en la capital; esto es, proporcionar cierta diversion . . . á personas que no pueden procurarse nuestros espléndidos recreos" ("The custom of keeping watch over *mondongos* fled the city and settled in the countryside, playing there the same role as it did in the capital, that is, to provide some amusement . . . to people who are not able to secure for themselves our splendid recreations") (364). Betancourt goes on to justify the eccentric tendencies of country mores as an attempt to eke out a living within a harsh environment: "La gente del campo, dedicada de contínuo á regar con el sudor de su frente la tierra, no puede divertirse del mismo modo que los ricos ciudadanos: toscas y campestres son sus diversiones, toscas y campestres como los prados que cultivan" ("Country people, dedicated to continually watering the earth with the sweat of their brows, cannot be amused in the same manner as rich city people; their entertainment is coarse and country-like, similar to the fields that they till") (364).

Because Merlin cut off these preliminary remarks, the sketch's opening scene in *Viaje a la Habana* duplicates in the reader the violence enacted by the *matador* as he slaughters his unsuspecting prey, for the tale also begins *in medias res* (65; Betancourt 365). Though the debt to the original author is not directly acknowledged, as is also the case in a later Villaverde adaptation, it is nevertheless signaled in the interstices of the text by means of *repression*: the absence of any logical transition to the next episode other than the mention that it takes place in the countryside warns the reader of its derived and contrived nature (65). Merlin signals her debt to Betancourt with another curious device: she displaces local color terms (such as *guaticero* for *guatíbere*) in order to endow her narrative with a greater degree of authenticity, hence "unsettling" the testimonial value of the original, in a manner similar to what Roland Barthes called the effect of the real.

This device is particularly effective in the French edition, where there is a conscious effort to represent or *graft* a local dialect, the language of the *guajiros*, onto the dominant narrative.[28] According to Bakhtin, this "ideologeme" or linguistic cluster is incorporated in narrative texts to simulate the language of a specific social group; in this case, the rural population of Cuba.[29] But in Merlin's rendering of Betancourt's "Velar el mondongo," the use of a "local" ideolect alters the relationship between model and copy, between external reality and literary imitation, to such an extent that it produces a hypermimetic effect anticipating Severo Sarduy's "pulsión de simulación" where the drive toward simulation manifested in the copy ultimately takes over the original work.[30]

Nowhere is this technique more evident than in Merlin's daring move to change the name of the popular country dance, the *zapateo* (Betancourt 367) to one of her own invention, "el famoso *zapateado*" ("the famous country tap dance") (Merlin 67). Implied in this translation is the desire to understand the figure of the *guajiro*, who appears as the Other from the Romantic, Creole perspective that Merlin embraced. At first glance, Merlin's tale seems to follow Cirilo Villaverde's judgment that the *guajiro's* dance and habitat are the best means to acquire knowledge of his difference within the emerging insular community. In his terms, "En nuestra tierra, fuera del zapateo . . . el mejor medio á mi juicio, para conocer las costumbres y el carácter de nuestros campesinos, es observar la manera que tienen de levantar sus casas" ("In our land, beside the *zapateo* . . . the best way in my opinion, to know the mores and the character of the country people, is the way in which they raise their homes").[31] As in the *velorio/velar* association, the renaming of the *zapateado* dance in *Viaje a la Habana* suggests a conscious ploy destined to represent an alternative view of countryside culture. Moreover, Merlin's change of terms affects the manner in which the dance is portrayed, best seen by comparing the vividness of Betancourt's description with Merlin's more static image:

Se ve á un diestro zapateador hurtar la vuelta al que baila, y sucederle escobillando para atrás y para adelante con admirable presteza, obteniendo en premio que alguna de las presentes le arroje al paso un pañuelo cifrado con sus iniciales y varios bordados alegóricos; mientras la compañera, de ojos negros y graciosas formas, de suelta y garboso talle, viva, ligera . . . á veces persiguiendo al *hombre*, (que así llaman al bailador), otras huyéndole, escapándose después para cruzar por sus espaldas y esperarle á la vuelta de frente, se asemeja á un pez que meneando la cola parece volar entre dos aguas sin que la vista pueda seguir sus movimientos, y que torna con igual rapidez al punto de donde partió. (Betancourt 367)

El mas ligero quita el sitio á su rival y le sucede en él, resbalando ligeramente sus pies hácia atrás y hácia adelante, y meneándose con una ligereza que le aturde. Alguna de las muchachas le tira su pañuelo bordado y perfumado, con las iniciales en un pico y con cien festones emblemáticos al rededor [*sic*]; . . . sigue, huye y vuelve á seguir sucesivamente al *hombre*, clavando en él sus ojos negros, deslizándose de entre sus manos con su cintura delgada y ligera, provocándole y burlándole con una encantadora coquetería. Y vuelve á acercársele, y vuelve á escaparse con una vivacidad camastrona, agitándose en las mil vueltas de su baile característico, como el pez en el agua . . . hasta que se cansa y se sienta. (Merlin 67)

(A skillful *zapateador* is seen stealing a turn from the dancer, and following him, dancing quickly back and forth with such admirable speed, securing as an award a handkerchief bearing her initials as well as some allegorical embroidery which one of the women present might throw at him as he goes by; while her companion, whose black eyes and gracious shape, of loose and graceful figure, lively, bright . . . sometimes chasing after the *man*, other times avoiding him, escaping only to cross later behind his back and wait for him at the front turn, resembles a fish who, moving its tail, seems to fly between two waters without the eyes being able to follow its movements, and which returns with equal speed to the point from which it departed.)

(The swiftest man takes away his rival's place and follows him, lightly sliding his feet to the back and to the front, and moving with such swiftness that he is dazed. One of the girls flings to him her embroidered and perfumed handkerchief, with her initials highlighted with a hundred emblematic garlands all around; . . . she pursues, flees and continues to pursue the man in quick succession, fixing on him her piercing black eyes and sliding away from his hands with her light and slender waist, provoking him and mocking him with charming flirtatiousness. And she returns to approach him, and she escapes again with such sly liveliness, fluttering in the one thousand whirls of her dance which is as natural to her as a fish in the water . . . until she gets tired and sits down.)

Missing in Merlin's rewriting is the poetic charge of the original, the heightened sense of the dance, and the whirling description which doubles precisely the dancers' fast pursuit. The paleness of the derivative version obliges Merlin to preface her flat rendition of Betancourt's original with an acknowledgement of her own authorial limitations: "No os lo pintaré yo; ya vos habeis visto el paso menudo é infantil de este baile, que expresa de una manera admirable la agilidad, la vivacidad, la naturalidad de los bailarines" ("I will not describe it to you; you have already seen the short and infantile steps of this dance, which expresses in an admirable manner the agility, the liveliness, the naturalness of the dancers") (67). Though displaced onto the narrative voice, this statement is, nevertheless, an important admission on Merlin's part that her role is not to be an authentic *costumbrista*, but rather his faithful imitator.

In her role as a twice-removed spectator, Merlin succeeds in her task of "artistically representing language . . . the image of a language," the language chosen by Cuban *costumbristas* to convey an emerging sense of insular community.[32] In duplicating this scene onto her text, the image of the dance is distorted by excessive loyalty to the source-text. Hence, the verisimilitude dear to the *costumbristas* is here supplanted by an alternative, hypermimetic narration, which creates the effect of mimicry or distortion of the original text. Mimicry thus turns back on itself as the dance scene accrues additional representative power; it enacts, not the typicality of the local color sketch, as Betancourt himself proposed, but rather an important cultural transaction: the shift between "barbarous" customs and "civilized" ones.[33] What was only a temporal succession at the level of plot—the killing and collective consumption of the animal followed by ritual dancing—is seen in Merlin's version as a qualitative change from the prosaic to the poetic; put in anthropological terms, the *lechón/zapate(ad)o* sequence signifies the transition from the raw to the cooked: "Con esto acabó la loa gastronómica, y empezó la fiesta poética. El mondongo no es mas que un pretexto; el verdadero objeto son el baile, la música, el amor y la libertad" ("With this, the gastronomical part ended and the poetic celebration began. The *mondongo* is only a pretext, for its true object is the dance, the music, love and freedom") (66).

The representation of Otherness in *Viaje a la Habana* is riddled by other curious associations, equivalences, and displacements. Throughout her appropriated tale, Merlin throws markers of her own peculiar conception of the Other and of his role in Cuban culture. A *criada de mano* that in Betancourt's account serves cups of sweetened coffee to all the feast's participants is magically transformed into a "negrita" in Merlin's rendition (366; 66, respectively). Why this inclusion of the black in a tale so obviously identified with the rural sector of the population? The clue to this change is found in another one of Merlin's alterations of Betancourt's original. When the prototypical *guajiro* "ño Pepe el mocho" appears, a sweet young girl runs out to greet him; her age is poetically depicted: "una guajirita que no ha visto parir mas que seis ocasiones el coco que su padre sembró el día de su nacimiento" ("a young country girl who has only seen the coconut tree that her father planted on her birthday bear fruit six times" [Betancourt 366]). Not content with merely repeating the original, Merlin doubles the girl's age to twelve, thereby literalizing the metaphor in the same way that she had tamed the energetic swirls of the *zapateo* into its unlikely double: "La guajirita apenas tendría doce años, ó como se dice poéticamente en el pais, no habia visto brotar el cocotero planteado por su padre el dia de su nacimiento" ("the young country girl must have only been twelve years old; as one would say it poetically in our country, she had not yet seen the buds of the coconut tree which her father had planted at her birth") (Merlin 66). In the absence of direct contact with rural scenes and characters, Merlin makes up for the gap not only by conscious imitation of *guajiro* speech, but also by her own willful imagining of what the racial and social strata of Cuban culture should look like. Through accumulation of detail and by tampering with accepted versions of reality, Merlin hoped not only to render an inclusive image of the nation, but also to signal at least a "zero degree" of originality, thereby forging her own version of the literary vernacular and inscribing herself, however obliquely, into tradition.

Such a sign of difference is likewise evident at the conclusion of the tale. Betancourt ends his version with a grotesque detail in which the beauty of its female participants is marred by association with the heavy odors of the pig roast.[34] By contrast, Merlin avoids such gender specificity to highlight a *carpe diem* theme that emphasizes the connection made between two previously unrelated cultural practices: "de la velada del mondongo, como de la velada del muerto, no queda mas, mi querida Mercedes, que nuevos gérmenes de vida, agradables recuerdos, ilusiones nuevas, matrimonios y amores" ("of the soirée of the *mondongo* as well as for the funeral wake, nothing is left, my dear Mercedes,

but new traces of life, which are nice recollections, new hopes, marriages, and loves") (Merlin 69). By inserting herself onto the text as a
fictional character in her own narrative, Merlin thus accomplishes her
task of *resembling*, albeit by mimicry and simulation, the original *costumbristas*.

The effect of mimicry is not only created in the text by Merlin's
reabsorption of master-narratives, but also by the manner in which these
tales are appropriated. In this sense, the *guajiro* theme that resurfaces
in "Carta VI" of *Viaje a la Habana* is patterned, for the most part, after
Cirilo Villaverde's *El guajiro*, first published in serial form in the *Faro
Industrial de la Habana* in 1842.[35] But instead of copying the published
version of Villaverde's novella, Merlin inserted into "Carta VI" an anonymous sketch entitled "Amoríos y contratiempos de un guajiro" ("Love
Affairs and Mishaps of a Country Bloke") which had appeared in the 1839
volume of *La Cartera Cubana* under the section "Costumbres."[36] Despite
its anonymity, this tale was, indeed, the first draft of Villaverde's *El guajiro*, which was not published in its entirety until 1842, two years after
Merlin's visit. The story appears in truncated form because Merlin apparently only had access to the first draft of Villaverde's novella, published
a year before her journey.

The plagiarism of "Amoríos y contratiempos de un guajiro" in
"Carta VI" of *Viaje* shows the effect of such abrupt transformations. José
María's serenade to his girlfriend is brusquely interrupted by the appearance of a wild dog that he kills in self-defense, thus arousing both the
household and, worse yet, the ire of the girl's father.[37] Because Villaverde's
sketch concludes at this climactic point, Merlin necessarily leaves the
lovers in the lurch, apologizing to the reader with the naive assertion:
"espero poderos dar en breve la continuacion de la historia de José María"
("I hope to soon be able to give you the rest of the story of José María")
(46). By finishing the tale with the conventional phrase used by Cuban
costumbristas to signal that their tale will continue in the next issue of the
serial publication, Merlin is, once again, patterning herself after her male
precursors.

Following her earlier technique of "radial reading," Merlin com-
pensated for this lack of (re)sources by "fattening" her chapter on rural
types and mores found in other Villaverde texts. Thus the love story of
José María *el guajiro* inserted into "Carta VI" is the filler of a narrative
"sandwich" whose top and bottom halves include sections from Cirilo

Villaverde's *Excursión a Vuelta Abajo*, which had originally appeared in
serial form in the pages of *El Álbum*.[38] Specifically, the opening scene of
Merlin's "Carta VI," aptly entitled "Los guagiros [*sic*]," includes topics
directly lifted from the fifth section of the first part of Villaverde's *Excursión*; mainly, the description of a typical rural habitat and the *guajiro's*
predilection for women, horses and *machetes* (*Viaje*, 34–39; *Excursión*,
84–89). Likewise, the concluding scene of a *guajiro* who throws himself
into the river to save his dog is the same as Villaverde's ending anecdote
(*Excursión*, 1891 edition, 83–84, 87–89, 90–94, respectively; *Viaje*, 47–48).

The pedagogical thrust of *costumbrista* narrative is evident in
Villaverde's *Excursión*, which nostalgically projects the image of a ver-
dant, pastoral Cuba to counter the ravaging effects of industrialization.
A yearning for a past Golden Age is particularly evident in the narrator's
lament at the cutting down of trees that had once graced the eastern part
of the island: "No queda en pié ni un jagüey, ni un ácana, bajo cuyas copas
tantas veces en su mejor mocedad se guareció de los ardores del sol de
Junio" ("Neither a tree of yellow wood, nor an acana stands now,
under whose branches he would in his youth so often protect himself
from the heat of the June sun").[39] This sense of inclusion, communal well-
being, and harmony with nature is echoed as well in the landscape descriptions which open and close Villaverde's inner travelogue, a Romantic
notebook of his return to his native land, the "little Cuba" of the tobacco
fields. The poetic thrust of the narration enacts a veritable inscape of
insular life, as at the end of the tale Villaverde describes a group of young
girls who playfully run by a nearby maze, a pastoral anecdote that allows
him to *name* the natural *topoi* of trees, fruits, and scenery in a fleeting
attempt to hold them fixed in time:

> El limpio en que el viejo y yo estábamos hablando, era un círculo bas-
> tante espacioso; asi que, el aparecimiento repentino de aquellas cabezas,
> coronadas de flores, de entre las *maníguas* ásperas del potrero, llenas de
> *guisazos* sus ropas, y arañadas sus caras de las espinas, no pudo menos de
> arrancarnos un grito de alegría. . . . Pero es lo bueno que sucias y llenas
> las bocas de las más de guayabas y otras frutillas del campo, como *pita-
> hayas* y *avellanos*, producía un ruido tan desapacible sus risas y zumos,
> que las reduje a completo silencio echándoles en rostro su golosina.

> (The clearing in which the old man and I were talking formed a very
> spacious circle. Suddenly, the appearance of flower-crowned heads in

the midst of the rugged jungles of the pasture-ground, their clothes full of prickles, their faces scratched by thorns, made us shout with joy. . . . But the good thing was that because their mouths and hands were dirty and full of guava and other wild fruits, such as tree-cactus and hazelnuts, their laughs and juices produced such an unpleasant noise, that I was able to silence them completely by tossing sweets into their faces.) (78)

Hence, Merlin's recasting of Cirilo Villaverde's *Escursion á la Vuelta-Abajo* shows her controversial vision in contrast to the *costumbristas'* idealization of rural types and mores. Whereas Villaverde's *Excursion* represents a longing for a pastoral world that is rapidly vanishing, Merlin's pronounced rewriting in "Lettre XXXV" of *La Havane* harbors a more modern project of the nation in looking beyond the confines of *Cuba pequeña* toward a more encompassing nationalist goal. This rewriting thus amplifies the parodic appropriation of the *guajiro* theme initiated in "Carta VI" of *Viaje a la Habana*, particularly through Merlin's refashioning of the episode surrounding Don Tiburcio, a rural patriarch whose ungrateful heirs had dwindled his lands away in countless lawsuits.

Within the framework of his own interior voyage to his native Pinar del Río, in Villaverde's *Excursión* the character of Don Tiburcio acquires special significance as one of the last representatives of the cultural values of *Cuba pequeña*. Tucked away as he is in a faraway *potrero* beyond the river, Don Tiburcio's blindness and isolation is emblematic of the decline of tobacco agriculture that made *Vuelta Abajo* famous. Yet Tiburcio stands amid the arid corner of his plot as a "leal centinela," "faithful sentinel" or guardian of cultural values in the face of the onslaught of modernization, an attitude which the narrator values as ethically correct: "El, como leal centinela, parece destinado por el cielo para dar testimonio de la manera como la industria y la planta del hombre, hacen mudar la faz de los paises más incultos é inaccesibles" ("He, like a faithful sentinel, seems destined by heaven to testify as to how man's ingenuity and schemes are capable of changing the face of even the most uncivilized and inaccessible of countries") (*Excursión*, 66).

Whereas Villaverde's description of San Diego de Núñez appears written "con los colores de la verdad" ("with truthful colors") (61), Merlin's rewriting revises not the truth but the verisimilitude of the original in order to project an alternative version of country life that stems from her position as woman and exile. In "Lettre XXXV" of *La Havane*,

Don Tiburcio becomes, not a "real centinela" representing both the inherited legacy of the land and an unshakable tie to the origin, but rather a kind of inverse counterpart to Merlin's own experience of exile and banishment.[40] If in the *Excursión* Villaverde accents the decline of land and patrimony of Don Tiburcio's clan, Merlin, by contrast, projects onto the past a utopian notion of order and concordance in the founding family: "C'est dans ce site agreste et sauvage, loin des hommes rassemblés, de leurs passions et de leurs vices, que cette nouvelle tribu présenta, dans toute sa simplicité primitive, le bonheur dans la vie de famille, riche des bons de la nature et d'affections hônnetes" ("Here in this rural and wild site, far from congregations of men, from their passions and vices, that this new tribe presents in primitive simplicity the happiness of family life, richly endowed with the gifts of nature and of honest affections").[41]

Following Villaverde's account to describe how Tiburcio's family dispersed and ultimately lost its lands and riches, Merlin extracts the main points without narrative embellishment, transforming the provocative tone of the first author into an impersonal sequence of events. For example, Villaverde's humorous anecdote on the lawsuits and legal battles that embittered the brothers is reduced to a dry, brittle commentary in Merlin's account:

He oido decir a algunos de los hijos del patriarca, que la testamentaría, [*sic*] de su padre había parido tantas testamentarías, que ya era preciso cargarlas en carretones, las veces que han tenido necesidad de sacarla del oficio para que les pasase vista el abogado defensor (65).	Les papiers concernant les litiges étaient portés par des charrettes chez l'avocat défenseur, et au bout de trente ans, la famille du patriarche s'éteignit dans la pauvreté et dans la douleur (377; *La Habana*, 390).
(I have heard some of the children of the patriarch say that their father's executrix had given birth to so many executrices that, indeed, it was necessary to carry them in large carts, every time that they needed to get the papers out of their official place so that the defense lawyer might look them over.)	(Documents concerning the many lawsuits were brought in carts to the defense lawyer, and, at the end of thirty years, the patriarch's family became extinct due to poverty and pain.)

Though portions of the letter emulate Villaverde's ecstatic descriptions of the hills and valleys of his native province, at other points Merlin departs from the original, adding her own (inventive and invented) response to a countryside that she never personally visited. A significant shift in literary code occurs here, for whereas Villaverde appears as the most Romantic given his recourse to reverie and contemplation of nature, Merlin resorts to a pragmatic approach to landscape. Whereas Villaverde contrasts Tiburcio's past as a *montero* with his present impoverished existence as a critique of the effects of increasing industrialization (69–70), Merlin exalts the virtues of institutions that could channel the bounties of nature into a more plentiful society (*La Havane*, 386; *La Habana* 393). Not only does this turn in the narration attest to the fact that Merlin has abandoned Villaverde's travelogue and is now registering her own impressions, but it also echoes Merlin's program of reform, and particularly her resistance to the idealization of *Cuba pequeña*. Though in these passages she echoes the pedagogic thrust of the del Monte circle by gearing the description of landscape into a vision of social welfare, this vision stems not from the natural bounties of the Cuban countryside, as in Villaverde's text, but from a more forward-looking, modernist goal of harnessing the riches of the land. In her rewriting of Villaverde, then, Merlin's gesture of establishing an "imagined community" follows the *costumbristas'* overvaluation of the rural, but charts a different course: unlike her Cuban precursor, Merlin upholds a vision of an emerging nationalist industry, another point of contention between her enterprise and that of the del Monte circle.

Merlin's plundering of Betancourt's original ultimately points to the woman writer's problematic relationship to the male master text: she can neither assimilate it to her purpose nor depart from it in a way that establishes once and for all her own narrative authority. The one literary debt that Merlin directly acknowledges is included, precisely, in "Lettre XXXV" of *La Havane*, almost as if Villaverde's interior journey patterned her own return to her native city. Villaverde's appearance as a character in the *Excursión* seems to permit this strategy of recognition, particularly the scene when the narrator, clearly a mask for the real author, goes to meet the famous Don Tiburcio. Blinded by fate, as it were (the victim of his father's downfall and loss of his dominions), Don Tiburcio nevertheless has retained his ability to recognize every one of his guests by name, including extended family and servants. When the narrator, in his function as Villaverde's mask, approaches him, the old man is disturbed at first, then makes a supreme effort to identify the person before him by sheer power of recall ("Yo quiero acertar con tu nombre sin necesidad de que me lo anuncies") ("I want to hit upon your name correctly without your needing to proclaim it") (73). Anticipating a technique used in his masterpiece, *Cecilia Valdés*, Villaverde plays with the symbolic legacy of the name as sign of individual and collective identity. After a moment's hesitation, the old man's face lights up as he recognizes in the apocryphal Villaverde not only a long-lost family friend but also the companion of his deceased son, in this way establishing a relation of metaphorical paternity with the narrator: "¡Dame un abrazo, camará! Yo que te vi nacer, que te cargué tantas veces en estos brazos ahora flacos y débiles, que te ví jugar con mi difunto hijo, . . . ¿yo no había de reconocerte?" ("Give me a hug, comrade! I who saw you at your birth, who carried you around so often in these arms so thin and frail now, I who saw you playing with my now-deceased child. . . . How could I not recognize you?") (74). When the old patriarch embraces and accepts him into the inner circle of the Vuelta Abajo region's founding families, this gesture represents the cultural value of the text as mark of *pertenencia*, the sense of belonging to a broader regional community. The scene also dramatizes Villaverde's affirmation of *Cuba pequeña*, which values the private, intimate realm of the countryside over the public bustle of industry and commerce represented by Havana.

Though up to this point Merlin had faithfully followed the contours of Villaverde's plot, there is a significant departure in her rendering of the recognition scene between the aging Tiburcio and a more youthful Cirilo. This scene is duplicated or inversely transposed in "Lettre XXXV" of *La Havane* to reveal Merlin's own (covert) identification with the original author. Although in earlier parts of the letter she had appropriated herself of the narrator's function with the use of the first-person narrative voice, here her gender seems to prevent any further identification with Villaverde's authorial position. In an ingenious move, Merlin displaces herself onto an unnamed but reliable cousin who offers to take her to meet the venerable last descendant of the San Diego tribe. Then, in a second turn of the screw, this imaginary cousin further displaces the original narrator onto another fictional character, an imaginary friend who coincidentally is called Cirilo Villaverde (381). For the first time and with a mixture of fear and delight that belies her authorial anxiety, Merlin—as much a character in her own text as Villaverde's fictionalized author, who had doubled himself as the first-person narrator in *Excursión*—recognizes both her precursor and the merit of his work:

> —*Cirilo Villaverde*! m'écriai-je, celui qui fait de si jolis vers, et des ouvrages si excellents! sur les moeurs de ce pays, [*sic*] Il est au nombre des hommes qui font honneur à notre pays, et je serai enchantée de le connaître avant de retourner en Europe (381; *La Habana* 391).

> (—*Cirilo Villaverde*! such a wonderful poet, and the author of such excellent works! about the mores of this country, [*sic*] He is a man whose name honors our country, and I would be delighted to meet him before returning to Europe.)

By connecting this scene to the later scene of recognition in which Tiburcio accepts the fictional Villaverde without naming him, Merlin effectively binds herself to the latter's creative powers at the same time that she acknowledges his literary fame. Moreover, this second gesture of recognition helps to neutralize whatever criticism might come her way in the event that her "crime" of literary plagiarism were discovered. Positing herself as both a fan and successor of the Creole writer, Merlin avoids confrontation at the same time that she articulates a hidden wish-fulfillment: to meet Villaverde in person, a desire that undoubtedly cloaks her—perhaps unconscious—ambition to *be* another Villaverde. Yet, because Merlin could not aspire to be one of the "founding fathers" of Cuban letters due to her gender, the displacement characteristic of the nativistic writer is here one step removed by fictionalizing both original and secondary authors, and by "translating"—or rather mutilating—Villaverde's text into disconnected fragments.[42] In this way, the tactic of assimilation from source-book to secondary text allows Merlin to further distance herself from Villaverde all the while marking her fundamental debt to him.

The end of the Tiburcio scene clearly establishes the status of *La Havane* as a "double discourse" marking the woman writer's paradoxical relationship to the male literary tradition.[43] Merlin loosely adapts Section VI of the first part of *Excursión a Vuelta Abajo*; in her version, Don Tiburcio woefully pets his dog Galeano, wounded in the eyes the night before and hence just as blind as his master (388–90; *La Habana*, 393–94).

Whereas Villaverde's text ends on an optimistic note—the narrator attempts to assuage the old man's grief by assuring him that the dog is not hurt—Merlin turns the scene into melodrama, as both dog and master appear bound to the same fate, blind to the vagaries of time and surpassed by the winds of change in their forsaken corner of country (*Excursión* 110–11; *La Havane* 338–90; *La Habana* 393–94). At another level, the metonymic relation between man and animal reads as a double inscription of another tie: the symbiotic bond that this letter of *La Havane* establishes between Merlin and Villaverde. Like a literary mongrel, the women writer has devoured the master text in order to feed her own monster-narrative, "Lettre XXXV" patterned on the scraps of *Excursion a Vuelta Abajo* and yet appearing, in simulated fashion, as an original. The pathetic scene thus reads as a projection of Merlin's authorial anxiety, her hesitation when appropriating the works of a male precursor. Though undaunted in her systematic use of this technique, the end of this letter signals Merlin's heightened awareness of her own literary secondariness, her conscious mimicry of the works of male authors in order to forge her own imagined and Imaginary version of Cuba.

A similar tactic of textual pillage is evident in "Carta VI" dedicated to "Los guagiros" in *Viaje a la Habana*, which closes with a scene echoing the end of Villaverde's *Excursión*: a clumsy sketch narrating a *guajiro*'s daring attempt to save his dog. In the Villaverde original, the tale is prefigured by the narrator's announcement that his sisters had interrupted his writing and urged him to take a walk along the river (Villaverde, *Excursion* 90); however, in *Viaje a la Habana*, these characters are transposed as Merlin herself, and her cousins appear on the scene (46). Such contrast points out the different authorial intentions playing in each case: whereas from Villaverde's anecdote the reader derives the simple fact that a man who risked his life for his dog had the good fortune to come out alive (93-94), Merlin, instead, has a black man save the desperate swimmer (48). Thus, in Merlin's rewriting, this apparently trivial anecdote is used didactically to emphasize cultural differences as well as similarities: "Ya veis, pues, que el guagiro ó montero de Cuba tiene los mismos instintos y el mismo valor que los africanos, suavizados por todo lo que hay de dulce ó de tierno en el carácter criollo" ("As you can see, the country bloke or backwoodsman of Cuba has the same instincts and courage as the Africans, who have been tamed by everything sweet and tender in the Creole character") (48). Rather than uphold the strict hierarchy of

race and class proper of the colonialist writer, Merlin prescribes here
to a transculturated vision of Cuban nationality that goes beyond the *costumbristas'* sustained idealization of *Cuba pequeña*. Though unfamiliar
with the regions charted by Villaverde, in this letter, and in the other *costumbrista* sketches incorporated into *Viaje a la Habana*, Merlin imagined
for herself a *"tierra de promisión"* that would cancel out the lack and distance of exile and replace it with an image of harmony encompassing
both the natural and social worlds. That her vision may be comparable
to the *costumbristas'* in its degree of idealization is not as important as the
fact that she, too, dared to invent an island.

Alone with Aurora: Merlin's Rewriting of Palma

More important perhaps than Merlin's plagiarism of both Betancourt
and Villaverde is her rewriting of Ramón de Palma's *Una Pascua en San
Marcos* (1838) in "Carta IX" of *Viaje a la Habana* (69–103).[44] Merlin lifted
nearly the entire text of Palma's novella essentially unchanged into her
autobiographical narrative, with the notable exception of the drastic
rewriting of its ending. In what can only be identified as a gesture of
female solidarity, Merlin alters both the name and the fate of the main
character, Aurora, saving her Conchita from an unhappy marriage with
the libertine Claudio. For better or worse, Conchita remains alone to
face her fate as a free woman rather than remain forever bound to the
man who had first seduced and then betrayed and abused her (*Viaje a la
Habana*, 103).

In order to appreciate the significance of Merlin's rendering of
Palma's tale, it is necessary to point out the impact Palma's novella had
on Creole intellectual circles. Perhaps for the first time in Cuban letters,
Palma's *Una Pascua en San Marcos* had unabashedly revealed the "forbidden" themes of seduction and extramarital flirtation among the Creole youth. Within the pedagogic model of the del Monte circle, Palma's
novella of romantic intrigue stood out as the first attempt to veer away
from the idealization of Cuban scenes and types and to gain proximity
to the realists' character introspection and social critique. The novella
had originally appeared in the pages of *El Album* (1838), a journal directed
by Palma and José Antonio Echevarría, which had published the *costumbrista* sketches of Cirilo Villaverde, Anselmo Suárez y Romero, José
Zacarías González del Valle, José Victoriano Betancourt, and José Ja-

cinto Milanés—in short, all the luminaries of the del Monte circle.[45] Palma's novella exemplified how the Cuban Romantics had successfully adapted the descriptive sketch to the Balzac model in order to depict more true-to-life accounts of customs and mores.[46] In a letter to del Monte dated May 17, 1838, José Jacinto Milanés exalts Palma's novella as representative of realist art: "Es indecible el gozo que me causó la lectura de una cosa tan criolla y tan llena de verdad" ("You have no idea of the delight I felt at reading something so Creole and so full of truth").[47]

Both the "effect of the real" caused by Palma's novella and the furor generated by Merlin's rewriting is borne out by a quick rundown of its plot. *Una Pascua en San Marcos* takes place in Artemisa during the Christmas dance of 1818.[48] An atmosphere of festivity and gaiety surrounds the initial encounter between the dashing Don Claudio de Meneses and the young Aurora, the adolescent daughter of Don Antonio Paciego, a rich landowner from the district of San Marcos. Don Claudio flirts with Aurora during the dance, pressing her for favors and engaging her with amorous tones. In complicity with Aurora's slave, that same night Claudio forces himself into her bedroom, notwithstanding Aurora's resistance and the violation of trust of her father Don Antonio, who had welcomed Claudio into the family estate. The next morning, in a pleasure trip through Don Tadeo Amirola's coffee plantation, the frivolous Don Claudio declares his admiration for Rosa, wife of the Spanish Captain Irum. Upon their return to the Paciego estate, a taciturn Aurora, aware of her lover's inconstancy, decides not to attend the evening festivities. She reproaches Claudio for his great dishonor, but the youth, unaffected by her claims, boasts to his friend Valentín of his future conquest, none other than the wife of Captain Irum. The scene shifts back to Amirola's coffee plantation, as the party of guests prepare a horseback ride through the fields. When Rosa Miranda accidentally falls from her horse, Don Claudio seizes the opportunity to rescue her and declare his passion. Later on that evening, Aurora, conscious of Claudio's betrayal, feigns disdain for him, but this only spurs him to seduce Doña Rosa under the *guardarraya* (boundary line). Aurora's instinct guides her to discover the illicit lovers' embrace, in a key scene that provoked moral uproar among Palma's contemporaries. A desperate Aurora cries out against Claudio, at which moment Rosa flees from the scene of seduction, leaving the Cuban Don Juan in the throes of a struggle with his first conquest. Upon hearing the dogs of the search party that Don Antonio had sent out to ensure Aurora's return, the frightened Claudio forces the girl to silence and renders her unconscious with his blows. Thinking that he killed her, Claudio then follows Rosa's example and abandons his victim. When he returns to the estate, Claudio is about to turn himself in and declare the truth, but he is checked by the resourceful Valentín, who assures Claudio that no one, except Rosa, had noticed his part in the scuffle. In complicity with Claudio's romantic adventures, Valentín had persuaded Don Antonio's *mayoral* (slave overseer) not to look any further for Aurora's tracks in the dark. In this way Claudio's "crime" is artfully concealed, in that Aurora's parents attributed her unconscious state to the effect of wine and the evening's merrymaking.

At this point in the novella, Palma's peers anxiously awaited the story's denouement, for on it hinged the moral fabric of Creole society. Will Aurora's honor be repaired in marriage? Will the libertine Don Claudio receive due punishment? Better yet, will Rosa repent her momentary "fall" into temptation? Palma disappointed detractors and defenders alike with the final resolution of the plot. After the climactic scene (discussed at length by his contemporaries José Z. González del Valle and José Jacinto Milanés), Palma has his female protagonist fall ill, during which time Claudio repents his past cruelty to her and vows to marry her upon her recovery (*Una Pascua en San Marcos*, 86–88). The cause of Aurora's affliction is never revealed, because Claudio's mistreatment of the girl is unknown even to her parents, a development that prolongs the moral ambiguity of the tale. True to the expectations of a Romantic reader, the two lovers ultimately reconcile themselves and their wedding is celebrated (ironically enough) in Don Tadeo's coffee plantation. Yet, toward the end, the marriage between Aurora and Don Claudio eventually fails, a twist occasioned by the fact that Claudio had wasted the family fortune in gambling, causing Aurora's reproaches for his moral excesses. Aptly enough, Claudio ends his days as a drunkard in the hospital of San Juan de Dios (Palma, 97–102), and his female protagonist is rightfully returned to the parental home. Though Palma's character meets his moral ruin and atones for his past life as a libertine, Aurora remains bound to the expectations of the period regarding a forsaken wife's respectability.

Two points of view are evident in the response to Palma's novella, which I will encode in terms of gender so as to better illustrate the effect which Merlin's rewriting must have had on her literary peers in Cuba.

José Z. González del Valle responded to the novella from a masculine perspective, a position that sees Claudio as representative of male values and behavior, which the moral ambiguity of the plot puts into question. In a letter González del Valle sent to Anselmo Suárez y Romero on June 15, 1838, González del Valle tried to salvage Palma from Suárez y Romero's negative opinion regarding the contrived plot of *Una Pascua en San Marcos*. From this letter we glean that Suárez y Romero, author of the antislavery novel *Francisco o los ingenios del campo (Francisco, or the Delights of Country Life)* (1839; published 1880), objected to the narrative inconsistency of Palma's novella evident in the scene when Aurora discovers Claudio's seduction of Rosa Miranda. Why is Aurora so ready to denounce her outrage against Claudio, argues Suárez y Romero, when in the previous episode she had showed him absolute indifference? González del Valle answered him by insisting that Aurora's action was justified in terms of her desire to avenge herself against Claudio. The question of plot obviously leads to the moral dilemma dramatized by Palma, inasmuch as Don Claudio's abandonment of Aurora leaves the character in the untenable position of seducer, criminal and deserter, at least in the narrator's view (Palma 75–76). Not surprisingly, González del Valle shifted his sympathies to Claudio, answering Suárez y Romero's objection by extricating the character from his moral responsibility:

> A la objeción de ¿cómo pasaron tantas cosas después que cayó Aurora al suelo y no se cuidó Claudio de huir, oyendo a los voceadores? contesto que ni fueron tantas, ni . . . dejan de poder suceder en muy corto espacio de tiempo.

> (To the charge of how so many things could happen after Aurora fell down, and why Claudio did not escape right away as soon as he heard the search party, I would answer that they weren't so many, nor . . . was it impossible for these things to happen in such a short span of time.)

In this way González del Valle implies that Don Claudio was right to flee and cover his crime, to the point that both character and novelist are redeemed by their ingenious "plotting": "Su artificio llega a poner tan en peligro a Claudio, que casi se pregunta uno a sí mismo—*¿porqué no se escapa este diablo? y se teme que lo cojan junto a Aurora*" ("His artifice puts Claudio in such danger, that the reader almost asks himself—'*why doesn't this poor devil escape? for one fears that he be caught next to Aurora*'").[49]

If González del Valle lightly dismissed Claudio's "mistakes," Tanco, by contrast, denied in his *Refutacion* the character's function as a type and the fact that Claudio's moral lassitude stemmed directly from the contradictions of Creole society (54). In his zeal to criticize Merlin's transformation of Claudio into a "Latin lover," Tanco went so far as to disclaim the work's representative value, recognizing only the verisimilitude of an individual prone to excess and vice. Consequently, Tanco also denied that Palma meant to make Claudio a type:

> En efecto, el autor de una Pascua en San Marcos [*sic*] pintó con todos los coloridos a veces demasiado vivos, con todo el nervio de su poético talento, pero siempre con verdad, los estravíos de un libertino, de un hombre disoluto, sin que pudiese jamas haber sido su idea demostrar que abundaban semejantes seres en nuestro pais. . . . [J]amas podrán admitirse estas producciones de la imaginación . . . del deseo de corregir las costumbres ó de denunciar los estravíos del espíritu humano, hechos aislados, apéndices por decirlo asi de la sociedad, como el resultado de las costumbres de nuestro pais, como tipo de nuestras sociedades.

> (In effect, the author of Christmas in San Marcos [*sic*] painted with a wide palette sometimes excessively vivid, with all the nerve of his poetic talent, but always with the truth, the excesses of a libertine, of a licentious man, without it ever having crossed his mind to prove that such types are common in our country. . . . Never could these products of the imagination . . . be recognized as the result of the desire to correct customs or denounce the excesses of the human spirit; [never could] isolated cases, what we could call appendixes of society, [be seen] as the result of the customs of our country or as types of our societies.)[50]

Neither Tanco nor González del Valle recognize that what Palma depicts as "immoral" is Aurora's destruction by the seducer—the physical injury and psychological harm which Don Claudio inflicts on his female victim. Seen from another perspective, her metaphorical "death" in the novella would be a warning to potential victims of such tropical Don Juans as Don Claudio. Such a "feminine" reading is, in fact, suggested by José Jacinto Milanés in a letter to Del Monte dated May 17, 1838:

> Veamos el desenlace que Palma le dá y luego diremos si es ó no inmoral: veamos en que para don Claudio. Pero entre tanto, (si concluye como espero), imagino que Palma está haciendo un eminente ser-

vicio á nstras doncellas en abrirlas [*sic*] los ojos y hacerlas mas cautas. Tal es la opinion que me he formado de su composicion.

(Let's see what outcome Palma gives [the novel] and then we can judge whether it is immoral or not: let's see what fate befalls Don Claudio. But, in the meantime, [if it ends as I think it should] I imagine that Palma is doing our maidens a great favor in opening their innocent eyes and making them more cautious. Such is the judgment that I have reached regarding the novel's form.) (*Centón epistolario*, III, 158–159)

For daring to reveal "the decadent life of idleness and excess led by the sugar and coffee plantocracy,"[51] *Una Pascua en San Marcos* soon earned the reputation of being an "immoral" work, provoking a lively polemic among the highbrow members of the *tertulia*. Milanés came once again to his friend's defense on the grounds of the novel's forceful realism:

Echeverría me dice que se decía que es inmoral la novela y que pensaba hacer un juicio crítico de ella. —Inmoral! en qué es inmoral esta obrita? En revelar ntras costumbres? En pintar tales cuales ntros libertinos, idiotas y viciosos? En retratar nuestras novelescas muchachas, cuya inocencia peligrosa se nutre de lecturas caballerescas, y luego quiere buscar los tipos europeos en ntra sociedad llena de corrupción y barbarie?

(Echeverría tells me that it was said that the novel was immoral and that someone was thinking of writing a critical commentary of it. —Immoral! In what sense is the novel immoral? In revealing our habits? In depicting our idiotic and vice-ridden libertines just as they are? In describing our women as fictional heroines, whose innocence is alarmingly fed by chivalric romances, so that later they go in search of the European types in our society, so full of corruption and barbarism?") (*Centón epistolario*, III, 158)

In his reply to Milanés, which, according to critic Imeldo Alvarez, is dated May 28, 1838, del Monte stressed once more the importance of *Una Pascua en San Marcos* as the first authentic portrait of social relations among the Creole upper class:

[P]or su colorido local, la buena observación y pintura de nuestras costumbres, y la naturalidad y sencillez del lenguaje, ha hecho aquí mucho ruido, y la gente cubana que es la primera vez que se ve retratada al

natural se ha escandalizado de su propia figura y ha tachado de
inmoral al pintor.[52]

(Given its local color, the acute observation and representation of our
native habits, and the naturalness and simplicity of its language, it has
caused great uproar here, and the Cuban people, seeing themselves for
the first time photographed 'in the nude,' are so scandalized of their
own image that they have dismissed the painter as immoral.)

In a second letter to del Monte dated May 28, 1838, Milanés notified the
tertulia leader that Félix Tanco y Bosmeniel was planning to publish a
critique of Palma's novella: "Tanco parece que se prepara a dar a
Palma una zurra que cause misterio" ("Tanco apparently is getting ready
to give Palma a real beating"), to which Milanés was violently opposed—
"yo no soy de la opinión de Tanco en cuanto a la novelita de dho
amo"[53] ("I am not of Tanco's opinion with respect to our said friend's
novella"). Whether that critique was going to be as severe as his future
allegation against Merlin is uncertain; we do know, however, that in the
Refutacion, Tanco hints at a mildly negative response to *Una Pascua en
San Marcos,* but is careful to suppress any criticism of the work because
of his friendship with the author.[54]

Safely hidden under the pseudonym "Amaranto," the *matancero*
Miguel Costales was first to publicly take up the charge of "immorality"
directed against Palma, writing in the June 17, 1838, issue of the *Diario
de la Habana.* For Costales considered "immoral" not the ending of the
novella, in which the libertine don Claudio is finally brought to moral
ruin, but the behavior of the women in the novel. Costales' charge of
"immorality" thus clearly highlights the typically male stance of the argument. Unlike Merlin's "feminist" adaptation of Palma's novella, in
Costales's interpretation the women characters are blamed, whereas the
male ones remain practically unscathed. Costales was especially harsh
with the amorous inclinations of Rosa Miranda, the wife of the Spanish
Captain who lets herself be swayed in the arms of the seducer, calling her
"una mujer sin decoro, sin amor a sus deberes, sin respeto a su marido ni
a la sociedad, descuidada de su honra, fácil en fin a entregarse al exceso
de sus deseos"[55] ("a woman without decorum, without love of duty, with
no respect for her husband or society, careless of her honor, in short,
more than willing to give herself over to the excesses of desire"). Apparently, Costales seems to have overlooked the fact that in the novella Rosa

Miranda never commits adultery. Moreover, Palma goes to great lengths to explain the psychological motivation of a woman who did not marry for love and was entitled to an episode of authentic passion (59).

But what must have scandalized Costales and the righteous *criollos* was that Palma blames the Captain of his wife's inclination to infidelity: "Al lado de un hombre que le hubiera hecho comprender la importancia de sus deberes, Rosa Miranda habría sido una esposa ejemplar; pero su marido le era muy inferior en entendimiento, y no se cuidaba de otra ciencia ni otros principios que los que podía cifrar en la punta de su espada" ("Next to a man who would have made her understand the importance of her duties, Rosa Miranda would have made a perfect wife, but her husband was much inferior to her in intellect, and had no other care nor values but those he could put on the tip of his sword") (Palma 59). Palma's humorous depiction of the Spanish Captain as a moral weakling and a potential cuckold was bound to have political repercussions.[56] "Amaranto's" censorship could thus possibly warn the Spanish authorities against Palma, and put the novelist in a politically sensitive position.

For this reason del Monte and his group rallied to Palma's defense, inasmuch as yet another criticism of the novel, such as the one planned by Félix Tanco, would surely compromise the Palma family's honor and social reputation (*Centón epistolario*, III, 158). This also explains why Lorenzo de Palma, the author's brother, wrote an impassioned plea to del Monte on June 13, 1838, asking him to exert influence on Tanco to prevent the latter from publishing his intended attack on the much debated piece (*Centón epistolario*, III, 164–65).[57] Did del Monte come to Lorenzo de Palma's aid and save the novelist further humiliation? The only clue to the affirmative is that Tanco's allegation was not, in fact, published in the *Diario de la Habana*.[58] Further proof is a letter from José Luis Alfonso to del Monte from Paris on July 3, 1838, in which he judges the Palma episode to be a closed issue, but one that left its mark on the national spirit: "La 'Pascua en S. Marcos' me ha gustado . . . y si ha alborotado a ciertas gentes es por aquello de que las verdades amargan" ("I liked Palma's 'Pascua in S. Marcos' . . . and if it has riled up certain people it is because, as the saying goes, truth is a bitter pill to swallow") (*Centón epistolario*, III, 172).

By contrast, Countess Merlin did not fare so favorably in the eyes of her compatriots. To begin with, in his *Refutacion al folleto intitulado*

Viage [*sic*] *a la Habana* (*Argument against a Pamphlet Entitled Voyage to Havana*), Félix Tanco y Bosmeniel harshly objected to Countess Merlin's blatant plagiarism of Cuban authors of the period. Tanco's indignation was particularly sparked by Merlin's rewriting of "a novel previously written and published in Havana by one of our most notable friends."[59] In the *Refutacion*, Tanco justified his vitriolic attack on the grounds that he felt compelled to correct "[las] innumerables inexactitudes, las infinitas equivocaciones de tiempo, lugar, forma y circumstancias de que está plagado este folleto" ("the innumerable inaccuracies, the infinite errors of time, space, form and circumstance with which this pamphlet is plagued") (4).[60] That Tanco was motivated as well by an antifeminist sentiment is evident in his equally unfair strike against Gertrudis Gómez de Avellaneda (258–59).

   Tanco's violent attack against the *habanera* from Paris can thus be mildly interpreted as a negative response to Merlin's literary talent. Though his stated objective was to correct the discredit heaped on Cuba by Merlin's travelogue, his real motive is revealed toward the end of *Refutacion* when he claimed that he was merely trying to save "the ladies' reputation" (58), supposedly tarnished by certain love scenes in the book. As we saw in chapter 4, Tanco relinquished responsibility for his writerly authority at the end, when he depicts a group of respected matrons entrusting him with the charge of saving honor and country by writing the text of the *Refutacion* (59) in their name. The implication, of course, is double: not only were women sheltered in the home impeded from taking up the pen, but Merlin, the only one who had dared to criticize the Creoles, was cast as morally suspect.

   Clearly, the violence of Tanco's attack is due to the fact that the visitor from France, and a woman at that, had dared to emulate a novel that had caused great stir in Cuban literary circles. Because 1844 was the year of both "La Escalera" and the publication of *Viaje a la Habana*, Tanco's indignant response could not then be tied directly to political factors, as the del Monte circle had ceased to meet by then. Apparently, some, though not all, Cuban intellectuals were familiar with the French edition of *La Havane*.[61] Why did these readers, who must have included Luz y Caballero, Merlin's mentor and a close family friend, not come to her aid and prevent Tanco's bitter pen from flowing against her *Viaje a la Habana*? Like the fictional Aurora with whom she identified, Merlin was forced to face alone the many criticisms leveled against her, whereas the male members of the del Monte circle prevented any blemish to fall on Palma as cherished peer and model. Undoubtedly these blatant differences in reader response can be accounted for where gender and literature intersect, and has to do with the way in which Countess Merlin wove into her narrative the main threads of Palma's romantic plot. For Merlin's dramatic twist of Palma's exemplary Creole masterpiece transgressed the accepted limits for a literary critique of Creole customs in colonial society.

Merlin's adaptation of Palma's novel into "Carta IX" of *Viaje a la Habana* reveals a different interpretation of the amorous plot rendered by Palma's original. This reversal is hinted at in Merlin's change of the title to read "Costumbres íntimas—Las Pascuas" ("Intimate Customs—Christmas") (*Viaje*, 69). The hint of intimacy in Merlin's title could have derived from Cirilo Villaverde's *Excursión a Vuelta Abajo* (1839 and 1842; 1891), which refers to the "afecto íntimo de familia" ("intimate family affection") proper of the *campesino* (country folk) (97). Superficially, in Merlin's version only the names of the characters are changed: Aurora becomes Conchita; Rosa Miranda is rendered Carmen Marena; Valentín is dubbed Manolo, and the principal male characters suffer a change in surname as Don Antonio Pacheco and Don Claudio de Pinto. Throughout "Carta IX," Merlin follows the narrative plot drawn by Palma to the smallest of details, including the flirtation over Aurora's glove in the first scene at the dance, and the episode of Carmen Marena's fall in horseback. But what is significant is Countess Merlin's rendition of the climactic scene and its consequences for the two protagonists. Like Palma, Merlin has Conchita discover the lovers under the *guardarraya* (boundary line) and has her cry out against Claudio. A comparison between the two versions of this crucial scene which so affected González del Valle shows the degree to which Countess Merlin attaches herself to Palma's original. "Carta IX" of *Viaje a la Habana* reads:

> Claudio no estaba en sí; ardía su cerebro, sus sienes latían con fuerza; no pudiendo por fin contener a la joven cuyo furor crecía mas y mas, la agarró con las dos manos por el cuello, y la empujó con violencia diciendo: "¡Furia del infierno!"—. La pobre niña cayó sin movimiento al pie de un yaya como la pobre gacela herida en el corazón. (96)

> (Claudio was not himself; his brain was ablaze; his temples were throbbing furiously; not able to refrain the young woman whose fury was

growing more and more, he seized her by the neck with both hands and pushed her violently, exclaiming: 'Fury of hell!'—. The poor girl fell motionless at the foot of a *yaya* tree like a poor gazelle wounded to the heart.)

The same episode is recounted in Palma with identical imagery and hyperbolic dramatism:

> Claudio no sabía por su parte lo que le pasaba, se había apoderado un vértigo de su cerebro que lo tenía desatentado y oyendo aproximarse la gente, y que la joven continuaba batallando con la misma furia, hubo un momento en que la sangre se le inflamó, sus miembros adquirieron dobles fuerzas, y por un impulso involuntario, aferrando a la desventurada con ambas manos por el cuello, la sacudió dos o tres veces con violencia diciéndole: —¡Ah, furia del infierno . . . ! Luego la soltó, pero la tierna niña cayó desmadejada en el suelo, a la manera de la garza cuando herida en el corazón desciende del ramo que la sostenía.

> (For his part, Claudio did not know what was happening; he was possessed of a fit of madness in his brain that unbalanced him; hearing people closing in, and seeing that the young woman continued to fight with the same fury, there was a moment in which his blood was inflamed, his limbs doubled their strength, and, with an involuntary impulse, holding on to the unfortunate [girl] with both hands on her neck, he shook her violently two or three times exclaiming to her: — 'Ah, fury of hell!' Then he let her go, but the tender girl fell languishing to the floor, in the manner of a gazelle that when wounded to the heart darts from the branch that had supported her.) (Palma, *Una Pascua en San Marcos*, 75)

At the point where Claudio hides his offense with the help of his friend Manolo, Merlin's rendition departs from Palma in a significant way. To begin with, and like Palma's heroine Aurora, the girl Conchita falls ill as a consequence of Claudio's attack, but this illness is protracted after the six days stipulated by Palma into a longer "enfermedad de languidez" ("a languishing illness") (*Viaje a la Habana*, 102). In Palma's account, Aurora relives the scene of cruelty in her coma, but she finally grants Claudio her pardon upon his confession of guilt, and adds insult to injury by consenting to marry him (Palma, 91–96). This same scene is depicted in Merlin's "Carta IX" with the significant introduction of a melodramatic element, which bears directly on the different moral implications of the second version. During her illness, Conchita is afflicted by the mysterious appearance of "manchas negras en su rostro, en sus brazos, y particularmente alrededor del cuello" ("black blemishes in her face, arms, and particularly around the neck"), which look like "señales como de dedos" ("finger marks") (*Viaje a la Habana*, 100). In this way Claudio's mistreatment of the girl becomes marked in her body, a detail that has two important consequences for Merlin's rewriting of Palma's romantic story. On one hand, Merlin's Conchita internalizes the extent to which Claudio has hurt her, although she does not reveal the nature of the offense—"guardó el mas profundo secreto sobre el acontecimiento del que había sido víctima" ("she kept the event that had rendered her a victim a most hidden secret") (*Viaje a la Habana*, 102). On the other hand, and despite the protagonist's reserve, the apparition of the telltale "blush" on Conchita's face alerts her parents to the gravity of their daughter's injury, thus revealing to society—and to the reader—the extent of Claudio's guilt. It is also true, however, that Merlin allows only a partial revelation of proof, inasmuch as at this point in the tale Claudio's misdeeds are covered by Manolo, the faithful friend, who blames a slave for the supposed attack against Conchita. But although the *criollo* Don Juan is spared full social indictment, in Merlin's alternative reading Claudio is not "rewarded" for his aggressive behavior. Unlike Palma's Aurora, her double Conchita refuses to comply with Claudio's request for her hand.

If Palma resolves the moral problem by a marriage of appearances, suggesting society's implicit sanction of female victimization, Merlin's heroine acknowledges her suffering and carries it to its ultimate consequences. "Carta IX" of *Viaje a la Habana* ends on a melodramatic note, which echoes the "fantastic" overtones of Conchita's illness scene. After atoning for her sins, the young protagonist dies in a swoon before an altar of "la Virgen de la Merced" ("the Virgin of Mercy"). Because this religious figure is, in fact, the author's namesake, the scene could very well signal Merlin's "feminist" sentiments toward her heroine as well as indicate her conscious parody of Palma's original (*Viaje a la Habana* 103). Toward the end, Merlin has Claudio squander his days in Paris and London, leading a life full of luxury but empty of the heart, in what could be interpreted as a warning to her Creole peers not to look to Europe for ethical models or cultural standards.

The Last *Costumbrista*: Merlin as Post-Colonial Double

Countess Merlin does to *costumbrismo* what Gertrudis Gomez de Ave-llaneda does to antislavery narrative in *Sab* (1841), another "scandalous" novel that dared to show a black slave in love with his white mistress. Both women invert the literary code in order to point out the contra-dictions faced by the marginal character, whether woman or slave. Was it valid, however, for Merlin to appropriate herself so unabashedly of the writings of her Cuban contemporaries? That she was conscious of her "borrowing" is obvious from her letters to Philarète Chasles, the false erudite who helped her edit the voluminous French edition of *La Havane*.[62] This practice, however, was not uncommon for Cuban authors of the period; for example, Antonio Zambrana "rewrote" Suárez y Romero's *Francisco* and called his novel *El negro Francisco* (*The Black Francisco*) pre-cisely to emphasize the slave's heightened black identity.[63] In much the same way, Countess Merlin refashioned Palma's novella from a feminist perspective in order to subvert the male code of seduction and betrayal.

This underlying defense of the victimized female protagonist undoubtedly motivated Tanco's vitriolic attack against Merlin's parody of Palma. The last word is to be had, however, by an anonymous com-mentator of *La Cartera Cubana* who did not hesitate to couch his fear of female authorship in praise of "the feminine mystique." With the clever ploy of denial, he went on to denounce "the slander raised by some detrac-tors of women's [literary] talent, who claim that Mrs. Merlin has relied on a man's help to write her works," in effect sarcastically undercut-ting the authenticity of her memoirs.[64] But little did this critic know that his strike against Merlin, artfully concealed in rhetoric, corrects the error done her in Cuban literary history:

> Ahora como entonces, en París como en la Habana, su imaginación ardiente y atrevida no ha podido estrecharse jamás en ningún círculo y *lanzándose fuera de los límites que la rodean, si no sabe una cosa, la adivina.*[65]

> (Now as before, in Paris and Havana, her fervent and daring imagina-tion has never been able to be confined within any sphere, and *throwing herself beyond normal limits, if she does not know something, she invents it.*)

What the anonymous commentator of *La Cartera Cubana* inadver-tently discovered was Merlin's capacity for invention, but he failed to see that her obsession with origins would lead her, like Carpentier's protagonist in *Los pasos perdidos*, into a "jungle of books."[66] In her journey home of 1840 Merlin found not the "real" island but that imagined before her by her precursors. If, in contrast to Carpentier, she chose to suppress rather than acknowledge her debt to tradition, it was due to her painful awareness of not belonging completely to the tradition she strove to imitate. Given the prohibition against female authorship, Merlin may very well have hesitated to reveal her sources, for to do so would have sustained the false claim ironically voiced by the commentator of *La Cartera Cubana* that she was not the "real" author of her works.[67]

In a real sense, Merlin's imitative gesture reverses the founding movement of Spanish American literature toward Europe and back, because she imitated neither the Romantics nor the early French realists but Cuban authors who were, in turn, assimilating European novelistic trends. *Viaje a la Habana* is, then, an imitation of an imitation, a textual copy that, like Borges's "Pierre Menard" who pretended to be "author of the Quijote," shows up the nature of literature as always and already a rewriting, in that every literary text originates only by virtue of the tradition that preceded it. Yet, paradoxically, Merlin's duplication, her authorial duplicity, becomes a symbol of the colony described in the travelogue, for Cuba was, in fact, a "copy" of Spain, its parodic double. Like Palma and Villaverde, who were developing a style with which to convey their "Cubanness" from foreign models, Merlin strove to speak with a language not her own but that became hers by way of imitation. "To invent a reality or to salvage it?" ("¿Inventar la realidad o rescatarla?") asks Paz in his essay on a Latin American "literature of foundations."[68] La Comtesse Merlin may have discovered, years before Paz, that the only real Santa Cruz y Montalvo was the one she had invented.

7. Tacón Theater. Pierre Touissant Frédéric Mialhe, *La Isla de Cuba Pintoresca* (Havana: Imprenta Litográfica de la Real Sociedad Patriótica, [1838?]). Special Collections Department, Otto G. Richter Library, University of Miami, Coral Gables, Florida.

CHAPTER 6

BOUND TO THE (MALE) BOOK

Gender, Colonialism, and Slavery in *La Havane*

Nowhere is la Comtesse Merlin's class extraction more evident, many feel, than in her views on slavery. Indeed, critics like Salvador Bueno have presumed a determining link between her life story and the history of the hated institution based simply on the fact that Merlin was born in 1789, the same year that the slave trade was authorized.[1] Such accusations of a proslavery stance have been used to undermine the status of Merlin's *La Havane* as a valid historiographical document, allowing it to be dismissed, in Bueno's words, as merely "una versión a ratos superficial tal como podía entregar una mujer formada en los ámbitos frívolos europeos" ("An often superficial version as only a woman raised in frivolous European circles could deliver").

Most of these accusations are based on "Lettre XX" of *La Havane*.[2] More dependent perhaps than any of the other letters of *La Havane* on an external source, "Lettre XX" evidences Merlin's reliance on the definitive essays of José Antonio Saco on the polemical subject of slavery. In this letter, Merlin clearly manifests her own authorial hesitancy and "anxiety of influence" which led her to appropriate the male master-story or book.[3] To quote Bhabha: "Hybridity is a *problematic* of colonial representation and individuation that reverses the effects of the colonialist disavowal, so that other 'denied' knowledges enter upon the dominant discourse and estrange the basis of authority—its rules of recognition."[4] Because Merlin's slavery letter derives its authority from other documents and texts of the period, it appears to adopt more eclectic "rules of recognition," which resist, according to Bhabha, the colonizing discourse of power. The polemical "Lettre XX" raises the question as to the ideological status of the text: does it mark a clear "colonialist disavowal" of the black presence in Cuba, a case of unmediated "colonialist authority," as critics from Bueno to Martin claim, or, on the contrary, is the discourse of power effectively undermined by its textual composition? In other words, does the rhetorical organization of Merlin's slavery letter, based primarily on a recurring intertextual debt to José Antonio Saco, reenact the "violent dislocation" or suppression of the Other implicit in colonialist discourse,[5] or does its pretended lack of authority as a "woman's text" render it ideologically ineffective? I hold that Merlin's own treatise on slavery represents a hybrid discourse, one that, by displaying the fissures and mechanisms of colonial authority, subverts—even belies by exaggeration—its negative portrayal of the black presence in Cuba. The distortions, inaccurate disproportions, and rhetorical "twists and turns" of the slavery letter are the signs of such narrative ambivalence.[6]

Merlin and the Debate on Slavery

The slavery letter of Merlin's *La Havane* forms part of a broader debate in nineteenth-century Cuban literature: at one extreme are the defenders of slavery like Juan Bernardo O'Gavan, and at the other is the group of "enlightened" Creole intellectuals led by Domingo del Monte who identified themselves with the plight of the black and promoted a series of works that depicted the sufferings brought about by slavery.[7] As William Luis has shown in his masterful study of Cuban antislavery narrative, the positions assumed in the slavery debate had a stake on colonialist rule because "any opposition to the slave trade was considered a threat to the government."[8]

With the slavery letter Merlin consciously inserted herself into this debate, situating herself in the double role of historian and political analyst. Though Merlin is usually regarded as an ideological spokes-

(wo)man of the sugar planter class, she was closer, in some regards, to
the liberal wing represented by José Antonio Saco and Claudio Martínez
de Pinillos, both of whom were followers of Francisco Arango y Parreño,
who had established sugar production in the island a generation earlier.[9]
Yet Merlin also held affinities with the more conservative faction represented by Juan Bernardo O'Gavan, author of an 1821 treatise which
argued the benefits of transporting Africans to the tropics to serve as
labor force.[10] Not only did Merlin defend the principle of slavery in similar terms, but she even went so far as to dedicate the entire book to Captain-General Leopoldo O'Donnell, the man responsible for the cruelest
episode of black repression in Cuban colonial history. It was obviously
an embarrassment for Merlin to place her work under the banner of "one
of the most hated men in the history of Cuba," but this sad fact is ame-
liorated by Merlin's biographer, Domingo Figarola Caneda, who argues
in her favor that *La Havane* appeared in February 1844, one month before
the notorious events of La Escalera.[11] It is helpful to quote Figarola
Caneda's defense in full, for it helps to put the Creole countess in a more
positive light, hence tempering the accusations as to her procolonialist
and proslavery stance:

> La Merlin [*sic*] no conoció á [*sic*] O'Donnell en La Habana, pues el
> primer viaje de ella fué en 1840, y aquél no comenzó a gobernar la colo-
> nia hasta Octubre [*sic*] de 1843. Además, en tanto que la dedicatoria (A
> mes compatriotes) está fechada en 1842, las páginas a O'Donnell no lle-
> van fecha ninguna; y como *La Havane* vió la luz pública en Febrero
> 1844, y las hazañas del déspota no comenzaron a evidenciarse hasta el
> mes siguiente, la autora, probablemente que termina su libro y después
> de consulta[r] [con] . . . D. Salustiano Olózaga, entonces embajador
> español en París . . . consideró que era de toda oportunidad diplomática
> abrir su libro con un llamamiento preliminar al "nom" . . . de quien ya
> tenía en sus manos los destinos de la isla.

> (Merlin did not meet O'Donnell in Havana, since her first trip was in
> 1840, and he did not start governing the colony until October 1843.
> Moreover, while the dedication [To my compatriots] was dated in 1842,
> the pages dedicated to O'Donnell do not bear a date; and since *La
> Havane* reached the public in February of 1844, and the despot's deeds
> did not make themselves evident until the following month, the author,
> who probably finished her book and then consulted . . . [with]
> D.Salustiano Olozaga, the Spanish Ambassador in Paris at the time . . .

considered it a diplomatic gesture to begin her book with a preliminary call to the 'name' . . . who already held in his hands the destiny of the Island.)[12]

Though sympathetic to Figarola Caneda's defense, I hold here that Merlin nevertheless does not fit neatly into any of the categories or ideological positions available at the time; rather, she drew on the ideas of both Saco and O'Gavan in composing the slavery letter, resulting in a necessarily contradictory and unsettled stance vis-à-vis the hated institution. As Martin has aptly put it, "Merlin appears to be torn between articulating an 'enlightened,' humanitarian, and paternalistic view of slavery and representing the more pragmatic concerns of colonial landowners on the brink of losing the foundation of their wealth through the emancipation of slaves."[13] I argue here that the obvious ambivalence of her position is due, in part, to the constant "slippage" between "original" text and source document; in short, to her dependency on the male book, represented primarily by Saco, but also, at the other end of the ideological spectrum, by the British abolitionist David Turnbull. This ambivalence, I believe, is the mark of gender difference, a byproduct of Merlin's consciously adopting a feminine position of mediation between metropolis and colony. As depicted in "Lettre XXIV" of *La Havane*, the tie between metropolis and colony becomes almost a metaphorical extension of the slavery system.[14]

It is safe to conjecture that it was the slavery issue that blighted Merlin's reception among the del Monte circle, a group bent on resisting the authoritarian tendencies of Spanish colonial administration as well as the increasing social threat represented by slavery. To get around the strong censorship of the colonial government, del Monte and the other *tertulianos* voiced their opposition to the slavery system largely within their circle by writing and promoting literary works with a strong abolitionist sentiment.[15] Merlin, on the other hand, was more overt. Not only did she commit the grievous offense of proposing a conciliatory position vis-à-vis slavery—Merlin unabashedly called herself a "créole endurcie" ("a callous Creole"), thus identifying herself with the principle of slavery[16]—but she also committed, in the eyes of Creoles in the island, a far more serious crime: she dared to step out into the public arena and not only address the polemical subject of slavery but voice her own views convincingly.[17] Indeed, it could be conjectured that the ironic barbs directed at Merlin, particularly Félix Tanco's vitriolic *Refutacion*

(1844), may have been due, in part, to the fact that Merlin's views on slavery so publicly and fundamentally contradicted the tenets espoused by the more liberal *delmontinos*.

Even though they were well aware of her position, the del Monte critics did not challenge the French-Creole countess directly on the issue of slavery. Indeed, at least some of the members of the del Monte group would have been familiar with the Spanish version of the letter, which had appeared in 1841 as a separate volume under the title *Los esclavos en las colonias españolas.*[18] And though Merlin geared her travelogue to a European audience, primarily to the addressees of her letters as privileged readers, *La Havane* invariably had an impact in the island. But restricted as they were in the expression of any open hostility against the colonial regime, the members of the del Monte group prudently silenced whatever criticism they may have had regarding Merlin's brazen defense of the principle of slavery, choosing instead to mount the rest of their attacks against Merlin, during and after her visit to Havana, on the grounds of her *performance* of gender difference.[19]

The del Monte group erected their dominant position as the "founding fathers" of Cuban culture based on the suppression of any alternative discourses that may have contested their dominant view of colonial society. As William Luis argues, "Del Monte and the authors of the antislavery narrative were among the first to define Cuban culture, which, by its very nature, developed in opposition to the Spanish colonial discourse."[20] In spite of this opposition, both Saco and del Monte carefully articulated their positions within the limits established by the hegemonic, colonialist discourse of the time, a fact explained by William Luis: "Although Saco's and Del Monte's ideas were antithetical to the antislavery cause, they were aware of the discourse of power and chose to challenge it not by going outside of the rhetoric of slavers but by appropriating their ideas and showing the fallacy of the sugar discourse. . . . Saco and Del Monte employed the same strategy as those who supported slavery and the slave trade to reveal a different truth. . . . Any questioning of the hegemonic discourse was interpreted as a threat to the slavers' power."[21]

As Luis's study shows, del Monte sidestepped this power and took the more courageous stance of incorporating blacks within literary discourse, specifically through the genre of the antislavery novel; in contrast, Saco's more cautious position was that "slavery . . . was an impediment to forging a Cuban nationality."[22] Despite these important differences, the novels commissioned by del Monte, as well as Saco's ideological writings, are read as cultural texts that define the origins of Cuban culture.

Though utilizing similar strategies, Merlin's proslavery manifesto has been systematically excluded from the canon of Cuban literature and the discourse of Cuban nationality. Rather, Merlin's letter has been interpreted as a systematic apology for *Cuba grande* (Big Cuba), the Cuba of the slave owners, which Luis contrasts to del Monte and Saco's claims from the *Cuba pequeña* or the Little Cuba closer to the land.[23] As was the case with the development of *costumbrista* narrative, Merlin and the del Monte circle parted ways in their respective representations of the Other and of literary language. In the slavery letter not only does Merlin appear to reject the black presence in Cuba promoted by del Monte, but she also moves beyond even Saco by exhibiting what can be interpreted as a moderate to extreme racism in her dismissal of the harsh conditions of life in the plantations. For example, at one point she compared the regimented life of the Cuban slave to that of farm workers in France. After asserting an initial empathy with the field slave, who was submitted to a grueling routine of overwork timed by the relentless sound of the bell, Merlin glibly concluded that in Cuba "si l'esclave est surveillé plus sévèrement, il est sans contredit mieux nourri" ("if the slave is severely supervised, he is unquestionably better fed") (*La Havane*, vol. 2, 149; *La Habana*, 174).

Though from a contemporary perspective the slavery letter is insensitive to the plight of the blacks, from another vantage point the polemical "Lettre XX" exhibits the defensive strategies by which many Creoles of that time tried to cope with the black presence in Cuba. Earlier we saw that the Creole landed aristocracy was in a period at which its members feared their very disappearance as a class. The Creole's anxious disavowal of the black as a cultural element in the construction of Cuban nationality indirectly confirmed that black presence. Merlin's defensive stance enacted the same reversal, at times contradicting the authoritative position for which it presumably stood—the denial of the black. In the interstices of the text, in fact, one can sense the mechanisms of "splitting, denial, and repetition" that erode the presumed authority of her argument, almost as if Merlin were writing a parody of herself.[24] The effect on the reader is an antithetical one because, contrary to the letter's desired intention, blacks are acknowledged as a force to be reckoned with precisely because of the density and rhetorical force of the argument constructed to dismiss them.

Editorial Variants of the Slavery Letter

That Merlin sought a dialogue both within and outside Cuba regarding the institution of slavery is proven by the multiple editions of the letter. Though the text remained fundamentally the same, each edition of the letter was geared toward different linguistic and national constituencies, always in an effort to gain a sympathetic audience for her views. This textual proliferation also served Merlin's mediating stance: by printing the letter in both Spain and France, she hoped to mollify the French promoters of abolition even as she countered the growing Spanish sentiment against the hated institution.[25]

The original French version of the slavery letter appeared in 1841 in the influential *Revue des Deux Mondes*, one year after Merlin's visit to Havana and three years before the definitive edition of *La Havane* was published.[26] Though we cannot know for sure what kind of reception the letter garnered in French circles, there is a slight clue in the discreet editorial note that is attached to the first printing of the letter in the *Revue des Deux Mondes*. This note is ostensibly added on to identify the author and also to attest to her recent visit to the island. Though the French editor states that Merlin gathered many documents regarding slavery during her recent trip, a statement that at first glance gives legitimacy to her account, he raises a question as to the veracity of her impressions by pointing out Merlin's "enthusiastic" use of this documentation and the manner in which she addressed island affairs.[27] This last comment not only erodes Merlin's author/ity but also ensures a reading of the piece in light of women's tendency for enthusiasm or sentimentality. In this light, the French editor of the *Revue des Deux Mondes* undermines the validity of Merlin's account with the same gender-based bias exhibited by her Creole readers.

Besides this introduction, the only substantial difference between the piece published in *Revue des Deux Mondes*, duplicated in the separate Spanish edition entitled *Los esclavos en las colonias españolas*, and "Lettre XX" of *La Havane* is found in the latter's introductory paragraph. Neither the French nor the Spanish version opened with a dedication, which suggests that Merlin intended her original text to reach the broadest possible audience. However, the letter in *La Havane* is dedicated to the noted French abolitionist, M. le Baron Charles Dupin, and opens with an appeal to his mercy. In addition to these slight but significant variations, the later version included in *La Havane* has a different date of entry. The temporal slippage between texts—the version in *Revue* is dated July 15, 1840, at the site of Havana, whereas the *La Havane* text has an earlier date, June 10 (the Spanish edition has no differentiating marks) simply confirms the fictitious nature of these dates, a practice in keeping with Merlin's method of fictionalizing or inventing the historical scene. Paradoxically, though, the change of dates adds greater authenticity to the *La Havane* letter by dating the definitive version of the slavery letter at an earlier point in her journey, thus suggesting an immediacy between event and writing.

Historical Context

Whatever the precise originating date, Merlin's polemical solution to the slavery issue clearly responded, first of all, to the set of historical contradictions facing the Creole elite in 1840, not the least of which was the pressure felt from the Spanish-British treaties of 1817 and 1835 that officially abolished traffic in slavery. For the Creole planters, no slaves meant no sugar: without the slave trade, they faced imminent ruin and, ultimately, the dissolution of their class. This situation was particularly acute in the case of "the old oligarchic families of Cuba," owners of sugar mills since the late eighteenth century who, for the most part, still maintained more primitive methods for the extraction of sugar than newer planters; among this group are counted the members of Merlin's family, including the Montalvos, Cárdenas, and O'Farrills.[28] Moreover, the anxiety of the saccharocracy was compounded by the threat of uprisings and the fear of slave revolts such as the one that culminated in the 1791 Haitian revolution.[29] Meanwhile, Captain-General Miguel Tacón's repressive policy was firmly in place in Cuba, snuffing out the efforts of liberal Creoles to reinstate the Spanish Constitution of 1812.[30] After their 1837 defeat in the Spanish Cortes, where they had sought to gain lawful representatives, the Creoles felt weakened before the increasingly despotic Spanish rule.

One year later, the British Parliament approved the immediate and absolute end of slavery.[31] As historian Franklin W. Knight points out, this act brought the debate on the illegal trade to "a feverish pitch," leading the Spanish authorities to make "a concerted effort to foster white immigration" on the island and so dispel the prevalent idea that the extensive labor required in sugar production was unsuitable for whites.[32]

The policy of white immigration, it was hoped, would also lessen the threat of revolt from the exploited slaves in the Cuban plantations, an idea expounded primarily by Saco.[33] Although the year of Merlin's visit to Havana, 1840, was also the year signaled by the British to mark the completion of a plan designed to attain the gradual end of slavery,[34] the slave trade nevertheless continued in Cuba because it was the only source of brute labor force for the sugar industry.

Merlin's text also responded to a specific set of historical events; mainly, the abolitionist campaign led by British Prime Minister Lord Palmerston and the assignment of David Turnbull as counsel to Havana with the specific mission of fulfilling the objectives of the queen.[35] The names of Palmerston and Turnbull not only figure in the appendixes attached to the third volume of *La Havane*, but they also serve as interlocutors or textual interfaces of the slavery letter itself, in which Merlin consciously responded to Turnbull's own narrative, *Travels in the West. Cuba; with notices of Porto [sic] Rico and the Slave Trade*, published in London in 1840. Turnbull's visit to Havana in November 1840, months after Merlin's departure, was especially threatening with respect to the *emancipados*, those slaves liberated by the British when they seized slave ships coming into the Havana harbor under the right of visitation called for by the treaty with Spain.[36] The Creoles reacted with alarm to Turnbull's presence, representing as it did the potential violation of their property rights and a corollary loss of fortune.[37]

Cuba's political destiny after 1840 hinged on the solution to the slavery problem. In order to ensure their property, the planters had either to seek protection from Spain or ally themselves with Southern slave owners in a potentially annexationist move.[38] The political ramifications of the slavery question were taken even further by Saco, who at the end of his *Paralelo entre la isla de Cuba y algunas colonias inglesas* (1837) proposed two avenues for the island's political future: either independence or annexation to the United States.[39] The same position was voiced by John S. Thrasher, the American journalist who translated Alexander von Humboldt's essay on Cuba,[40] and Richard Kimball, author of the noted *Cuba and the Cubans* (1850). Thus, Merlin's "proslavery" views can be seen as forming part of a broader project that sought to defuse the annexationist spirit by reinforcing the tie between Spain and the colony, primarily by celebrating shared cultural factors such as language and tradition.[41] Read in historical context, then, Merlin's letter, though ostensibly fostering the anti-abolitionist cause, also represents, albeit indirectly, an energetic stance against annexation.

Textual Oppressions: Enslaved to the Male Text

Saco's writings stand as the source and subtext of Merlin's slavery letter. Merlin's fundamental argument in "Lettre XX"—an immediate stop to the illegal slave trade and the gradual elimination of slavery with the substitution of the black labor force by a policy of white immigration[42]—can be traced, fundamentally, to Saco, who from 1837 to 1845 made similar pronouncements in a series of essays published in Europe. Writing in a rambling, digressive style in which the surety of her views is often contradicted by the hesitancy of her expression, Merlin nevertheless managed to insert her own "personal narrative" into Saco's ideological program. The coiled arguments in Merlin's letter often take a circuitous route, which can be briefly summarized as follows: (1) she first considers the equivocal nature of the term *liberty*; (2) she makes her main point in favor of suppressing the illegal slave trade without, however, banishing the institution of slavery, arguing fundamentally in favor of protecting the life and property of the white planter class; (3) she then critiques Britain's pro-abolitionist campaign, adding an incisive analysis of the violations on the part of the Mixed Commissions set up by Britain and Spain to control the illegal slave trade; (4) she briefly compares the institution of slavery as practiced in antiquity with the practice by modern nations; and (5) she makes an impassioned plea for the promotion of a vigorous policy of white immigration, primarily from Europe.

In structuring her text, Merlin leans heavily on Saco's work as her primary subtext while positing Turnbull and the British abolitionists as the principal targets of her attack. Only in the last part of the letter does Merlin present what can be interpreted as an "original" point of view by offering a benign (and historically false) interpretation of the practice of slavery in Cuba, demonstrating by concrete examples the unwavering loyalty felt by the island's slaves toward their masters. The letter ends with a vision for the future, in which Merlin again draws on previous written sources which discuss the social consequences of black emancipation in the Caribbean colonies.

The dispersed nature of Merlin's argument surely signals the "splitting" that produced the characteristic ambiguity of colonialist texts. With its "rules of recognition" exposed, Merlin's slavery text can thus be seen as comparable to "those social texts of epistemic, ethnocentric, nationalist intelligibility which cohere in the address of authority as the 'present'."[43] This is due to the rhetorical force of the letter, which ambitiously aspired to the status of an authoritative, exhaustive treatment of the institution of slavery and of all its social, political and economic ramifications.

While in the "literary" portions of the travelogue, Merlin suppressed her debt to Creole *costumbrista* authors, in the slavery letter she openly acknowledged her debt to Saco, citing as her primary sources the latter's *Mi primera pregunta* (1837) and *Examenes analítico-politicos* [*sic*] (1837).[44] Despite these specific references, however, Merlin incorporated ideas from other essays by the "illustrious patriot," as she called him, which are not explicitly recognized in her text. It is this hidden reliance on the male text, or textual enslavement, that marks the site of ambivalence and subverts what would otherwise be read as an authoritative discourse. Indeed, the suppression of other references to Saco can be seen as a form of denial generated by this authorial anxiety. Thus, Merlin's appropriation of Saco makes her text appear as discursively transparent: outwardly rigid and dictatorial, yet inwardly concealing an underside—the hidden texts (f)used in its composition and only partially gleaned in her acknowledgment of Saco as master author.[45]

Seen from the perspective of colonialist discourse, both Saco and Merlin are "hybrids," caught between their need to sustain a connection to the metropolis and their need to assert their own separate identity, a position that would later blossom into independence. The dislocations, repetitions, and correspondences between Merlin and Saco's views in their mutual self-presentations are emblematic of Creole cultural values. However, whereas Merlin identified herself as a "créole endurcie," unabashedly siding with the cause of the Cuban sugar aristocracy in defense of the principle of slavery, Saco maintained a position of impersonal authority, permitting a personal note only toward the end of his essay.[46] Saco was careful to cloak his argument in the guise of impartial judgment—thus investing his text with the male marker of objectivity—while Merlin justified her stance by adopting a purely subjective position, replacing reason with justice and impartiality with feeling.[47] Saco could automatically assume that his voice encompassed the collectivity of Creoles, but Merlin had to justify her self-definition as a Creole and a woman speaking in the public arena.

Similar hesitancies are revealed in both writers' mode of address to their real and virtual audiences. Merlin began her letter with an appeal to Dupin in a brazen rhetorical opening motivated to gain her addressee's—and by extension, her audience's—sympathies. This explains the outright apology that serves both to anticipate and include the reader's expected response, which would most likely be one of opposition: "Ne criez pas anathème contre moi, créole endurcie, élevée dans des idées pernicieuses, et dont les intérèts se rattachement au principe de l'esclavage" ("Do not sentence me, callous Creole, raised with pernicious ideas, and whose interests are tied to the principle of slavery") (*La Havane*, vol. 2, 87).[48] Here the feminine artifice of apology for authorship that was practiced throughout the nineteenth century becomes a useful instrument of persuasion and ideological combat. Contrast this strategy with Saco's own apology at the beginning of *Mi primera pregunta*, where he also anticipated his reader's negative judgment. Whereas Merlin personalized her apology to a specific male interlocutor, following the tactic of other women authors of the period, Saco assumed a general readership, "adversaries" who were personified instead as the collective judgment of History or the accumulated memory of the Archive.[49]

The way in which Merlin addressed the complex issue of slavery from the vantage point of Saco, including her conscious strategies and her rhetorical (mis)organization, turned her into an obvious object of attack. It is as if her enslavement to Saco's text here produced the discriminatory effect of female victimization, something she consciously repudiated earlier in her previous rewriting of Ramón de Palma's *Una Pascua en San Marcos* (1838).[50] Textual "blind spots" carefully avoided by Saco in the formulation of his arguments come glaringly to light in Merlin's letter. The most notorious of these involves the philosophical justification for their mutual stance on slavery, a theme introduced in Saco's *Examen analítico* by means of a reflection on the ambiguous meaning of the term *liberty*. The *Examen analítico* is a historically grounded text written in response to the 1837 decision of the Spanish government to ban representatives from the colonies to the Spanish court.[51] In this pamphlet Saco sums up the dilemma faced by Creoles of the period, where slavery was seen as tied to the political destiny of the island. Saco first paraphrases the thinking of colonial authorities in the following cryptic manner: "Si quereis ser libres, dejad de tener esclavos, pero si estos quereis conservar, renunciad á la libertad" ("If you desire freedom, give up your slaves, but if you want to keep these, then you must pay the price of free-dom") (19). From this point he goes on to define two types of freedom, individual and political, but conflates these two categories in terms of his first definition: "La primera [libertad], que es la que realmente consti-tuye la felicidad de los pueblos, consiste en el respeto sagrado a la propiedad, en la inviolable seguridad de las personas, y en la pacífica posesión de los demás derechos individuales" ("The first type of freedom, which is what really constitutes the happiness of the people, consists in a sacred respect for property, in the inviolate security of the individual, and the peace-ful possession of all other human rights") (19).

The Spanish edition of Merlin's slavery letter also opens with a dis-quisition on the term *liberty*, obviously extracted from Saco's *Examen analítico*, but the extraction was made in apparent disregard for the original pamphlet's historical context, a textual surgery sure to condition a negative response from the reader. Though Merlin drew from Saco's first definition of liberty to substantiate her claim that abolition would constitute a serious violation of property, she emphasized the slaveown-ers' rights in a manner that exaggerated the import of Saco's argument. Even though the letter frankly acknowledges the abuse implicit in the ille-gal slave trade, Merlin's rhetoric opposing abolition is abrasive, as in the passage quoted below where she contests it on the grounds of the slave-owners' right to property.[52] Merlin also derived from Saco her justifica-tion of the abstract principle of "happiness,"[53] a term that, according to Leví Marrero, was used as a metaphor for the progress and material wealth aspired to by the Creole upper class.[54] In both cases of appropriation, Mer-lin placed herself in an extremely vulnerable position as a speaking sub-ject by confronting the reader directly and decontextualizing the argument.

The same vulnerability appears in what has been interpreted as the most scandalous tenet of the slavery letter: Merlin's outspoken resistance to the liberation of all slaves even as she favored the gradual end of the hated institution. Perhaps the most glaring passage in the whole letter is the following statement, which aptly summarizes Merlin's position on slavery:

> Rien de plus juste que l'abolition de la traite des noirs; rien de plus injuste que l'émancipation des esclaves. Si la traite est un abus révoltant de la force, un attentat contre le droit naturel, l'émancipation serait une violation de la propriété, des droits acquis et consacres par les lois, une vraie spoliation.

(There is nothing more just than the abolition of the African slave trade; there is nothing more unjust than the emancipation of slaves. If the slave trade is an insulting abuse of power, an assault against natural law, emancipation would be a violation of property, of rights acquired and consecrated by the law, a true spoliation.) (*La Havane*, vol. 2, 88)

Again, these ideas are not original to Merlin but rather are derived from Saco's ideological program—particularly the position assumed toward the end of *Mi primera pregunta* that the treaties between Spain and Britain be rigorously enforced to assure the end of the illegal slave trade.[55] In contrast to Saco, who carefully positioned himself as aligned with the slavers but also as voicing a concern for Cuba's prosperity,[56] Merlin failed to give her argument any kind of subtle shading. Moreover, because, in the eyes of her readers, her foreign residency disenfranchised her from her class of origin, her claim to represent the slaveholders' interests could only be interpreted as a sign of her underlying wish to be wholly accepted into the insular community. No such accusations could be made against Saco. In proposing his argument, "Saco reassures his readers that he is on their side and is defending their interests," a persuasive stance that makes him appear in favor of emancipation without being labeled an abolitionist outright.[57]

Although Merlin's letter antedates the Conspiración de la Escalera, or Ladder Conspiracy, the severity with which she stated her views recalls Saco's more extreme position in *La supresión del tráfico de esclavos africanos en la isla de Cuba* (1845), an essay that revises *Mi primera pregunta* from the point of view of the crucial events of March 1844. In *La supresión*, Saco makes an urgent call for an immediate end to the illegal slave trade, arguing that the very security of the island depends on abolition, given the increased threat of slave rebellions.[58] Merlin's position, in one sense, anticipated the heightening of racial tensions in the island, while also appearing as almost anachronistic in its discounting of the cruel reality faced by the slaves. In spite of its overt tone of disavowal, the rhetoric of the slavery letter is, in truth, a product of denial, a denial motivated by fear of the blacks and by the overpowering need to suppress the signifier of slave revolt—which, rather than going unmentioned, is reversed toward the end of the letter in Merlin's "fantastic" portrayal of slavery.

Like Saco's essays, Merlin's slavery letter responded to the heightened anxiety in the Spanish colonies caused by the 1838 decree abolishing slavery in Britain.[59] Merlin's letter echoes the solution reached at the time: to foster a policy of white immigration that would at once solve the labor needs for the sugar industry as well as attenuate the danger of revolt on the part of the blacks.[60] Though Merlin wrote in support of Saco's argument in *Mi primera pregunta* regarding the advantages of a European labor force, her position appears weaker by comparison. Whereas Saco's intention in *Mi primera pregunta* was to prove that the sugar industry could survive with an alternative labor supply,[61] Merlin contended that even imported white workers would fall prey to the dangers of slavery. Saco weighed the relative merits of black and white workers, all the while arguing for the superiority of the latter.[62] In contrast, Merlin essentially undermined a similar argument by claiming that upon their arrival in the islands, European workers would automatically hire slaves themselves![63]

Again on the trail of Saco, Merlin made a strong plea in favor of white immigration, thus following to the letter the Spanish policy of the time, which stipulated the creation of incentives to import permanent farmers to the island and not merely a "floating" labor force.[64] In this part of the letter Merlin softened the argument she had developed earlier against abolition, attempting to arrive at a conciliatory position similar to the one Saco took in his essays.[65] More than an effort "to lure Europeans to invest and work in the island and, of course, to increment the white population," as Martin claims, both Saco and Merlin's writings were attempts to reverse the attitudes prevalent at the time, which held that white workers were unsuitable for the sugar plantations.[66] According to Knight, the attempted Spanish policy of white immigration ultimately failed, in part because negative attitudes toward blacks prevailed,[67] a fact that is also strongly documented in Merlin's letter.

The argument for a policy of white immigration also reveals the ambivalence of Merlin's text if considered as colonialist discourse, because in that argument she critiqued as well the deficiencies of the colonial administration in successfully carrying out this policy. To illustrate the failure of the policy of white immigration, Merlin included the strange anecdote of an anonymous Creole planter who subsidized fifty Castillian workers to labor in the cane fields, only to be treated with disdain by a Spaniard who resided in the island (*La Havane*, vol. 2, 106–7; *Los esclavos*, 21–22). This section of the letter illustrates Merlin's characteristic dependence on the male book, for Saco had also argued in both *Paralelo entre la isla de Cuba y algunas colonias inglesas* and *Clamor de los cubanos* in favor of a policy of white immigration.[68]

From Saco, Merlin derived two subarguments developed in her slavery letter: (1) the critique of Britain and its abolitionist policy as fundamentally tainted by an imperialist thrust, mainly its desire to compete in an expanded sugar market (*La Havane*, vol. 2, 91–92; *Los esclavos*, 5–7) and (2) the comparative historical view of the practice of slavery from antiquity to the modern period. The latter argument contains the faulty historical logic that the slave would prefer his own servitude rather than be the victim of tribal practices such as cannibalism (*La Havane*, vol. 2, 91; *Los esclavos*, 5). Such statements situate Merlin closer to the conservative proslavery faction represented by O'Gavan than to the more liberal wing that had Saco as its spokesman,[69] a vacillation related to her dependency on the male text and perhaps to her own insecurities in handling a decidedly masculinist discourse.

The contrasts in tone and rhetorical address between Merlin's and Saco's writings underline a strong gender difference in their respective historiographical approaches. Though they shared a fundamental vision of the slavery problem, their methods of exposition and their constructions of a political argument make for two very different types of texts, a difference reflected, in part, in the reception afforded each one in literary history. Whereas Saco has received a place in the archive of foundational texts of Cuban nationality, Merlin not only has been excluded from this canonical edifice but has been severely chastised for her classist position and her alleged misrepresentation of the lower strata of Cuban society.[70] This strong admonition stems more from a paternalistic historiography that readily curtails women's appropriation of the genre rather than from the contents of the writing itself.

Although Merlin did not entirely break free from the confines of male textual authority (except perhaps in the last part of the letter), she was not merely a passive recipient of the male book. She also engaged in active ideological battle, writing portions of the slavery letter specifically with the British counsel David Turnbull in mind. Elected head of the Mixed Commission established by the British and Spanish governments to supervise and enforce the treaties suppressing the illegal slave trade, Turnbull became directly involved in Cuban affairs and was even suspected of a plot to foster independence and bring slavery on the island to an end.[71] As a representative of British interests in the Caribbean and as a strong-minded abolitionist, Turnbull served as the opposite pole to Merlin's conciliatory and apologist's position vis-à-vis slavery. Those passages of the letter that discuss the status of the Courts of Mixed Commission directly address the writings of British abolitionists, particularly Turnbull's *Travels in the West*, which was coincidentally published in 1840, the same year as Merlin's visit. Her letter thus establishes an intertextual dialogue between Saco and Turnbull with herself as mediator, echoing the manner in which she earlier had mediated between Saco and O'Gavan by simultaneously drawing from their ideas and moderating them to suit her purposes. The same position of mediation is evident in the letters of *La Havane* that effectively critique the cumbersome Spanish colonial administration, and particularly the abuses of litigation suffered by Creoles.[72] In the slavery letter, the "cross-dialogue" between Saco and Turnbull as ideological extremes results in a multivocal, performative text that breaks up the polarized options for and against slavery. Despite its overt rhetoric of domination, Merlin's slavery letter thus transgresses the discursive norms of the period, which prescribed the limits of the slavery debate in terms of two mutually exclusive positions.

In her response to Turnbull, Merlin followed almost to the letter Saco's analysis where he examined the immediate results of the 1817 and 1834 treaties between Britain and Spain. In *La supresión* Saco had anticipated the concerns of the Creoles regarding the expansion of the rights and duties of the Courts of Mixed Commission in 1840. Although Merlin fundamentally followed this position, she was by far more resistant to the treaties than Saco was. Further, Merlin took a more aggressive tactic when she attacked the *derecho de visita* (right of entry), which granted British authorities the right to inspect ships suspected of carrying slaves as well to take possession of their human cargo (*La Havane*, vol. 2, 113–16; *Los esclavos*, 28–31). Like Saco before her, Merlin's criticism of the *derecho de visita* was based solely on nationalistic grounds. Britain's ultimate goal was to identify and grant liberty to all the slaves introduced in Cuba since 1820, which for Saco constituted a serious threat to the island's plantation economy.[73] Writing in a tone of self-defense, Turnbull in his travelogue focused on the corruption of British functionaries who, with the aid of equally corrupt Spanish authorities, had the audacity to actually purchase slaves themselves.[74] In a reply to Turnbull, clearly meant to challenge his ethical authority to criticize his countrymen's complicity with the illegal slave trade, Merlin pointed out the excesses of zealous British officials who went so far as to hang or shoot Spaniards suspected of participating in slave commerce (*La Havane*, vol. 2, 115; *La Habana*, 163). Merlin continued to fan the flames of the nationalist argument by showing that the *derecho de visita* represented a violation of Spain's maritime boundaries (*La Havane*, vol. 2, 115; *La Habana*, 163). Adding a hyperbolic touch, she even described the fate of a Catalan merchant who was stripped of his fortune on his trip back to Spain on the suspicion of trading with the African coast (*La Havane*, vol. 2, 116–17; *Los esclavos* 31–32). This anecdote is obviously geared to exaggerate the threat represented by the expansion of the Courts of Mixed Commission and of British abolitionist efforts. In the intertextual dialogue that Merlin established with Saco and Turnbull as interlocutors, she departed significantly from the Saco model: rather than focus almost exclusively on the effect of this policy on the white elite, Merlin drew attention as well to its transnational repercussions.

Moreover, instead of simply transcribing into her text Saco's opinions regarding the Spanish/British alliance, Merlin actively refuted Turnbull's description of the conditions of slaves working on Cuban sugar plantations. Where Turnbull identified with the slave who lived in torment under the constant threat of the whip, Merlin distanced herself by appealing to the abstract principle of law to justify the master's excesses, thus glossing over the slaves' real circumstances. Compare in this regard the following passages from Turnbull and Merlin:

Under the tender mercies of the Mayoral, [the slave] knows well before leaving the Havana [*sic*] that he has no thing to expect in the plantation but a wretched existence of over labour and starvation, accompanied by the application, or at least the constant terror, of the lash as an incentive, relieved only by the hope of that dissolution, which sleepless nights and incessant toils are so speedily and so surely to accomplish.[75]

L'esclave ne doit être soumis qu'à un travail modéré, et seulement de *sol á sol*, c'est-à-dire pendant le jour, et á condition qu'il aura, dans le courant de la journée, *deux* heures de repos. . . . [Le maitre] est défendu d'infliger des peines corporalles aux esclaves, à moins de fautes graves, et mème, dans ce cas, le châtiment est borné par la loi.

(The slave should not be submitted but to moderate work and only *from sunrise to sunset*, that is, during the day, and on the condition that he will have, during the course of the day, *two* hours of rest.

... [The owner] is forbidden to inflict corporal punishment on the slaves, unless there are serious errors; even then, in this case, the punishment is limited by the law.) (*La Havane*, vol. 2, 126–27; *Los esclavos*, 40–41. Emphasis in original)

In short, Turnbull's and Merlin's accounts stand in ideological counterpoint one with the other, as the first basically refutes Merlin's "benign" view of slavery:

[A]s I had frequently been told that the slave owners of the Havana [*sic*] were the most indulgent masters in the world, I was not a little surprised to find . . . that in this particular I had been most miserably deceived. . . . [I]n no forth . . . is the state of slavery so desperately wretched as it is at this moment on the sugar plantation of the queen of the Indies, the far-famed island of Cuba.[76]

La douceur du colon de Cuba pour son esclave inspire à ce dernier un sentiment de respect qui approche du culte. . . . Le maître est pour l'esclave la patrie et la famille.

(The sweetness of Cuban masters toward their slaves inspires in the latter a feeling of respect that resembles worship. . . . The owner is to the slave both his homeland and his family.) (*La Havane*, vol.2, 156; *Los esclavos*, 68)

Despite their ideological and rhetorical discrepancies, Merlin's and Turnbull's accounts converge in their respective discussion of the fate of the *emancipados*, the slaves liberated upon the confiscation of a slave ship by a British or Spanish arbiter. After seizing a slave ship, Spanish authorities randomly distributed these unfortunate men to individuals who exploited them as slave labor. They remained bound to their employers in perpetual servitude as they lacked the legal right to buy their freedom that was at least potentially available to other slaves (*La Havane*, vol. 2, 118–19; *Los esclavos*, 33–34). In this regard, Merlin followed Saco in depicting the fate of the misnamed *emancipados* (freed men) as worse than that of the slaves. This position is echoed in Turnbull's account, as he emphatically declares that "the fate of the *emancipados* is worse than ordinary slavery."[77] Despite the fact that they represent extreme positions vis-à-vis the slavery question, both Turnbull's and Merlin's texts operate under the same "political unconscious:" a critique of colonialism that reveals the desire for dominance implicit even in the abolitionist cause.

Constructed with Saco as subtext and Turnbull as rhetorical target, the slavery letter in *La Havane* evidences an intermediary position in the debate waged over the destinies of the sugar plantation in the Spanish colonies. Siding at times with the most ardent defenders of slavery and at other times with the proponents of reform, Merlin's text is never ideologically "settled," but rather wavers as if in search of its own source of grounding as historical argument. This vacillation can be traced to Merlin's double rhetorical strategy: at one extreme an overdependence on Saco as master-author, and at the other extreme an "aborted" rebellion against Turnbull as political antagonist. Aborted, because Merlin's picture of slavery violates readers' expectations by its distortion of historical "truth"—its misrepresentation of the real conditions of slave labor in a plantation society. Enslavement to a male text (en)genders a double vision, the "negative transparency" of a colonial text that reverts back on itself to the point where the discourse of exclusion cloaks Merlin's own defensive stance when positioning herself in relation to the Other.

"Fantastic" Enslavement: The Daughter's Wish-Fulfillment

> ¡Dulce Cuba! en tu seno se miran
> en el grado más alto y profundo,
> las bellezas del físico mundo,
> los horrores del mundo moral.[78]
> —José María Heredia

Toward the end of her letter Merlin abandoned herself to her own personal description of slavery, making it appear as a paternalistic institution or pseudo-family of kindly white "fathers" and gently submissive black "sons." What Tanco in his *Refutacion* characterized as a "fantastic" reverie depicting conditions in the sugar plantations is really Merlin's belated attempt to break the dependency on the male book. Likewise, as farfetched as Merlin's idyllic vision of master/slave relations may seem,[79] it did have a corollary in the few depictions of kindhearted masters which appeared in nineteenth-century Cuban literature; the one notable example is Juan Francisco Manzano's *Autobiografía* (English edition, 1840), where the former slave describes his experiences with both good and bad masters.[80] Merlin's benign vision of slavery owed much more to Saco than to antislavery narrative, however. Saco's perspective was further complicated by his prevailing belief that abolition would result in Cuba's becoming a predominantly black nation, with similar consequences to the disasters faced by the neighboring island of Santo Domingo.[81] Yet in his *Examen analítico*, the text most intimately connected to *La Havane's* slavery letter, Saco denied the fear shared by the Creole planters that a racial revolt such as the one that shook Haiti in 1791 could erupt in Cuba; asserting instead that political reform and liberalization would be the surest antidote to racial unrest.[82] Such a statement suggests that both Merlin's and Saco's texts were responding to the collective anxiety felt among the Creole upper class about the possible loss of life and fortune implicit in the threat of slave uprisings.

Thus the crisis surrounding the illegal slave trade in the 1840s provoked in the Creoles a sense of the "potential disintegration" of their world and consequently of the images created to represent it.[83] Hence, the stereotyping of the slave by both Saco and Merlin doubtless corresponds to their deep need to project onto blacks the anxiety generated by the tensions and strife of the historical moment.[84] Furthermore the image of the black slave construed in these texts becomes the very *cause* of conflict and loss of control over the social world. Attitudes that would otherwise be labeled as racist spring from these historically determined "projections of anxiety," to use Sander Gilman's term.[85] Indeed, for Knight, Saco represents "the most intelligent and articulate of Cuban racists," and goes so far as to label the latter's policies as tantamount to apartheid, a charge that would necessarily have to apply to his female counterpart as well.[86] This perspective can be balanced if we keep in mind that Saco was manipulating the discourse of the slavers to suit his own agenda, that is, to bring about the gradual end of slavery without threatening the prosperity of island.[87] Situating Merlin and Saco as colonial hybrids allows their texts to be read not as overt racist arguments, but rather as articulations of "root-metaphors" of race that characterized a particular historical epoch.[88]

A comparison of Saco's and Merlin's representations of racial difference reveals different categories of stereotypes operating in their texts. In *Mi primera pregunta*, Saco constructed his energetic argument in favor of white immigration on the basis of the supposed superiority of European workers, which, in his view, is directly proportional to the alleged inferiority of black workers. Using Gilman's terms, Saco's argument operates according to the "root-metaphor" of illness and pathology. His rhetorical strategy is to equate the blacks' physical vulnerabilities—their alleged propensity toward contracting fatal diseases like cholera and their higher mortality rate—to moral deviations like "indolence," thus drawing an analogy between the physical and the ethical planes.[89] Although Merlin's text also falls within from this model, repeatedly echoing the received opinion as to the inherent "indolence" of the Africans,[90] there are noticeable differences in her representation of race. Whereas Saco conceived of the Cuban nation as two races in fundamental opposition to each other, essentially locked in a rigid hierarchy ("Si en Cuba hay una humanidad negra, también hay una humanidad blanca, muy superior a la primera por muchos títulos sociales, y por lo mismo más digna de la vida y bien estar") ("If in Cuba there is a black humanity, there also is a white humanity, far superior to the former by way of its social attributes, and consequently more worthy of life and well-being"),[91] for Merlin the antipathy of whites and blacks derived from a "primitive division" originating in nature:

> Ce superbe dédain des hommes blancs envers les nègres n'est pas seulement produit par le mépris attaché à l'esclavage, mais par le stigmate de la couleur, qui semble perpétuer au delà de l'affranchissement la tache d'una condamnation primitive. On dirait que la nature a signé de sa main l'incompatibilité des deux races.

> (This great disdain of whites towards blacks is not only produced by the contempt attached to slavery, but by the stigma of color that seems to perpetuate a kind of primitive flaw, even beyond manumission. One could say that nature has signed with its own hand the incompatibility of the two races.") (*La Havane*, vol. 2, 107; *Los esclavos*, 22)

This typically Romantic metaphor moderates the determinism of Saco's position for, unlike Saco, Merlin at least envisioned the possibility of a "fraternal union" among the races.[92] This notion anticipated, however hesitatingly, José Martí's universalist stance in "Nuestra América," which sweeps away the notion of race in favor of a humanist, though gender-marked, valorization.[93]

Despite their many correspondences, Merlin departed from Saco in her categorization of race when she transmuted the "illness" metaphor into a stereotypical version of the slave's promiscuous sexuality, a slippage conditioned by the fact that, according to Gilman, "disorder and loss of control, the giving over of the self to the forces that lie beyond itself," are inevitably crystallized in the sexual dimension.[94] Echoing the worst stereotype about black sensuality, Merlin suggested in her account that marriage is an irrelevant institution among the blacks, a conclusion derived from what she fathomed was an uncontrolled sexual urge among the slaves.[95] This untenable view clearly reverses the image of the repression of love among the slaves depicted in the antislavery novel, a genre considered the counterdiscourse of the period. Anselmo Suárez y Romero's *Francisco*, written in 1838, and Cirilo Villaverde's *Cecilia Valdés* (1882) reveal how the oppression of slavery extended even to the slave's emotional and sexual life, for the conditions in the sugar estates impeded a stable family unit or normal exchanges of affection among the slaves. As dramatized in these novels, particularly in *Francisco*, the domestic female slave is tormented by the lust of the master, often leading to tragic love triangles where the woman is forced to repudiate her love for a black man.[96] Contrast this to Merlin's scandalous description of the plight of a pregnant slave woman: "Une pauvre fille devient-elle grosse, le maître, s'il a des scrupules, en est quitte pour infliger, au nom de la morale, une punition à la délinquante et pour garder le négrillon chez lui" ("A poor girl becomes pregnant; the owner, if he has any scruples, is free to inflict a punishment to the delinquent girl in the name of morality, and to keep the young black boy with him") (*La Havane*, vol. 2, 132; *Los esclavos*, 46–47). In this passage, Merlin glosses over the fact that the pregnancy probably resulted from the master's sexual assault. Not only does the master get to keep the child, but the unfortunate female slave has to endure punishment on top of the violence already inflicted on her. Compared to the more sympathetic view of the female slave in antislavery narratives, where she often appears as a victim, Merlin's stance is totally lacking in gender identification.

In depicting the sexuality of the slaves, other travelogues are by far more faithful to historical fact. Notable in this regard is Turnbull's dramatic description of hordes of male slaves held captive in the fields with no healthy outlet for passion because the disproportion between male and female slaves was so great. In his account, Turnbull linked this cruel deprivation to the planters' greed: "There are some so totally regardless of human sentiment, save the sordid sense of their own pecuniary interests, that they people their estates with one sex only, to the total exclusion of females, taking care to prevent the nocturnal wanderings of men, by locking them up in their plantation prisons, called also barracoons, as soon as their daily labour is concluded."[97] If the slavery system operated symbolically under the notion of the Master as a "'good' other," provoking a "positive stereotype," with the slave as the "bad" Other or "negative stereotype," this equivalence has been turned around to suit Turnbull's didactic purposes.[98] Turnbull's and Merlin's travelogues radically part ways here: whereas Turnbull's text uses the "root-metaphor" of sexuality to reverse the stereotypical portrait of the black and consequently to tarnish the master's "whiteness" (in the figurative sense of innocence), Merlin's text conforms to more conventionally held notions, where the Other receives the projections of a sexuality outside social control.

Besides the "root-metaphor" of race based on sexual excess, Merlin's text also subscribes to the theory of "juridical benevolent paternalism," which held that Spain's judicial system protected the slaves against mistreatment by their masters and the cruelties implicit in the institution itself.[99] From a psychoanalytical point of view, Merlin's embrace of this paternalism stemmed from her fundamental adherence to the Law of the Father, a symbolic submission made poignant by her continued need to compensate for the absence of her real father, Don Joaquín de Santa Cruz. The belief in the protective power of the Law was a wish-fulfillment reflecting Merlin's own need for a compassionate father figure. This psychological motivation is suggested in her early works, particularly in *Mes douze premières années* (1831), where parental mercy toward domestic slaves was a means to disguise the young Mercedes's mistreatment at the hands of her father, female slaves becoming projected figures for her own childhood abandonment.[100] In *La Havane*, the psychological subtext is "lifted," as it were, onto the collective plane, thus endowing the white Master with a surrogate paternal role. Spain as substitute father/land becomes metaphorically invested as a guarantee of a stable symbolic order for all its citizens, whether slaves or freemen.

As at other points in the memoir, this benevolent metaphor belies historical fact. Indeed, Knight has addressed the gap between theory and practice in the slave laws, arguing convincingly that "the laws and decrees promulgated in Spain cannot be seen as a description of 'real' conditions in the Indies."[101] Moreover, Knight states that the 1824 slave laws were tied to the increased repression of blacks at a time when slaveholding societies were becoming more scarce and were submitted to increasing external pressures, such as the British abolitionist campaign.[102] In the slavery letter, Merlin's defense of corporal punishment is clearly aligned with the planters' desperate need to maintain their estates and a plantation economy based on slave labor. Knight's cryptic statement—"To deny the Cuban planters their slaves at that time was like bleeding their lifeblood"[103]—provides the underside to Merlin's apologist position justifying the cruel treatment of slaves: "Cette cruelle condition nous révolte; elle est pourtant d'une impérieuse nécessité, le nègre étant accoutumé à cette rigueur en Afrique dès sa naissance" ("This cruel condition revolts us; it is nevertheless extremely necessary, since the black man was accustomed to this rigor in Africa where he was born") (*La Havane*, vol. 2, 127; *Los esclavos*, 41). This reversibility from revulsion to necessity makes her text appear as a "negative transparency" of colonial discourse. As if repenting of her previous justification of corporal punishment, she quickly produced legal arguments to prove that the slave could redress his injuries by legal means (*La Havane*, vol. 2, 126–28; *Los esclavos*, 41–42). Again, Knight's classic study belies this version: though the slave was protected by the letter of the law, in reality he was unable to utilize the system to his defense because colonial officials at every level were firmly tied to the sugar *hacendados*.[104] The same duplicity between legal theory and practice holds true in Merlin's description of the famous statute of *coartación*, which stipulated that a slave had the right to buy his liberty at a fixed price (*La Havane*, vol. 2, 128; *Los esclavos*, 43) but which historians see more as an economic stipulation than as a legal or moral one.[105]

Seen in the context of other travelogues of the period, it is clear that Merlin's account by no means constitutes a realistic portrayal of master/slave relations. Indeed, her benevolent vision sharply contradicts Turnbull's near-naturalistic depiction of daily life in the *ingenio*, a cruel picture of slaves submitted to a beastly routine of corporal punishment and overwork.[106] Not only avowed abolitionists like Turnbull but other foreign visitors to the island—particularly women travelers like the North American Julia Ward Howe and the Swedish Fredrika Bremer—also expressed outrage at the deplorable condition of slaves in the sugar plantations.[107] And in his novel *Francisco*, Suárez y Romero's minutely described the physical and mental sufferings endured by the field slave, the sadism of the *mayoral* or overseer, and the depravity of the white master, leading to a tragic fate for both male and female slaves. In short, Merlin's "fantas-tic" representation of slavery opposes not only the subgenre of the travelogue but also one of the dominant literary forms of the period, the antislavery novel.

Is the "fantastic" nature of Merlin's slavery letter due to literary naïveté or rather to the "ill-conceived and self-serving" nature of la Comtesse's "literary and political adventure"?[108] To answer that question fairly, her text needs to be inscribed in what Gilman calls the "fantasy life of the culture," that other scene where stereotypes are "perpetuated, resurrected, and shaped" according to deep-seated collective needs.[109] At one level, the apparent distortions, glaring contradictions of historical facts, and reversals of roles evident in the slavery letter are markers of psychological projection whereby the Other becomes endowed with the rejected characteristics of the self.[110] This process, in turn, reverts the "violent dislocation" of colonial discourse, so that the misrepresentation of the black reads as the reverse, opaque side of the Creole's need to erect an authoritative—or, more accurately, a *self-determining*—discourse in light of their oppression under Spanish colonial rule.[111] At another level, however polemical it may be, Merlin's letter on slavery represents, like her historical letters, an alternative stance on a complex social problem—a gendered rhetoric that is concerned not so much with historical accu-racy but rather with passionate debate. Seen in this light, the hesitancies and inconsistencies evident in the slavery letter stem not so much from Merlin's attempt to mediate between the proslavery faction and Saco's more liberal ideas, but rather from the fact that she was the first Cuban woman to dare to speak in the public arena about a controversial topic.

Moreover, the charges of "fantasy" and "unreality" that Tanco and other male critics have leveled at Merlin can be tempered if one keeps in mind that she constructed her version of slavery on the basis of her con-tact with domestic slaves in Havana. Based on her experiences at the time of her journey and on her (un)conscious recollections of maternal black nannies (*La Havane*, vol. 1, "Lettre XV," 303), Merlin structured her vision of slavery by transposing the milder destinies of the domestic, urban slave to the harsher life of the rural slaves in the plantations, a the-sis corroborated by Knight's assertion that the living conditions of slaves were determined by whether they lived in the city or in the country.[112] Thus, the apparent distortion is, in part, an effect of invention substi-tuting for experience: presumably, Merlin would not have had direct knowledge of the real conditions in the sugar plantations as she limited her visit to Havana only. This, and her attachment to her parents, particularly to her father, may explain her depiction of the supposed "humanity" of white sugar planters, an Imaginary vision which conjured up an equally idealized image of Don Joaquín de Santa Cruz.

By shifting the town/country opposition, Merlin's travelogue dissolves traditional categories of historical thought.[113] In the same way that she based her vision of slave society on the urban, domestic model, Merlin reversed the existing hierarchy between metropolis and colony to confirm her belief in the Creole's benevolence toward the blacks; in her words, "les blancs créoles dans nos colonies sont plus humaines envers les nègres que ne le sont les Européens . . . soit que sa vie patriarcale le porte à entendre jusqu'aux noirs la pitié paternalle du foyer domestique" ("the white Creoles of our colonies are more humane towards the black than the Europeans . . . perhaps because their patriarchal life inclines them to extend to the black the paternal piety of the domestic hearth") (*La Havane*, vol. 2, 107–8; *Los esclavos*, 22–23). The representation of racial difference using the primary metaphor of a "pseudo-family" created by slave and master is fundamentally patriarchal and corresponds to Merlin's acquiescence to paternal Law. Indeed, in the last pages of the slavery letter, the master/slave bond is redefined in terms of a father/son metaphor, an analogical structure that absorbs the previous categories of white and black:

> Il se montre non seulement plus doux, mais moins altier enver ses esclaves. Tout en les traitant avec l'autorité du maître, il y mèle je ne sais quelle nuance d'adoptive protection, je ne sais quel mélange de la sollicitude paternelle et de l'autorité seigneuriale.

> (He appears not only sweeter, but less haughty towards his slaves. While he treats them with the authority of a master, he blends in a certain adoptive and protective shading, a certain mixture of paternal solicitude and of noble authority.) (*La Havane*, vol.2, 108; *Los esclavos*, 23)

Curiously enough, and in spite of the many contradictions in their respective visions, this paternalistic view of slavery is echoed in Turnbull's text, which describes town or city slaves as forming "almost a family with the master."[114] In what is clearly a mechanism of denial, antithetical to historical truth, Merlin tried to argue that "L'esclavage, à Cuba, n'est point, comme ailleurs, un état abject et dégradé" ("Slavery in Cuba is, like elsewhere, neither an abject nor a degraded state"),[115] but a kind of extended family in which the white considers the free mulatto as a brother. This idealized picture is undermined, however, by the conditions necessary for such a fraternal alliance to take place: the mulatto's free status and educated bearing: "le Havanais . . . traite la mulâtre en frère, *pourvu qu'il soit libre et bien élevé*" (*La Havane*, vol. 2, 123; *Los esclavos*, 38, emphasis added). This image of master and slave bonded in symbolic kinship is repeated in other works of the period, best illustrated in Villaverde's classic novel *Cecilia Valdés* (1882), whose protagonist is a mulatto woman. Yet, unlike Villaverde's text, which depicts the confluence of white and black as a tragedy, a tale of incest, murder, and miscegenation, Merlin's letter paints a sentimental and inaccurate picture that presents the slave's submission as an unchangeable historical given.

Using Gilman's notion of the stereotype as "an idealized definition of the different" and of texts as the site of (re)production of such stylized images,[116] *La Havane* can be viewed as an example of a "complicated text" that "consciously form[s] a fiction of the world" in response to the historical situation of a particular group—in this case, the contradictions of the Creole condition.[117] Merlin's curious wavering between imaginative play and distortion of fact corresponds to a particular type of fictional text, one exhibiting parodic distortion of both the external world and its own self-referential composition.[118] That Merlin's fictional text is indeed "an attempt to provide an image of control"[119] is borne out by the fact that in her "fantasia for slaveholders," the slave repeatedly declares his unswerving devotion to a kind master. Salient among these anecdotes is the story of her cousin Don Rafael, whose slaves revolted during his absence, causing his wife and children to fear for their lives. In Merlin's account, an elderly female slave comes to her mistress's aid, urging her to remain safely behind closed doors and reassuring her that she has already alerted the master. Though the shouts below confirm that the slaves' are exacting vengeance against the *mayoral*, the master soon reappears like "el ánjel esterminador [*sic*]" ("an exterminating angel"), discharging the slaves with stern and angry look.[120] In instant repentance, the slaves clamber back to their places in the *casa de purga* (sugar house), their heads held low in submission. The white family then flees, stopping only to pick up an anguished and half-dead *mayordomo*, the man responsible for the estate during the master's absence. This story, which Bueno rightfully called "a mixture of the bizarre with the ridiculous,"[121] can only be explained in terms of a fictional representation that enacts a desire for power and control.[122] In light of the historical juncture at which the Creole elite found itself, Merlin's text served the defensive function of dispelling, if not the possibility of slave revolt, which was imminent and real, at least the fear that such rebellions would have harmful or disastrous results for the white master and his family. The Creole readers of "Lettre XX" could then maintain the illusion of control and safeguard in their minds the plantation society under threat. If seen in response to this Imaginary function, Merlin's text is a palliative analogue to Saco's impassioned warnings in "Clamor de los cubanos."

Other tales of revolt included toward the end of the slavery letter were written with a similar purpose in mind, though they succumb more to the tone of hyperbole on which the whole text is based. In the next one, one slave offsets a rebellion by saving his master's life and dying at the hands of his fellows, a generosity matched by the rioting slaves' courteous gesture of turning off the steam engine in order not to damage the machinery of production (*La Havane*, vol.2, 161–63; *Los esclavos*, 72–74). The story suggests the slaves' complicity with the mechanistic force that keeps their bodies in submission, that is, with the sugar mill as both economic and psychological "deep structure." Another tale that reads as equally "fantastic" is nevertheless based on a true anecdote.[123] When General Tacón gave a splendid dinner, he was so impressed with the talents of Antonio, a black cook under the service of the marquis of Casa-Calvo's daughter, that he wanted to acquire his culinary talents for himself. Though Tacón went so far as to offer the slave his freedom, Antonio's emphatic response was: "Dites au gouvernour que j'aime mieux l'esclavage et la pauvreté avec mes maîtres que la liberté et la richesse avec lui" ("Tell the governor that I prefer slavery and poverty with my masters to freedom and riches with him") (*La Havane*, vol. 2, 168–69; *Los esclavos*, 78–79). Its recounting of such a brazen response further confirms that Merlin's slavery letter was geared more to a patriotic end—the affirmation of a cohesive sense of Cubanness—than to a position that categorically excluded blacks from the picture of Cuban nationality.

The "fantastic" anecdotes included in "Lettre XX" suggest that Merlin's apparently distorted view of slavery was tied to her procolonial stance and to the necessity of upholding a metonymical image of the nation: the belief (still held by the majority of Creoles) that Cuba must remain part of Spain so as not to break the continuity of language, culture, and tradition (*La Havane*, vol. 2, 121–22; *Los esclavos*, 37). Thus, the rigidity of her views was more a result of her concern that Cuba remain tied to the maternal/cultural matrix that Spain represented than to an overt racism in and of itself. In this light, Merlin's (re)version of slavery is consistent with her avowal of Cuba's colonial condition, which Saco described using the metaphor of slavery.[124] Instead of representing an authoritative colonialist text, then, Merlin's *La Havane* reveals the hesitancy and deep ambivalence generated by the condition of hybridity, traits that subvert the discourse of power while marking the gradations of gender difference.[125]

Such an interpretation helps explain the ambivalence underlying Merlin's problematic representation of the black, for the negative portrayal of Africans in "Lettre XX" is countered in other sections of *La Havane* by positive, even endearing images of domestic female slaves. Such is the case with the sympathetic portrait of Mamá Agueda, the venerable nanny of Teresa Montalvo, whom she encounters at the home of her maternal uncle in a tender scene of recognition (*La Havane*, vol. 1, "Lettre XV," 303). These extremes conform to the "bipolar" or "double-edged" stereotype that conjoins the negative image of the Other with "a positive idealization."[126] The ambivalence at the heart of Merlin's representation of race is tied, then, to the parallel sentiment that colors her version of the colony, making her text a "negative transparency" that shows the *traces* of colonial domination rather than simply (re)enacting it.

From a psychoanalytic point of view, Merlin's transformation of the cruelties of slavery into a kind of paternalistic "golden age" stemmed from her desire to reconstruct an imaginary country whose contours had faded in more than thirty years of exile. If Merlin granted the slave an unshakable tie to a master who encompassed for him the absolutes of country and family—"Le maître est pour l'esclave la patrie et la famille" ("The master is to the slave his homeland and his family") (*La Havane*, vol. 2, 156; *Los esclavos*, 68)—this is only a displacement of her own deep-seated need to compensate for the loss of her own.

Between the Old World and the New: The Rhetoric of Mediation in *La Havane*

In "Lettre XXIV" of *La Havane*, the tie between metropolis and colony is represented as an extension of the slavery system. Merlin's basic image of the colonial government as a pyramid of power that is inversely proportional to the hierarchy of race and caste constituting slave society is, once again, derived from José Antonio Saco. It was Saco who first described the relationship between colony and peninsula in terms of a dependency dangerously resembling the institution of slavery: "¡Cuán cierto es que, si esta isla depende de España, esta misma dependencia . . . es hasta cierto punto *la esclavitud de su métropoli*" ("How true it is that, if this island depends on Spain, this dependence . . . makes it to a certain extent *enslaved to its metropolis*").[127] Following Saco's argument, Merlin compares Spanish American colonialism to a subtle form of "slavery" experienced by the whites: "L'esclavage des blancs est le premier élément politique de cette île à laquelle on reproche l'esclavage des noirs" ("The slavery of whites is the first political factor of this island, which is blamed for the slavery of blacks").[128] This metaphor acquires rhetorical force in Merlin's political letters in that it permeates her analysis of the organization of political power in Cuba, and, most of all, her representation of the institution of the Captain-Generalcy.

Nowhere is the contradiction between Merlin's procolonial position and her nationalistic fervor more evident than in her critique of Spanish colonial administration. Though later she will argue for the cultural continuity between Spaniards and Creoles—"Quant à nous, je le répète, nous sommes profóndement, exclusivement Espagnols" ("As far as we are concerned, I repeat, we are Spaniards through and through")[129]—here she affirms, instead, a sense of the colony's "historical uniqueness," and goes so far as to denounce the need for separate institutions, forms of government, and laws. Attacking first the feudal vestiges implicit in Spanish bureaucracy, Merlin then attacks the institution of the Captain-Generalcy, pointing out its despotic and absolutist nature. Her scathing critique seems almost prophetic from a contemporary vantage point: "Le gouvernement de l'île de Cuba se réduit à un pur despotisme militaire, concentré sur la tête d'un seul homme, sans contrôle, sans responsabilité, sans surveillance" ("The government of the island of Cuba is reduced to a military despotism, concentrated solely on the head of one man, without controls, without responsibilities, without supervision").[130] Merlin denounces the absolutism and the abuse of power implied in the person of the Captain-General: "sa toute-puissance est inévitablement contraire l'intérêt de la colonie qu'il regit." ("his omnipotence runs inevitably counter to the interests of the colony which he rules").[131] This tempers, in part, her polemical dedication to Leopoldo O'Donnell. In a short, cryptic passage Merlin compresses the experience of three absolutist rulers—

Las Casas, Vives, and Tacón—into the abstract principles which apply
to the Captain-Generalcy as a whole:

> Ainsi, vous me demanderez, après tout, quels sont les pouvoirs
> représentatifs dans l'île de Cuba, quelle est la balance de ces pouvoirs,
> comment ils s'équilibrent. Je vous repondrai en peu des mots:—Nous
> avons un roi: —c'est le capitaine général; —il y a pour conseil de minis-
> tres: —le capitaine général, —lequel se sert à lui-même de chef de la
> justice, de ministre de la marine et de préfet de police. Il constitue aussi
> sa chambre haute et sa chambre basse; tel est notre gouvernement
> représentatif; il n'est pas compliqué, comme vous voyez.

> (So you ask me, after all, what are the representative powers in the
> island of Cuba? what is the balance of power? how are these distrib-
> uted? I would answer in just a few words: We have a king: he is the
> Captain-General; his council of ministers: the very same Captain-
> General, who serves as well as the Chief of Justice, Minister of Marines
> and Head of Police. He constitutes as well the Upper and Lower
> Houses; such is our representative government. Not very complicated,
> as you can see.)[132]

On closer look, it was Tacón's reign that provoked Merlin's overarching criticism of Spanish colonial administration. Whereas on one
hand Merlin is energetic in her appraisal of Tacón as a despotic ruler
who alienated the Creole upper class, on the other hand she is careful to
acknowledge his reform of the colonial city, including notable improve-
ments in public lighting, transportation, and the use of police force to
suppress robbery and other crimes.[133] Despite this somewhat sympathetic
picture, "Lettre XXIV" also documents the clash ensuing between Tacón
and the Creoles, and the widening rift between *peninsulares* and *criollos*.
For, despite her later assertion of Hispanic cultural legacy on the island,
Merlin evidences an equally pronationalistic stance, siding as she does
with the Creoles' righteous indignation against Tacón's abuses. Moreover, she situates the pivotal point of the Creoles' continued resistance:

> C'etait dans la confiance des Havanais, et non dans une volonté despo-
> tique, que le général Tacon aurait dû chercher le levier de sa politique.
> Rien de plus étranger à nos caracters que la persécution et la dureté. Il
> y a chez nous tant de pitié pour le malheur, une tendresse d'âme su
> facile à émouvoir, que nous prenons toujours le parti du faible et du
> condamné.

(It is the trust of the people of Havana, and not a despotic will, in which General Tacón has found leverage for his rule. There is nothing more alien to our character than persecution and harshness. There is among us so much pity for misfortune, a tenderness of soul so easily stirred up, that we always take up sides with either the weak or the condemned.)[134]

As this passage shows, the analysis of Tacón's political failures stands Merlin in good stead, as from this position she safely assumes the collective "we" which embraces and transcends her inner division, thus casting her wholly within the insular "imagined community."

In describing the consequences of Tacón's rule, Merlin clearly signals the widening breach between Spanish commercial interests, on the one hand, and Creole nationalistic ones, on the other. This rift, in turn, was represented in terms of loyalty or disloyalty to the Captain-General, for "[l]e commerce, les classes moyennes, les employés espagnols, se groupèrent autour de ce chef qui était en horreur à la propriété foncière et agricole de la haute aristocratie" ("[b]usiness[men], the middle classes, Spanish employees, all grouped themselves around their chief who was simply horrified at the agricultural and landed property of the high aristocracy.")[135] Though this analysis at first glance seems to contradict her later statement that "sa colonie, qui n'est plus une conquête, mais une fraction de l'Espagne" ("Cuba is not a conquest but a part of Spain"),[136] the description of class antagonisms in Creole society anticipates her version of a crucial event in Cuban colonial history; mainly, the break between Tacón and his Minister of Finance, Claudio Martínez de Pinillos, known as the Count of Villanueva. In Merlin's version, the *intendente* fostered at first the Captain-General's program of reform and then ultimately cut himself off from the latter's rule.[137] However, Merlin glosses over the split between these two powerful men (in contrast to her earlier, detailed account of the rift between Velázquez and Cortés), an omission that may have more to do with her own discretion than with her siding with Pinillos or his Creole constituency. Indeed, the rift between Tacón and Villanueva worsened on account of General Lorenzo's uprising in Santiago in favor of Spain's liberal constitution, an uprising thwarted by Tacón himself. Villanueva, in turn, seized this opportunity to mount a campaign against the hated Captain-General that eventually led to his resignation and forced return to Spain.[138]

There was also a powerful economic reason for the break: Tacón had opposed construction of the Havana railroad, a project dear to

Villanueva and other enterprising members of his class.[139] That Merlin ultimately aligned herself with Pinillos's position on this issue is made evident in her letter on commerce: "Donnez à l'île de Cuba deux choses, des chemins et une législation, aussitôt l'ordre matériel et l'ordre moral vont changer" ("Give the island of Cuba two things: roads and laws, and the material and moral order will change").[140] By siding with Pinillos, Merlin aligns herself again with the landed aristocracy and with those liberal-minded Spaniards interested in fostering island prosperity; however, her omission of the real cause of tension between Tacón and his ex-minister may have been due to the hesitancy of her gender position, which inhibited her from revealing the conflicts and strains behind current political events. Likewise, her mention of Pinillos and Francisco Ramírez, another Spaniard responsible for fostering education and commerce as well as the policy of white immigration, signals her acknowledgment of Spanish influence in shaping the educational and intellectual institutions in the island.[141] Though she herself may not have dared to intervene rhetorically in the Tacón-Pinillos split, her intention was clearly to mark this event as responsible for a growing breach between Spaniards and Creoles, thus complicating—and also deepening—her own sense of insular belonging.

Merlin's mediating stance is also prevalent in "Lettre XXIII" dedicated to M. Berryer and concerned exclusively with the *foro* or colonial administration of justice. In his monumental *Cuba: economía y sociedad*, Leví Marrero documents the fact that Merlin's description of the legal system is based on a report which Saco prepared for her.[142] This is corroborated as well by a letter that Saco wrote to José Luis Alfonso from Paris and dated October of 1842, where Saco refers to the project of *La Havane* in these terms: "De la obra de la Merlin quiero decirte á ti y a los demas amigos dos palabras. Yo le he dado muchas noticias, y ademas dos articulos, uno sobre *foro*, y otra sobre la *forma del gobierno* de la isla de Cuba" ("About Merlin's work, I'd like to simply say two words to you and our other friends. I have given her many news, as well as two articles, one on the law, and the other on the form of government of the island of Cuba").[143] Saco's article is presumably the source of "Lettre XXIII" of *La Havane*, although Saco had also spoken against the abuses of the legal system in his "Clamor de los cubanos."[144] Hence, Saco's second document would presumably underlie most of "Lettre XXIV," which centered on colonial government and followed immediately in *La Havane* after the chapter on the law. As in the slavery letter, hints that Merlin intended to hide her dependency on Saco is shown by the dates given: "Lettre XXIII" is dated July 20, toward the end of her journey, and "Lettre XXIV" on June 12, at the beginning of her trip. This temporal slip was perhaps meant to deceive the reader into thinking that there is no apparent connection among the two succeeding letters, when the fact that they obviously come from the same source and deal with similarly charged topics suggest a direct link between the two. These letters pertaining to the political destinies of the island and to its internal organization hence tie together with the slavery letter to develop in *La Havane* a consistent, political argument structured around the idea of mediation, primarily, the mediation between island and metropolis.

Besides the rhetoric of mediation present in these texts, Merlin's "letter of the law" has other ramifications for nineteenth-century Latin American literature. For this letter counters the dominant discourses of Latin American literature based on legal texts. In this light, Merlin reverts the usual practice of Latin American colonial writers, whereby self-presence is attained by "compliance with the rhetorical mold" in "a legal kind of ontological gesture" in which the use of legal formulas guarantees "the symbolic link with family and territory, with lineage and the state."[145] Orphaned herself and without a stake in the reigning symbolic order, Merlin resists this notion by attempting another kind of ontological move: a return to the law as univocal guarantee of a stable society.[146] The thrust of Merlin's letter-of-the-law is based, at one level, on a Romantic notion of an ideal society modeled after Nature (as in Chateaubriand's *Paul et Virginie*); at another, on her own need to acknowledge silently the Count of Jaruco's paternal authority. Behind her yearning for a single, all-encompassing law that would bind together the members of one social body is hidden, no doubt, her secret desire for the Law of the Father; in Lacanian terms, the Name of the Father as a deep, unconscious structure underlying individual and collective identity, and associated with the figure of the count.

Instead of assuming the viability of the law as a legitimizing and mediating discourse, as in Latin American colonial narratives, Merlin undermines its pervasive influence in all layers of society. Not only this, but she argues convincingly that the unwieldy domain of the law stifles what should constitute the moral end of the legal process, that is, the attainment of justice. Nowhere is Merlin's confrontational stance more evident than in this scathing critique of the abuses perpetrated by judicial bureaucracy: "Les patrimoines se perdent, les mois et les années s'ensevelissent, les générations des plaideurs y usent leurs forces, et jamais la sentence attendue ne vient couronner de son dénoument l'équité de la cause la plus évidente" ("Patrimonies are lost, months and years are buried, generations of litigants use their forces, and never is a verdict attained that crowns by its outcome the righteousness of even the most evident of cases").[147] In typical epigrammatic style, Merlin sums up the nature of the colonial legal system by setting up a contradiction: "L'administration de l'injustice remplace ici l'administration de la justice" ("The administration of injustice replaces here the administration of justice").[148] Historian Leví Marrero recalls this quote when he acknowledges the value of Merlin's travelogue in documenting the cumbersome legal system operating in the colony: "La Condesa de Merlin . . . fue explícita, directa y enérgica en su denuncia del sistema de justicia—de injusticia, lo llamaría ella—del que la opulenta clase alta criolla era también víctima" ("Countess Merlin . . . was explicit, direct and energetic in denouncing the abuses of the system of justice—of injustice, she would say—of which the Creole upper class was also made victim").[149]

The reversal at the core of Merlin's argument also has repercussions in terms of how she conceived of the relations between metropolis and colony. In her terms, the confusing and contradictory nature of the law could result in a civil war, were it not for the complacent nature of the Creoles: "Je vous l'ai dit, mon ami, il faut les âmes les plus douces, les plus nourries de miel, les plus désireuses de paix, pour que la guerre ne soit pas aux quatre coins d'île" ("I have said it to you, my friend, they have the most sweet, the most honey-nurtured, the most peace loving, of souls, which is why war has not yet broken out in the four corners of the island").[150] Her idealistic image of the Creoles lends itself to an utopian vision of social harmony: "La douceur des moeurs, l'heureuse nature des caractères et la facilité des âmes conservent à la Havane une sorte de bien-être social, en dépit des plus étranges abus qui aient jamais été organisés et enracinés pour la destruction de toute société humaine" ("Their sweet manner, the happy nature of their characters and their spiritual ease preserves in Havana a kind of social welfare, despite the strangest abuses that have ever been organized and established to ensure the destruction of all human society").[151]

Such an idyllic vision can only respond to Merlin's own deep-seated need to reconcile her Creole past with her own exiled condition, while presumably addressing the pressing demands of colonial society. Hence, the need to imagine a harmonious community leads her not to attack Spain's inflated overseas bureaucracy but rather to feel compassion for the mother country's inability to rule over her vast dispersed dominions.[152] Such a conciliatory move hearkens to a prototypically feminine stance of mediation, and must temper the view of Merlin handed down in literary history as simply a procolonialist writer.

Merlin's rhetorical reversal of justice serving injustice upsets not only the status of legal discourse itself but also the way in which it was assimilated into other types of writing, particularly during the colonial period. The legalistic nature of the Spanish empire converted it into a "self-enclosed, self-regulating machine whose grist was paper and which was oiled in ink."[153] Merlin's slavery letter had echoed the notion that the patriarchal lord personified in the slaveowner was the paradigm of social authority, thus suggesting a continuity between public and private spheres. As González Echevarría has shown, this collapse between external and domestic authority is what sustained the Spanish empire as a "patrimonial bureaucratic state," which was initially modeled on a paternalistic (and patriarchal) authority but later transformed into "an entelechy" by the heavy weight of a cumbersome law.[154] Writers like Garcilaso de la Vega sought legitimation within this codified system, thus hoping to resolve their cultural disenfranchisement by appeal to a higher authority.[155] This appeal reads as a "letter the individual writes to [an] absent father," the father usurped by the codification of law and whose authority was yet adjudicated by the King himself.[156] Within this system, the languages of history and law were permeated by notarial rhetoric, forming a tight web of texts impermeable to marginal discourses.[157]

The critique of the legal system developed in "Lettre XXIII" of *La Havane* contests this view, and, consequently, runs counter to the legacy of Latin American colonial letters. Merlin's picture of the endless proliferation of paper, codes, and lawyers implied in the judicial system, shows not only the lucrative nature of the law, but also its arbitrary influence, its unwieldy power: "plus il se salit de papier timbré, et plus, lorsque ce papier sali se débite, il tombe de piastres fortes dans les caisses du fisc et dans les trésors des juges, des avocats et de leur suite" ("the more he soiled stamped paper, and then, when the soiled documents were sold, he dropped strong piastres in the coffers of the exchequer and in the treasury of the judges, the attorneys and all their sort").[158] A similar criticism of colonial law is echoed by Leví Marrero, who explains that: "[l]a actividad de los agentes del Foro, desde los letrados hasta los *papelistas*, continuaría en grado tal que el *papel sellado*, vendido por la Real Hacienda e indispensable para todo tipo de documentos, vino a ser uno de los ramos más productivos del Erario" ("the activity of the legal representatives, from the attorneys on down to the scribes, was pitched to such a high degree that stamped paper, sold by the Royal Treasury and indispensable for every kind of legal transaction, was one of the most lucrative activities of the Exchequer").[159]

More pointed for our argument in support of Merlin's controversial stance is the tongue-in-cheek irony used to describe the Edifice of Books, which regulated power relations within the colony as well as the constraining tie to the metropolis. In one apt rhetorical move, Merlin crumbles the entire (male) paradigm equating Law and Book, emblematized in the notion of an infinite, incessant Archive:

> Imaginez, mon ami, quel édifice, ou plutôt quelle masure barbare ce doit être que ce monument sans fenêtres et sans lumières, qui a pour base les vieilles lois gothiques du *fuero-juzgo*, pour premières assises, les lois espagnoles des *fueros-viejos*, et pour étage supérieur, les lois féodales et romaines des *siete partidas, la novísima recopilacion*,—mélange indigeste de lois et d'arrêtes concernant toutes les races et toutes les époques; puis, pour couronnenement ridicule d'une si absurde fusion, les lois des Indes,—*leyes de Indias*—les ordonnances des intendants de la Nouvelle Espagne—*intendentes de la Nueva España*,—sans compter un nombre infini d'arrêts rendus par des tribunaux supérieurs dans toutes les circonstances et pour tous les cas possibles, jugeant noir demain ce qu'ils avaient jugé blanc hier.

> (Imagine, my friend, such a building, or perhaps instead that barbarous hovel which it must be resembling a windowless and lightless monument, that has as its basement the old gothic laws or *fuero-juzgo*, as its first floor, the Spanish laws of the *fueros-viejos*, as its last floor, the feudal laws or the Roman seven laws, or new compilation—an undigested mix of laws and decrees concerning all races and all periods; then, to ridiculously crown such an absurd combination, the laws of the Indies—*leyes de Indias*—the ordinances of the intendants of New Spain, *intendentes de la Nueva España*—without counting an infinite number of decrees rendered by the higher courts on all circumstances and for all possible cases, judging black tomorrow that which they had judged white yesterday.)[160]

This passage plays on the double meaning of *assise* as both archi-
tectural "foundation" and its broader meaning of "foundation of society," an irony made even more acute by the connotations of the word
pertaining to a particular type of law.[161] Underlying this description is
the rhetorical ploy of antithesis, where "à toute loi répond une loi contraire" ("for each law there is a contrary one"),[162] thus enacting, once
again, a reversal in colonialist discourse that restrains the authority of
the Archive, if not completely rendering it useless. For Merlin signals
the gap between law and social praxis, as is the case with the *Leyes de Indias*,
whose authority has been voided by present social reality: "Applicables
aux populations vaincues, elles sont lourdes aujourd'hui aux populations
descendant des anciens conquérants " ("Applied long ago to the conquered populations, these laws weigh heavy today for the populations
that descended from the ancient conquerors").[163] If the colonial writer
complies with the rhetorical mold patterned on the notarial act, thereby
usurping a place by acquiescence to authority,[164] Merlin enacts a gender difference by completely (a)voiding the letter of the law, emptying
it of its presumed authority. Her parodic gesture, then, is not to mimic
colonial discourse but rather to flaunt it by divulging its inefficacy.

Merlin focuses on the multifaceted character of the legal process,
which she describes as an interminable labyrinth of parchments, cases, and
jurisdictions. This description has a curious postmodern ring to it, for the
legal complex is pictured as a metaphorical paper mill, a multilayered
machinery of judges, scribes, and counsels: "Quels sont, dites-vous, les
pivots de cette étrange machine?—L'intérêt du Fisc, l'intérêt des avocats,
l'intérêt des juges, des greffiers, des huissiers, des assesseurs, et de toute la
tourbe qui vit de la loi" ("Tell me, what are the pivots of such a strange
machine?—The treasury's interestes, the attorneys' interests, the judges'
interests, those of the clerks of court, of the bailiffs, of the assessors; in
short, of the entire rabble that makes a living from the law").[165] That this
picture is historically accurate is proven by the following assessment of
the practice of the law in colonial Cuba by historian Leví Marrero:

> A socaire del ánimo pleitista profundamente arraigado, y manejando
> arbitraria y dolorosamente las leyes confusas y contradictorias, un
> ejército de abogados, procuradores, escribanos y *papelistas o picapleitos* se
> adueñarían del foro para hacer interminables los litigios, mientras se
> paralizaba la justicia y se arruinaban los litigantes.

(By means of a deeply rooted spirit of litigation, and by arbitrarily and painfully manipulating the set of confusing and contradictory laws, a veritable army of attorneys, procurators, scribes and writerly or overly feisty lawyers would take over the Law in order to make litigation end-less; in the meantime, real justice was paralyzed and the litigants brought to ruin.)[166]

Emblematic of the abuses perpetrated by the legal system is the scathing critique of the *juez pedáneo*, rural judges who heavily fined the people for every conceivable procedure, thus exercising "cette tyrannie des petits, mille fois plus oppressive que le despotisme suprême" ("the tyranny of the small-minded, which is a thousand times more oppressive than the most extreme form of despotism").[167] Leví Marrero explains these abuses, usu-ally confined to the countryside, in terms of class extraction: "Los pedá-neos, en el escalón más bajo de la pirámide judicial, y a enorme distancia geográfica de la autoridad que les designaba, ejercían su poder abusivo sobre los estratos más humildes e indefensos de la población rural" ("The rural judges, who found themselves at the bottom of the judicial hierar-chy, and also at a great geographical distance from the authority which had entrusted them, would exercise their abusive power over the lowest and humblest strata of the rural population").[168] Merlin's mediating stance shows, then, her ability to empathize with the ordinary citizen, and par-ticularly with the victims of such outrageous legal abuses: "La victime, c'est la masse de la population elle-même, qui n'a ni titre, ni autorité, ni pouvoir pour échapper à cette saignée permanente et secouer toutes les sang-sues attachées à chacun de ses membres" ("The victims are most cer-tainly the bulk of the population, who have neither the title, nor the author-ity, nor the power to escape such permanent bleeding nor to shake off the leeches attached to its limbs").[169] These passages show us a Countess Mer-lin fully able to abandon her own class interests and able to identify as well with the marginalized sectors in the countryside, a flexibility partly owing to gender difference and partly to her affiliation with Saco, the presumed author of the manuscript on which the *foro* letter is based.

This emphatic position is a response, most probably, to Merlin's own attempt to settle her claim to the Nazareno sugar mill, which was unsuccessful (cf. p. 24). It is also, in the last analysis, an effect of Merlin's mediating stance on the relationship between island and peninsula. For the proposed revamping of the legal administration is part of a broader program of reform, as in her suggestion that the judges' greed be curbed so that a portion of the high cost of legal paper be destined to the general welfare of the colony: "Pour rendre la vie à cette colonie magnifique, il faudrait le sacrifice d'une partie de ce tribut, mais d'une partie seulement,—car le papier timbré serait toujours d'usage" ("In order to make the life of this colony simply magnificent, all it would take would be a sacrifice of part of this tribute—but only part of it—because stamped papers will always be useful").[170] It is at the end of this letter where Merlin expresses her epigrammatic solution, noted earlier, that would reverse the fabric of colonial society, arguing that the whole material and moral order of the nation would change if given roads and law.[171]

With the letter on the law, Merlin not only stresses her role as mediator but also inserts herself effectively into the project of the "imagined community," a gesture that complements her earlier attack on colonial administration. She herself construes her gendered subjectivity as the motivating force of her act of mediation: "—Que je serais heureuse, mon ami, si les germes que contiennent ses observations d'une femme guidée par le simple bon sens et l'amour du pays pouvaient devenir fertiles pour une des régions du monde les plus mal administrées et les plus faciles à régir" ("How happy I would be, my friend, if the seeds that contain these observations of a woman guided only by common sense and love of her country would spring for one of the worst administered but easiest to rule regions of the world").[172] Thus, Merlin's position is not that of other reformists who stopped short of envisioning a break with the peninsula, but can even be construed as politically advanced in the context of the period. Not only does Merlin express a repressed wish to destroy the existing corrupt system, but she even accedes to a social vision in which each class would have restored to it its inalienable right to justice: "[S]i je pouvais hâter la destruction, sans violence, de ce système barbare, ruine des familles, plaie du pays, nuisible à la métropole, où la loi est muette . . . où l'esprit des corps, entretenu et fomenté par les *fueros*, donne à . . . chaque classe sociale une forteresse pour s'y deféndre sans craindre le châtiment de ses délits" ("If I could hasten the destruction, without violence, of such a barbarous system, the ruin of families, the country's plague, harmful to the metropolis, [and] where the law is mute, where the collective spirit, maintained and promoted by the attorneys, give . . . each social class a fortress in which to defend itself without fearing punishment for its misdemeanors").[173] If Merlin could speak as her own advocate, this passage would surely be her best defense in Cuban literary history.

8. Colonial horse-drawn carriage (el quitrín). Frédéric Mialhe, *Viage pintoresco alrededor de la isla de Cuba dedicado al Señor Conde de Villanueva* (Havana: Litografía de Luis Marquier, ca. 1840). Special Collections Department, Otto G. Richter Library, University of Miami, Coral Gables, Florida.

7

CREOLE WOMEN

The Other as Self

It is ironic that the only selection from *La Havane* widely known to Creole readers was the "feminist" "Lettre XXV" of the 1844 standard edition, which was published as a series entitled "Cartas dirigidas por la Sra. de Merlin a Jorge Sand" ("Letters sent by Mrs. Merlin to George Sand") in both major newspapers of the period, the *Diario de la Habana* and the *Faro Industrial*.[1] In this letter, Merlin addresses the women of Havana with the tenderness and affection of a prodigal daughter. Merlin, however, had returned home to find not a mirrored self-image, but a difference in style of living that forced her to confront her destiny as expatriate and female intellectual.

Among all the letters of *La Havane*, "Lettre XXV," dedicated to George Sand, most dramatically reveals the author's internal conflict and perhaps even the compelling drive that motivated her writing, for in these pages Merlin confronts at last her divided identity. Can she find the young Mercedes Santa Cruz y Montalvo, or has she forever faded into the mask of "la Comtesse Merlin"? Whose face stares back in the mirror: Creole or countess, Romantic or early feminist? This set of contradictions is inscribed already in the letter's opening dedication to Sand, an apt rhetorical move that placed the text into the hands of one of the most important figures of French Romanticism, and certainly the one most relevant to Merlin's experience. With the appeal to Sand, Merlin obviously anticipated a negative readers' response, as if she knew she was placing herself at the mercy of her peers on the island by addressing as polemical a topic as women's domestic role.

Indeed, the publication of Merlin's "feminist" letter caused quite a stir in the intellectual circles of colonial Havana. Not only was the letter important within the orbit of the period, but it also has unquestionable historical value as a pioneer text of early feminist consciousness. Merlin's letter is one of the few documents to shed light on the role assigned to women in nineteenth-century Spanish America.[2]

Its central theme is the representation of Creole women, who are pictured both as extensions of the self and as the Other who embodies the desired traits of the tropics. The ideal of femininity is explored in diverse representations of Creole women, ranging from the carefree, unmarried youth to the still blooming wife and mother and culminating in a portrait of the stately matron who rules over her extended family. Merlin's attempts to go beyond the cult of domesticity prevalent at the time were riddled with tensions as she struggled to reconcile her past and present selves, as well as conflicting images of female subjectivity. Most probably written upon her return to Europe from Havana, the letter to Sand was the medium through which Merlin tried to resolve her divided identity, a conflict heightened by her recent direct contact with Creole women, who appear in her text as mirror images or doubles of herself— not only of the girl that she was before her departure from the island, but also the talented creative artist she had become. As Carmen Vásquez so aptly puts it, "la más importante de las mujeres cubanas de la Condesa de Merlin es ella misma" ("the most important of la Condesa de Merlin's Cuban women is herself").[3]

In truth, Merlin projected onto her female doubles in Cuba the idealizing gaze that early French Romanticists indulged in when dealing with non-European zones. Much like a female Bernardin de Saint-Pierre or François René de Chateaubriand, Merlin echoes here what had been a recurrent *topoi* in the political letters: the image of the island as a harmonious social order in which the bounties of nature are reflected primarily in the beauty and exorbitant graces of its women. This natural grace goes on to find its external counterpart in Merlin's discussion of

marital mores, for in her letter the institution of marriage consolidates
the union between the female, originating world and the secondary order
represented by a male-dominated and class-conscious society. Thus, the
letter to Sand recasts the nature/culture debate in terms of an opposition
between women in the Old World and the New.[4] Creole and European
women stood at opposite ends of the spectrum, the first staying close to
home, watching the hearth, whereas the second either read or roam happily throughout the world. Because the latter stereotype with its obvious
allusions to the writer or traveler must ultimately revert to la Comtesse
herself, the possibility of resolving the split between traditional and non-
traditional female roles was *embodied*, as it were, in her own person.
The letter to Sand conveys a hope for a more fully integrated ideal of
womanhood that would cancel out these opposites. Hence, Merlin attempts
through this letter to reconcile the backward glance at the past with her
present condition as *femme du monde*, or world-weary traveler, as well as
to sustain a delicate balance between the double feminine role of wife and
mother, on the one hand, and writer and artist, on the other.

As was the case with the slavery letter, the letter to Sand underwent a series of editorial transformations. The "Cartas dirigidas por la
Sra. de Merlin a Jorge Sand" published in the Havana colonial press basically follows the text included in the definitive French edition. However,
there are slight but significant differences. For one thing, the Spanish
version published in the *Diario de la Habana* has additional editorial comments, quite clearly included for the benefit of local readers. In effect,
the *Diario* version incorporates an ideological censor who summons up
Creole attitudes toward the potentially subversive themes of Merlin's
letter, those involving the benefits and drawbacks of women's domestic
role. These marginal notes not only attest to the impact which Merlin's letter had on the Creole elite, but they may very well have been the
means by which the author of the notes engaged in a secret polemic with
the visiting countess.

In addition to these covert signs of resistance, Merlin's feminist
letter provoked a lively public debate. A series of articles entitled "Cartas a Chucha. Las mugeres de la Habana" ("Letters to Chucha. The
Women of Havana"), all signed with the pseudonym "Serafina," appeared
in the literary section of the *Faro Industrial* on September 21, 24, and 28,
1843, very shortly after Merlin's letter was published. This response inaugurated a feminist polemic between Merlin (as the absent target) and her

until then silenced Creole counterpart. With the exception of a brief mention in Salvador Bueno's essay, this polemic has received virtually no critical attention, obviously because traditional literary history has deemed it unimportant, pertaining as it does to women's issues.[5] In my view the exchange between Merlin and "Serafina" constitutes an early feminist dialogue, notwithstanding the fact that the two women never had face-to-face contact with each other. Although in part this lack of communication stemmed from the obvious factors of physical and temporal distance between Europe and America, I claim that it was also caused by the restrictions placed on them and their discourse by the patriarchal order.

The exchange is structured rhetorically as a series of letters from "Serafina" to "Chucha," these names concealing an identity crisis as serious as that of Merlin herself: who is hiding behind the veil of such deceptively simple pseudonyms? Although "Serafina's" repetitive style and tendency toward circumlocution suggests a young girl making earnest attempts to write but lacking literary training, "Chucha's" letters conjure up the much more stereotypical image of a lazy adolescent without the slightest intellectual pretensions. I suspect that "Serafina's" identity has to be linked to the editor of the newspaper where the letters appeared or, at the very least, to the author of the marginal notes appended to the *Diario* version of Merlin's letter. This hypothesis is corroborated by the fact that in her letters "Serafina" refers to her father as a practical philosopher who is erudite in literary matters. Would not this shadowy influence point to a member of del Monte's *tertulia*? If so, one could imagine a Creole intellectual thrusting his daughter with a copy of Merlin's forbidden letter, urging her to write in defense of all Creole women— a strategy already put into practice at the end of Félix Tanco's *Refutacion*.[6] Or was this reply done entirely at the girl's own initiative? If so, this would have been a daring step for the time, even if, as seems to be the case, "Serafina" in her answers merely echoed the editor's (or her father's) opinion. In either case, the polemic instigated in the pages of the *Faro Industrial* suggests a father/daughter complicity that reveals the mechanisms of patriarchal control over women's literary vocation.

The mystery surrounding the polemicist's identity increases when we consider that, in addition to the "Cartas a Chucha," other responses to Merlin's letter appeared in the Havana press of the period. Most relevant to the feminist controversy are two anonymous articles published in the *Diario de la Habana* on September 24 and October 1, 1843, the work of a curious character who called himself "el cronista del Buen Tono," or the Cultured Chronicler. This person was in charge of a section of the *Diario* dedicated to topics of supposed interest to women—for example, the latest Parisian fashions or lively descriptions of the customs of elegant Creole society—themes that supposedly catered to "la educación del bello sexo" ("the education of the fair sex"). Under this rubric were hidden repressive tactics aimed at controlling the behavior of women and children, regarded as the most vulnerable members of society. This type of sentimental education typically involved constricting instincts and repressing emotions into accepted formulas that insured patriarchal dominion over women's bodies.[7] Hence, "el cronista del Buen Tono" acted as spokesman of the patriarchal Symbolic, interfering in women's affairs yet mediating his influence by means of subtle mockery and ironic detachment.

Not only did this anonymous commentator severely judge Merlin's opinions, but he also bestowed on himself the role of final arbiter, ending the polemic with the clear intent of minimizing its importance, thereby suppressing any further discussion of women's traditional role. Moreover, the self-designated Cultured Chronicler also obstructed any possible dialogue between Merlin and her interlocutors, "Serafina" and other young Creole women like her who were eager to define and understand their position in society. It is not by chance, then, that the identity of the commentator should be none other than Ramón de Palma, famous author of *Una Pascua en San Marcos* (1838). Did his charge against Merlin derive from reading her version of his novel rewritten in the pages of *Viaje a la Habana* (1844), or was he genuinely responding to the threat posed by an intelligent woman's questioning of her socially proscribed role?

Besides these direct replies to Merlin's letter, a lively article appeared in the pages of the *Faro Industrial* in December 19, 1843, which, though anonymous, had to have been written by Merlin's translator. The article reveals intimate knowledge of Merlin's work, comparing the letter to Sand with another fragment which, in the writer's judgment, is marred by the same stylistic defects as the former.[8] The question arises, which one of two translators is involved here? Was it Agustín de Palma, who had diligently edited and translated *Mis doce primeros años* (1838), or was it Rosa Aldama, Domingo del Monte's wife, who in her own humble way endeavored to translate Merlin's work from within that predominantly male literary circle and under her husband's supervision?[9] The emphatic and resolute tone of the article, however, leaves no doubt as to the author's gender identity: a knowledgeable male commentator who, unlike the eclectic "cronista del Buen Tono," considered himself a literary critic. It could be none other than the latter's cousin, the venerable Agustín de Palma.

Thus, on the one side of the feminist debate stands "Serafina," who resists Merlin's idealizing gaze yet also manifests a secret rebellion against the repressive tactics constricting the "ángel del hogar" ("domestic angel"). At the other extreme is the "cronista del Buen Tono," a representative figure of patriarchal control who in his function as male superego persuades women to follow accepted paradigms of female behavior. Defenseless and in the middle lies Merlin herself, laying her soul bare in a text meant to picture the Other, but only as a means to come home to herself, an intimate self-portrait that outlined as well the contours of her sister's face.

Needless to say, the feminist polemic must be seen as developing in the context of the ambivalent reception afforded Merlin by the members of the del Monte circle. An echo of these ambivalent reactions are found in the writings of "Serafina," for she vacillates between accepting Merlin as a model to emulate and criticizing her for alleged misrepresentations of colonial affairs, an opinion sounding like a caricatured version of the *tertulia's* views. The many contradictions evident in "Serafina's" position, however, suggest that a curious relationship was enacted between the two female figures, despite the fact that their voices could never confront one another directly.

Nevertheless, even as "Serafina" contradicts the virulent "Verá-filo" with her mild defense of the letter to Sand—"yo encuentro alguna parte de verdad en sus descripciones, y mas aun cuando prescindo de la exageracion con que se han escrito" ("I see some truth in her descriptions, and more so when I disregard the exaggeration with which they have been written.")[10]—she clearly is obliged to adopt the criteria of verisimilitude so dear to the del Monte circle. In short, "Serafina" shared Tanco's and the other *tertulianos'* opinion as to Merlin's propensity for exaggeration. For example, in the first letter—dated September 21, 1843—"Serafina" supposes that the many inconsistencies and inaccuracies of Merlin's letter must be due to her long absence from the island.[11] A similar concern with accuracy is revealed in an editorial note written by the critical commentator of the *Diario* version: "Hemos copiado esta carta de la Sra. condesa de Merlin sin deternos en comentarios, porque el público podrá juzgar con la misma exactitud que nosotros de lo que en ella hay de ideal y de verdadero" ("We have copied this letter by Lady Countess of Merlin without stopping to comment on it, because the public will be able to judge with the same accuracy as ours what is ideal and truthful in it").[12] Like "Serafina," the editor excuses Merlin's alleged inventiveness on the grounds of her protracted absence and notes as well the limited period of her stay. These concerns are also voiced in the "Cartas a Chucha" by means of what Bakhtin calls "represented speech" or reported indirect discourse, such as this claim attributed to "Serafina's" father: "la Condesa que apenas nos conoce, carece de los medios necesarios para hablar con exactitud y tino de nuestras cosas" ("the countess, who barely knows us, lacks the necessary means to speak with accuracy and good aim about our issues").[13] Such echoes seem to confirm the thesis that the editor of the *Diario* and the polemicist's father were one and the same. In this light, the father used the daughter as a convenient mouthpiece for a more incisive critique of Merlin than was permitted him in his public role.

"Serafina's" appeal to a paternal figure and her repeated technique of grafting her father's discourse into her text by way of direct citation speaks to the restrictions imposed on women in the symbolic mode. In other words, "Serafina" subscribes to the Law in order to gain legitimacy for her own (tentative) critical discourse, mildly exerting her own "author/ity" only by recourse to a parental "pre-text". Read as indirect discourse, "Serafina's" reliance on the father generates a "double-voiced" effect, which erects him into an invisible authority, thereby undermining the feminist arguments and setting the polemic within restrictive discursive parameters. "Serafina" is thus incapable of trusting her own feminine intuition that would otherwise lead her to sympathize with Merlin, given the fact that they both shared a common destiny as women.

This lack of trust can be explained in part by the resistance mounted against the intruding traveler by "Serafina's" immediate family and friends, all members of the Creole elite. This external authority not only denied any validity to Merlin's letter but went so far as to render it an object of mockery and even of light diversion, almost as if it were the perfect excuse for escaping the daily tedium of the tropics. Under the crushing weight of public opinion, "Serafina" had no choice but to censure herself, unabashedly confessing her fear of rejection to her more carefree interlocutor: "No me atreveria, amiga mia, á expresar esta idea á [sic] presencia de ellas [amigas y familiares], porque me atraeria alguna indignacion" ("I would not dare, my friend, to express this idea in their presence [that of lady friends and relatives], because it would bring indignation upon me").[14]

These pressures created in "Serafina" an internal division comparable to the identity conflict suffered by Merlin herself. Both women felt the need to authorize their writing. While "Serafina" had no other recourse than reliance on paternal authority, Merlin, by contrast, chose to ground her text under the shadow of Sand. This gesture not only legitimized her writing but also served to protect her from the critical barbs she very well may have anticipated, as Sand's established reputation as defender of women's rights would theoretically serve to safeguard her against any possible attacks.

Nowhere is Merlin's call for protection more evident than in the opening rhetorical question:

> ¿A quien mejor que a V. podré yo dirigir mis observaciones sobre las mugeres de mi país, y sobre su modo de vivir y de sentir; a V. que sabe comprender tambien [sic] mi sexo, y cuya elocuente pluma ha interesado tantas veces las almas generosas en favor de las mugeres que padecen en las sociedades civilizadas?

> (To whom else better than you could I direct my observations about the women of my country, and above all about their way of dressing and feeling; to you who understands my sex so well, and whose eloquent pen has so often interested generous souls in favor of the sufferings of women in civilized societies?)[15]

Though critics have insisted that between Merlin and Sand existed a literal friendship, I argue that they formed above all a literary partnership.[16] Indeed, Sand showed herself to be an avid reader of *Mes douze premières années* (1831), a work to which she dedicated a chapter of *Questions d'art et de littérature*.[17] Although definitely praising Merlin's primitive autobiography, Sand also used Merlin as an example of how women need an intellectual education, clearly an ironic statement meant to undermine the French-Creole woman's literary talent. The same underhanded tactic or sense of female rivalry is also subtly deployed by Gertrudis Gómez de Avellaneda in her prologue to *Viaje a la Habana*.[18]

The image of Creole women that Merlin offered to her readers on the island was from the other shore; in the words of the *Diario* editor, "[Merlin] nos ha pintado como se lo figuró su imaginación, que podemos llamar europea" ("[Merlin] has painted us as we figured in her imagination, which we could call European").[19] Almost as if she were compressing the past, Merlin composed a summary view of the physical and spiritual traits of Creole women: "[C]asta, aunque dotada de un alma y de una naturaleza ardientes" ("Chaste, though endowed with an ardent soul and nature"), a miniature statue whose "estremidades son finas y delicadas como las de un niño" ("limbs are as fine and delicate as a child's").[20] This Romantic ideal of a tropical species was evocative of her own self-portrait, included in her first book of memoirs, *Mes douze premières années*. The reader may well profit from a direct comparison:

La Habanera, en general, es delgada y de mediana estatura; pero por delicadas que sean sus formas, estas están vivamente pronunciadas. . . . La libertad que gozan desde la infancia, el dulce y constante calor de la atmósfera, mantienen sus miembros en toda su frescura y flexibilidad primitivas, y dan cierto aire dulce, tierno y suave á su piel, muchas veces de una blancura macilenta, pero a través de la cual se puede distinguir un reflejo cálido y dorado como si hubiesen penetrado por ellas los rayos del sol. Sus movimientos llenos de cierta languidez voluptuosa, su voz dulce y cadenciosa contrastan á veces con la vivacidad de su fisonomía y con los rasgos [*sic*] [rayos] de fuego que despiden sus ojos negros y rasgados, cuyas miradas no tienen igual.

(In general, the woman from Havana is thin and of medium height; but as delicate as their shape may be, it is sharply

A los once años ya había llegado a todo mi tamaño, y aunque muy delgada, estaba tan formada como cualquiera otra a los dieciocho. Mi color de criolla, mis ojos negros y animados, mi pelo tan largo que me costaba trabajo sujetarle, me daban un cierto aspecto salvaje, que se hallaba en relación con mis disposiciones morales.

(By the age of eleven I had already grown to my full height, and though I was very thin, I had the shape of an eighteen-year-old. My Creole coloring, my black and lively eyes, my hair that was so long that it was hard to keep it fastened, gave me a certain savage air, that was well suited to my moral disposition.)[22]

delineated. . . . The freedom they enjoy from infancy, the sweet and constant heat of the atmosphere, keep their limbs in all of their freshness and primitive flexibility, and bestows their skin with a certain sweet, tender, and soft air, which often has an extenuated whiteness, but one through which a warm and golden reflection can be discerned, as if the rays of the sun had penetrated them. Their movements are full of a certain voluptuous languor, their sweet and harmonious voice sometimes contrasts with the liveliness of their features and with the lines [sic] [rays] of fire that their black and almond eyes emit; eyes whose gazes have no equal.)[21]

In accordance with the cultural stereotype, woman is portrayed in Merlin's writing as a universal and homogenous subject, lacking in any distinguishable individual features beyond a generalized passionate nature whose perfect symbol is the searing black eyes and fiery look.[23] Still, the similarity between both portraits is so striking that it can serve as proof of Merlin's desire to identify herself as a Creole: the *habanera* appears as the primitive female archetype, while young Mercedes unabashedly proclaims herself the incarnation of this ideal. This identification persisted despite the deep gulf that divided Merlin from her compatriots. She had already been marked by the "wild" stamp of the woman artist— the "madwoman in the attic" proclaimed by Sandra Gilbert and Susan Gubar. In contrast, the Creole's more docile attitude and apparent lack of interest in art readily conformed to the "languor" or passivity traditionally assigned to women.

These differences notwithstanding, both descriptions subscribe to the image of the noble savage, European Romanticism's ideation of New World inhabitants. Bridget Aldaraça has examined how this topic was assimilated in Romantic literature: "Women, and by extension the place where they reside, are filled with primitive grace, an image reminiscent of the biblical Eden prior to Adam's fall from grace. . . . The idea that the female is more natural than the male, that is, uncorrupted by the per-

nicious influence of urban civilization, effectively designates the former as a kind of noble savage and provides the justification for isolating
women from modern history under the guise of protecting and preserving the purity of their natural nobility."[24] Despite her good intentions,
Merlin evokes in her letter to Sand the tropics imagined by Saint-Pierre
in *Paul et Virginie* (1788), that idealized representation of a harmonious
society founded on Nature, the original world of feeling prior to the fall
into History or the contaminated civilized world.[25]

Paradigmatic in this regard is the following description of the effect
of a tropical climate onto the same sexed body: "Mientras dura el ardor
del sol es imposible que [la habanera] pueda dedicarse a nada. Apénas da
unos pasos, y pasa en el baño ó comiendo una fruta una parte del día, y
el resto del tiempo meciendose en la butaca" ("While the heat of the sun
lasts, it is impossible for a woman from Havana to do anything at all. She
just takes a few steps and goes to the bathroom, or eats fruit during
part of the day, and the rest of the time she rocks in a easy chair").[26] This
description appears almost as a parodic translation of the "natural life"
of the infants in *Paul et Virginie*[27] or of the American natives idealized by
Chateaubriand in his *Atala* (1801), an analogy pointed out by none other
than Sand herself in her comments on *Mes douze premières années*: "La
muchacha havanaise nageant dans le ruisseau avec ses compagnes comme
la jeune sauvage de Chateaubriand" ("The girl from Havana swims in
the creek with her companions like Chateaubriand's young savage").[28]
Sand, like Merlin, had internalized the European perspective of the American Eden, except that Merlin, unlike Sand, would struggle between her
need to identify with the Creole world and the idealization demanded
by her dream, between the *locus amenus* of the *contradanza* (a stately waltz
derived from Spanish influence) and the hospitality of "the homes of the
New World."[29]

It is no wonder that this reflection of themselves made the Creole
women indignant, and they reacted strongly to the narrow characterization of themselves made by, in their eyes, an outside observer. In the
"Cartas a Chucha," the female commentator denies the ideal of the
habanera which Merlin traced so superficially in her letter to Sand. She
does this using two rhetorical devices: one, by displacing her own opinion onto a fictionalized character, and two, by means of repetition and
citation. An example of the first tactic is the appearance of an indignant
Lola who appears in the first of the "Cartas a Chucha" angrily raising the

current issue of the newspaper and shouting aloud Merlin's scandalous description of Havana women, an image which provokes general laughter.[30] By repeating in her writing Merlin's original stereotypical description, Serafina makes use of direct quotation as a rhetorical device to show up the range of Merlin's own (ideological) "excesses." In spite of this critical goal, repetition and intertextual echo have a contrary effect, for instead of serving the polemicist's purpose, it reinforces Merlin's point about the "languor" of Creole women. Thus, when faced with opposition from friends and family, "Serafina" finds that she can side with Merlin without risking additional censorship. Proof of this is her warning to "Chucha" that introduces the supposedly hyperbolic representation of Creole women:

> Tú sabes, Chucha, que siempre he sido tolerante, y en esto he seguido las reflexiones de Papá, y aprovecharme de sus juiciosos consejos [*sic*]. Pues bien, tú no te puedes formar una idea de cuanto se me ha reconvenido, porque no podia ménos que convenir con alguna ú otra cosa de las que contiene la carta.

> (Chucha, you know that I have always been tolerant, and in this I have followed Papa's thoughts, and have profited much from his judicious advice. And so, you do not have an idea of how much I have been reprimanded because I could not but agree with some of the things that the letter contains.)[31]

Thus, despite the commentator's naïveté, her discomfort in taking up the pen, and the paucity of her style, clearly Merlin's letter must have struck a chord in her heart.

This is why at the end of the first letter she uses denial as a defense mechanism, contrasting the image of "languor" with the domestic activity of her peers. Resisting Merlin's stereotype of an "uncivilized" colonial subject, "Serafina" holds up the domestic ideal that relieves women of all responsibility for their own development, making "Chucha" herself the embodiment of the *ángel del hogar*: "tan hacendosa, tan incansable" ("so diligent, so indefatigable").[32] However, proof that this model is not at all satisfactory comes at the end of the letter when "Serafina" admits that she divides her attention between her routine chores at home and her fledging attempts at writing. This conflict is made even more pronounced when "Serafina" acknowledges that writing serves as a means to widen the limits of the home, all the while she ironically denies Merlin's stereotypical characterization:

> Adiós, Chucha, de mi vida, aunque son las diez de la mañana, dura el ardor del sol y soy habanera, ya ves que no es imposible dedicarme á nada, como dice la Condesa cuando te escribo esta larga carta, y que no paso el día en el baño, comiendo fruta, ni sentada en la butaca, *cuando dejo la aguja por un momento para dirigirte los presentes renglones.*

> (So long, my dear Chucha. Though it is only ten o'clock in the morning as I write this letter, the heat of the sun continues and because I am from Havana, it is impossible to do anything, as the Countess says, and I don't spend the whole day in the bathroom, eating fruit or sitting in an easy chair, *when I stop my needlework for a moment to send you these lines.*)[33] (Emphasis added)

The conflict dissolves, however, with the introduction of the male point of view, represented by the lively "cronista del Buen Tono." Agreeing with Tanco's characterization of Merlin in his *Refutacion*, the ubiquitous commentator in the *Diario* considers Tanco's description of Creole women as a "crónica fantástica extrangera."[34] More sophisticated in literary matters than the youthful "Serafina," a clear sign of his gender identity, the improvised chronicler then mercilessly dismantles Merlin's idyllic portrait by means of parody and biting wit:

> En esas vaporosas regiones del cerebro, la criolla aparece frágil como la caña, flexible como el bejuco, lánguida como el sauce, su cabellera negra y lustrosa debe cobijarle hasta los pies como el manto de la noche; y de sus ojos rasgados y húmedos como los de la gacela, solo en circunstancias extraordinarias, en que la emocion le da fuerza para alzar los párpados, se escapan miradas relampagueantes [d]e pasion o de fiereza.

> (In those ethereal regions of the brain, the Creole woman seems fragile as sugar cane, as flexible as rattan, as languid as a willow, her black and lustrous hair covers her down to her feet like a night veil; and her almond and humid eyes similar to a gazelle's, only in extraordinary circumstances, when emotion gives her strength to raise her lids, emit sparkling gazes of passion or fierceness.)[35]

By means of a persistent tone of mockery, the Cultured Chronicler associates the feminine "languor" with the stereotypical excess of passion that
supposedly lumps all women into a single subject category. Nevertheless, the effect of such irony and hyperbole is not to liberate women, but,
on the contrary to cast a shadow across any attempt at female independence, however slight. Even the smallest step toward liberation from
women's traditional role, claims the witty commentator, already threat-
ens to produce a monster:

> Por una rara contradiccion, este mismo ser en quien está poetisada la
> debilidad y la indolencia, de pronto se despierta, y despliega las más
> enérgicas facultades, como la serpiente dormida sobre las flores, al sen-
> tir la huella del viagero, desenvuelve de pronto sus anillos, y se agita
> con la velocidad flameante de las llamas.

> (Because of a rare contradiction, this same being in whom weakness
> and indolence are poeticized, suddenly awakens, and she unfolds the
> most energetic faculties, like a snake sleeping on a flower bed that,
> upon sensing the traveler's footstep, suddenly unwraps its coils and
> moves about at the blazing speed of a flame.)[36]

These exaggerated and grotesque images conjure up the woman writer,
who alone can "unfold the most energetic faculties" in self-defense as
well as to champion her own sex and condition. Read in this light, the
passage from the *Diario* could very well cloak a veiled allusion to "Serafina" herself, who had unmasked her innocence in public and even sided
with woman's creative spirit—a plausible explanation inasmuch as her
replies had appeared in the *Faro Industrial* three days previously. The last
quotation could also refer to Merlin, given the obvious mockery of the
"madwoman in the attic's" intellectual fire, which is clearly a parody of
the flaming self-portrait traced in *Mis doce primeros años*, a work widely
circulated in Havana and hence familiar to readers in the island.[37]

Despite his downplaying of women artists, the "cronista del Buen
Tono" recognized in Merlin's writing the usual preoccupation of European Romanticism with America as a bountiful paradise; hence, of all
her commentators he was the only one who did not attribute to her a lack
of knowledge of local affairs, but rather a rhetorical excess. In keeping with
the del Monte circle's penchant for realism yet introducing his own light-
hearted tone, he transmutes in his review the famous image of a woman

sensually eating fruit to a second parodic degree, creating an effect of mimicry meant to undermine the originating force of Merlin's stereotype:

> El ardor de nuestro clima exige tambien el refrigerio de las frutas, que la naturaleza ha producido en nuestro suelo para el caso. Pero de esto á pintar á las habaneras, cual las almas del paraiso de los indios, siempre meciendose y comiendo frutas, hay tanta distancia, como en suponer que del encierro en que vive, se lanza a arrastrar los ardores del sol, cual otro héroe la furia de las balas, en cuya atrevida metafora me parece que se exaltó la vena épica de la escritora.

> (The heat of our climate also demands the refrigeration of fruits that nature has produced in our soil to soothe us. But to go from this to depict Havana women as souls from the Indians' paradise, always rocking and eating fruits, is as great a gap as supposing that the confinement in which she lives leads her to drag along the heat of the sun, just as a hero would seek the fury of the bullet, a metaphor in which, it seems, the epic vein of the writer was by far too exalted.)[38]

The writer topples in one fell swoop Merlin's stereotypical characterization and then proceeds "to put her in her place"—that is, the place ideologically destined to Everywoman, that of the domestic angel—by juxtaposing his critique of artistic creation with a monotonous litany of domestic chores:

> ¿Y quién cose la ropa? ¿quién gobierna la casa? ¿quien atiende a los chiquillos? ¿quién dispone la comida? ¿quien cuida [a] los enfermos? ¿quien corre con el gasto? . . . Confesemos que al escribir tan bello idilio, la señora Merlin se olvidó de todas las necesidades de la vida.

> (And who sews the clothes? Who manages the household? Who tends to the children's needs? Who prepares the food? Who takes care of the sick? Who is responsible for the expenses? . . . Let us confess that when writing such a beautiful pastoral poem, Mrs. Merlin forgot all of life's basics.)[39]

Though "Serafina" had also resisted Merlin's idealization by means of the domestic ideal, this commentator passes judgment on the woman who transgresses the fulfillment of her domestic duties, thus keeping her enclosed within the narrow confines of the patriarchal order.

By far the most controversial part of the letter to Sand pertains
to marriage rites. The overt discrepancy here between Merlin and her
Creole interlocutors with regard to the feminine ideal reflects the difference in perspective between Europe and America. Though earlier she
had praised the sensuousness of the Creoles, Merlin adopted a more
repressive standpoint when she described the white women's voluptuous
excess alongside the slaves' unabashed nudity: "los negros que estan en
una completa desnudez hasta la edad de doce años" ("the blacks go completely naked until they are twelve years old").[40] However, if we believe
the critical notes appended by the *Diario*'s editor, such a view is a distortion of reality:

> Sentimos tener que rectificar esta opinion de nuestra apreciable compa-
> trióta [*sic*] porque no es cierto que estén en completa desnudez y á la
> vista de todos la gente de color hasta la edad de doce años. Solo en las
> miserables chozas en que reina la indigencia dejan de cubrirse las
> carnes de los muchachos ni aun de dos años.

> (We regret having to rectify the opinion of our esteemed compatriot
> because it is not correct to say that the people of color go completely
> naked in front of everybody until the age of twelve. It is only in the
> most abject huts, where indigence reigns, that they allow children less
> than two years of age to go around with uncovered flesh.)[41]

Likewise, a smart "Serafina" voices the same objection through Lola,
though she reserves for herself an opinion similar to Merlin's:

> [E]mbellecida por el bello matiz del pudor, [Lola] raya en intolerancia a
> veces y no cesa de preguntarnos ¿donde, en que parte, en cual familia
> habrá visto la Condesa esos negros desnudos continuamente hasta la
> edad de doce años? *Yo guardo silencio,* y cuando la veo tan apurada, ó la
> distraigo con una ligera sonrisa, ó le repito estas palabras de Papá.

> ([A]dorned by the beautiful color of modesty, [Lola] is at times almost
> intolerant and she never stops asking us: Where, in what place, in what
> family must the Countess have seen those black people continually
> naked until the age of twelve? I remain silent, and when I see her so
> bothered, I either distract her with a sunny smile, or repeat Papa's
> words to her.)[42]

Thus both Serafina and other Creole women resisted the stereotype of tropical nudity evoked by Merlin in racial terms. In terms of gender, however, this relaxed attitude toward the body, plus "[l]a constante publicidad de la vida privada" ("the constant public exposure of private life") would, in Merlin's opinion, represent a grave danger for any non-Creole woman. Returning to the charge of overdeveloped sensuality, Merlin writes that only their modesty saves Creole women from sinking into depravity, a quality seen as natural in contrast to the bookish tendencies of her European counterparts.[43] Merlin thus sets up an opposition between nature and culture as the analogue of a greater breach between Europe and America. The passage has further ramifications, as Merlin seems to fall into the ideological trap of adopting modest behavior as the only safeguard against social criticism. As Aldaraça puts it in her analysis of the *ángel del hogar*: "The idea that modesty is a natural (i.e., ontological) characteristic of women is a reiteration of the belief in the essential difference between the male and the female nature. . . . A woman's modest behavior is her only protection against public opinion and . . . her self-restraint is all that prevents society's watchdog, *el qué dirán*, from consuming her. . . . The ultimate social authority, public opinion, is an impregnable power."[44] This need for constraint sets up an impossible dichotomy between the Creole's avowed sensuality and her innate tendency toward virtue: "A pesar de los riesgos de una sangre quemada por el sol, de la franqueza de la vida íntima y de los hábitos sensuales de las mugeres, estas son púdicas por un profundo instinto de honradez natural" ("In spite of the risks of a sun-burnt blood, of the frankness of intimate life and of the sexual customs of the women, they are modest due to a deep instinct for natural virtue").[45]

When faced with such a frank description of the Cuban woman's sexuality, "Serafina" pretends to blush in innocence—pretends, because later she will show herself as very knowledgeable about intimate matters—and points out Merlin's contradictory move of making the *habanera* modest and sensual both. She affirms female modesty as the only socially accepted behavior:

> Aunque yo no comprendo que la franqueza de la vida íntima, sea obstáculo á la honradez y el pudor, á menos que por esas palabras se entienda otra cosa, y aunque no alcanzo tampoco cuales los hábitos sensuales de las mugeres de la Habana, es una contradiccion notoria,

una anomalía que no puede esplicarse, decir á la vez que son púdicas por un profundo instinto de honradez natural.

(Though I do not fathom that the candidness of intimate life might be an obstacle to virtue and modesty, unless one understands something different by those words, and though I cannot also begin to understand which are the sensual customs of the women of Havana, it is a notorious contradiction, an anomaly that cannot be explained, to also say that their modesty is due to a deep instinct for natural virtue.)[46]

But she also resorts once again to her father's authority to reinforce the patriarchal mold, quoting him as saying "procuremos educarla para que profundamente conozca sus deberes y sepa llenarlos en bien de su familia y de la sociedad á que pertenece" ("let us try to educate her so that she is deeply aware of her duties and knows how to fulfill them to the benefit of her family and of the society to which she belongs").[47]

In logical progression, Merlin adds her views on marriage to the previous discussion of tropical sensuality. Marriage is described as an exogamous ritual among members of one class, excluding all outside suitors other than the ones admitted into the family line. In fact, Merlin projects onto her peers on the island an idealized version of romantic love, where marriages obeyed solely the dictates of the heart despite the fact that they were severely circumscribed to one class or extended clan. In effect, the bucolic description Merlin gives of lovers united since infancy is clearly an echo of the infants in *Paul et Virginie*, who fell in love at a most tender age. In Saint-Pierre's novel, the heroine suffers a tragic destiny, dying in a shipwreck just before landing on the shores of her native island to meet her childhood sweetheart, a fate that symbolizes both the destructive influence of Europe as well as the fleeting nature of romantic love. Merlin's version reverses this destiny, for Cuba, comparable in beauty to Saint-Pierre's elusive isle, allows the dream of eternal union and social harmony to remain untainted:

[Las] uniones entre dos jovenes de una misma familia, educados [criados] uno con el otro, tiene [sic] casi siempre felices resultados. El amor mutúo, confundiéndose con la tierna afeccion de la infancia, y semejante al amor fraternal que le sobrevive, no da lugar en caso alguno ni al olvido ni á los malos procederes.

([The] union between two young people of the same family, who have been raised together, always has a happy outcome. Mutual love blended

with tender childhood affection is similar to fraternal love which out-
lives it; it does not, under any circumstances, allow for forgetfulness
nor for evil doings.)[48]

Hence, in Merlin's scheme, what is denied to Saint-Pierre's juvenile protagonists is fulfilled in the New World.

The resourceful "Serafina," however, once again belies this vision,
dismantling the illusion of romantic passion for a more materialistic
account: "no es el amor mútuo lo que se confunde con la afeccion de la
infancia, el que preside a estas uniones . . . que a esas rancias preocupa-
ciones del linaje más o menos esclarecido, se inmola la felicidad del corazon" ("it is not mutual love fused with childhood affection, which takes
precedence in these unions . . . rather, the happiness of the heart is sac-
rificed . . . to time-honored preoccupations of a more or less illustrious
lineage").[49] Contrary to Merlin's benevolent view of marriages freely
established within a specific class, "Serafina" condemns this practice,
since it almost always results in disastrous effects, negating "la felicidad
del alma" ("the soul's happiness") and making women victims of social
convention and economic advantage.[50]

Both Merlin and "Serafina" acknowledge the sad consequences
that strict adherence to the monogamous code of marriage brings to many
women. Merlin again compares the case of the Creoles, who appear to
suffer neither the pain of adultery nor the decline of passion, with that
of European women, who are far more knowledgeable of life and
hence more predisposed to find happiness in a fleeting amorous episode.[51]
Contradicting Merlin's benevolent version of a mutual affection among
Creole couples that is hardly ever marred by extramarital flirtations, "Serafina" insists, "asegurar que esas pasiones no tienen lugar en nuestros
enlaces, es mas que un error" ("it is a mistake to insist that those passions
have no place in our relationships").[52] Moreover, she goes on to demys-
tify the "bello ideal" which Merlin offers as the prototype of Creole womanhood, where the wife reigns supreme as absolute owner of the home
and of her husband's loyal affection:

Como para la eleccion de su marido no se ha consultado jamas ni la ambi-
cion, ni la vanidad, ni la codicia, el hombre con quien se casa tiene siempre edad y gustos correspondientes a ella, la cual le ama, y no llega nunca
al lecho conyugal con el corazon alterado ni con una imaginación incli-
nada a otros lazos ni otros deseos.

(Because in selecting a husband, ambition, vanity or greed has not intruded, the man she marries is always of age and interests that correspond to hers; because she loves him, she never arrives at the marriage bed with an excited heart or imagination that would incite her to other relationships or desires.)[53]

Refuting Merlin's idealization of Creole marriage, "Serafina" exposes the disjunction between the romantic ideal and reality by sadly resigning herself to the fact that "[n]o está en manos de la muger, mi dulce amiga, escojer el compañero eterno de su vida; tampoco está siempre en manos del hombre, esta que por ventura debiera reputarse" ("it is not in women's hands, my sweet friend, to choose life's eternal mate; but neither is it always in a man's hands, the one that chance had allotted to him").[54] She goes on to dismantle Merlin's most cherished illusion of a marital union untroubled by the temptation of illicit desire. Though Merlin seems to deny this darker reality among Creole circles, "Serafina" speaks with such bitter candor about male infidelity that it could spring only from personal experience:

> [La criolla] [n]o se ha visto castigada del amante por el marido, ni del marido por el amante. Severamente juzgada por la opinion y por ella misma, digustada [*sic*] ante todo, *abandonada en el interior de su casa*, no trata de indemnizarse de las privaciones de la vida haciendo participar á los demas de las amarguras de su corazon.

> ([The Creole woman] has never found herself punished by the husband's lover, nor by the husband through the lover. Severely judged by public opinion and by herself, upset above all, *abandoned inside her house*, she does not try to compensate for life's deprivations by telling all the other women about her heart's bitternesses.) (Emphasis added)[55]

More radical in her feminism than Merlin herself, "Serafina" bluntly addresses the bleak realities of the suppression of woman's desire in a patriarchal order where the woman is often forced to marry as a social obligation: "¿como decir que no llega al lecho conyugal con el corazon alterado. . . ? En donde, amiga mia, en que parte del mundo existe un pais en que sea la muger tan venturosa?" ("How can it be said that she does not arrive at the marriage bed with an excited heart. . . ? Where, my friend, where in the world is there a country where woman is so fortunate?")[56] After these reflections, she reaches the realistic yet inconsolable conclusion that "[el] matrimonio ha sido con frecuencia el sepulcro del corazon" ("marriage has often been the grave of the heart") because within the rigid patriarchal confines to imagine a free choice of partner "[es] atribuirnos una felicidad que creo irrealizable en la tierra" ("is to attribute us a happiness that I think is unattainable on earth").[57] In short, the discreet "Serafina" adapts a feminist position quite advanced for her time and presumably her level of experience when, addressing the issue of women's education and marriage, she confesses to "Chucha" that "si la primera me ha llenado alguna vez de amargura, el segundo me ha hecho temblar" ("if the first [topic] once filled me with bitterness, the second has made me tremble").[58]

The last point of the controversy involves the topic of children's education, a point much debated in the press of the period, particularly in *La Moda ó el Recreo Semanal del Bello Sexo*, a journal whose avowed purpose was to mold women into their nurturing role. Articles such as these repeatedly stressed the mother's sole mission as inculcating sound moral precepts in her children, thus preparing them for life in society:

> El primer preceptor del niño . . . ha de ser la misma madre que le suministró el primer alimento corporal. Cuide ella también de alimentar su entendimiento y su corazon en aquellos tiernos años, y cumpla en esta parte con la naturaleza, con la seguridad de que cogerá el fruto de sus dulces tareas.
>
> (The mother, who provided the child's with the first corporal nourishment, must be his first teacher. She must also be careful to nourish his intellect and his heart during those tender years, and to comply with nature as far as these things are concerned, with the assurance that she will reap the fruit of such sweet tasks.)[59]

Merlin's letter to Sand reveals many contradictions between this proscribed role and the real practices observed inside the Creole household, and thus stands as a valuable documentary for prevailing domestic rules and norms. The letter depicts a young Creole mother who is totally dominated by an unruly son whom she cannot discipline, in sharp contrast to the cultural ideal declared in the *La Moda* articles. An amusing scene is narrated in the third *Diario* entry, when the distressed mother begs her capricious "little gentleman" not to venture from the house, a request that the son greets with outspoken insolence and disregard for his mother's wishes. The boy, apparently a preadolescent, then storms out of the house with an obstinate goodbye, furtively fleeing his mother's embrace and eager to taste forbidden worldly pleasures, even at age twelve.[60] After presenting this scene, Merlin judiciously comments on the factors that in Creole society impeded the proper education of minors, thus sustaining her European perspective:

> La estremada juventud de la madre, y el desarrollo precoz de la infancia, perjudican estraordinariamente [sic] á la primera educacion. El niño tiene á su madre por una compañera suya, al paso que la negligencia criolla priva á esta de la energía indispensable para recobrar sus derechos y gravedad de madre.

> (The mother's extreme youth, and the precocious development of infancy, damage primary education to a great degree. The child considers his mother as his own playmate to such an extent that Creole negligence deprives her of the needed energy to recover a mother's rights and seriousness.)[61]

Conscious of the cultural difference that governs the education of boys and girls, Merlin sees them as already determined by socially assigned gender roles: "Con la debilidad maternal, el hijo sale voluntarioso y exigente. El mal es ménos grave en cuanto á la educación de las hijas, cuyo carácter dulce, tierno y suave, se exalta tiernamente por sus padres" ("Given maternal weakness, the child turns willful and demanding. The damage is less serious in the education of daughters, whose sweet, tender and mellow character is tenderly exalted by her parents").[62] Then, in a series of rhetorical questions, she exhorts young Creole women to correct the excesses of motherly love so as to suppress those future character defects that inevitably stem from such unbounded affection. As if anticipating the Creoles' reaction to such a criticism, a solicitous Merlin finally asks forgiveness of her peers in the name of "la simpatia de vuestra hermana" ("your sister's affection") and, in a paradoxical move, goes on to praise the tight bonds that unite parents and children in colonial Havana: "la ternura filial es aquí mas viva que en cualquier otro pais" ("filial tenderness is more alive here than in any other country").[63]

   Despite the fact that in this portion of the letter Merlin provided a realistic picture of domestic affairs, her commentators reacted defensively by insisting on the superiority of the Creole family. Whereas "Serafina" criticizes the negative portrait of the mother who overprotects her children, the "cronista del Buen Tono" adopts a more positive attitude, granting Merlin's point that the *criollas* are "algo estremadas en el desempeño de sus deberes como madres" ("somewhat extreme in the performance of their maternal duties").[64] However, and in contrast to Merlin's opinion, the commentator attributes these relaxed standards of upbringing to the negative influence of European ideas. More concretely, he claims that Jean Jacques Rousseau's essays on education resulted in a shift in mothering styles from "strict" to "indulgent" as mothers absolved themselves of all responsibility for caretaking by claiming that they were merely following reforms that came to them from the outside. In the last analysis, he sides with "Serafina" with respect to the superiority of children's education in America, citing the example of moral rectitude set by the parents.[65] Thus, in this part of the polemic as well, polarized arguments in terms of gender positions—the "cronista del Buen Tono" as representative of the masculine and "Serafina" as the feminine—are joined together against Merlin's sensible critique of the deficiencies of domestic life in colonial Havana.

The polemic reaches its climax when it treats the feminine ideal. In Merlin's view, it is the mother or, more specifically, the matriarch who stands out as the single guiding moral principle of Creole society:

> ¡Es cosa sumamente tierna ver el respeto que se tiene aquí a las madres cuando han llegado a una edad avanzada! La abuela, orígen fecundo de una numerosa posteridad, es el objeto de atencion y de la veneracion general. En su casa se celebran las fiestas y los banquetes; ella es quien sencillamente vestida, con los cabellos blancos que jamas ha tratado de ocultar, levantados y trenzados, preside la mesa. Todo lo mejor, lo mas esquisito, es ó viene de ella, y cuando llega el día que debe poner fin a esta vida patriarcal, se apaga dulcemente sin dolor y sin remordimientos, como ha vivido.

> (It is such a tender thing to see the respect that they have here toward mothers when they have reached an advanced age! The grandmother, fruitful source of a numerous posterity, is the object of attention and of general veneration. At her home, parties and banquets are celebrated; she is the one who, plainly dressed, with her white hair which she has never tried to hide raised and braided, presides over the table. The best, the most exquisite, is hers or comes from her, and when the day

comes when she must end this patriarchal life, she dies away sweetly
with no pain or remorse, just as she has lived.)[66]

However, is Merlin here advocating an idealized version of the feminine,
as Carmen Vásquez claims?[67] Or is Merlin evoking and paying homage
in these pages to her venerated great grandmother, Doña Luisa Herrera
y Chacón, who raised her with the loving affection of a surrogate mother?[68]
Undoubtedly this portrait also coincides with the sentimental memories
of "Mamita" included in *Mes douzes premières années*, a figure which also
captivated Sand in her review of Merlin's early memoirs. Note the resemblances between Sand's evocative image of "Mamita" with Merlin's own:

> Elle traverse les rues de l'Havane d'un pas rapide, et va se jeter dans le
> sein de Mamita, poétique figure d'aïeule, dont un demi-page de
> description charmante nous fait aimes les longues tresses d'argent, la
> beauté majestueuse, le vêtement toujours blanc et d'une properté
> recherchée, la grâce bienveillante et la bonté inaltérable.

> (She crosses the streets of Havana with a quick step, and throws herself
> at *mamita's* bosom, a poetic figure of a grandmother, the charming
> half-page description of whom makes us love the long silver tresses, the
> majestic beauty, the ever-white dress of an affected propriety, of a
> benevolent grace and an unfaltering kindness.)[69]

If we compare the description of the matriarch with the praise that
Merlin gives to her compatriots elsewhere in the letter, it seems evident that the author is celebrating the prestige that the Creole women
enjoy in their social setting. However, the elevated status of aristocratic
women is directly and inversely proportional to the humble position of
the slave; moreover, it even seems to depend on the slave's condition:
"como en todos los paises de esclavos, la mujer está mas considerada que
en cualquier otra parte. Reina de un vasallaje esmerado, rodeada de con-
sideracion y de amor, con influencia en su casa, rara vez es accesible a un
mal pensamiento" ("just as in all slave countries, woman has a higher status here than anywhere else. Queen to a conscientious group of vassals,
surrounded by love and consideration, with the ability to exercise
influence at home, she rarely falls victim to any evil thoughts").[70] In effect,
the Creole appears as "queen and lady," the emotional center of her home,
a privilege unattainable to the woman who lives in the more agitated met-

ropolitan centers of Europe. Both in this portrait and in the earlier one of the venerated matriarch, Merlin contrasts the emotional validation and filial affection of the women from Havana with the worldly preoccupations of her European counterparts, who more often than not are devoted to social frivolities and the cultivation of self rather than to family intimacy.[71]

Moreover, Creole matriarchs experience aging in a more dignified manner than does the "woman of the world," who "es muchas veces digna de compasion cuando la edad viene a borrar los atractivos de la juventud, porque es raro que sepa envejecer" ("often deserves compassion when age comes to erase the attractiveness of youth, because it is rare that she knows how to age").[72] In contrast to the relative serenity enjoyed by the elderly woman in the New World, Merlin laments the emptiness of a life scattered among myriad activities and the squandering of affection among superfluous relationships, all of which seems to be the lot of the European woman:

> ¿[C]uando solo ha consagrado todos sus momentos a las agitaciones de la vanidad y de la galanteria, y cuando despues de haber pasado toda su vida en los placeres facticios [*sic*], se los ve arrebatar sucesivamente por la juventud que la rodea, ¿qué es de ella? Entónces mira alrededor de sí, y se apercibe [*sic*] por la primera vez que no estando habituada á la abnegacion, que habiendo vivido por ella misma y solamente para sí, nadie se cree obligado a considerarla.

> (When she has dedicated her entire life to the stirrings of vanity and politeness, and when after having spent all of her life in artificial pleasures, she sees these successively being taken over by the youth that surrounds her, what is left of her? She then looks around and perceives for the first time that since she has not been used to abnegation, since she has lived for herself and for herself alone, no one feels obligated to consider her.)[73]

This contrast between the Creole and the European woman replicates, in effect, the Romantic debate between nature and culture: whereas the *habanera* is depicted as closer to the first pole, the European typifies the second, and each is stereotyped accordingly.

In the last analysis, the tensions evident in Merlin's letter to Sand, as well as in the responses in the Havana press of the period, respond to the patriarchal division between public and private spheres. If women are restricted to the inner realm of the home, any attempt to introduce themselves into the outer world, whether in business, arts, or social activity, puts them in an irresoluble conflict.[74] This is precisely the dilemma Merlin suffered. After performing brilliantly in French salons and in musical *soirées* in Havana, she seemingly felt the need either to fulfill the impossible ideal of domestic bliss or to mourn the loss of it (for the death of her husband had essentially eliminated recreating that world again).[75] Do we not hear in these melancholy pages a regretful echo for the course Merlin's own life had taken? Indeed, the following passage from the letter to Sand seems to uncannily prefigure Merlin's tragic fate during her last years when, abandoned by the perfidious Philarète Chasles, she felt "[a]islada y llena de amargura" ("isolated and full of bitterness").[76] In speaking of European women, then, Merlin seems to project her own grief over a life that remained unfulfilled: "[la europea] muere como ha vivido corriendo en pos de la felicidad por medio de estériles é impotentes agitaciones" ("the European woman dies just as she has lived, in pursuit of happiness [and] in the midst of sterile and impotent stirrings").[77] Such a level of disillusionment explains, then, Merlin's nostalgic desire to belong to an affectionate family circle—which in the text of *La Havane* becomes the perfect symbol of a Creole "imagined community."

Seen from the other shore, how does "Serafina" and other Creole readers respond to the idealized conception of family life drawn in Merlin's letter? To begin with, "Serafina" bravely attempts to remove woman from her servile condition of economic dependency and argues furthermore for allowing young girls a wider range of action and an opportunity to develop their talents. In the second letter to "Chucha," "Serafina" reveals her wish for women to attain certain basic rights, mainly education, which in her view is given too little attention in Cuba. Up to date with the many essays published in the *Faro*, *El recreo* and other publications geared solely to women, "Serafina" proposes a series of changes that would help transform women into more integrated selves, mainly through the establishment of academies and special schools where they could learn "á coser, cortar, bordar y hacer labores de todas las clases" ("to sew, cut, embroider and do all kinds of needlework").[78] Though at first glance, these activities only enhance traditional female domestic roles, in "Serafina's" view they also could provide a handy source of sustenance under adverse circumstances, particularly after a divorce.[79] Although "Serafina's" ideas do not transcend nineteenth-century norms of training girls primarily for domestic duties,[80] they appear almost daring within the context of Creole society. The anonymous early feminist proposed a unique blend of public and private roles that would conceivably forge a new feminine ideal—"¿qué conquista mas bella, qué lauro mas hermoso podria ofrecer la civilizacion en aras de la humanidad?" ("What more beautiful conquest, what more beautiful fame could be offered on the altar of humanity?")—an ideal thoroughly permeated with incipient nationalist pride: "quien rivalizaria entonces con la muger nacida bajo el brillante sol de Cuba?" ("Who would then rival the woman born under Cuba's radiant sun?").[81] Hence, "Serafina" responded to Merlin's idyllic portrait with her own conception of a new femininity, not yet freed from the patriarchal conception that woman's role is to serve the universal male subject, but at the very least aware that she herself deserved the right to self-fulfillment and self-determination.

If "Serafina" comes close to a feminist position, the opposite is true of "el cronista del Buen Tono," who falls back on the most traditional notions of female behavior. Relegating women to their maternal role only, the chronicler's words are a striking example of the way in which patriarchy twisted the full range of feminine feelings. Almost as if to mock Merlin's sentimental portrait of the elderly matriarch, this nineteenth-century ideologue traps middle-aged women in the stereotype of the undesirable female: "La tradicion cuenta que estas señoras [las damas criollas] cuidaban bien de alimentarse, y de estar nutridas y saludables, para creerlo conforme a los mandatos de la iglesia" ("Tradition has it that these [Creole] ladies were careful to eat well, and to be well-nourished and healthy, for they believed this was according to the church mandates").[82] Instead of celebrating the figure of the matriarch, then, the male position is to reduce her to the stereotypical *mamá grande*, showing her empire to be founded on genealogical lines rather than on inherent moral strength:

> [E]stas antiguas matronas tenian una energia de carácter, una actividad de cuerpo y un don de gobierno tan especiales, que sus hijos y criados eran ejemplos de buena crianza y sumision, las casas, modelos de arreglo y de limpieza, y los negocios estaban tan bien administrados que el caudal iba siempre en aumento.

> ([T]hese older matrons had such force of character, such physical stamina and governance skills, that their children and servants were examples

of good upbringing and submission, their houses, models of organization and cleanliness, and their businesses were so well administered that
they always increased their profits.)[83]

This derogatory discourse, in which mature motherhood is negatively
associated with the denial of female sexuality, is reversed, in part, in Plácido's famous poem, written as a homage to Merlin upon her departure
from the island. After identifying Merlin as the "Angel de Santa Cruz,"
a metaphor evoking the domestic ideal, Plácido begs her to remain among
her own folk. Despite its sentimentality, this poem is the only text published in the colonial press that depicts Merlin's return to Europe in a
favorable light. For Plácido interprets the countess's final farewell as
an unselfish act responding to her deepest maternal feeling; here the
poetic first-person voices Merlin's moral imperative to embrace her children whom she was forced to leave behind in Paris, thus dispelling any
possible criticism of her action:

>—¡Tente, iluso cantor, no es el deseo
>De lucir en brillantes reuniones
>El que me impele á repasar los mares,
>Ni yo desdeño los paternos lares
>Por lucir de Paris en los salones.
>La mas noble de todas las pasiones,
>El amor maternal, el que me hiciera
>Volar tambien á la Siberia fría,
>Es quien mi ausencia proxima reclama:
>Pasion eterna, y de tan gran valía
>Por el fulgor de su divina llama,
>Que ni la puede minorar la fama,
>Ni la alcanza á pintar la poesía.

>(Stop, deluded singer, it is not the desire
>to shine in brilliant gatherings
>which impels me to cross the seas again,
>neither do I disdain the paternal places
>to shine in the halls of Paris.
>The most noble of all passions, maternal love,
>is what would also make me fly to cold Siberia.
>It is the one who demands my next absence:
>Eternal passion, and of such worth
>by the radiance of its divine fire

which not even fame is able to diminish
nor poetry able to depict.)[84]

In writing these verses Plácido failed to see that Merlin's children were already grown and that perhaps she was ready to reclaim another life for herself, despite the deep affection that bound her to her daughter, one of the privileged addressees of *La Havane*. Without a doubt, Plácido's ode reveals how in the patriarchal conception the maternal archetype erases all traces of an individual destiny for women, contrary to a woman's subjective experience of motherhood. Although Plácido's poem pays her a tender tribute, it freezes Merlin for all time as a "woman, faceless, without any identifying characteristics," who "can be safely put away and forgotten."[85]

This was precisely Merlin's destiny in colonial Cuba. Merlin's departure from the shores of Cuba was marked only by a few honorary verses, most of them lacking any literary quality, a cycle that was closed by Plácido's cherished ode.[86] Was the celebratory tone of the odes of departure a sign that the Creoles secretly wished to keep Merlin at a distance? For the countess's continued presence in Havana would have forced a necessary reevaluation of the private/public dilemma of the female subject who sought artistic expression.

Ironically enough, it was the ubiquitous "cronista del Buen Tono" who had the last word in the feminist debate with his judgmental declarations against any change in women's roles. His last intervention effectively silenced the discussion of Merlin's letter to Sand in the colonial press, and no one heard from Merlin again in Cuban literary history until she was resurrected later on in the century in Serafín Ramírez's *La Habana artística* (1891).[87] In a moving evocation of Merlin that highlights her superlative operatic talents, Serafín Ramírez posited Merlin as a model for her female peers on the island, thus echoing the opinions of her early autobiography by the del Monte circle's commentators: "¡Si fuera dable, por uno de aquellos inexcrutables y divinos arcanos, señalar en cada cubana una Merlín!" ("If it were possible, by one of those inscrutable and divine mysteries, to detect a Merlin in every Cuban woman!").[88] In doing so, this later critic offset, in part, the negative trace left behind by the feminist controversy that resisted Merlin's influence as a possible role model for future generations of Cuban women.

It is ironic, then, that Ramón de Palma in his role as the "cronista del Buen Tono" was the only one who grasped Merlin's work as a poetic rendering of reality rather than as a "fantastic" distortion of land-scape and mores. As if to respond to "Serafina's" father, to Tanco and to other members of the del Monte circle who repeatedly accused Merlin of hyperbole, Palma exhorts them rather to

> hacer imparcial justicia á la buena intencion de nuestra paisana y con-siderar que su carta llena de gracia y fantasia en su orijinal, si es un poco indiscreta y aun inexacta para la Habana, para Paris, no solo es el mas poetico elojio de nuestra tierra, sino una noticia mas completa y satisfactoria que la que acostumbran dar comunmente los viageros.

> (do impartial justice to the good intention of our compatriot and to consider that her letter, full of grace and fantasy in its original, if it is a bit indiscreet, and perhaps inexact for Havana, for Paris, not only is it the most poetic praise of our land, but it is also the most complete and satisfactory account of those usually given by travelers.)[89]

This assessment appears to coincide with George Sand's, who finds in *Mes douze premières années* the poetic essence distilled only by women: "[Les femmes] ne son pas poëtes, elles sont la poésie. Rien ne peut être mieux appliqué au recit de l'enfance de Mercedès Merlin." ("[Women] are not poets, they are poetry itself. Nothing can be better applied to the story about Mercedes Merlin's childhood").[90] Though this last statement could be seen as an internalized patriarchal conception of an essential feminine, Sand nevertheless correctly addressed the function which Mer-lin played in Cuban literary history as trace and symbol of an ethereal, though equally strong, womanly presence.

9. Montserrate Gates. Havana. Frédéric Mialhe, *Viage pintoresco alrededor de la isla de Cuba dedicado al Señor Conde de Villanueva* (Havana: Litografía de Luis Marquier, ca. 1848). Special Collections Department, Otto G. Richter Library, University of Miami, Coral Gables, Florida.

**10. Portrait of María de las Mercedes Santa Cruz y Montalvo,
Condesa de Merlin.** Jorge Yviricú, private collection.

C H A P T E R 8

La Comtesse Stares Back

The Many Faces of Merlin in Cuban Literature

Most accounts of Cuban Romanticism downplay and even deny the contribution of women writers to the forging of the national bond. Influential books such as Cintio Vitier's *Lo cubano en la poesía* (1958), which trace the origin, development, and fulfillment of *lo cubano*, a term denoting a distinctive insular sensibility, have systematically excluded women writers from the process of defining a national identity. The notion of *lo cubano* remains ambiguous in Vitier's study, inasmuch as it refers to neither a fixed essence nor an absolute notion of insular destiny. Resisting the term's obvious connotations, Vitier claims that it should be associated with neither patriotic emotion nor a mirroring of historical emplotment:

> No hay una esencia móvil y preestablecida, nombrada *lo cubano*, que podamos definir con independencia de sus manifestaciones sucesivas y generalmente problemáticas. . . . *Lo cubano* . . . no es, centralmente, la emoción patriótica ni el reflejo de nuestra poesía en las vicisitudes políticas y sociales del país.

> (There is not a mobile and preestablished essence, called *Cubanness*, that we might be able to define independently of its successive and generally

217

problematic manifestations. . . . *Cubanness* . . . is not fundamentally patriotic emotion nor is it the reflection in our poetry of the political and social vicissitudes of the country.)[1]

Vitier defines *lo cubano* rather as a sediment that has risen from an archeological depth at various turning points of Cuban history: at peak expressions of a spiritual collectivity. Nineteenth-century poetry provides the means for identifying the strata that compose these insular foundations:

> La poesía va iluminando al país. . . . Primero fue la peculiaridad de *la naturaleza* de la isla. . . . Muy pronto . . . aparece *el carácter*: el sabor del vernáculo, las costumbres, el tipicismo. . . . Más adentro empieza a brotar el sentimiento, se empiezan a oir las voces del alma. Finalmente, en algunos momentos excepcionales, se llega a vislumbrar el reino del *espíritu*: del espíritu como sacrificio y creación.

> (Poetry started to illuminate the country. . . . First there was the peculiarity of nature in the Island. . . . Soon . . . the emergence of national character: the flavor of the vernacular, the customs, the typical attitudes . . . deeper within emotion springs, the voices of the soul begin to be heard. Finally, in some exceptional moments, we catch a glimpse of the kingdom of the *spirit*: of the spirit as sacrifice and creation.)[2]

This exceptional moment is categorically denied to the woman writer, despite the fact that prolific poets like Gertrudis Gómez de Avellaneda clearly deserve to be included within the spiritual plenitude, which, for Vitier, constitutes the height of national expression. Because in the Cuban tradition exceptional women writers have been inevitably faced with the dilemma of exile, the exclusion of female talent has been justified by casting doubt on their "true" literary nationality, as Vitier does when he asks whether Gómez de Avellaneda is: "Gallarda y criolla, sí . . . pero ¿cubana de adentro, de los adentros de la sensibilidad, la magia y el aire? . . . Confieso llanamente mi impresión: no encuentro en ella ese registro" ("Graceful and Creole, yes; . . . but Cuban from within, from the depths of sensitivity, magic and the air? . . . I openly confess my impressions: I do not find in her that register").[3]

The systematic denial of a woman's access to the discourse of nationhood stems from the fact that poets like Gómez de Avellaneda violated the male code relegating woman to the symbolic equivalent of the nation. In Vitier's view, women cannot form an insular bond because they lack men's ability to appropriate themselves of either the lyrical or narrative variants of historical discourse. Because traditionally the metaphor for the island has been female—José María Heredia's comparison of the palm tree with the stylized shape of woman and Cirilo Villaverde's mulatto protagonist as an archetype of the Cuban nation are two notable examples— woman can partake of nationality only as a symbol and not as an active agent.[4] Hence, the female poets recognized as valid in *Lo cubano en la poesía* are those who *incarnate* this metaphor, either by physical attachment to the island or by proximity to nature. At one point, Vitier compares Gómez de Avellaneda to Luisa Pérez de Zambrana, a late Romantic poet:

> El ímpetu de la Avellaneda nos parece profundamente americano, mientras que la delicadeza de Luisa tiene una luz específicamente insular. Pero lo que no descubrimos en ella [Avellaneda] es una captación íntima, . . . de lo cubano en la naturaleza o en el alma.

> (The impetus of Avellaneda seems to us deeply American, while the refinement of Luisa has a particular insular light. What we cannot find in her [Avellaneda] is an intimate intuition . . . of what is Cuban in nature or in the soul.)[5]

Because Pérez de Zambrana never left the island, she becomes in Vitier's account a transparent echo of *lo cubano*, in exact reverse proportion to Gómez de Avellaneda, who in the famous sonnet "Al partir," written upon her departure from Santiago de Cuba in 1836, bestowed symbolic value instead to the act of separation.[6]

Because in Vitier's account woman signifies the source and center, nature and homeland, then the destiny of exile shared by both Gómez de Avellaneda and Merlin is interpreted as arbitrary proof of their non-involvement with the insular bond. In contrast, Vitier grants full literary and political authority to José María Heredia and José Martí, both of whom were also exiles.[7] Indeed, Vitier's recognition of Heredia and Martí as major poets in the canon and as founders of the Cuban national spirit is based on their mutual convergence of the exile experience into *lejanía*—the diffused perspective from afar that imagines the island as symbolic space.[8] In contrast, women writers who suffered geographic exile, like Gómez de Avellaneda and Merlin, are forced to undergo a second, and perhaps more radical, exclusion: marginalization from the canon, or literary exile. Vitier's *Lo cubano en la poesía* implicitly states that the only women with a place in the tradition are those who stayed close to the source and who translated in their poetry the traditional symbolic equivalence between nation and femininity.

The notion of distance or *lejanía*, which Vitier coins, in fact can serve as a frame within which to reevaluate the role of women writers in Cuba's Romantic period. In reply to Vitier, I propose an alternative tradition to be placed alongside the "virile" poetics represented by Heredia and Martí. The feminine imprint in the process of discovery and poetic definition of an insular identity can be traced by uniting Gómez de Avellaneda and Merlin in literary sisterhood, a filial connection not only marked by biographical similarities between the two authors but also sealed by the fact that Gómez de Avellaneda wrote the prologue to the Spanish edition of Merlin's *Viaje a la Habana* (1844). Though both women left Cuba at an early age and initiated their literary careers in Europe, each one marks a distinct literary as well as political generation. From Paris, Merlin maintained an oblique although polemical association with the del Monte circle, while Gómez de Avellaneda in Madrid apparently remained "neutral" in regard to the island's fledgling autonomist sentiments.[9] After many years of absence, both women returned to the island in voyages colored by the political implications of their links to peninsular authority: Merlin's scandalous dedication to Captain-General Leopoldo O'Donnell in the opening pages of *La Havane* (1844), and Gómez de Avellaneda's return in 1860 at the side of her husband, Domingo Verdugo, who formed part of the entourage of the Spanish Captain-General Francisco Serrano. Although Gómez de Avellaneda's inclusion in the Captain-General's company contradicted the political climate at the time, which favored separation from Spain, Merlin's dedication was seen as an embarrassing concession to one of the cruelest figures in Cuban history, one associated with both the repression of blacks and the dispersion of the enlightened circle of Creole intellectuals that figured in Cuba's literary boom. Despite the fact that Gómez de Avellaneda herself lamented not having met la Comtesse in person, some critics still hold that the link between these two notable nineteenth-century women was a literal friendship.[10] Their similar life experiences and shared artistic vocation reinforce, however, the notion of a female poetic tradition operating in Cuban literature distinct from, but necessarily linked to, the dominant canon explored by Vitier.

Though made tense by literary rivalry, the link between Gómez de Avellaneda and Merlin and their shared poetics of memory and longing complement the vision from afar established in Vitier's account as the exclusive domain of male poets, traced in particular in the poetic correspondences between Heredia and Martí. Before the advent of political nationhood, poets like Heredia and later Martí were required to *imagine* the *patria*, conceiving it in a double dimension both as a meeting place of nature and community (what I have called here *pertenencia*) and as a future aspiration: the unreachable island that must be turned into an "imagined community" from a faraway mainland shore. In Vitier's terms: "La primera iluminación lírica de Cuba se verifi[ca] desde el destierro. . . . Heredia hace que la isla . . . se convierta en patria, pero no simplemente como tierra natal, sino en patria que brilla distante, lejana, quizás inalcanzable" ("The first lyrical illumination of Cuba is verified from exile. . . . Heredia causes the Island . . . to be turned into motherland, not simply as native land, but as the homeland that radiates from the distance, remote, perhaps unreachable").[11] In the male poets, the notion of national identity implied necessarily the political imperative of autonomy, as declared in the prophetic final verses of Heredia's "Himno del desterrado" ("Hymn of the Exile").[12]

Complementing the vigorous political pronouncements of Heredia and Martí is the vision of women poets like Gómez de Avellaneda and Merlin, who inscribed into the Cuban tradition the poetry of memory or *la poesía de los recuerdos*. Both women applied a sentimental first layer to the perspective of *lejanía* without which the political dimension would be perhaps unthinkable. This "original" sediment is found in Gómez de Avellaneda's poetry and in Merlin's autobiographical works, texts that trace the departure from and return to the island as the symbolic foundation of *lejanía*. Gómez de Avellaneda's "Al partir" should be placed alongside Heredia's "Himno del desterrado" as a foundation poem for the distanced perspective of *lejanía* inasmuch as both poems initiate the tradition of viewing the island as a desired object and mediating absence. In a moving essay dedicated to "Al partir," Severo Sarduy signals the space of mourning opened up by Gómez de Avellaneda's sonnet as a premonition of loss: "en mil ochocientos treinta y seis Avellaneda deja la isla, sale de Santiago de Cuba para Francia; cuando las velas se izan y el ancla se alza presiente la ausencia prolongada y la oquedad del exilio."[13] The same register of loss that Sarduy attributes to Gómez de Avellaneda is applicable as well to Merlin's early autobiography, for Merlin also described the scene of departure from the island in terms of anticipated loss, in passages which almost read as prose transcriptions of Gómez de Avellaneda's famous sonnet:

> Impelida nuestra barca por una brisa ligera, hendía las alas, todavía agi-
> tadas por la marea. . . . Alejándome de mi país, dejaba todo lo que me
> había amado, todo lo que yo había amado hasta entonces, y sentía ya . . .
> cuán doloroso es para el alma el paso que separa las afecciones pasadas
> de las nuevas.

> (Our boat, impelled by a light breeze, was blowing its sails, still agitated
> by the tide. . . . As I was leaving my country, I was also leaving every-
> thing that had loved me, all the things that I had loved to this moment,
> and I could already feel . . . how painful is for the soul the step that sepa-
> rates past and new affections.)[14]

This departure scene from *Mis doce primeros años* (1838), quoted at length
in Gómez de Avellaneda's autobiographical sketch, stimulated in the
younger poet such an avowed identification with her precursor that she
read herself as a double in Madame Merlin's life story: "Todas las impresiones que nos pinta la autora nos son conocidas: todos aquellos placeres,
todos aquellos pesares los hemos esperimentado [*sic*]" ("All of the sensa-
tions that the author depicts are well known to us: we have experienced
the same pleasures, the same sorrows").[15] Thus it was Gómez de Avellaneda herself who first acknowledged the spiritual affinity linking her
with the countess both as woman and exile forced to cross the sea.

Furthermore, the memorable verses from "Al partir" which every
Cuban knows by heart—"¡Adios, patria feliz, edén querido!/¡Doquier
que el hado en su furor me impela,/tu dulce nombre halagará mi oído!"
("Farewell, blessed fatherland, beloved Eden!/Wherever destiny in its
fury impels me/your sweet name shall gratify my ear!")[16]—have even
greater import. From Severo Sarduy's postmodern perspective, these
verses imprint *lo cubano* as sonorous image, as a veritable *signifier* of
absence[17]:

> La presencia de lo sonoro puede seguirse desde su fundación hasta su
> corona barroca, el *Enemigo rumor* de Lezama; su epifanía en el romanti-
> cismo está en *Al partir*: . . . Cuba, en la premonición de la lejanía, no se
> le presenta [a Gómez de Avellaneda] ni como una imagen ni como una
> nostalgia, sino como un sonido, como una palabra: lo que significa a
> Cuba, lo que la representa y la contiene, . . . es su *nombre*: "¡tu dulce
> nombre halagará mi oído!"

> (The presence of the sonorous can be followed from its foundation to its
> baroque crown, Lezama's "Enemigo rumor"; this Romantic epiphany is

found in "Al partir:" . . . [where] Cuba, in the anticipation of distance, is not represented neither as an image nor as nostalgia but rather as a sound, as a word: What signifies Cuba, what represents and contains it, . . . is its *name*: "Your sweet name shall gratify my ear!")[18]

If Gómez de Avellaneda, as the "stronger" poet, could make the *sound* of Cuba stand for the symbolic associations of the origin, Merlin represents a synecdoche of the source, for she has come down in Cuban literary history (and almost in literal fashion) as a *voice*. Nearly all of Merlin's commentators, particularly early biographers like Serafín Ramírez, emphasize not only the quality of her operatic voice but also its prodigious range of feeling, a gift that constituted a living sign of a vivid artistic temperament and that was seen to emanate from nature itself.[19] Moreover, it is Merlin's renown as a singer—with all its duplicities—that provides a symbolic inscription of nationhood: in the terms of an early commentator, "su nombre es un elogio," a kind of walking hymn to the republic.[20] Thus, Merlin has been granted full stature in Cuban literary history for her performative power as a *singer*, almost as if her voice still echoed down through time.

As a writer, however, she has received less privileged treatment, condemned to the margins of a tradition that values the textual (or pedagogic) over the performative. In this light, there is poetic justice in the fact that it was Gómez de Avellaneda herself who reversed the patronizing opinion of *La Cartera Cubana*'s anonymous commentator when he claimed that Merlin's writings were not equal to the charm of her conversations.[21] Allying herself with her generational precursor, Gómez de Avellaneda assures us in her prologue to *Viaje de la Habana* that Merlin's speech and writing are both on par with each other: "su conversacion no tiene menos encantos que sus escritos."[22]

The shared recollection of loss and the prevalence of the sonorous are not the only signs of a poetic partnership between Gómez de Avellaneda and Merlin. By writing the autobiographical notes that preface the 1844 edition of *Viaje a la Habana*, Gómez de Avellaneda signaled that she was, indeed, a conscious *reader* of Merlin. Evident here is a complicity of readership serving as a means for women writers to enter the literary tradition as well to appropriate it for themselves. Indeed, in linking Merlin to Heredia, Gómez de Avellaneda strangely anticipated Vitier's notion of *lejanía*, by pointing out the curious fate that, in the Cuban tradition, drives writers into exile: "Desgracia es de Cuba que no florezcan en su suelo muchos de los aventajados ingenios que sabe producir. Heredia vivió y murió desterrado, y apenas llegaron furtivamente á sus compatriotas los inspirados tonos de su lira" ("It is unfortunate for Cuba that many of the advantaged geniuses that she knows how to produce do not flourish in the land. Heredia lived and died in exile, and the inspired tunes of his lyre were able to reach his compatriots only clandestinely").[23] From a gender perspective, Gómez de Avellaneda recognized in the French-Creole countess the same contradiction between the woman and the writer's role that she herself must have felt: "Grandes modificaciones . . . han esperimentado [sic] el talento y el carácter de la persona que nos ocupa; y si no han sido ventajosas á su originalidad como escritora, creemos que lo debieron ser útiles en su destino de mujer" ("The talent and the character of the person who occupies us now has experienced great modifications . . . and if these have not been advantageous to her originality as a writer, we believe that they must have been useful in her fate as a woman").[24]

Despite these correspondences, however, Gómez de Avellaneda's prologue is far from innocent in its acknowledgment of Merlin's personal and literary merits. Though at first she censured Merlin for writing in a foreign language ("las vemos con disgusto destinadas á enriquecer la literatura francesa"), in the same breath Gómez de Avellanada then acknowledged these works as part and parcel of the Cuban tradition ("son timbres honoríficos para el pais que la vió nacer").[25] More importantly, Gómez de Avellaneda explained Merlin's linguistic difference not as an alienating factor but rather as an inevitable consequence of a cultural malaise, suggesting that Cuba seemed to squander its considerable literary and artistic talents abroad: "La señora Merlín escribe en un país extranjero y en una lengua extranjera, como si favoreciesen diferentes circunstancias la fatalidad que despoja á la reina de las Antillas de sus más esclarecidos hijos" ("Mrs. Merlin writes in a foreign country and in a foreign language, as if different circumstances would favor the fate that the queen of the Antilles strip herself of her most distinguished sons").[26] When evaluating Merlin's works in the light of tradition, however, Gómez de Avellaneda opted to declare her own critical abilities mute, as if by doing so she held out the claim of her own superior talent. Rather than present her individual opinion, she cast the reading public as sole arbiter of the literary value of Merlin's works, reserving for herself the far humbler role of ordinary reader: "Nada dirémos de las sus obras que el público ha juzgado, y que nosotros pudiéramos relatar de memoria: tanto nos hemos recreado leyendo repetidas veces aquellos cuadros de delicadas medias tintas. " ("We will not say anything about the works which the public has already judged, and which we could relate by heart; we have entertained ourselves so much by reading over and over again those sketches of delicate half tones").[27] The same subversive tactic appears a paragraph later when she with subtle ambiguity summed up her own reader's response to her predecessor:

> Si no hay en las obras de nuestra compatriota creaciones estupendas, contrastes maravillosos, poseen la ventaja de que no dejan en el alma ni terror, ni desaliento. Si no hacen vibrar, hasta romperse, las fibras del corazon; si no fascinan al juicio, ni exaltan la imaginacion, hablan al sentimiento; simpatizan con la razon; agradan siempre; muchas veces conmueven, y algunas cautivan poderosamente el ánimo.

> (If the works of our compatriot do not abound in wonderful creations, marvelous contrasts, they at least have the advantage of marking the soul with neither terror nor dismay. If they do not make us throb until they break our heartstrings; if they do not bewitch our judgment nor exalt our imagination, they do speak to emotion; they are congenial to reason; they always delight; they often move, and some even powerfully captivate the spirit.)[28]

Progressively building up to the final *tiro de gracia* that debunks Merlin's literary artifice in one fell swoop, Gómez de Avellaneda's concluding comment is proof that behind a seemingly solid female literary partnership lay the shadow of the same competitive strategies at work in the male canon. For Gómez de Avellaneda summarized Merlin's endeavors with the following ironic question: "¿Qué se puede pedir al escritor que nos dá un libro que despues de leido veinte veces todavía se abre sin fastidio?" ("What can we ask of a writer who gives us a book that, after having been read twenty times, is still opened without boredom?")[29]

These barbs and rivalries notwithstanding, both women join together within the larger context of the Cuban literary tradition by articulating the experience of departure and return to the island—Gómez de Avellaneda in her sonnet "Al partir" and in her romance "La vuelta a la patria" (1860), Merlin in the two Cuban travelogues tracing her sentimental journey to and eventual separation from the source. The many affinities between the two women, and particularly Gómez de Avellaneda's final defense of Merlin's literary nationality as a Cuban writer, reinforce their symbolic sisterhood. Indeed, the last phrases of the prologue make it seem as if Gómez the Avellaneda anticipated that she herself would face a similar charge among her Cuban peers, for she affirmed, above all, Merlin's right to figure in an insular "city of letters."[30]

If seen from the perspective of Vitier's *lejanía*, then, Merlin's auto-biographies encompass the three ways in which nineteenth-century poetry "illuminated" the nation: nature, character, and spirit.[31] *Viaje a la Habana* in particular distills a vision of nature wherein the seeing subject, enthralled with the *noche insular*, the perennial green of a valley, or vastness of the ocean, wants to hold close the object of its attention by *fusing* with it, an experience of ecstasy missing for the most part in the accounts of male travelers. Recall in this regard this moving passage written at dawn upon sighting the island's shores:

> El buque se deslizaba suavemente, y el agua, dividida por la quilla, mur-muraba y se deshacia en blanquísima espuma, dejando tras de nosotros largos rastros de luz. Todo era resplandor y riqueza en la naturaleza; y cuando yo, hombre [sic] débil y mortal, con los ojos fijos en la bóveda del cielo, distinguia las oscilaciones de las velas . . . cuando veia las estrellas arrojando raudales de luz agitarse é inclinarse muellemente ante mí, me sentia arrebatada de un extásis embriagador y divino.

> (The ship was gliding gently, and the water, divided by the keel, would ripple and break into a very white foam, leaving behind us long trails of light. Everything in nature was radiance and richness; and when I, a weak and mortal man [sic], my eyes fixed on the vault of heaven, was able to distinguish the oscillations of the sails . . . when I could see the stars throwing torrents of light, shaking and tilting softly before me, I would feel enraptured by an intoxicating and divine ecstasy.)[32]

Likewise, Merlin's memoirs attest to the presence of a *criollo* identity that is much different from that of the Spaniard. Thus *La Havane* anticipated national cohesion in its picture of a community of privilege among the white landowner class. Only later does this emerging sense of Creole identity, glimpsed in the poetic scenes of colonial Havana, give way to political demands in a rhetorical reinforcement of the peninsular tie.

According to Vitier, the last degree of poetic illumination, and perhaps the most elusive one, pertains to the realm of the spirit. By ideat-ing the tie to insular territory in terms of a maternal metaphor, Merlin transformed the patriarchal conception identifying nation with fatherland by casting the motherland as locus of origin and imagining it in feminine terms:

> Salud, isla encantadora y virginal! Salud, hermosa patria mia! En los latidos de mi corazon, en el temblor de mis entrañas, conozco que ni la distancia, ni los años han podido entibiar mi primer amor. Te amo, y no podria decirte por qué; te amo sin preguntar la causa, como la madre ama á su hijo, y el hijo ama á su madre; te amo sin darme, y sin querer darme cuenta de ello, por el temor de disminuir mi dicha.

> (Enchanting and virginal Island, I greet you! Greetings, oh beautiful motherland! In the beating of my heart, in the trembling of my innermost parts, I know that neither distance nor time has been able to dampen my first love. I love you, I could not tell you why; I love you without asking why, as a mother loves a son, and a son loves his mother; I love you without giving myself, and without realizing it, because of the dread of diminishing my happiness.)[33]

Though Merlin also engaged the image of the nation as site of prosperity and of racial strife, in these ecstatic passages she nevertheless reversed the *language* by which the nation is conceived, in this way contributing to a female Symbolic.

Merlin's role has not been confined solely to the Romantic period. Instead, she has resurfaced in Cuban literature at critical junctures of our national history; particularly after the impact of the 1959 revolution, la Condesa de Merlin has emerged in the works of contemporary exiled novelists as an eloquent symbol of an ephemeral national identity. Seemingly inspired by Merlin's plagiarizing thrust, Cuban writers of today reappropriate the figure of the countess for their own parodic purposes, thus elevating to a third degree the connections revealed in her travelogues between mimicry and colonialism. Not only are the allusions to Merlin in the works of contemporary authors grossly hyperbolic and parodic in nature, but they also display a wide array of expression, which ranges from simple citation to more elaborate scenarios in which Merlin stars as a caricature of herself. Thus, the parodic appropriation of Merlin's life and works resembles, strangely enough, the very mechanisms she used in her own endeavors to imitate the vernacular language of an emerging Cubanness.

My contention, however, is that such disfiguration cannot proceed but from the strongly misogynous basis of Cuban culture, which fundamentally resists the entry of any woman writer into the Cuban "hall of fame." Merlin's emblematic personality and marginalized status have made her a kind of symbolic scapegoat in Cuban literary history, marking both a resistance to the woman author as well as a troubled transition to modernity. Postmodern authors like Severo Sarduy, Guillermo Cabrera Infante, and Reinaldo Arenas have used Merlin as a site of projection for their own (un)fulfilled fantasies, thus representing her as a radical Other available for literary consumption. Underlying this extreme parodic trend is the traditional *choteo*, which levels the serious and the sacred to an everyday occurrence. However, in Merlin's case I believe there is another powerful psychological factor at work, for by embodying both the maternal and the feminine, she becomes a near-perfect target for the male writer's unconscious anxiety about the origin—a kind of figurative Lacanian object a supplanting the (real or imagined) connection to the mother. This psychological factor must be taken into account when examining Merlin's inevitable status in Cuban literary history as a talented woman who still confirms to the "madwoman in the attic" stereotype invented by the male Imagination. In the Cuban tradition at least, talented women are seen as deviations from the norm of female sexuality, figures having an eerie masculine aura, who never quite attain definitive identity as women.[34] In spite of the fact that Merlin's life story belies such a projection, she has figured in Cuban literary history as an extension of a collective male self that is considered the only valid speaking subject. This projection is further complicated in the work of contemporary writers when they channel Merlin into their own homosexual fantasies, as is the case with Arenas, thus probing a psychological complex at the heart of Cuban culture, a deep-seated primal Oedipal struggle marred by ambivalence to the mother and rejection of the (absent) father.[35]

Merlin appears in Cuban letters first of all through direct allusions to the writer, in which the venerable nineteenth-century figure is remembered as a prototype of patriotic sentiment. Such is the case in Severo Sarduy's *De donde son los cantantes* (1970), specifically the second section of the novel titled "La Dolores Rondón," which is structured as a dramatic dialogue between a quintessential mulatta from Camagüey and two relentless narrators. When Dolores Rondón declares her ardent desire to move to Havana, a move that implies a climb up the social ladder and potential fame, one of the ubiquitous narrators compares her to Merlin: "¿Lo estás oyendo? La Habana. Ella lo ha querido, ella misma precipita su destino. . . . Quiere Habana, quiere gran vida, quiere, como dice, imitar a nuestro ilustre clásico, la condesa de Merlín" ("Do you hear? Havana. She wants it, she accelerates her own fate. . . . She wants Havana, she wants the great life, she wants, as it is said, to imitate our illustrious classic, the Countess of Merlín").[36] An undaunted Dolores announces her departure with her lover Mortal's political entourage, a parodic version of the fate of many provincial women who were forced to work as domestic servants in Havana during the republican years. At this point, the second narrator twists the reference to the nineteenth-century author, a mutation that reads as a sign of Dolores's excess: "Allí está, haciéndose abanicar por dos negras obesas a la salida de un baño de ron. Igual que la 'Condesa de Berlín', dice. ¡Válganos!" ("There she is, allowing herself to be fanned by two obese black women after a rum bath. Just like the 'Countess of Berlin,' she says. Good heavens!").[37] It is typical for these twentieth-century authors to confuse Merlin's name, almost as if they were (un)consciously repeating the negative image cast by Félix Tanco that Merlin was the kind of writer of whom readers could only expect a long list of mimetic mistakes, glaring omissions and misrepresentations. With this logic, then, Merlin herself is turned into a mistake, an "error-at-the-margin" of the entire Cuban tradition. In attempting to surpass her humble origins, Dolores here apes the habits of the aristocracy in a passage that is vaguely reminiscent of Merlin's letter to George Sand. The class contrasts could not be more evident, for it is highly ironic that Dolores, as a mulatto woman, should consent to being fanned by two black female slaves. Not only is Dolores's unbridled ambition critiqued, but the distortion also reinforces the stereotypical image of Merlin as prototypical aristocrat that has come down in Cuban literary history.

A similar tactic is evident in Guillermo Cabrera Infante's "Meta-Final," an epilogue to *Tres Tristes Tigres* (1965) that narrates the sea burial of la Estrella, a black singer in Havana's cabarets who has accidentally died in Mexico during a tour. Cabrera Infante's tale takes off when the "three trapped tigers" discuss la Estrella's final destiny, in the midst of which appears the reference to our author: "Discóbolo que le da la razón a Cerpentier (o a la Condesa de Marlín, no sé: tal vez a los dos) cuando dijo que los cubanos estaban todos grisés, diciendo así quizás en francés que Cuba es una isla rodeada (por todas partes) por un mal de genios o genios de mar."[38] ("A discus thrower who confirms Cerpentier (or the Countess of Marlin—I don't know which, perhaps both) when he said that all Cubans are grisés, meaning maybe in French that Cuba is an island surrounded (on all sides) by an ocean of geniuses, or *sí*-men") (145). Obviously, the association between Merlin and Carpentier stems from the fact that they both represent "the French connection" in Cuban culture, a trait Cabrera Infante ridicules as an affectation rather than a merit. Hence, the confusion between Merlin and Carpentier, and the "fishy" transmutation of their names, levels them both to the same diminished status within the Cuban tradition: they are parodically turned into cultural appendixes rather than central figures. Moreover, Cabrera Infante's ploy underlines the predominantly male bias on which Cuban culture is built. The parodic allusion to the French-Creole countess in "Meta-Final" proves that, in Cabrera Infante's fiction, all women who dared to swim with the tides of literature are considered "odd fish in the sea," as the inversion of her name into "Marlín," a sport fish, clearly suggests.[39] This is further emphasized in the contrastive word play between the Spanish original and the English translation, which puns "semen" and *"sí*-men."[40] Explaining why Cabrera Infante turned *mar de genios* into *mal de genios*, given the tendency in Cuban speech to mispronounce *l* for *r*, Roberto González Echevarría then ventures to suggest that "[*M*]*al de genios* can also mean to suffer from too many geniuses; that is, that Cuba is in the clutches of *men* who think they are geniuses but are instead a plague."[41] What is implied here is that the creative urge sides exclusively with the male gender and not the female.

If in Severo Sarduy the erroneous reference to Merlin marked Dolores's arrival at the apex of *lo barroco*,[42] so, too, does la Estrella signify baroque excess and distortion.[43] According to González Echevarría, it is no coincidence that all the "monstrous" characters in Spanish American fiction should be female: "As women they are representations of nature, within the conventional ideology of Latin American literature, and by being authoritative they reveal the connection between authority and the concept of nature in that ideology. Of course, *there is an obvious contradiction in their being at the same time female and authoritative, which the texts exploit and expose*."[44] Such a statement reveals a strong masculinist bias in the Cuban tradition, including male-authored critical texts that prohibit women from partaking in both the cultural code and the natural realm. Hence, any author who, like Merlin herself, managed to transcend this division would be depicted in distorted and disfigured ways, as is the case with Arenas's parodic caricatures of Merlin (Mercedes Santa Cruz). At another level, and even though Cabrera Infante's piece does not make this connection, Merlin functions as an inverted figure for la Estrella herself, "given her aura as a kind of Orphic voice issuing from the earth,"[45] a description that could also apply to Merlin's operatic voice. The association between Merlin and la Estrella marks the gap between high culture and low, a fissure also signaled by racial difference and historical discontinuity.

Among all contemporary writers, Arenas is the one who most systematically absorbs the figure of the countess to suit his own autobiographical/literary purposes; indeed, in his writing Mercedes Santa Cruz appears either as an alter ego to Arenas himself, or as a kind of projection for unresolved homosexual fantasies. It is telling that Arenas signed his clandestine letters to fellow writers in Cuba with the pseudonym "la Condesa de Merlín," a pseudonym that served the purpose of concealing Arenas's identity in the event the letter was intercepted by the security police.[46] Whether Arenas's attachment to Merlin stems from a profound psychic identification that associates her as an emblem of femininity, and hence of the feminine within, or whether she served him rather as a gendered alter ego in the same sense that Fray Servando Teresa de Mier played the role of authorial double in *El mundo alucinante* (1969), are open possibilities derived from the readings of his texts.

In any case, Arenas's mimetic identification with la Condesa de Merlin ranges from the self-conscious use of her best-known work in a modern-day version of *Viaje a La Habana* (1990) to outlandish representations of the countess in his later fictional works.[47] In the first instance, it is not by chance that in his retelling of "Viaje a La Habana," the third story in the triptych, Arenas tells the story of father-son incest occurring within the context of the homophobic paranoia of postrevolutionary Cuban society. The exile returning now is not a woman in search of her past, but a middle-aged Cuban man from New York named Ismael who is also a repressed homosexual. Longing to be reunited with his wife and son, the errant exile wonders why he has made the journey back, for the mirage of the island only offers him deflected images of his youth and past.[48] The crucial scene of recognition between father and son, which evokes a similar scene in *Cecilia Valdés* when sister and brother almost come to understand their common bond under the paternal name, nonetheless rewrites Villaverde's classic insofar as the son claims that the incest was willingly and consciously consummated.[49]

However, *La loma del ángel* (1987) is where Arenas rewrites Villaverde's masterpiece, *Cecilia Valdés* (1892), from a postmodern perspective. Merlin's presence in *La loma del ángel* is, first of all, a hyperbolic enlargement of a passing allusion to the countess included in Villaverde's original. Second, it is a clear anachronism, since Arenas's ironic novel follows Villaverde's realistic depiction of the Vives period in Cuban history, which took place approximately one decade before Merlin's visit.[50] In keeping with the parodic tone that characterizes Arenas's version of the antislavery novel, Merlin appears as her quintessentially aristocratic self in a chapter titled "El Paseo del Prado," alluding to the famous *volanta* strolls that took place in a corner of colonial Havana and which were forever immortalized in Frédéric Mialhé's prints as well as in "Carta X" of Merlin's *Viaje a la Habana*.[51] In Arenas's version, Merlin's magnificent entry into the Paseo del Prado atop the Montalvo carriage gives way to a primal struggle between the slave Dolores Santa Cruz (whose master had to have been the Count of Jaruco, Joaquín Santa Cruz, Mercedes's father) and the impeccably dressed visitor from France.

First, the countess is described in hyperbolic terms that recall the baroque excess associated with both Sarduy's Dolores Rondón and Cabrera Infante's la Estrella:

> Tal vez debido a las gigantescas proporciones de la falda que portaba la Condesa ninguna otra persona venía en el carruaje. Llevaba la distinguida dama, además de la falda gigantesca . . . relucientes botines de fieltros tachonados de oro, chaqueta de fino talle pero de mangas inmensamente acampanadas, largas cintas violetas, azules y rojas que desprendidas del cuello partían hacia todos los sitios; el brillo y color de diversos collares resaltaban aún más la blancura de aquellos pechos aún turgentes y casi descubiertos por la gigantesca manta que la hábil condesa dejaba caer graciosamente.

> (Maybe due to the huge proportions of the skirt that the Countess was wearing, there was no one else with her in the carriage. Besides the huge skirt, the lady was wearing . . . shiny felt half-boots studded in gold, a small-waisted jacket with huge bell sleeves, long, violet, blue and red ribbons which unfastened at the neck, going every which way; the sparkle and color of various necklaces emphasized even more the whiteness of those breasts that were still turgid and almost uncovered by the huge shawl that the skillful countess was allowing to fall gracefully.)[52]

The most salient part of this description is, however, of Merlin's black hair, which copiously drapes her shoulders and spreads itself over the carriage and which is topped by a gleaming, diamond-studded comb worn in the Spanish manner.[53] Not only is this description imbedded with literary resonances—"una peineta calada incrustrada de diamantes" ("a carved, diamond-studded ornamental comb") is an oblique reference to Villaverde's *La peineta calada* (1843)—but the presence of the monkey adds a bizarre element that fantastically colors the entire scene.

Arenas thus imaginatively duplicates what must have been the initial reaction of Creoles in the island to Merlin's visit, particularly the initial, enthusiastic response to her performance at the Concierto de Peñalver: "Evidentemente la Condesa había cautivado a toda la sociedad habanera, desde los modestos empleados del gobierno . . . hasta las grandes damas nobles o las distinguidas señoras que la contemplaban embelesadas" ("Evidently the Countess had charmed the entire Havana society, from the modest government workers . . . to the great nobles and distinguished ladies who contemplated her, spellbound").[54] Continuing her afternoon stroll in the midst of a heightened excitement, which peaks with the appearance of none other than the Captain General and the Bishop, Mercedes Santa Cruz soaks in the crowd's admiration, until the black slave Dolores Santa Cruz makes her sudden appearance. The slave then swiftly proceeds to rob her aristocratic namesake of her most precious possession, her luxurious black hair, almost as if to avenge herself for the harm done to her by her ex-master, the Count of Jaruco[55]:

> Pero Dolores Santa Cruz, evidentemente más hábil en la técnica de apoderarse de una peineta que la Condesa en el arte de conservarla en su cabeza, pudo finalmente tomar la prenda, llevándose consigo la hermosísima cabellera aristocrática, y quedando María de las Mercedes de Santa Cruz [*sic*], Condesa de Merlín, tal como era: absolutamente calva.

> (But Dolores Santa Cruz was evidently cleverer in the technique of appropriating an ornamental comb than the Countess was in the art of keeping it on her head. She was finally able to take the jewel, which came along with the beautiful aristocratic hairpiece, leaving Maria de las Mercedes de Santa Cruz [*sic*], Countess of Merlin, just as she was: completely bald.)[56]

In a historical and political interpretation of this scene, Olivares contends that Mercedes Santa Cruz, playing the role of master's daughter, and the *Other* Santa Cruz, who represents a humiliated slave branded as the offender's property, wage an ideological struggle between anti-abolitionist and pro-abolitionist factions.[57] This interpretation hinges on the tie between Merlin's anti-abolitionist sentiments and the Creole sugar aristocracy's involvement in the illegal slave trade, and on the famous finale of the Sociedad Filármonica dance, a scene narrated later in *La loma del ángel*.[58] According to Olivares, when at the dance the British consul willfully steps on the monkey's tail—representing not only a miniature countess but also, by extension, her pronounced proslavery views—this signifies a British victory over the Spaniards and consequently the demise of the illegal slave trade, an ideological ending prefigured by Dolores Santa Cruz's earlier humiliation of the countess during her stroll through the Paseo del Prado.[59]

Not only does this interpretation fail to take into account Merlin's own complex views on slavery, but it also overlooks the psychoanalytical ramifications of the parody of Merlin embodied in Arenas's *La loma del Angel*. Because in biblical legends an abundance of hair is equated with sexual potency, the passage at the Paseo del Prado can be rightfully seen as enacting a powerful castration scene. The intensity of the primal rivalry between Dolores Santa Cruz and Merlin has other than ideological overtones; if we remember the scene, the slave is impelled by a prodigious energy in her strike against the countess, after which she then throws herself naked into the sea, only to be given chase by Merlin bent on recuperating her lost object.[60] Arenas describes with magical-realist flair how Merlin's skirts billow out to form a sail: "en pocos segundos, la regia señora adquirió la configuración y eficacia de un enorme y poderoso velero que impulsado por el viento abandonaba ya la bahía y atravesaba el Golfo de México internándose, a vela tensa, en el océano Atlántico" ("in a few seconds, the regal lady acquired the configuration and speed of an enormous and powerful sailboat that, propelled by the wind, was abandoning the bay and crossing the Gulf of Mexico, penetrating the Atlantic Ocean with its taut sail").[61] The scene ends with Merlin's happy return to France, where she vows to a surprised Philarète Chasles that she will never again return to Cuba.[62]

According to Olivares, "la 'otra' Santa Cruz, la 'negra' Dolores . . . es responsable de la expulsión de la 'blanca' Santa Cruz, enriqueciéndose con este agresivo acto no sólo ella y su causa política sino también el texto" ("the 'other' Santa Cruz, Dolores the 'black woman' . . . is responsible for the expulsion of the 'white' Santa Cruz, enriching with this aggressive act not only herself and her political cause, but also the text").[63] Understood on a purely literary level, however, it is telling that this fantastic scene evokes the distortions that Tanco y Bosmeniel and other critics attribute to Merlin's own travel account. At another level, such an "expulsion" from the text suggests, once again, a notion of female castration, as in Arenas's novel both Merlin's person and work are banished forever from the island's borders. If the countess can never return to the island of Cuba, the male imagination can keep on fantasizing with increased assurance about the creative impotence of the woman writer, echoed in Arenas's *El color del verano* when the narrator maliciously affirms the nineteenth-century claim made in *La Cartera Cubana* that Merlin was not the true author of her works.[64] In this sense, then, the black voice represented by Dolores Santa Cruz, instead of being a liberating force, plays rather into the male-dominated tradition and its consequent exclusion of women authors from the text.[65] Recalling Cabrera Infante's terms, when faced with the impossibility of becoming "sea/men," Merlin is necessarily forced ashore, settling down with the mediocre Chasles and "the signifying monkey," passively resigned to pass the rest of her days in silence.

Arenas's later fiction, written in exile, progressively distorts the image of Merlin in Cuban literature. In *El color del verano* (1991), a fantasy of homosexual eroticism set in a futuristic Cuba still ruled by Fidel Castro, Merlin's person is converted into a "floating signifier" in the same way as la Estrella in Cabrera Infante's "Meta-Final."[66] The most experimental of Arenas' fiction, *El color del verano* is composed of fragments that spread out in radial fashion, forming part of the narrative pentagon with which Arenas deployed the historical cycle of the Cuban revolution. In the midst of carnival celebrations in Havana, a series of aggressively effeminate gays or "locas de atar" ("drag queens"), go in search of adventure in the night, colliding with official representatives of the regime and with Castro's elaborate rituals of power. After the revolution, Arenas's narrator assures us, the graceful Montalvo mansion suddenly gets converted into a gigantic urinal, thanks to the wise property distribution supervised by the Urban Reform laws.[67] To the critique of Cuban socialism is added the subversive charge of the eschatological, for it is there that hordes of Havana homosexuals carry out their nightly orgies. In the midst of this

hedonistic splendor, Arenas pictures Merlin's dramatic second return to
her parental home:

> En ese instante, una voz de mezzo-soprano, tan potente que paralizó a
> todos los que orinaban, retumbó en el gigantesco urinario. Todos los
> urinantes . . . se volvieron y contemplaron con asombro a una
> esquelética dama ya de edad madura completamente ataviada al estilo
> francés de mediados del siglo XIX quien, colocada en el centro del uri-
> nario, cantaba. Era María Mercedes de Santa Cruz [sic], condesa de
> Merlin, quien ciento cincuenta años después, conminada por la nostal-
> gia y la furia, regresaba a su casa habanera por segunda vez con el fin
> específico de cantar de nuevo allí la opera Norma compuesta por
> Bellini en 1831.

> (At that moment, a mezzo-soprano voice, so potent that it paralyzed
> everybody who was urinating, resounded in the gigantic urinal. All the
> urinating men . . . turned around and stared in amazement at the skele-
> tal lady of ripe old age decked out in the French style of the mid-nine-
> teen hundreds who, placed at the center of the urinal, was singing. It
> was Maria Mercedes de Santa Cruz [sic], Countess of Merlin, who after
> one hundred and fifty years, threatened by nostalgia and fury, was
> returning to her Havana home for the second time with the specific
> aim of singing there again the opera *Norma* composed by Bellini in
> 1831.)[68]

During the summer of 1999, in Arenas's parodic account Merlin tri-
umphantly stages a repeat performance at her old palatial home:

> Ninguna *Norma* alcanzará jamás la altura y el rigor, el sentido armóni-
> co y el matiz dramático, que María de las Mercedes de Santa Cruz [sic]
> le insufló a esa ópera en aquel gigastesco urinario. La magia inundaba
> todo el palacio; la Condesa de Merlin volvía a triunfar.

> (No *Norma* would ever be able to reach the height and rigor, the har-
> monious sense and the dramatic nuance, that Maria de las Mercedes de
> Santa Cruz [sic] breathed into that opera in that gigantic urinal. Magic
> inundated the whole palace; the Countess of Merlin had triumphed
> once more.)[69]

This hyperbolic (mis)representation at the very least honors the historical import of the countess's talent, for the famous Concierto de Peñalver

had precisely featured Merlin and her rival Sra. Osorio singing a duet from *Norma*.[70] Madame Merlin's operatic triumph amidst the delighted sighs of the copulating men could thus signal the victory of the transgressive and the marginal as forms of resistance to the oppressive Castro regime. This positive evaluation is countered, however, in those portions of *El color del verano* than deny Merlin the basic right to authorship; following the earlier reversion of the *La Cartera Cubana* article, Arenas adds that "se le había entregado [a Merlin] también el Premio Nobel de Literatura precisamente por aquellas novelas que nunca había escrito" ("she had won the Nobel Prize for Literature precisely on account of those novels she had never written").[71] In an earlier fragment of the novel dedicated to "La Condesa de Merlin," Arenas gives a capsule summary of her autobiography, quoting passages in French from *Souvenirs et Mémoires* and endowing the countess with the gift of longevity; in this version, she survives not only her exile in Paris but also the intense rivalry of "Zebro Sardoya," a writer from Camagüey nicknamed "la Chelo" who is described as "uno de los maricones más temibles de la tierra" ("one of the most deadly faggots to ever walk the earth"), an unfair, if clear, allusion to Severo Sarduy.[72]

Yet another scene of *El color del verano* presents a powerful rewriting of Merlin's *Mis doce primeros años*: there, "la Tétrica Mofeta" ("The Sullen Skunk"), one of Arenas's many alteregos, ruthlessly destroys the famed convent of Santa Clara where the young Mercedes Santa Cruz was temporarily held captive under her father's orders. In a scene pointedly entitled "El hueco de Clara" ("Clara's Cave"), Arenas first of all transgresses notions of historical accuracy, for he alters the tale of juvenile entrapment and escape into one of outright violence. The four homosexual characters find themselves not in Old Havana, as they supposed, but rather "en la sede central del convento de las Monjas de Santa Clara, sede en la cual se habían refugiado las monjas villaclareñas luego que la Condesa de Merlin le pegó fuego al convento provincial" ("inside the main convent of the nuns of Santa Clara, in which the nuns from Villaclara had taken refuge after the Countess of Merlin had set ablaze the provincial convent").[73] Second of all, when la Tétrica Mofeta discovers the lost treasures of the convent, the scene acquires pronounced sexual overtones, beginning with the allusion to the female sex already indicated in the title and ending with the suggestion of feminine intimacy: "Esto es una verdadera mina—dijo Mahoma la astuta" ("This is a true gold mine—said Mahoma, the astute one").[74] The sacred zone of the convent distils an aura of virginity accumulated over time by the many nuns whose lives silently transpired there—"aunque era imposible hacer un inventario de todo lo que durante siglos las monjas habían acumulado pacientemente y habían tenido que abandonar en menos de veinteicuatro horas" ("though it was impossible to make an inventory of everything that the nuns had patiently accumulated throughout the years, and which they had to abandon in less than twenty-four hours") [75]—thus reinforcing the metaphorical equation between cloistered space and female sanctuary.

When the motley crew of invaders attempts to sack the convent of all its treasures, they must enlarge the space in order to get the booty out: "Casi todos se dieron a la tarea, ya no tan difícil, de agrandar el agujero de Clara para poder realizar el tráfico" ("Almost everyone took upon himself the now not so difficult task of enlarging Clara's cavity in order to do the trading").[76] They do so with the help of protruding objects like the empty green bottles stored in a cellar which la Tétrica venerates in a public display of phallic devotion: "Eran cientos de botellas de un verde primaveral, gruesas y resistentes. La Tétrica Mofeta se arrodilló ante aquellas botellas vacías con tal devoción (nunca antes allí manifestada) que hasta las paredes del viejo convento parecían estremecerse") ("There were hundreds of bottles the green color of Spring, thick and resistant. The Sullen Skunk knelt down before those empty bottles with such devotion [as was never disclosed before] that the walls of the old convent seemed to shake").[77] Hence, if the convent itself evokes the sumptuous folds of female sexuality, the bottles stand supreme as obvious symbols of phallic domination that pierce the inner sanctuary of the female space. The convent is systematically demolished by "locas, cheos, niños, putas y ancianos" ("crazy women, *cheos*, children, whores, and old people") who sacrilegiously tear down statues, wooden crosses, religious books, and other time-venerated artifacts, a scene which suggests the invasion of the inscrutable female by male homosexuals in an obsessive search for their own (impossible) femininity.[78] Since the *loca de atar* or drag queen inhabiting Arenas's fiction secretly identifies himself as a woman trapped in a male body—hence his intense desire to be(come) a woman[79]—the destruction of the Santa Clara convent suggests the transsexual's violent appropriation of the feminine in a desperate attempt to establish at least a precarious sense of an alternative sexual identity.

The destruction of the Santa Clara convent also incorporates a harsh social critique of "the culture that the revolution created,"[80] for the once sacred place is swiftly and mercilessly ransacked in defiance of any sense of propriety and cultural value, a transgression made worse by the complicity of the neighborhood committees.[81] The character of la Tétrica Mofeta even goes so far as to use the precious wood to construct (her)himself a *barbacoa*, a makeshift attic used to alleviate the severe housing shortage in Havana.[82] This fictional scene has its "real" counterpart in Arenas's autobiography, *Antes que anochezca* (1992); however, the relentless destruction of the Santa Clara convent in both novel and memoir bear so many curious resemblances that it is impossible to distinguish fact from fiction.[83] Such systematic erosion of traditional cultural values goes hand in hand with Arenas's transgression against the heterosexual norm; these passages move the reader with regret for the loss of the Convento de Santa Clara both as a residue of the colonial past and as a nostalgic trace of Mercedes Santa Cruz.[84]

Toward the end of *El color del verano*, the eschatological portrait of the Romantic visitor is subsumed into a final apocalyptic scene. At the climactic moment when they are about to topple Castro's regime, the Cubans consider the many political options open to them, weighing in their minds the energetic appeal from Madame la Comtesse Merlin: "que había izado la bandera francesa en su volanta, [y] proclamaba que Fifo debía ser guillotinado" ("that the French flag was flying in a big wheeled cart [and] it was proclaiming that Fifo [Fidel] must be guillotined").[85] At this point, and without reaching any concerted solution, the Cubans finally manage to pry the island off its terrestrial platform, floating on the high seas with their portable nation only to sink forever into the depths of the ocean.[86] The nihilistic overtones of this scene place it as a counter-discourse to the utopian ending of Cabrera Infante's *Vista del amanecer en el trópico* (*View of Dawn in the Tropics*) (1974), where the island remains intact even after enduring the strain of every conceivable kind of oppressive regime—from Spanish colonialism to the present.[87] This apocalyptic scene, then, seals the fate of the Cuban nation as a perpetual battle of wills.

Arenas's problematic translation of Merlin into his own novelistic idiom suggests, at one level, a psychological projection and, at another, a deep identification springing from his own tortured sense of gender and cultural marginality. Hence, Merlin's marginalized condition as a woman expatriate becomes, for this trio of contemporary Cuban novelists, the most eloquent symbol of their own elusive nationality.

La Comtesse stares back, perhaps most faithfully, in the contemporary account of her life given by poet Lourdes Gil, who pictures her retracing the steps of her beloved Havana in the midst of the warm embrace of family and friends. In Gil's prose poem, the allure of memory is tinged not so much with nostalgic recall of people and places, but rather with Merlin's sad acknowledgment that her countrymen will perhaps forget or refute her.[88] Echoing the prediction made by Gómez de Avellaneda in her biographical sketch of *Viaje a la Habana*, this twentieth-century countess laments the series of misreadings that is sure to accompany her famous travelogue throughout the ages: "Los pequeños descubrimientos que he hecho con tanto afecto; mi asombro y placer en las costumbres de mi país . . . mis observaciones sobre las mujeres de mi país y sobre su modo de vivir y de sentir, ¿qué harán de todo éso en esta isla que todo lo arroja lejos de sí?" ("The many little discoveries that I made with such tender affection; my sheer delight and pleasure at the customs of my country; . . . my observations on the women of my country and their way of living and feeling, what will they do with all that in this island that throws everything far away from it?").[89] By restoring la Comtesse to Cuban literary history, this book has been written in an effort to counter that trend and preserve what has been lost.

NOTES

BIBLIOGRAPHY

INDEX

N O T E S

I would like to thank the journal editors who have granted permission to use portions of three of my articles, which form an important component of this book: "'Las mugeres de La Habana': Una polémica feminista en el romanticismo hispanoamericano" appeared in *Revista de Estudios Hispánicos* 24, no. 2 (May 1990) and is the original version of chapter 7; "A Journey to the (Literary) Source: The Invention of Origins in Merlin's *Viaje a la Habana*" appeared in *New Literary History* 21 (Spring 1990) and was important to the development of chapters 2, 4, and especially 5; and "Voyage to *La Havane:* The Countess of Merlín's Preview of National Identity," *Cuban Studies* 16 (1986), ed. Carmelo Mesa-Lago (Pittsburgh: University of Pittsburgh Press, 1986), forms an integral part of chapter 2 and part of chapter 8. These articles are used by permission of the publishers.

CHAPTER 1: FROM THE MARGINS OF HISTORY

1. Joan Wallach Scott, *Gender and the Politics of History* (New York: Columbia University Press, 1988), 16.

2. Samples of this growing critical corpus include the chapter on Merlin in Sylvia Molloy's *At Face Value: Autobiographical Writing in Spanish America* (Cambridge: Cambridge University Press, 1991); Silvia Delfino's penetrating essay on the Argentine patriot Mariquita Thompson, "Conversar, escribir: dos tramas de un secreto," *Escribir en los bordes: Congreso Internacional de Literatura Femenina Latinoamericana* (Santiago de Chile: Ed. Cuarto Propio, 1990), 117–126; Mary G. Berg, "Rereading Fiction by 19th Century Latin American Women Writers: Interpretation and Translation of the Past into the Present," *Translating Latin America: Culture as Text*, ed. William Luis and Julio Rodríguez Luis (Binghamton: SUNY, 1991), 127–133, and, last, Francine Masiello, *Between Civilization and Barbarism: Women, Nation, and Literary Culture in Modern Argentina* (Lincoln and London: University of Nebraska Press, 1992).

3. Francine Masiello echoes this opinion when she states that "a vast world of women's responses to nationhood and culture remains to be unearthed" in the Latin American tradition (Masiello, 3).

4. This point is amply developed in Doris Sommer, *Foundational Fictions: The National Romances of Latin America* (Berkeley: University of California Press, 1991), 12–27. See especially p. 15: "Without a proper genealogy to root them in the Land, the creoles had at least to establish conjugal and then paternity rights, making a *generative* rather than a *genealogical* claim. They had

to win America's heart and body so that the fathers could found her and reproduce themselves as cultivated men" (emphasis added).

5. For a discussion of this association in Fenimore Cooper and Sarmiento, see Sommer, 56–62.

6. I use the term in the Lacanian sense of constructing the realm of the Symbolic; that is, the sphere of symbol-making activity of which culture and history form a part. Throughout this book, I refer to the Lacanian categories of the Imaginary and the Symbolic, often encoding them in terms of gender.

7. "In the nineteenth century, autobiography is usually validated as history and . . . justified for its documentary value" (Molloy, *At Face Value*, 141).

8. Roberto González Echevarría describes the relationship between Sarmiento the biographer and Facundo as "the Other within" in *Myth and Archive: A Theory of Latin American Narrative* (Cambridge: Cambridge University Press, 1990), 96, 125.

9. González Echevarría, 147. See also Molloy's reading of *Recuerdos de provincia* in *At Face Value*, 26–35.

10. "Sarmiento is not only an exemplary Argentine but he is Argentina, forming with his country one, inseparable body" (Molloy, 148).

11. Molloy, 8.

12. González Echevarría, 7–9.

13. Sidonie Smith, *A Poetics of Women's Autobiography: Marginality and the Fictions of Self-Representation* (Bloomington: Indiana University Press, 1987), 17, 12.

14. See Delfino's incisive analysis of the role played by Mariquita Thompson's literary salon in the forging of Argentine independence. Delfino develops the thesis that Thompson entered the ranks of written history by converting oral speech into a secret written code, thereby establishing her agency as historical subject by means of political and textual subterfuge.

15. Sara Castro-Klarén, "Introduction," *Women's Writing in Latin America*, ed. Sara Castro-Klarén, Sylvia Molloy, and Beatriz Sarlo (Boulder: Westview Press, 1991), 3–4.

16. Examples of this genre include Frances Calderón de la Barca's *Life in Mexico* (1843) and Flora Tristan's *Mémoires et pérégrinations d'une paria* (1838).

17. Scott, 24.

18. "From these private seats of selfhood, Graham and Tristan depict themselves emerging to explore the world in circular expeditions that take them out into the public and new, then back to the familiar and enclosed" (Mary Louise Pratt, *Imperial Eyes: Travel Narrative and Transculturation* [London: Routledge, 1992], 160).

19. Scott, 24.

20. The most recent translation of the entire three-volume French edition is Amalia E. Bacardí's: Condesa de Merlin, Mercedes Santa Cruz, *La Habana* (Madrid: Cronocolor, 1981).

21. Díaz stresses that "Merlin creates a hybrid text whose meaning cannot be fully comprehended outside the system of Cuban literature" (58).

22. Cintio Vitier uses the term *lejanía* in *Lo cubano en la poesía* (Havana: Universidad Central de Las Villas, 1958) to signify the poetic unveiling of the island by exiled Cuban poets.

23. Díaz, "Merlin's Foreign House," 58.

24. Díaz considers that "Merlin's plethora of names is problematic" and questions the use of Merlin's multiple identities as well as my critical gesture of enacting la Comtesse's self-fashioning. He suggests that the name "Mercedes Merlin" is "the one which best expresses her habitation in two worlds," but stops short of pronouncing "any single name as Merlin's true identity." Interesting as Díaz's discussion of Merlin's "paratexts" is, I must respond that this attempt to "tame" Merlin's existential and cultural heterogeneity stems from a phallologocentric concern with one meaning, that is, one primary signifier. Insofar as it is possible in the language of criticism, I have chosen another mode, which is to approach Merlin from the point of view of Cixous's multivocal, multivarious female "sexte," rich in meanings, rich in textures. My conscious use of Merlin's names is meant to express that fullness of meaning which she herself embodied, thus enhancing, rather than detracting from, "her authorial integrity." See Roberto Ignacio Díaz, "Paratextual Snow; or The Threshold of Mercedes Merlin," *Colby Quarterly* 32, no. 4 (December 1996): 247, 251.

25. Scott, 20.

26. Scott, 19, 20.

27. Scott, 17.

28. Scott, 20.

29. González Echevarría, 96 ff.

30. González Echevarría, 96.

31. Louis A. Pérez, Jr., *Slaves, Sugar, and Colonial Society: Travel Accounts of Cuba 1801–1899* (Wilmington: Scholarly Resources, 1992).

32. See the section entitled "Havana," Pérez, 1–39.

33. Nara Araújo, ed., *Viajeras al Caribe* (Havana: Casa de las Américas, n.d.), 7–10.

34. "La condesa de Merlin ofrece una visión colonizante de su ciudad natal" (Salvador Bueno, "Una escritora habanera de expresión francesa," *De Merlin a Carpentier: Nuevos temas y personajes de la literatura cubana* [Havana: UNEAC Contemporáneos, 1977], 48).

35. Bueno, 48.

36. Condesa de Merlin, *Mis doce primeros años*, ed. Nara Araújo (Havana: Editorial Letras Cubanas, 1984), 24.

37. Díaz, "Merlin's Foreign House," 68. He then adds: "Merlin's views often contradict the notions of social and political progress underlying much of

Cuban literary historiography. On several major issues, Merlin rejects the nationalistic ideals espoused by such canonical figures as Heredia, Cirilo Villaverde, and José Martí" (68). Merlin's subversive relationship to the Del Monte circle's nationalist project is discussed in chapter 4.

38. For a description of the political climate at the time, I have drawn on Consuelo Naranjo Orovio and Miguel Angel Puig-Samper Mulero, "El legado hispano y la conciencia nacional en Cuba," *Revista de Indias* 50, no. 190 (September–December 1990): 790, 798.

39. In her essay on Mariquita Thompson, Delfino characterizes the Argentine patriot as occupying "una posición femenina de mediación" (*Escribir en los bordes*, 119).

40. "The colonial hybrid is the articulation of the ambivalent space where the rite of power is enacted on the site of desire, making its objects at once disciplinary and disseminatory . . . a negative transparency" (Homi K. Bhabha, "Signs Taken for Wonders: Questions of Ambivalence and Authority under a Tree Outside Delhi, May 1817," in *"Race," Writing, and Difference*, ed. Henry Louis Gates, Jr. [Chicago: University of Chicago Press, 1986], 173).

41. Homi K. Bhabha, "Of Mimicry and Man: The Ambivalence of Colonial Discourse," *The Location of Culture* (London: Routledge, 1994), 88.

42. Díaz, "Merlin's Foreign House," 58–59.

43. Bhabha, "Signs," 173.

44. Díaz, "Merlin's Foreign House," 58.

45. I borrow the concept of female text from Hélène Cixous, "The Laugh of the Medusa," *New French Feminisms: An Anthology*, ed. Elaine Marks and Isabelle de Courtivron (New York: Schocken Books, 1981), 245–64.

46. Marianne Hirsch uses this term to refer to female-gendered narratives constructed around the experience of motherhood. See *The Mother/Daughter Plot: Narrative, Psychoanalysis, Feminism* (Bloomington: Indiana University Press, 1989).

47. This is the thrust of Roberto Ignacio Díaz, "La habitación contigua. Extraterritorialidad y multilingüismo en la literatura hispanoamericana," Ph.D. diss., Harvard University, 1991, 1–4. For a discussion of the conscious use of French in the narratives of Eduarda Mansilla de García, an Argentine nineteenth-century writer, see Masiello, 40–46.

48. Díaz, "La habitación contigua," 8.

49. See the title essay in Bueno's *De Merlin a Carpentier*, 9–55.

50. Gómez de Avellaneda's nationality—literally and literarily—is put in question in Salvador Bueno's *Figuras cubanas: Breves biografías de grandes cubanos del siglo XIX* (Havana: Comisión Nacional Cubana de la UNESCO, 1964), 365, and in José Antonio Portuondo's "La dramática neutralidad de Gertrudis Gómez de Avellaneda," *Capítulos de literatura cubana* (Havana: Editorial Letras Cubanas, 1981), 227.

51. Díaz, "La habitación contigua," 20.

52. Max Henríquez Ureña, *Panorama histórico de la literatura cubana*, vol. 1 (New York: Las Americas Publishing Co., 1963), 233–34.

53. José Antonio Portuondo, *Bosquejo histórico de las letras cubanas* (Havana: Ministerio de Relaciones Exteriores, 1960).

54. Bueno, *De Merlin a Carpentier*, 55. Cf. Díaz, "Merlin's Foreign House," 61.

55. Bhabha, "Signs," 173.

56. Delfino's study shows how Argentine patriot Mariquita Thompson managed to (re)define herself as a female subject through an ingenious rhetorical maneuver: "enunciar que mira como una mujer y autorizar su discurso por el receptor masculino" ("by enunciating her womanly gaze and authorizing her discourse by means of a male interlocutor") (*Escribir en los bordes*, 121). This tactic is similar to Merlin's directing her letter to specific addressees, thus persuading the interlocutor toward her political cause. Despite the resistance to the term "feminine" in Anglo-Saxon academic circles, this category of analysis is certainly viable in the Latin American tradition, for it suggests an assertion of woman's gendered self and of sexual difference and not merely a passive adoption of masculinist views.

57. See González Echevarría's analysis of Garcilaso de la Vega's *Comentarios reales* in *Myth and Archive*, 46–84.

CHAPTER 2: THE RETURN OF THE PRODIGAL DAUGHTER

1. La Condesa de Merlin, *Viaje a la Habana* (Madrid: Imprenta de la Sociedad Literaria y Tipográfica, 1844), 2.

2. Salvador Bueno, "Una escritora habanera de expresión francesa," *De Merlin a Carpentier: Nuevos temas y personajes de la literatura cubana* (Havana: UNEAC Contemporáneos, 1977), 12. Francisco Xavier de Santa Cruz y Mallén, *Historia de familias cubanas*, vol. 2 (Havana: Ed. Hercules, 1942), 305.

3. Bueno, 12.

4. Francisco Calcagno, *Diccionario biográfico cubano* (New York: Imprenta y Librería de N. Ponce de Leon, 1878), 345. This date is also confirmed in Santa Cruz y Mallén's *Historia de familias cubanas*, 305. In an otherwise scathing version of Teresa Montalvo's life, Joaquín de la Lastra points out that she was short of her seventeenth birthday when she married Santa Cruz y Cárdenas; "Teresa Montalvo: Una habanera en la Corte de España," *Revista Bimestre Cubana*, 48: 11 (July–August 1941), 75. Lastra's attempt at a literary biography not only casts Teresa Montalvo as the stereotype of the lascivious Creole who squandered her life in the Spanish court (79–82), but also unfairly suggests that Merlin merely followed in her mother's footsteps (88).

5. Leví Marrero, "El Conde de Mopox y Jaruco: Noble, cortesano, empresario y mercader (1769–1807)," *Cuba: Economía y sociedad*, vol. 13 (Madrid: Ed. Playor, 1986), 251.

6. Marrero, 250, 254–55.

7. Marrero, "Realidad y mito en la comisión científica encargada al Conde de Mópox y Jaruco en Cuba," *Cuba: Economía y sociedad* 13: 255–56.

8. Marrero, 255, 259.

9. La Condesa de Merlin, *Mis doce primeros años*, ed. Nara Araújo (Havana: Ed. Letras Cubanas, 1984), 38; Bueno, 14.

10. *Mes douze premières années* was published in Paris by Gautier-Laguione in 1831. Agustín de Palma was the first to translate the work into Spanish in an 1838 Philadelphia edition; *Mis doce primeros años* was later reprinted by the Imprenta de la Unión Constitucional in 1892. Later versions include a 1922 edition published by the Imprenta el Siglo XX in Havana, which is the basis for Nara Araújo's 1984 edition.

11. Madame la Comtesse Merlin, *Histoire de la Soeur Inés* (Paris: Imp. de P. Dupont et Laguione, 1832). *Mis doce primeros años* ends as follows: "Volví a mi cuarto entregada a una agitación muy viva; rompí el sello y empecé a leer aquel precioso manuscrito, cuyo recuerdo no debía borrarse de mi alma en todo el resto de mi vida" ("I went back to my room and gave myself over to a lively emotion; I broke the seal and started to read that precious manuscript, whose memory whould not be erased from my soul for the remainder of my life") (1984 ed., 96). *Histoire de la Soeur Inés* is reprinted in the fourth volume of Merlin's autobiography, to which was attached an appendix and various historical notes pertaining to the French occupation of Spain.

12. Sylvia Molloy, *At Face Value: Autobiographical Writing in Spanish America* (Cambridge: Cambridge University Press, 1991), 89.

13. Molloy, 89.

14. Madame la Comtesse Merlin, *Souvenirs et Mémoires de Madame la Comtesse Merlin, publiés par elle-même*, 4 vols. (Paris: Charpentier 1836). The first volume starts with the text of *Mes douze premières années*, then continues the autobiography with *Souvenirs et Mémoires*, recounting Mercedes's residence in Madrid. A Spanish version of the four-volume autobiography, *Memorias y recuerdos de la Señora Condesa de Merlin*, was translated by Agustín de Palma and published in Havana in 1853.

Merlin's emotive encounter with her mother is narrated from Teresa Montalvo's viewpoint in De la Lastra, 83.

15. *Souvenirs et Mémoires*, vol. 2, 31–32; *Memorias y recuerdos*, vol. 1, 107–8.

16. *Souvenirs et Mémoires*, vol. 1, 197–201, 251–53. *Memorias y recuerdos*, 6–8, 36–37. Marrero, "Realidad y mito," 261.

17. *Souvenirs et Mémoires*, vol. 1, 251–53; *Memorias y recuerdos*, vol. 1, 336–37; Marrero, "Realidad y mito," 261.

18. *Memorias y recuerdos*, vol. 1, 36–37; *Souvenirs et Mémoires*, vol. 1, 251–53. Leví Marrero, 261–62.

19. Bueno, 16.

20. According to de la Lastra, this marriage was arranged "sin tomar en

cuenta los deseos de la niña, sacrificándola a su ambición, en un nuevo rasgo egoísta, de los muchos que tuvo en su vida" ("without taking into a consideration the young girl's wishes, thus sacrificing her to her [Teresa Montalvo's] ambition, in a new egotistic gesture, among the many which she showed throughout her life.") (87).

21. *Souvenirs et Mémoires*, vol. 2, 277–78.

22. *Souvenirs et Mémoires*, 280.

23. Molloy, 89.

24. These were Merlin's feelings after her wedding day: "je le dirai dans toute la sincérité de mon coeur, j'avais du chagrin à l'idée de quitter ma mère, mais je n'avais pas de craintes pour mon bonheur" ("I would say with utmost sincerity that I was sad at the thought of leaving my mother, but I did not fear for my happiness.") *Souvenirs et Mémoires*, vol. 1, 294. As Molloy states, "Mercedes Merlin finds her identity as a writer in exile and because of exile" (86).

25. Domingo Figarola Caneda, *La Condesa de Merlin. María de la Merced Santa Cruz y Montalvo. Estudio bibliográfico e iconográfico, escrito en presencia de documentos inéditos e de todas las ediciones de sus obras. Su correspondencia íntima (1789–1852)* (Paris: Ed. Excelsior, 1928), 35.

26. *Souvenirs et Mémoires*, Vol. 3, 147 ff.

27. "[S]es concerts [de la Comtesse Merlin] étaient cèlébres par toute l'Europe, et il ne venait pas un musicien chez nous sans qu'il se crût obligé de se présenter d'abord chez elle, afin d'en recevoir un passe-port de célébrité" ("These concerts [of the Countess Merlin's] were famous throughout Europe, and there was not a musician who came to us who did not feel obliged to request an introduction at once in her home, with the purpose of receiving a celebrity passport" [Comtesse de Bassonville, *Les Salons d'autre fois* {Paris: P. Brunet, 1866.}, quoted in Figarola Caneda, *La Condesa de Merlin*, 48]).

28. Bassanville, *Les Salons d'autrefois*, quoted in Carmen Vásquez, "*Histoire de Soeur Inès*, de la Condesa de Merlin, relato de una mujer crítica de su época," *La Torre* 6: 21 (January–March 1992): 88, 86–88.

29. "Air espagnol," a fanciful melody with a Spanish flair, is reproduced in Figarola Caneda, *La Condesa de Merlin*, on pp. 48, 50, and following; I am indebted to Prof. Richard Bloesch of the School of Music at the University of Iowa for playing the piece. The list of musical events appears on pp. 45–46. Merlin sang soprano in Bellini's *Norma* in 1844, the year her works were published in Cuba.

30. Figarola Caneda, 42. Don Gonzalo Merlin, Merlin's firstborn son, noted that his mother was the first to organize benefit concerts in Paris.

31. Madame la Comtesse Merlin, *Les loisirs d'une femme du monde*, 2 vols. (Paris: Librairie de L'Advocat et Comp., 1838). The biography was published in English as *Memoirs of Madame Malibran* (London: Henry Colburn, 1840). According to Figarola Caneda, *Madame Malibran*, 2 vols. (Bruxelles: Société Typographique Belge, 1838) is an apocryphal edition (64).

32. Figarola Caneda, 65.

33. Figarola Caneda, 7, 68.

34. The episode is beautifully documented in Belkis Cuza Malé, "Viaje a la Habana: la Condesa de Merlin," *Linden Lane Magazine* 2 (1983): 11–12.

35. Carmen Vásquez claims that *La Havane* "conoció un éxito bastante notable" ("the work enjoyed considerable success"), comparable to the level of success achieved by Merlin's first two books of memoirs, which were highly acclaimed by the Parisian reading public (91—92, 93). However, this opinion is not shared by most of Merlin's biographers, including Figarola Caneda and Salvador Bueno.

36. Madame la Comtesse Merlin, *La Havane*, 3 vols. (Paris: Amyot, 1844).

37. The Chasles episode is documented in poignant pages of Merlin's *Correspondencia íntima*, a collection of letters edited by Emilia Boxhorn and translated by Boris Bureba (Madrid: Industrial Gráfica Reyes, 1928). The Merlin/Chasles correspondence is extracted from Figarola Caneda, 181–313.

38. Figarola Caneda, 66, 69.

39. Figarola Caneda., 63, 129, 144–45, 176–79; Bueno, 25–27. *Lola* was reproduced in serial form in the *Faro Industrial de la Habana* on May 2, 5, 7, 8, 9, 11, 13, and 15, 1845, translated by "P.D.E." I am most grateful to my friend Yolanda Vidal, librarian at the Instituto de Literatura y Lingüística of the Academia de Ciencias in Havana, for sending me copies of the entire *Lola* series.

40. Dennis Porter, *Haunted Journeys: Desire and Transgression in European Travel Writing* (Princeton: Princeton University Press, 1991), 17.

41. *Boswell on the Grand Tour* represents this paradigm, as discussed in Porter, 25–68.

42. Porter points out that "[t]o deal adequately with the complex motivations that drive women to travel . . . would have to be theorized differently" (17).

43. *Mis doce primeros años* (1984 edition), 31.

44. *Viaje a la Habana*, "Carta III," 14–19; *La Havane*, vol. 2, 301–12. A Spanish version of *La Havane* is available in a recent edition: Mercedes Santa Cruz, Condesa de Merlin, *La Habana*, trans. Amalia Bacardí (Madrid: Cronocolor, 1981). *La Habana*, 105–9.

45. *Viaje a la Habana*, 26–27; *La Havane*, vol. 2, 332–33; *La Habana*, 115–16.

46. Marianne Hirsch, *The Mother/Daughter Plot: Narrative, Psychoanalysis, Feminism* (Bloomington: Indiana University Press, 1989).

47. Hirsch, 133.

48. *Souvenirs et Mémoires*, vol. 1, 324. "[Y]o, que mis palabras, mis acciones, mi vida entera no tenían mas objeto que hacerme querer de ella y merecer su confianza, yo, que ponía en esta conducta todo el entusiasmo y toda la exageracion de la juventud" (*Memorias y recuerdos*, vol. 1, 79).

49. *Souvenirs et Mémoires*, vol. 1, 206–7; *Memorias y recuerdos*, vol. 1, 11–12.

50. Alice Miller, *The Drama of the Gifted Child*, tr. Ruth Ward (New York: Basic Books, 1981).

51. Miller, 6.

52. Miller, 7–8.

53. Miller, 7–8.

54. *Souvenirs et Mémoires*, vol. 3, 81–82.

55. Hirsch, 160.

56. Hirsch, 161.

57. Hirsch, 84.

58. *Souvenirs et Mémoires*, vol. 3, 74. This passage curiously anticipates Severo Sarduy's theory of simulation, which was, in turn, strongly influenced by Jean Baudrillard's theories of simulacra in postmodern societies and art. Merlin's tropical pastiche strangely anticipates Sarduy's hyperreal (re)constructions in *Colibrí* (1984) and *Cocuyo* (1990). Further connections between Sarduy and his nineteenth-century precursor are traced in chapter 8.

59. *Souvenirs et Mémoires*, vol. 3, 74–75.

60. Hirsch discusses how the web of female relationships constructs "an alternative to patriarchy and the logos" in a "shared female knowledge and experience;" this "all female realm" can be defined as a "female family romance" (133).

61. "Only by accepting loss (an idea quite repugnant to many of her ambitious male contemporaries) does [Merlin] regain, on paper, her country and childhood" (Molloy, 86).

62. "Ma main tremble en écrivant ces détails; mais la douleur que renferment ces souvenirs est accompagnée de deux idées consolantes; le tableau des precieux et derniers moments que ma mère passa près de moi sur la terre, et le sentiment intime de les avoir adoucis" ("My hand quivers as I write these details; but the pain that is contained in these memories is accompanied by two consoling thoughts; the images of the last precious moments that my mother spent on earth, close to me and the intimate feeling of having softened them" [*Souvenirs et Mémoires*, vol. 3, 75].

63. *Souvenirs et Mémoires*, vol. 3, 85–89.

64. *Souvenirs et Mémoires*, vol. 3, 71.

65. *Souvenirs et Mémoires*, vol. 3, 88–96.

66. Hirsch, 160, 133. The daughter's name was María de las Mercedes Josefa Teresa Ana Manuela, combining her own name with her mother's and grandmother's. Figarola Caneda, 3, 7.

67. *Souvenirs et Mémoires*, vol. 3, 90–91.

68. Hirsch, 161.

69. *Souvenirs et Mémoires*, vol. 3, 91–95.

70. *Souvenirs et Mémoires*, vol. 3, 95–96.

71. *Souvenirs et Mémoires*, vol. 3, 182–87.

72. *Souvenirs et Mémoires*, vol. 3, 190–91. This last phrase refers to the

constant threat of guerrilla attacks as the French retreated from Spanish territory.

73. cf. Molloy, *At Face Value*, 88–89.

74. *Souvenirs et Mémoires*, vol. 3, 143. Throughout Merlin's autobiography, Spain is referred to as "mon pays" and even "le plus beau pays du monde" (197).

75. *Souvenirs et Mémoires*, vol. 3, 148–49.

76. *Souvenirs et Mémoires*, vol. 3, 365.

77. *Souvenirs et Mémoires*, vol. 3, 341–42.

78. *Souvenirs et Mémoires*, vol. 3, 373.

79. *Souvenirs et Mémoires*, vol. 3, 375.

80. The revolutionary idea of a female-centered Symbolic order is amply developed by the Milan Women's Bookstore Collective in its important book *Sexual Difference: A Theory of Social-Symbolic Practice* (Bloomington: Indiana University Press, 1990).

81. *La Havane*, vol. 1, 5.

82. See Hirsch's discussion of the conditions of narrativity generated by the male paradigm of separation from the mother (102–3).

83. C. Valdés (Plácido), "A la Señora DA María de las Mercedes Santa Cruz y Montalvo, Condesa de Merlin," *El Artista* 1, no. 1 (August 13, 1848): 20–21. Díaz's essay focuses more on Merlin's exiled condition than on the issue of gender; see "Merlin's Foreign House: The Genres of *La Havane*," *Cuban Studies* 24 (1994): 59, 74.

84. This is the topic of my last chapter.

85. Hirsch, 102, 133.

86. Hirsch, 102–3.

87. *Souvenirs et Mémoires*, vol. 3, 246.

88. I am using the terms *masculine* and *feminine* here as inner psychic polarities, much in line with Jungian analytical psychology, and not in the sense of innate essences or stereotyped roles. However, I do claim that the gender difference inscribed by Merlin accentuates a feminine component, and can be understood as a validation of the female experience. This position develops out of the pivotal text by Italian feminists, *Sexual Difference*, which asserts the possibility of a female Symbolic, as distinct from the phallocentric Symbolic theorized by Lacan.

89. *Correspondencia íntima*, 122, 136. Also quoted in Bueno, 47, 45.

90. Salvador Bueno also points out the omission of all political content in the Spanish edition (37–42).

91. Bueno, 32–34.

92. *La Havane*, vol. 1, iv–vi, 1–5. Bueno claims that the dedication to O'Donnell is also included in *Viaje a la Habana* (40–41); however, I have consulted both the Madrid original and subsequent editions and can find no trace of this preface.

93. Bueno, 41–42.

94. Robert L. Paquette, *Sugar Is Made with Blood: The Conspiracy of La Escalera and the Conflict Between Empires Over Slavery In Cuba* (Middletown, Conn.: Wesleyan University Press, 1988), 240.

95. Hugh Thomas, *Cuba: The Pursuit of Freedom* (New York: Harper & Row, 1971), 205.

96. Paquette, 263.

97. Emilio Bacardí Moreau, *La Condesa de Merlin* (Santiago de Cuba: Tip. Arroyo Hermanos, 1924), 38. The year indicated has to be 1844, the year that saw both the publication of *La Havane* and the Conspiración de la Escalera.

98. Silvina Delfino, "Conversar, escribir: dos tramas de un secreto," *Escribir en los bordes* (Santiago de Chile: Ed. Cuarto Propio, 1990).

99. Roberto González Echevarría, *Myth and Archive: A Theory of Latin American Narrative* (New York: Cambridge University Press, 1990), 44, 59, 70.

100. *La Havane*, vol. 1, vi.

101. The development of a sense of regional identity in Cuba is the subject of Jorge Ibarra's *Nación y cultura nacional* (Havana: Editorial Letras Cubanas, 1981). According to Ibarra, the sugar plantation did not foster a unified national conscience but rather a series of dispersed regional identities (14, 11).

102. *La Havane*, vol. 3, 421–78. See Bueno for a detailed account of the differences between the two editions (37–39).

103. The date is marked as "Día 5 de .... á las cuatro de la tarde ("The fifth day of ...., at 4:00 o'clock in the afternoon"); the month necessarily has to be in June, for in the French original the next dated entry is June 11, which corresponds to Carta III of the *Viaje*, erroneously dated July 11. Corresponding material in *Viaje a la Habana* 1, 14, is erroneously dated July 11; *La Havane*, vol. 1, 9, 301.

104. Bueno, 42–43. I discuss this aspect of the work more fully in chapter 5.

105. Bueno, 38. More will be said about Merlin's relationship to the del Monte circle in Chapter 4.

106. Bueno, 43, 31.

107. Roberto Ignacio Díaz, "Merlin's Foreign House: The Genres of *La Havane*," *Cuban Studies* 24 (1994): 80n.27.

CHAPTER 3: THE VIEW FROM THE HARBOR

1. Madame la Comtesse Merlin, *La Havane*, vol. 1 (Paris: Librairie d'Amyot, 1844), 265; Condesa de Merlin, Mercedes Santa Cruz, Condesa de Merlin, *La Habana*, tr. Amalia Bacardí (Madrid: Cronocolor, 1981), 93. Roberto Ignacio Díaz comments on the significance of the ship's name in his "Merlin's Foreign House: The Genres of *La Havane*," *Cuban Studies* 24 (1994): 63.

2. José Lezama Lima, *Las eras imaginarias* (Madrid: Ed. Fundamentos, 1971), 173.

3. Alexander von Humboldt, *The Island of Cuba*, rpt. 1826 ed., tr. J. S. Thrasher (New York: Negro Universities Press, 1969), 104; Alexander von Humboldt, *Ensayo político sobre la isla de Cuba*, prologue by Fernando Ortiz (1826; Havana: Publicaciones del Archivo Nacional, 1960).

4. Mary Louise Pratt, "Scratches on the Face of the Country; or, What Mr. Barrow Saw in the Land of the Bushmen," *Critical Inquiry* 12 (Autumn 1985): 121.

5. Mary Louise Pratt, *Imperial Eyes: Travel Narrative and Transculturation* (London: Routledge, 1992), 39.

6. According to Pratt, the sentimental account "narrates the journey as an epic-style series of trials and challenges, of various kinds of encounters—often erotic ones—where indigenous inhabitants occupy the stage alongside the European" ("Scratches," 131). In *Imperial Eyes*, Pratt situates the rise of sentimental travel narrative toward the end of the eighteenth century and suggests that its "[a]uthority lies in the authenticity of somebody's felt experience" (76). Merlin's travelogue, however, does not fit neatly into either category.

7. Ortiz, introduction, *Ensayo político*, 79–80.

8. Ortiz, 47.

9. Ortiz, 46, 72. Ortiz even goes so far as to suggest that Humboldt's maternal last name, Colomb, is the French-Provençal version of the Castillian Colón!

10. Díaz, "Merlin's Foreign House," 63, 67.

11. Pratt, "Scratches," 123.

12. Scott Slovic, "Alexander von Humboldt's Comparative Method of Landscape Description," *Publication of the Society for Literature and Science*, 5 (May 1990): 5.

13. Slovic, 6; Pratt, "Scratches," 124.

14. Pratt, "Scratches," 124; *Imperial Eyes*, 60.

15. Pratt, *Imperial Eyes*, 7, 60.

16. Evelyn Fox Keller, *Reflections on Gender and Science* (New Haven: Yale University Press, 1985), 79.

17. Victor Wolfgang von Hagen, *South America Called Them: Explorations of the Great Naturalists: La Condamine, Humboldt, Darwin, Spruce* (New York: Alfred A. Knopf, 1945), xi.

18. Roberto González Echevarría, *Myth and Archive: A Theory of Latin American Narrative* (Cambridge: Cambridge University Press, 1990),108, 112.

19. González Echevarría, 107.

20. González Echevarría, 108.

21. Díaz interprets Merlin's treatment of insular nature in terms of the chronicles of discovery; see "Merlin's Foreign House," 64–66.

22. Pratt claims that "in exploration writing . . . the reverie convention

often very specifically projects the civilizing mission onto the scene." "Scratches," 126.

23. Lezama Lima, 177. Thanks are due to Roberto Ignacio Díaz for rendering a more accurate translation of this phrase.

24. See my article "Voyage to *La Havane*: La Condesa de Merlin's Pre-View of National Identity," *Cuban Studies* 26 (1986): 71–99 and "*La Havane*: The Double Reading" in chapter 2.

25. González Echevarría, 10, 12, 102.

26. González Echevarría, 106.

27. González Echevarría, 96.

28. González Echevarría, 11–12.

29. For a discussion of Merlin's appropriation of the *crónicas de Indias*, see Díaz's "Merlin's Foreign House," 62–63.

30. González Echevarría, 107.

31. González Echevarría,, 108. The concept of the "Other within" is developed in a discussion of Sarmiento's appropriation of and/or identification with the *gaucho* (96).

32. The Milan Women's Bookstore Collective, *Sexual Difference: A Theory of Social-Symbolic Practice* (Bloomington: Indiana University Press, 1990), 38.

33. Humboldt's *Essai politique sur la île de Cuba* originally formed part of the longer account of his voyage with Bonpland titled *Voyage aux regions équinoxiales du Nouveau Continent*, published in Paris in 1807; it was later published separately in 1826 (Ortiz, 79). I cite here from the 1969 English translation, *The Island of Cuba*, translated by the American annexationist J. Thrasher, and refer to the 1960 Spanish edition for other relevant passages.

34. Alejo Carpentier, *Tientos y diferencias* (Havana: UNEAC Contemporáneos, 1966), 15.

35. This is Louis Mink's term in *Historical Understanding*, ed. Brian Fay, Eugene O. Galob, and Richard T. Vann (Ithaca: Cornell University Press, 1987), 50.

36. Mink, 183, 199. Mink later explores the relationship between history and fiction: "Narrative history borrows from fictional narrative the convention by which a story generates its own imaginative space; . . . but it presupposes that past actuality is a single and determinate realm, a presupposition which . . . is at odds with the incompatibility of imaginative stories" (197). Later in his essay Mink dissolves this claim and argues for the prevalence of a "disciplined imagination" to account for the *effect* of determinacy of the past (202).

37. Mink, 187–88.

38. Pratt, "Scratches," 125; *Imperial Eyes*, 61.

39. Pratt, *Imperial Eyes*, 120, 124.

40. Pratt, *Imperial Eyes*, 131.

41. Díaz, "Merlin's Foreign House," 65.

42. Mink, 77, 81–82.

43. Mink, 79.

44. For example, Humboldt claims to "clarify facts and give exact ideas, with the help of comparison and statistical tables" (282).

45. Pratt, "Scratches," 121.

46. Humboldt, *The Island of Cuba*, 283–87.

47. Such a diffuse combination could lead one to question the literary status of this discourse, and, in particular, to ask whether the overflowing river of Humboldt's prose can, indeed, be said to form a narrative: "The *Personal Narrative*, in fact, often veers so thoroughly in the direction of unchecked factual accumulation that it hardly seems any more to be a personal document of any kind—not even a narrative, since events and personal observations both tend to disappear when Humboldt embarks on an extended list of temperature, magnetic, or altitude measurements or a theoretical discourse on plant geography, the structure of mountain ranges, the manufacture of poison from plants, Indian languages, cannibalism . . . or the causes of earthquakes, among many other topics" (Slovic, 6).

48. Homi K. Bhabha, "Signs Taken for Wonders: Questions of Ambivalence and Authority Under a Tree Outside Delhi, May 1817," *"Race," Writing and Difference*, ed. Henry Louis Gates, Jr. (Chicago: University of Chicago Press, 1986), 173.

49. In chapter 5 I deal specifically with Merlin's free adaptation of literary sources.

50. *La Havane*, vol. 2, "Lettre XVIII," 4; *La Habana*, 126.

51. "J'ai avais lu peu de romans, et, je crois déjà l'avoir dit, mon goût s'étant porté de bonne heure vers l'histoire, l'exaltation de mon imagination s'était exercée de préférence sur les grands faits et sur les hommes illustres de l'antiquité" ("I had read few novels, and, as I think I have already mentioned, my taste had luckily been inclined toward history, the passion of my imagination had mostly taken as its object the great feats and the great men of antiquity" [Madame la Comtesse Merlin, *Souvenirs et Mémoires* vol. 1, {Paris: Charpentier, 1836}, 320]).

52. *La Havane*, vol. 1, 3.

53. *La Havane*, vol. 2, 4; *La Habana*, 126. Also quoted in Díaz, 62.

54. Lezama Lima, 27–28.

55. *The Island of Cuba*, 364–65; *Ensayo político*, 304–5.

56. *The Island of Cuba*, 370–72; *Ensayo político*, 379–80.

57. González Echevarría, 108.

58. *The Island of Cuba*, 365–66. "Efectivamente, una parte de aquellos pretendidos jardines es muy agradable; porque el navegante ve variar la escena a cada momento, y el verdor de algunos islotes parece tanto más hermoso cuanto hace contraste con otros cayos en que sólo se ven arenales blancos y áridos. La super-

ficie de éstos, calentada por los rayos del sol, parece ondear como la de un líquido; y por el contacto de las capas de aire de temperatura desigual, produce desde las diez de la mañana hasta las cuatro de la tarde los fenómenos mas variados de suspensión y del golpe de vista de refracción (mirage)" (*Ensayo político*, 305).

59. *The Island of Cuba*, 370; *Ensayo político*, 308.

60. *The Island of Cuba*, 375; *Ensayo político*, 311–12.

61. *The Island of Cuba*, 368; *Ensayo político*, 307.

62. *The Island of Cuba*, 376; *Ensayo político*, 312.

63. Antonio de Herrera y Tordesillas. *Historia general de los hechos de los castellanos, en las islas y tierra firme de el* [sic] *Mar Oceano*, vols. 1 and 2 (1726–1730; Asunción del Paraguay: Editorial Guaranía, 1944–1945). This book was first published in Madrid in 1601 to 1615 (González Echevarría, *Myth and Archive*, 64).

64. Quoted in Slovic, who calls this the "summit survey" perspective of mountaineers and scientific explorers alike (6).

65. *The Island of Cuba*, 378; *Ensayo político*, 313.

66. *Ensayo político*, 282.

67. *The Island of Cuba*, 378; *Ensayo político*, 313.

68. James Suchlicki, *Historical Dictionary of Cuba* (Metuchen: The Scarecrow Press, 1988); *Latin American Historical Dictionaries* 22: 10. Subsequent information on this event is derived from the same source. See also *Ensayo político*, 378n.1; Ortiz corrects the date in a subsequent note.

69. Von Hagen, 97.

70. Slovic, 6.

71. Díaz, "Merlin's Foreign House," 62.

72. José Antonio Echeverría, "Estudios históricos—Diego Velázquez," *El Plantel*, vol. 1 (Havana: Imprenta de R. Oliva, Editor: 1838), 15–20; J. M. de A., "Hernán Cortés," *El Plantel*, 158–61.

73. *La Havane*, vol. 2, 4–5; *La Habana*, 126.

74. Díaz, "Merlin's Foreign House," 62.

75. Consuelo Naranjo Orovio and Miguel Angel Puig-Samper Mulero, "El legado hispano y la conciencia nacional en Cuba," *Revista de Indias* 50 (Sept.–Dec. 1990), 792–93.

76. Jorge Ibarra, *Nación y cultura nacional* (Havana: Ed. Ciencias Sociales, 1981), 14, 11.

77. *La Havane*, vol. 2, "Lettre XVIII," 11; *La Habana*, 128.

78. *La Havane*, vol. 2, "Lettre XVIII," 22–23; *La Habana*, 131. It is rewritten from Echeverría, 19.

79. *La Havane*, vol. 2, "Lettre XVIII," 29; *La Habana*, 134.

80. *La Havane*, vol. 2, "Lettre XVIII," 27; *La Habana*, 133.

81. Echeverría, *El Plantel*, 20.

82. *La Havane*, vol. 2, "Lettre XVIII," 24; *La Habana*, 132.

83. *La Havane*, vol. 2, "Lettre XVIII," 30; *La Habana*, 134.

84. J. M. de A., 159.

85. *La Havane*, vol. 2, "Lettre XVIII," 28; *La Habana*, 133; J. M. de A., 159.

86. J. M. de A., 160.

87. Although, following the dictates of the del Monte circle, J. M. de A. claimed that his historical sketch corresponded to "nuestro sistema de imparcial veracidad" ("our system of impartial verisimilitude"), his writing is tinged by Romantic aggrandizement and fantasy. J. M. de A., 158.

88. R[amón] de Palma, "Don Francisco de Arango," *El Plantel*, vol. 1 (Havana: Imprenta de R. Oliva, Editor: 1838), 44–54.

89. "Su historia completa sería la de toda una época" ("His life story would complete a history of the era.") de Palma, 54. *La Havane*, vol. 2, 32, 34–35; *La Habana*, 135. See also Leví Marrero, *Cuba: economía y sociedad—Azúcar, Ilustración y conciencia* (1763–1868), vol. 9 (Madrid: Ed. Playor, 1983), 18–33, for a discussion of Arango's role in the establishment of the slave trade in Cuba.

90. González Echevarría, 112; *La Havane*, vol. 2, "Lettre XVIII," 36; *La Habana*, 136.

91. Salvador Bueno, "Una escritora habanera de expresión francesa," *De Merlin a Carpentier* (Havana: UNEAC Contemporáneos, 1977), 13.

92. Humboldt, *The Island of Cuba*, 229; *La Havane*, vol. 2, 36; *La Habana*, 136.

93. Manuel Moreno Fraginalls, *El ingenio*, 3 vols. (Havana: Editorial de Ciencias Sociales, 1978); Antonio Benítez Rojo, "Power/Sugar/Literature: Toward a Reinterpretation of Cubanness," *Cuban Studies* 16 (1986): 9–31.

94. *La Havane*, vol. 2, "Lettre XVIII," 40–41; *La Habana*, 137.

95. *La Havane*, vol. 2, "Lettre XVIII," 42; *La Habana*, 138.

96. Ortiz, introduction, *Ensayo político*, 22–23.

97. Humboldt, *Personal Narrative*, xl.

98. González Echevarría, 83–84.

99. González Echevarría, 100, 108, 112.

100. González Echevarría, 99–100.

101. Doris Sommer, *Foundational Fictions: The National Romances of Latin America* (Berkeley: University of California Press, 1991), 82.

102. Sandra M. Gilbert and Susan Gubar, *The Madwoman in the Attic: The Woman Writer and the Nineteenth-Century Literary Imagination* (New Haven and London: Yale University Press, 1979), 49.

103. Bueno, 48.

104. "Hybridity . . . is the name for the strategic reversal of the process of domination through disavowal" (Bhabha, "Signs," 173).

105. Humboldt, *The Island of Cuba*, 282.

106. Mink, 202.

107. Mink, 202.

108. See, for example, Jean Franco, "Un viaje poco romántico: Viajeros británicos hacia Sudamérica: 1818–1828," *Escritura* 4, no. 7 (1979): 133.

109. Pratt, "Scratches," 121, and *Imperial Eyes*, 39. See also Mary Louise Pratt, "Humboldt y la reinvención de América," *Nuevo Texto Crítico* 1 (1988): 37.

110. Evidence is a letter written from Paris on August 22, 1822, where Humboldt announces his retirement plans: "I have resolutely decided to leave Europe and live in the Hispanic American tropics, in a place where I have some memories left and where the social institutions are more in harmony with my wishes" (quoted in Ortiz, 74).

CHAPTER 4: A NATION INVENTED

1. Antonio Benítez Rojo, "Power/Sugar/Literature: Toward a Reinterpretation of Cubanness," *Cuban Studies* 16 (1986): 25.

2. Benítez Rojo, 17–23; William Luis, *Literary Bondage: Slavery in Cuban Narrative* (Austin: University of Texas Press, 1990), 29.

3. Larry R. Jensen, *Children of Colonial Despotism: Press, Politics, and Culture in Cuba, 1790–1840* (Tampa: University of South Florida Press, 1988), 129; Luis, 36–37.

4. Benítez Rojo, "Power/Sugar/Literature," 25–26.

5. Benítez Rojo, "Power/Sugar/Literature," 25–26; Luis, 36–37; Jensen, 129.

6. Jensen, 135–36.

7. Jensen, 96.

8. Luis, 29. Benítez Rojo states that "sugar is and has been the one factor determining Cuban political geography and demographic composition, shaping as well its economic, social, and cultural history" ("Power/Sugar/Literature," 13–14). He ends his argument with the notion of a "metafigure formed by the production of sugar" (28).

9. Anderson ties the rise of nationalist sentiment in eighteenth-century Europe to the phenomenon of "print capitalism," which allowed the spread of vernacular languages derived from Latin and so solidified a sense of close-knit communities. Benedict Anderson, *Imagined Communities: Reflections on the Origin and Spread of Nationalism* (London and New York: Verso, 1991), 43–46.

10. Anderson, 47.

11. "[L]a literatura hispanoamericana es una empresa de la imaginación. Nos proponemos inventar nuestra propia realidad" ("Spanish American literature is an imaginative enterprise. We set out to invent our own reality.") Octavio Paz, "Literatura de fundación," *Puertas al campo* (Mexico City: UNAM, 1966), 16.

12. I derive this notion of "performative" and "pedagogical" discourse from Homi K. Bhabha, "DissemiNation: Time, Narrative and the Margins of the Modern Nation," *Nation and Narration* (London: Routledge, 1990).

13. Anderson, 50.

14. "[E]ach of the new South American republics had been an adminis-

trative unit from the sixteenth to the eighteenth century" (from Gerhard Masur, *Simón Bolívar* [1948], in Anderson, 54).

15. Anderson, 58–59.

16. Anderson ties this development to the rise of the colonial press: "Cramped viceregal pilgrimages had no decisive consequences until their territorial stretch could be imagined as nations, in other words until the arrival of print capitalism" (61).

17. Paz, 41.

18. Quoted in César Leante, "*Cecilia Valdés*: espejo de la esclavitud," *El espacio real* (Havana: UNEAC Contemporáneos, 1975), 38.

19. Manuel Moreno Fraginalls, *The Sugar Mill: The Socioeconomic Complex of Sugar in Cuba*, tr. Cedric Belfrage (New York: Monthly Review Press, 1976), 82–84.

20. Fraginalls, 97, 83. Antonio Benítez Rojo, in *The Repeating Island: The Caribbean and the Postmodern Perspective*, tr. James Maraniss (Durham: Duke University Press, 1992), shows how the evolution of the *factoría* generated "a huge machine of machines" as the core structure common to all Caribbean islands (72). See also Benítez Rojo, "Power/Sugar/Literature," 13. The significance of the *máquina de vapor* in transforming the sugar economy is dramatically illustrated in Cirilo Villaverde's *Cecilia Valdés* (1882).

21. I am drawing here on the summary of these events in both Luis, 29, 35–36, and Benítez Rojo, "Power/Sugar/Literature," 22.

22. Benítez Rojo uses the term "discourse of resistance" to refer to an emerging sense of "Cubanness" ("Power/Sugar/Literature," 14, 17), whereas Luis labels it a "counter-discourse" (27).

23. Benítez Rojo, "Power/Sugar/Literature," 20–21.

24. Benítez Rojo, "Power/Sugar/Literature," 20–22.

25. Benítez Rojo, "Power/Sugar/Literature," 21.

26. Luis, 29.

27. Luis, 29; Benítez Rojo, "Power/Sugar/Literature," 22.

28. Benítez Rojo, "Power/Sugar/Literature," 23.

29. Benítez Rojo, "Power/Sugar/Literature," 23.

30. Jensen, 111.

31. Jensen, 111–12.

32. Luis, 35. For a description of the Lorenzo rebellion, see Jensen, 116–25.

33. Luis, 34.

34. Luis, 35.

35. Quoted in Jensen, 124.

36. Jensen, 124.

37. Luis, 34.

38. Anderson, 61.

39. Jensen, 21.

40. Jensen, 23–24.

41. Jensen, 131–32.

42. Jensen, 112.

43. Jensen, 126. Ironically enough, the traveler to present-day Cuba suffers the same fate.

44. Luis, 29.

45. Jensen, 127.

46. Luis, 29.

47. Jensen, 105.

48. Benítez Rojo, "Power/Sugar/Literature," 15.

49. Leví Marrero, *Cuba: economía y sociedad*, vol. 9 (Madrid: Ed. Playor, 1983), 18, 53.

50. Benítez Rojo, "Power/Sugar/Literature," 15.

51. Luis, 27.

52. Benítez Rojo, "Power/Sugar/Literature," 15.

53. Jensen, 104. This local "idiolect" roughly corresponds to Anderson's vernacular.

54. Not only did del Monte directly promote these works, but he also gave the books to British abolitionist Richard Madden to publish in England, inasmuch as they were obviously banned in Cuba. See Luis, 36–39.

55. Salvador Bueno, *Las ideas literarias de Domingo del Monte* (Havana: Comisión Nacional Cubana de la UNESCO, 1954), 10, 13–14.

56. In his prologue to *Cecilia Valdés*, Villaverde states: "In my writings I take pride in being a realist before all else, using this word in the artistic sense in which it is used today" (*Cecilia Valdés or Angel's Hill, A Novel of Cuban Customs*, tr. Sydney G. Gest [New York: Vantage Press, 1962]) On the basis of this prologue, Luis asserts that *Cecilia Valdés* is strictly a realist novel (103). However, I hold that this foundation text of Cuban literature is a hybrid combination of romantic novel, local color sketch, and European "high" realism.

57. Jensen, 128–29.

58. "The Cuban writer could not even live in romantic poverty by his craft" (133). Jensen shows how even the best of *contertulios*—including del Monte himself—had to seek other means of support in the stifling colonial atmosphere (133–35).

59. Jensen, 21.

60. Bhabha,"DissemiNation," 297.

61. Bhabha, "DissemiNation," 299.

62. Díaz, 32.

63. Jensen, 131–32.

64. The review appeared anonymously in the *Revista Bimestre Cubana* I: 3 (October 1831): 346–60, titled "*Mes douze premières années*. Paris: 1831. *Mis doce primeros años*," and it is attributed to del Monte.

65. Francisco Calcagno claims in his *Diccionario biográfico cubano* that "En el idioma de Voltaire, ménos rico, ménos flexible y sonoro que el de su pátria, escribio Mme. Merlín todas sus obras, pero éstas no por eso dejaban de ser leídas y apreciadas por sus compatricios, apenas salían de sus manos" ("Mme. Merlin wrote all of her works in the language of Voltaire, [which was] less rich, less flexible, and less sonorous than that of her homeland, but this was no reason for her compatriots not to read them and appreciate them, which they did as soon as they issued forth from her hands") (New York: Imprenta y Librería de N. Ponce de Leon, 1878), 582.

66. *Memorias y recuerdos de la Señora Condesa de Merlin, publicados por ella misma, y traducidos del francés por A. de P.*, vol. 1 (Havana: Imprenta de Antonio Ma Dávila, 1853); Domingo del Monte, "Una habanera en París," *Aguinaldo Habanero* (Havana: 1837), 69–72. "Fragmentos de 'Recuerdos de una criolla'" appears on pp. 73–84. Further references will be included parenthetically in the text.

67. Ramón de Palma, "Memorias y recuerdos de la Condesa de Merlin," *El Album*, 11 (1839): 5.

68. "María Malinbran Beriot," *Diario de la Habana* (May 28, 1840): 1–2.

69. Under the rubric *Variedades* appears "Concierto de la Sra. condesa Merlin [sic]," *Diario de la Habana* (December 21, 1839): 1, signed by B. I am grateful to Zoila Lapique of the Biblioteca Nacional José Martí for identifying the author as Antonio Bachiller y Morales, who apparently translated the review.

70. "N.R.B., 'Mis doce primeros años' por la Condesa de Merlin: obra traducida del francés por A. de P.—é impresa en Filadelfia con el mayor esmero," *Diario de la Habana* (January 30, 1839): 2.

71. Ibid., 2.

72. *Diario de la Habana*, April 22, 23, 24, 25, 26, 27, 28, 29, and 30, and May 1, 2, 3, 4, 1844. The pseudonym "Veráfilo" appears in the last article, along with an additional note to the editor of *La Revista de Madrid*. These articles were published together in *Refutacion al folleto intitulado Viage [sic] a la Habana por la Condesa de Merlin, Publicada en el Diario*, por Veráfilo (Havana: Imprenta del Gobierno y Capitanía General, 1844).

73. "La Condesa de Merlin. Mis doce primeros años," *La Cartera Cubana*, 2 (January 1839): 99–102.

74. Ibid., 100.

75. [Del Monte], "*Mes douze premières années*. Paris: 1831. *Mis doce primeros años*," *Revista Bimestre Cubana* (October 1831), 346. Subsequent references are included in the text.

76. "La Condesa de Merlin. Mis doce primeros años," *La Cartera Cubana* 2 (January 1839): 100.

77. Ibid., 99–102.

78. Palma, "Memorias y recuerdos," 5.

79. Chapter 5 contains a detailed analysis of Merlin's strategies of appropriation and develops the implications of this rewriting for nineteenth-century Creole culture.

80. "N.R.B.," 'Mis doce primeros años' por la Condesa de Merlin, obra traducida por A. de P. e impresa en Filadelfia con el mayor esmero" *Diario de la Habana* (January 30, 1839), 2.

81. [Agustin de Palma], introduction, *Mis doce primeros años por La Condesa de Merlin, traducidos del francés por A. de P.* (Philadelphia: 1838), 8–9.

82. Severo Sarduy, "Tu dulce nombre halagará mi oído," *Homenaje a Gertrudis Gómez de Avellaneda*, ed. Rosa M. Cabrera and Gladys B. Zaldívar (Miami: Ediciones Universal, 1981), 20.

83. Sarduy, 20.

84. "Poesía. A la Señora Condesa de Merlin," *Diario de la Habana* (July 12, 1840): 3.

85. Cf. chapter 8 for Merlin's trace in this contemporary tradition.

86. "La Señora Condesa de Merlin. Concierto del Sr. Conde de Peñalver," *Diario de la Habana* (July 12, 1840): 2–3. Reprinted in José de la Luz y Caballero, *Escritos literarios* (Havana: Universidad de La Habana, 1946), 99–105.

87. "Un concurrente," "La Señora Condesa de Merlin. Concierto del Sr. Conde de Peñalver," *Diario de la Habana* (July 12, 1840): 2.

88. Ibid., 2.

89. Ibid., 3.

90. "El efecto que hizo aquí la Merlin, al principio, fue muy favorable: después con sus *excentricidades* fue alborotando á nuestra gente, que es la mas intolerante del mundo,—de manera que si permanece aquí mas tpo le tiran piedras." ("Merlin produced at first a very favorable impression: later, with her quirks and *eccentricities*, she began to rile up our people, who are the most intolerant in the world—so much so that if she remains here much longer, they will probably stone her", emphasis added [Domingo del Monte, "Cartas a José Luis Alfonso," vol. 2 {1838–1847}, Manuscript Collection #39, Colección Cubana, Biblioteca Nacional José Martí, Havana]).

91. "Novedades en Nueva York," *Diario de la Habana* (June 17, 1840): 1–2. The following appeared in *Noticioso y Lucero*: "Puerto de La Habana" (June 10, 1840): 1; "Noticias de La Habana" (June 17, 1840): 2; "Tanto vales cuanto pesas" (June 24, 1840): 2; and "Noticias de La Habana" (July 3, 1840): 2.

92. The author, signed F., went on to suppose that it was only a temporary visit and not a longer stay. "Novedades en Nueva York," *Diario de la Habana* (June 17, 1840): 1.

93. Ibid.

94. "N.R.B., 'Mis doce primeros años' por la Condesa de Merlin," *Diario de la Habana* (January 30, 1839): 2.

95. Ibid., 2.

96. [Del Monte], *Mes douze premières années*. Paris: 1831. *Mis doce primeros años*" *Revista Bimestre Cubana* (October 1831), 346.

97. Bhabha, "DissemiNation," 299.

98. [Del Monte], *Mes douze premières années*. Paris: 1831. *Mis doce primeros años*," *Revista Bimestre Cubana* (October 1831), 346.

99. Bueno justifies del Monte's action by arguing that he was not guilty of the "sin" of omission. According to Bueno, del Monte genuinely did not know who the real author was and was only guessing himself, presumably from the passage quoted; "Una escritora habanera," 24.

100. Bhabha, "Signs Taken for Wonders: Questions of Ambivalence and Authority Under a Tree Outside Delhi, May 1817," in *"Race," Writing and Difference*, ed. Henry Louis Gates, Jr. (Chicago: University of Chicago Press, 1986), 173–75.

101. Benítez Rojo, "Power/Sugar/Literature," 21–22.

102. Domingo del Monte, "Una habanera en París," *Aguinaldo Habanero* (Havana: 1837), 69–72. Further references are included in the text.

103. Bhabha, "Signs Taken for Wonders," 174.

104. "La Condesa de Merlin," *La Cartera Cubana* (January 1839), 102.

105. [Ramón de Palma], "La novela," *El Album*, 1 (1838): 5–35.

106. Benítez Rojo, "Power/Sugar/Literature," 26–25.

107. Palma, "La novela," 22.

108. Ibid.

109. Ramón de Palma, "Introducción a *El espetón de oro* de Villaverde," *El Album* 4 (1838): 5–11. Further references are included in the text.

110. See note 72 for full reference to the series of articles as well as to the complete published version.

111. Further references to the *Refutacion* will be to the 1844 Havana edition and will appear parenthetically in the text.

112. "Nadie diria que la condesa de Merlin, natural de la Habana, con un talento despejado, acostumbrada á ver y á recibir impresiones en diferentes paises, ha pisado otra vez su tierra natal. Tales son los absurdos é inexactitudes de una obra, que no debia haber dado á luz, que no le hace honor alguno, y que quisiéramos no haber leido para no tener que ocuparnos del trabajo de refutarla; y decimos trabajo, porque lo es ciertamente emplear la pluma en defensa del pais y sus costumbres, y contra una persona que la urbanidad y otras circunstancias nos mandan respetar" ("It's hard to believe that Countess Merlin, a native of Havana, who is endowed with a clear talent, and is accustomed to seeing and receiving impressions from different countries, has visited again her native land. Such are the absurdities and the inaccuracies of a work to which she should not have given birth, which does not honor her in any way, and which we wish we had not read so as not to have to take the trouble to refute it. We say trouble because it is truly a bother to take up the pen in defense of a country and its mores, and against a per-

son whom we must respect out of decency and other circumstances") (11). Covered in this quote are the three arguments on which the exclusion of Merlin has been traditionally founded: linguistic difference, nationalism, and gender.

113. Bueno, "Una escritora extranjera," 32. Quoted from *Centón epistolario*, vol. 5, 75. My emphasis.

114. Domingo del Monte, "Cartas a José Luis Alfonso," Manuscript Collection #39, Colección Cubana, Biblioteca Nacional José Martí, Havana.

115. "[N]o te puedes figurar la demanda que hay de [el *Paralelo* de Saco]: yo todos los que he tenido los he regalado a viageros extranjeros, que deseaban conocer ntra isla política y social—" ("You can't imagine the demand there is here [for Saco's *Paralelo*]; I have given away all of my copies to foreign travelers who wished to know the state of our Island, both political and social.").

116. Bhabha, "DissemiNation," 312.

117. Enildo A. García, "Cartas de Domingo del Monte a Alexander H. Everett," *Revista de Literatura Cubana* 7, no. 13 (July–December 1989): 137.

118. García, 137.

119. García, 138.

120. I am referring here to Benítez Rojo's and Luis's interpretations, already cited in this chapter.

121. "Poesía. A la Señora Condesa de Merlin," *Diario de la Habana* (July 12, 1840): 3. I borrow from Jessica Benjamin's analysis of the Oedipal complex and particularly her idea that "the oedipal repudiation of the mother splits her into the debased and the idealized objects" (*The Bonds of Love: Psychoanalysis, Feminism and the Problem of Domination* [New York: Pantheon Books, 1988], 214–15).

122. A. A., "Justo elogio al mérito de la Sra. Condesa de Merlin," *Diario de la Habana* (July 17, 1840): 2.

123. Ibid.

124. *Diario de la Habana* (July 17, 1840): 2.

125. *La Havane*, vol. 3, 419.

126. See the section "A midi," *La Havane*, vol. 3 (Paris: Amyot, 1844), 418–19.

127. The *Lola* series was published on May 2, 3, 5, 7, 8, 9, 11, 13, and 15, 1845, in the *Faro Industrial de la Habana*; *Mis doce primeros años* was published in serial form in the journal *Cuba y América* from January 26 to March 9, 1902, followed by *Historia de Sor Inés*, which appeared from March 16 to April 27, 1902.

CHAPTER 5: (IN)VERSIONS AND (RE)WRITINGS

1. Jorge Ibarra, *Nación y cultura nacional* (Havana: Ed. Letras Cubanas, 1981), 11.

2. Octavio Paz, "Literatura de fundación," *Puertas al campo* (Mexico City: 1966), 11.

3. Roberto Ignacio Díaz, "La habitación contigua: Extraterritorialidad y multilingüismo en la literatura hispanoamericana," Ph.D. diss., Harvard University, 1991, 9.

4. Díaz, 44.

5. Salvador Bueno, "Una escritora habanera de expresión francesa," *De Merlin a Carpentier: Nuevos temas y personajes de la literatura cubana* (Havana: UNEAC Contemporáneos, 1977).

6. Quoted in Díaz, 32; Gastón Baquero, "Introducción a la novela," *La enciclopedia de Cuba*, vol. 3. (San Juan and Madrid: Playor, 1975), 8.

7. Díaz, 8.

8. "En las historias de la literatura cubana. . . no es la nacionalidad de la Condesa de Merlin lo que realmente se cuestiona, sino la nacionalidad de su escritura" ("In Cuban literary histories, . . . what is put into question is not so much Countess Merlin's nationality, but rather the nationality of her writing" [Díaz, 20]).

9. Juan Marinello, *Americanismo y Cubanismo literarios: Ensayo en Marcos Antilla, cuentos de cañaveral por Luis Felipe Rodríguez* (Havana: Editorial Hermes, n.d.), vi; author's emphasis. I cite Roberto González Echevarría's translation in *Alejo Carpentier: The Pilgrim at Home* (Ithaca: Cornell University Press, 1977), 15.

10. Marinello, vi–vii, xi–xii, xv; Paz, 41; Díaz, 35.

11. "Activating the original-as-new rather than the original-as-primitive paradigm, the undiscovered repetition, masquerading as newness, is an offense against the erudition of the institution, and its belated recognition must suffer the censure of criminality" (Marilyn Randall, "Appropriate(d) Discourse: Plagiarism and Decolonization," *New Literary History* 22: 3 [Summer 1991]: 530).

12. Antonio Benítez Rojo, "Power/Sugar/Literature: Toward a Reinterpretation of Cubanness," *Cuban Studies* 16 (1986): 24.

13. This tactic is akin to the practice of contemporary anti-colonial authors who mark their departure from the inherited history of oppression by debunking the entire span of its tradition; Randall, 537.

14. M. Bakhtin, *The Dialogic Imagination*, ed. Michael Holquist, tr. Caryl Emerson and Michael Holquist, (Austin: University of Texas Press, 1981), 336.

15. "Sarmiento's practice [made] plagiarism count for the most efficient originality by inverting the priority between model and revision" (Doris Sommer, *Foundational Fictions: The National Romances of Latin America* [Berkeley: University of California Press, 1991], 82).

16. "Sarmiento's rivalry with adoptive mentors allowed for something different than denial. . . . It allowed him to subordinate the master, gently and without eliminating him, so as not to lose the legitimacy of the master's approval that Sarmiento attributes to himself" (Sommer, 82).

17. "Los nombres que te pido son los del autor de *Vuelta Abajo* y el de la historia de *Luisa*; los dos se encuentran en los libritos del *Album* [sic], de La Habana; también la *nota de Drake*. ["I ask for the names of the authors of *Vuelta Abajo* and of the story of *Luisa*; they both appear in the little *Album* [sic] notebooks from Havana; as also, *Drake's Note*."] *Correspondencia íntima de la Condesa de Merlin*, ed. Domingo Figarola Caneda (Madrid/Paris: 1928), 183. This request echoes an earlier one Merlin made to Chasles the day before. Both are quoted in Salvador Bueno, "Una escritora habanera de expresión francesa," *De Merlin a Carpentier* (Havana: UNEAC Contemporáneos, 1977), 45.

The reference to Drake alludes to Saco, for his documentation was sent to Merlin at Drake's entreaties. Though Merlin inquires for José Zacarias González del Valle, author of the romantic novel *Luisa*, I have found no trace of the latter's influence on Merlin, nor are there any passages from *Luisa* copied onto the text of *Viaje a la Habana*.

18. Randall, 529–30.

19. Likewise, this letter is included in "Lettre XXII of *La Havane*, vol. II (Paris: Librairie d'Amyot, 1844), 211–37.

20. Anonymous, "El velorio," *La Cartera Cubana* II (January 1839), 47—51, and [José Victoriano Betancourt], "Velar un mondongo," *La Cartera Cubana* (December 1838), 363–68. Further references will be to this edition and will appear in the text. Bueno identifies Betancourt as author of the latter sketch in "Una escritora habanera de expresión francesa," 45–46.

21. "Lettre XXII," *La Havane*, vol. II, 214.

22. La Condesa de Merlin, *Viaje a la Habana* (Madrid: Imprenta de la Sociedad Literaria y Tipográfica, 1844), 59. Further references will be to this edition and will appear in the text.

23. For a discussion of this scene in the original French edition, see Roberto Ignacio Díaz, "Merlin's Foreign House: The Genres of *La Havane*," *Cuban Studies* 24 (1994): 66–68.

24. That Merlin was consciously playing with the connotations of the word is proven in her opening title, "Las dos veladas" ("The two soirées") (59).

25. "Me daba envidia de ver aquel buen hombre, bufon habitual de los velorios, carácter original que solo la Habana puede poseer, mostrarse tan alegre entre las imágenes y el aparato de la muerte" ("I was envious to see that good man, the buffoon of funeral wakes, an original character native only to Havana, appear so happy amid the images and ghostly apparatus of death.") (63).

26. Cf. *La Cartera Cubana* (December 1838), 363–68. Further references will be to this edition and cited in the text.

27. Gustavo Pérez Firmat, *The Cuban Condition: Translation and Identity in Modern Cuban Literature* (Cambridge: Cambridge University Press, 1989), 11.

28. Although in "Merlin's Foreign House," Roberto Ignacio Díaz also

notes the play of language created by the reproduction of Spanish Creole dialect within Merlin's *costumbrista* scenes (70–71), he does not, however, mark the hyper-mimetic effect the translation of the *guajiro* dialect has in the French text.

29. Bakhtin, 333.

30. Severo Sarduy, *La simulación* (Caracas: Monte Avila, 1982), 7.

31. Cirilo Villaverde, *Excursión a Vuelta Abajo* (Havana: Imprenta "El Pilar" de Manuel de Armas, 1891), 101.

32. Bakhtin, *The Dialogic Imagination*, 336. Author's emphasis.

33. "[E]l carácter poético que van poco á poco tomando hasta borrar insen-siblemente la parte vulgar y grotesca de la fiesta" ("The poetic character that they adopt little by little to the point of gradually erasing what is vulgar and grotesque in the celebration" [*Viaje a la Habana*, 67]).

34. "A pesar de la inocencia de esta diversion, es demasiado sucia, y muy prosáico ver una jóven, linda y fresca como madrugada de Mayo, en vez de exhalar los perfumes de la rosa despedir los edores del mondongo" ("In spite of the inno-cence of this entertainment, it is very dirty and prosaic to see a young lady fresh and beautiful as a May daybreak give off the smells of the *mondongo* instead of the sweet smells of the rose" [Betancourt 368]).

35. Cirilo Villaverde, *La joven de la flecha de oro y otros relatos*, ed. Imeldo Alvarez (Havana: 1984), 426–36.

36. "Amoríos y contratiempos de un guajiro," *La Cartera Cubana* II (April 1839), 229–38.

37. "Amoríos y contratiempos de un guajiro," 235–38; *Viaje* 43–45.

38. "Escursion [*sic*] á la *Vuelta-Abajo*," *El Album*, vols. 6–8 (1838–1839), 11–46, 89–108. In these *entregas*, the author's name does not appear.

39. Cirilo Villaverde, *Excursión a Vuelta Abajo* (Havana: Imprenta "El Pilar" de Manuel de Armas, 1891), 66. Further references will be to this edition and will appear in the text.

40. "De los hijos del patriarca, no restan más que cuatro. Uno de ellos par-ticularmente, el mayor, no ha querido alejarse un punto de los lugares de su ori-gen, queridos entrañablemente para él, por más que la fortuna le ha brindado con mayor vida en otros sitios" ("There are only four sons of the patriarch left. One of them, the eldest, has not wished to move one spot from his place of ori-gin, so dearly beloved by him, no matter what better life fortune may offer him elsewhere" [Villaverde, 65]).

41. Madame la Comtesse Merlin, *La Havane* (Paris: Librairie d'Amyot, 1844), vol. III, "Lettre XXXV," 374. Further references will be to this edition and will appear in the text.

42. Pérez Firmat, 5.

43. Bakhtin characterizes the novel as a "double discourse" that reflects the many sociolinguistic codes existing in society.

44. Also commented on in Díaz's "Merlin's Foreign House," 71.

45. Marguerite C. Suárez-Murias, "Cuba Painted by the Cubans: The Nineteenth-Century Journalistic Essay," *Essays on Hispanic Literature—Ensayos de literatura hispana. A Bilingual Anthology* (Washington, D.C.: University Press of America, 1982), 49–51.

46. José Zacarías González del Valle, *La vida literaria en Cuba, 1836–1840* (Havana: Secretaría de Educación y Cultura, 1938), 51. This volume collects the letters exchanged between González del Valle and Anselmo Suárez y Romero during the period in which the former edited the latter's antislavery novel *Francisco o las delicias del campo*. The work was commissioned by *tertulia* leader Domingo del Monte in order to promote the abolitionist cause.

47. Domingo del Monte, *Centón epistolario de Domingo del Monte*, ed. Domingo Figarola-Caneda, v. III (1836–1838) (Havana: Imprenta "El Siglo XX," 1926), 158. Future references to this volume of the *Centón epistolario* will appear parenthetically in the text, with original punctuation and spelling.

Milanés contrasts *San Marcos* to Cirilo Villaverde's *La peña blanca*, which, in his mind, was lacking in literary verisimilitude: "Esto no es la Peña blanca [*sic*] de Villaverde, en que si campea de vez en cuando una naturalidad de tono, sumamente original y cubana, también hay mucho de vaporoso y fantástico" ("This is not Villaverde's la Peña blanca [*sic*], in which, although every once and again there sounds a very natural note, highly original and Cuban, there is also a lot of fantasy and light-headedness" [Del Monte, 158]). Villaverde's *La peña blanca* was originally published in the *Miscelánea de Util y Agradable Recreo* in August, 1837. It is included in Cirilo Villaverde, *La joven de la flecha de oro*, ed. Imeldo Alvarez (Havana: 1984), 52–70.

48. Ramón de Palma, "Una Pascua en San Marcos," *Cuentos cubanos* (Havana: Cultural, S. A., 1928). Future references to Palma's novel will be to this edition and will appear in the text.

49. My emphasis; González del Valle, *La vida literaria en Cuba (1836–1840)*, 32–33.

50. Félix Tanco y Bosmeniel, *Refutacion al folleto intitulado Viage a la Habana por la Condesa de Merlin* (Havana: Imprenta de Gobierno y Capitanía General, 1844), 53–54.

51. Benítez Rojo, "Power/Sugar/Literature," 26.

52. Del Monte's reply is quoted in A. M. Eligio de la Puente, "Introducción" to Ramon de Palma, *Cuentos cubanos* (Havana: Cultural, 1928), xxvii.

In the prologue to a recent Cuban edition of Villaverde's *La joven de la flecha de oro*, Imeldo Alvarez quotes del Monte's letter but with a radically different ending. Instead of de la Puente's version, which reads "y ha tachado de inmoral al pintor" ("and [they] have dismissed the painter as immoral"), Alvarez renders it: "y ha tratado de inmolar al pintor" ("and (they) have tried to burn the painter at the stake"), 18. Which of the two versions of del Monte's letter is the accurate one? De la Puente's version echoes Milanés own words in his previous letter to del Monte of May 17, 1838, that Palma's novel was considered "immoral" gives its overt treatment of sexual themes. But neither de la Puente nor Alvarez can identify del Monte's addressee: was it Milanés himself or another member of the circle? It would seem that del Monte was, indeed, writing to José Jacinto Milanés, as the criticism of Palma's novel is a recurring topic of exchange. This can be proven by another letter of the *Centón epistolario*, dated May 28, 1838, in which Milanés answers del Monte's letter of May 21. In this letter del Monte apparently satirized the latest barbs of "estos pobres académicos" ("these poor academics") (III, 160). Is this the same letter in which del Monte passed judgment of Palma's novel, quoted by both Alvarez and de la Puente? If so, then the "poor academics" must have referred to critics like Costales and other detractors of *Una Pascua en San Marcos*. Assuming this were the case, Alvarez dated del Monte's first letter to Milanés on the same day as Milanés's response (May 28, 1838), but the correct date would have to be May 21.

53. *Centón epistolario* III, 160; partially quoted in de la Puente, "Introducción," Palma, *Cuentos cubanos*, xxvii–xxviii.

54. "[N]o es de este lugar hacer el juicio crítico de esta producción ingerta [sic] en los viages [sic] de la señora de Merlin; la amistad, las íntimas relaciones que llevamos con su legítimo autor nos sirven de obstáculo" ("[T]his is not the place to make a critical evaluation of this book grafted on Mrs. Merlin's travels; our friendship, our intimate bonds with its legitimate author serve as obstacles" [Tanco, *Refutacion*, 54]).

55. Quoted in de la Puente, "Introducción," Palma, *Cuentos cubanos*, xxviii.

56. Benítez Rojo, "Power/Sugar/Literature," 26.

57. Eligio de la Puente speculates that this letter must have been written on June 19, 1838, and not on June 13, inasmuch as Costales's criticism appeared on June 17. What is more, Lorenzo de Palma wrote again to del Monte on June 20 to press his case a second time, and here he referred to his previous letter as "mi carta de ayer" [yesterday's letter]. De la Puente, "Introducción," Palma, *Cuentos cubanos*, xxix n.1; ref. *Centón epistolario* III, 166.

58. De la Puente, "Introducción," Palma, *Cuentos cubanos*, xxxi.

59. Félix Tanco y Bosmeniel ["Veráfilo"], *Refutacion*, 53. Quoted in Bueno, "Una escritora habanera," 43.

60. See also "El comunicante del Faro" (*El Faro*, April 27, 1844), included in Luz y Caballero's *Escritos literarios*, 257.

61. Salvador Bueno was of this opinion in a personal communication made during my 1989 trip to Havana.

62. Bueno, 43–44.

63. William Luis, *Literary Bondage: Slavery in Cuban Narrative* (Austin: University of Texas Press, 1990), 39–40. Though Luis discusses at length the thematic and characterological echoes between both novels (46–50), he stops short of tracing the intertextual connection; that is, whether Zambrana strove to surpass, in Sarmiento fashion, the earlier master.

64. "Sus escritos están muy lejos de igualarse todavía al hechizo y origi-nalidad de sus conversaciones. Esta observación destruye la calumnia que han levantado algunos detractores del ingenio de la mujer, propalando que la Sra. Merlin se ha valido del auxilio de un hombre para escribir sus obras" (La Con-desa de Merlin, *Mis doce primeros años," La Cartera Cubana* II [183], 102, partially quoted in Figarola-Caneda, *La Condesa de Merlin*, 98).

65. "La Condesa de Merlin," *La Cartera Cubana*, 100.

66. Roberto González Echevarría, introduction to *Los pasos perdidos* (Madrid: Ed. Cátedra, 1985), 40.

67. Sandra M. Gilbert and Susan Gubar convincingly argue that patri-archal conceptions of Author and Text have excluded women from literary part-nership, in *The Madwoman in the Attic: The Woman Writer and the Nineteenth-Century Literary Imagination* (New Haven and London: Yale University Press, 1979), 3–7. Countess Merlin is one more case of that particular "anxiety of authorship" expe-rienced by the woman writer when confronted with the dominantly male liter-ary canon: "a radical fear that she cannot create, that because she can never become a 'precursor' the act of writing will isolate or destroy her" (Gilbert and Gubar, 49).

68. Paz, 19.

CHAPTER 6: BOUND TO THE (MALE) BOOK

1. "Precisamente en el mismo mes y año en que nació María de la Merced [sic] fue autorizado el comercio libre de esclavos africanos bajo todas las banderas" ("Precisely the same year in which Maria de la Merced [sic] was born, the trade of African slaves was authorized under all flags" [Salvador Bueno, "Una escritora habanera de expresión francesa," *De Merlin a Carpentier: Nuevos temas y personajes de la literatura cubana* {Havana: UNEAC Contemporáneos, 1977}, 12]).

2. For an engaging view of the slavery letter, see Claire Emilie Martin, "Slavery in the Spanish Colonies: The Racial Politics of The Countess of Mer-lin," an essay included in *Reinterpreting the Spanish American Essay: Women Writ-ers of the 19th and 20th Centuries*, ed. Doris Meyer (Austin: University of Texas Press, 1995), 37—45. Martin's reading emphasizes both the ideological and his-torical contradictions surrounding the slavery letter as well as the tensions evi-dent in Merlin's own political stance, though still privileging her class affiliation: "[Her] mercenary interests [were] tied to slavery" (40). As I was putting the fin-ishing touches on this book, I received a copy of this essay thanks to the courtesy of the author.

3. I translate to a Cuban context Bhabha's notion of "the emblem of the English book . . . as an insignia of colonial authority" (Homi K. Bhabha, "Signs Taken for Wonders: Questions of Ambivalence and Authority Under a Tree Outside Delhi, May, 1817," *"Race," Writing, and Difference*, ed. Henry Louis Gates, Jr. [Chicago: University of Chicago Press, 1986], 163). However, it is

crucial to keep in mind that both Saco and Merlin, along with the Creole intellectuals grouped around the del Monte circle, represented a counterdiscourse to colonial authority. See William Luis, *Literary Bondage: Slavery in Cuban Narrative* (Austin: University of Texas Press, 1990), 2–3, and his subsequent discussion of the relations between Saco and del Monte (28–34).

4. Bhabha, 175.

5. "Hybridity reverses the *formal* process of disavowal so that the violent dislocation, the *Entstellung* of the act of colonization, becomes the *conditionality* of colonial discourse" (Bhabha, 175).

6. Bhabha, 175.

7. Luis, 62–63.

8. Luis, 62.

9. I am indebted to Antonio Benítez Rojo for this insight.

10. See the section "Testimonios: 'No ha sido una desgracia para el negro sacarle de los horrores de Africa para transformarlo en labrador de nuestras islas,'" in Leví Marrero, *Cuba: economía y sociedad*, vol. 13 (Madrid: Ed. Playor, 1986), 184–85. O'Gavan was directly responsible for the expulsion of Saco from Cuba under Captain-General Tacón; Marrero, 185.

11. The quote is from Domingo Figarola Caneda, *La Condesa de Merlin* (Paris: Editions Excelsior, 1928), 158. Also quoted in Bueno, 41.

12. Figarola Caneda, 159.

13. Martin, 43–44.

14. Madame la Comtesse Merlin, *La Havane*, vol. 2 (Paris: Librairie d'Amyot, 1844), 277–312.

15. For a discussion of Domingo del Monte's efforts in promoting the antislavery novel, see Luis, 26–39.

16. *La Havane*, vol. 2, "Lettre XX (Paris: L'Amyot, 1844), 87. Subsequent references will be to this edition and will be included in the text.

17. Martin makes a similar point in the section of her article entitled "The Birth of a Nation: The Personal as Political," 37–38.

18. La Condesa de Merlin, *Los esclavos en las colonias españolas* (Madrid: Imprenta de Alegría y Charlain, 1841).

19. See chapter 4 for a discussion of the divergent nationalist projects of Merlin and the del Monte circle.

20. Luis, 28.

21. Luis, 32.

22. Luis, 28.

23. "Saco, who neither was from Havana nor had ties to the dominant sugar interest, was an exponent not of *Cuba grande* (Big Cuba), of sugar planters, but of *Cuba pequeña* (Little Cuba)" (Luis, 28).

24. "It is crucial to remember that the colonial construction of the cultural . . . through the process of disavowal is authoritative to the extent to

which it is structured around the ambivalence of splitting, denial, repetition—strategies of defense that mobilize culture as an open-textured, warlike strategy whose aim 'is rather a continued agony than a total disappearance of the pre-existing culture.'" Bhabha, 175. The quote is from Frantz Fanon, *Toward the African Revolution* (1967), 183.

25. British abolitionist pamphlets were being distributed in Spain in an effort to promote the cause in the Peninsula. See, for example, P.J. Alexander, *Observaciones sobre la esclavitud y comercio de esclavos e Informe del Dr. Madden sobre la esclavitud en la isla de Cuba* (Barcelona: Imprenta de A. Bergnes y Co., 1841). The Spanish editor of this volume calls for a popular uprising of "all honest men in Spain" in favor of the abolitionist cause (66).

26. "Les esclaves dans les colonies espagnoles," *Revue des Deux Mondes* (April–June 1841): 734–69. On the editorial history of the letter, see also Martin, "The Creation of a Literary Triptych," 38–40.

27. "Nos réserves faites, on ne s'étonnera ni de nous voir accueillir ces documents nécessaires au grand débat soulevé par la question de l'esclavage, ni de l'enthousiasme avec lequel l'auteur, créole de naissance et d'origine, parle du pays ou elle est née" ("Our reservations made, it will not surprise anyone that we welcome these documents, necessary to the great debate on the question of slavery, nor at the enthusiasm with which the author, a Creole by birth and origin, speaks about her native country" ["Les esclaves," 734]).

28. Hugh Thomas, *Cuba: The Pursuit of Freedom* (New York: Harper & Row, 1971), 152.

29. For a discussion of the relationship between labor demand and the illegal slave trade, see Franklin W. Knight, *Slave Society in Cuba During the Nineteenth Century* (Madison: University of Wisconsin Press, 1970), 91–92.

30. Ramiro Guerra y Sánchez, *Manual de historia de Cuba (económica, social y política)* (Havana: Cultural, 1938), 383. Cf. Luis, 35.

31. Guerra y Sánchez, 391–93.

32. Knight, 114.

33. Knight, 114.

34. Guerra y Sánchez, 379.

35. Guerra y Sánchez, 396–97.

36. Guerra y Sánchez, 398.

37. Guerra y Sánchez, 399.

38. Guerra y Sánchez, 427.

39. Guerra y Sánchez, 381–83. See also José Antonio Saco, "Paralelo entre la Isla de Cuba y algunas colonias inglesas," reprinted in *Ideario reformista* (Havana: Secretaría de Educación, Dirección de Cultura, 1935), 69–70.

40. Thomas, *Cuba: The Pursuit of Freedom*, 208.

41. Guerra y Sánchez, 427.

42. Guerra y Sánchez, 379–80.

43. Bhabha, 171.

44. *La Havane*, vol. 2, "Lettre XX," 151; *Los esclavos*, 63. Merlin's brief citation refers more exactly to the following essays: José Antonio Saco, *Mi primera pregunta—¿La abolición del comercio de esclavos africanos arruinará o atrasará la agricultura cubana?* (Madrid: Imprenta de Don Marcelino Calero, 1837) and *Examen analítico del informe de la comisión especial nombrada por las Cortes sobre la esclusión de los actuales y futuros diputados de Ultramar, y sobre la necesidad de regir aquellos paises por leyes especiales* (Madrid: Oficina de D. Tomas Jordan, 1837).

45. *La Havane*, vol. 2, "Lettre XX," 151; *Los esclavos*, 63. "[D]iscursive 'transparency' is best read in the photographic sense in which a transparency is also always a negative, possessed into visibility through the technologies of reversal, enlargement, lighting, editing, projection, not a source but a re-source of light" (Bhabha, 171).

46. "Abogando por la causa de una patria inocente y ofendida, algun esfuerzo me ha costado reprimir el fuego de la juventud y manejar la pluma con templanza[;] . . . dejando solo oir las voces de la razon, de la severa é imparcial razon" ("While advocating on behalf of an innocent and offended land, it has been somewhat of an effort to repress the fire of youth and to maneuver the pen with temperance[,]...only allowing the voices of severe and impartial reason to be heard" [Saco, *Examen analítico*, 32]). In his famous essay "Clamor de los cubanos," Saco introduced a personal note in the rhetorical opening; the essay was reprinted as "Carta de un patriota o sea clamor de los cubanos," in *Ideario reformista*, 15–16.

47. The gender specificity of this position is clearly evidenced in the following passage: "écoutez mes impartiales refléxions, et si vous me condamnez ensuite, je me livre à vous dans mon humilité, et demande grâce pour mon coeur en faveur de cet amour inquiet de la justice qui peut m'égarer, mais qui ne saurait jamais détruire la généreuse pitié dans le coeur d'une femme" ("heed my impartial reflections, and if you condemn me afterwards, I give myself humbly to you, and entreat you for this heart, this uneasy love of justice that may lead me astray, but which will never know how to destroy the generous compassion in a woman's heart" [*La Havane*, vol. 2, "Lettre XX," 87–88]).

48. The earlier Spanish version adopted a more diffused strategy where, as in Saco, an appeal is made to a more general reader—philosophers, public spokesmen, and other "enthusiasts" (*Los esclavos*, 2).

49. For a discussion of the Archive as articulated memory and accumulated code of history, see González Echevarría, *Myth and Archive: A Theory of Latin American Narrative* (Cambridge and New York: Cambridge University Press, 1990), especially the first chapter.

50. Cf. chapter 5, "(In)versions and (Re)Writings."

51. All further references to Saco's document will be to the 1837 edition cited in note 44 and will appear in the text.

52. "Si la trata es un abuso insultante de la fuerza, un atentado contra el

derecho natural, la emancipación sería una violación de la propiedad, de los derechos adquiridos y consagrados por las leyes, un verdadero despojo" ("If the
African slave trade is an insulting abuse of power, an assault against natural law,
emancipation would be a violation of property, of rights acquired and consecrated by the law, a true spoilation" [*Los esclavos*, 2; cf. *La Havane*, "Lettre XX,"
vol. 2, 88]).

53. In his "Advertencia," Saco asks his adversaries not to pass judgment
on him in the name of his "sacred devotion to Cuba's existence and to the happiness of her offspring" (*Mi primera pregunta*, i).

54. "La colonia de plantación, destinada según la generación de Arango a
promover la riqueza—*felicidad* en la semántica del Setecientos—, acrecentó indu-
dablemente la opulencia en los niveles más altos de la sociedad colonial, pero en
dramático contraste intensificaría la presencia de componentes negativos que
serían denunciados, coetáneamente, por las mentes criollas más lúcidas" ("The
plantation colony, destined according to the generation of Arango to promote
wealth—*happiness* in the semantics of the 1700s—, undoubtedly increased wealth
in the higher levels of colonial society, but in dramatic contrast, it would inten-
sify the presence of negative components which would simultaneously be denounced
by the most lucid Creole minds") (emphasis added). Marrero, *Cuba: Economía y
sociedad*, vol. 13, 1.

55. Saco, *Mi primera pregunta*, 62–63.

56. "Saco reassures his readers that his position is not to emancipate slaves
but to end the slave trade" (Luis, 33).

57. "Although Saco does not argue for the emancipation of slaves in Cuba,
this proposition is clearly implicit in his essay" (Luis, 32–33).

58. "Cuba, para hacer frente al porvenir, no solo debe terminar al instante,
y para siempre, todo tráfico de esclavos, sino proteger con empeño la colonización
blanca" ("In order for Cuba to face the future, it must not only end at once and
forever all slave traffic, but it must also diligently protect white colonization"
[José Antonio Saco, *La supresión del tráfico de esclavos africanos en la isla de Cuba.
Examinada con relación a su agricultura y a su seguridad* {Paris: Imprenta de Panckouke, 1843}, 54]). See also 47, 50: "Si el tráfico de esclavos continúa, ya en Cuba
no habrá paz ni seguridad" ("If the slave trade continues, Cuba will have neither
peace nor safety").

59. Knight, 113.

60. "The Spanish government hoped that the policy of white immigration would export displaced population, increase the supply of laborers in
Cuba and comply with British demands to end trade" (Knight, 114).

61. "[Saco] disarms the central issue that sugar production will decline if
the slave trade is eliminated" (Luis, 33).

62. Saco argued that whites were better fitted for the rugged conditions
of the sugar mill than blacks, who, in his view, were more prone to disease and

consequently to higher mortality rates. *Mi primera pregunta*, 6–16. The racism implicit in this view will be discussed later.

63. "Mais à peine les prolétaires europeéns arrivent-ils ici, qu'ils se voient confondus avec une race esclave et maudite. . . . Le premier usage que fait de ses premières épargnes un pauvre laboureur, c'est l'achat d'un nègre" ("But as soon as the European proletarians arrive here, they see themselves mixed with an enslaved and cursed race. . . . The first thing that a poor laborer does with his first savings is to buy a black person" [*La Havane*, vol. 2, "Lettre XX," 105–6; *Los esclavos*, 21]).

64. "[S]i queremos hallar una base sólida, estable y natural al aumento de la población blanca, la busquemos en la inmigracion de verdaderos colonos . . . familias labradoras y honradas" ("If we want to find a solid, stable, and natural base for the growth of the white population, we must find it in the immigration of true colonists . . . industrious and honest families") *Informe fiscal sobre Fomento de la población blanca en la Isla de Cuba y Emancipacion progresiva de la esclava* (Madrid: Imprenta de J. Martin Alegría, 1845), 37–38.

65. Merlin clearly echoes Saco's position when she states: "Si la prohibition de la traite était rigoureusement observée, et que la colonisation fût encouragée avec activité et persistance, l'extinction de l'esclavage s'opérerait sans secousse, sans dommage, et par le seul fait de l'affranchissement individuel" ("If the prohibition of the slave trade had been rigorously enforced, and colonization had been actively and consistently encouraged, the abolition of slavery would have been carried out smoothly, without personal injury, and for the single purpose of individual emancipation" [*La Havane*, vol. 2, 103; *Los esclavos*, 18–19]).

66. Martin, 43. This fact is corroborated by Knight, 113–14.

67. Knight, 115.

68. Saco, *Ideario reformista*, 32, 59–61.

69. "In 1821, don Bernardo O'Gavan published in Madrid a brief polemical essay against the dispositions destined to bring an end to the slave trade since 1817. This O'Gavan was an accomplished representative in the intellectual sector of criollo plutocratic supporters of the establishment of slavery, which attempted to justify affirming that all African slaves of the Antilles were happier in this state than when they enjoyed their liberty in their native continent" (José Antonio Fernández de Castro, *Tema negro en la literatura cubana* [Havana: El Mirador, 1943], 27–28, quoted in Luis, 62 [his translation]).

70. Typical in this regard is Marrero's appraisal of *La Havane* as a work containing "lamentables distorsiones en sus referencias a las clases y castas humildes y marginadas de la sociedad cubana" ("shameful distortions in reference to the humble and marginalized classes and castes of Cuban society" [Marrero, 259]).

71. Luis, 58.

72. Cf. last section of this chapter.

73. Saco, *La supresión*, 61.

74. David Turnbull, *Travels in the West. Cuba; With Notices of Porto [sic] Rico, and the Slave Trade* (London: Longman, Orme, Brown, Green and Longmans, 1840), 39–41, 76–77.

75. Turnbull, 52.

76. Turnbull, 48.

77. Turnbull, 75–77.

78. "Sweet Cuba! In thy bosom reflected/To the deepest and fullest extent/Of the physical world, all its beauty,/Of the moral world, all its horrors."

79. Martin rightfully claims that "Merlin unabashedly constructs a fairy-tale in describing the master/slave relationship" (43).

80. Luis, 86. That the difference is not caused by gender alone is proven by the fact that both of Manzano's masters were female.

81. This fear was voiced in the famous statement, "La isla de Cuba, si no es española, es negra," made by one of the Spanish delegates to the 1837 Spanish Cortes. ("The Island of Cuba, if not Spanish, would be black.") Quoted in Guerra y Sánchez, 376.

82. "Un gobierno liberal en Cuba, lejos de poder renovar las calamidades de Santo Domingo, será el medio mas seguro para preservarla de semejante catástrofe" ("A liberal government in Cuba, far from reproducing the disaster of Santo Domingo, will be the surest way to guard her against a similar catastrophe" [Saco, *Examen analítico*, 25]).

83. "The complexity of the stereotype results from the social context in which it is to be found. . . . The deep structure of the stereotype reappears in the adult as a response to anxiety, an anxiety having its roots in the potential disintegration of the mental representations the individual has created and internalized" (Sander Gilman, *Difference and Pathology: Stereotypes of Sexuality, Race, and Madness* [Ithaca: Cornell University Press, 1985], 19).

84. "When, however, the sense of order and control undergoes stress . . . an anxiety appears. . . . We project that anxiety onto the Other, externalizing our loss of control. The Other is thus stereotyped, labeled with a set of signs paralleling (or mirroring) our loss of control" (Gilman, 20).

85. Gilman, 22.

86. Knight, 99.

87. Luis, 32.

88. "We learn to perceive in terms of historically determined sets of root-metaphors, and they serve as categories through which we label and classify the Other" (Gilman, 22).

89. Saco, *Mi primera pregunta*, 7, 13–14.

90. "Aussi sa répugnance au travail et son indolence ne cèdent-elles qu'à la contrainte" ("Also his loathing of work and his idleness are not given up unless with the use of force" (*La Havane*, vol. 2, "Lettre XX," 127; *Los esclavos*, 42).

91. Saco, *La supresión*, 62.

92. "Peut-être un jour devrons-nous à la civilisation une fusion fraternelle; malheureusement elle n'est pas encore près d'arriver" ("It is possible that one day we will owe to civilization a fraternal union; unfortunately this has not yet arrived" [*La Havane*, vol. 2, "Lettre XX," 107; *Los esclavos*, 22.

93. "No hay odio de razas, porque no hay razas" ("Racial hatred does not exist because race does not exist" [José Martí, "Nuestra América," in *Literatura hispanoamericana: una antología*, ed. David William Foster {New York and London: Garland Publishing Co., 1994}, 460]).

94. "Human sexuality, given its strong biological basis, not unnaturally is often perceived as out of the control of the self. . . . For a secure definition of self, sexuality and the loss of control associated with it must be projected onto the Other" (Gilman, 24).

95. "Ils se marient rarement: à quoi bon? Le mari et la femme peuvent être vendus, d'un jour à l'autre, à des maîtres differents, et leur séparation devaient alors éternelle. Leurs enfants ne leur appartiennent pas. Le bonheur domestique, ainsi que la communauté des intérèts, leur étant interdit, les liens de la nature se bornent chez eux à l'instint d'une sensualité violente et désordonnée" ("They rarely get married: what for? The husband and wife can be sold from one day to the next to a different owner, and their separation must then be eternal. Their children do not belong to them. Domestic happiness as well as communal interests are prohibited to them; the bonds of nature are restricted to instinct, to a violent and disorderly sensuality" [*La Havane*, vol. 2, "Lettre XX," 131–32; *Los esclavos*, 46]).

96. For a discussion of triangulated desire in this novel, see Luis, 47–49.

97. Turnbull, 62.

98. "The Other is invested with all of the qualities of the 'bad' or the 'good'. . . . The 'bad' Other becomes the negative stereotype; the 'good' Other becomes the positive stereotype" (Gilman, 20).

99. Knight shows how this supposition has led other historians astray and argues consistently against the "benign" view of slavery based on legal grounds (95).

100. Sylvia Molloy expounds this brilliant thesis in *At Face Value: Autobiographical Writing in Spanish America* (Cambridge: Cambridge University Press, 1991), 91–92. Cf. chapter I.

101. Knight, 122–23.

102. Knight, 132.

103. Knight, 132.

104. Knight, 127–36.

105. As Knight describes it, the function of the *coartación* was to determine a set value for the slave (130–31).

106. Cf. p. 30. Turnbull, 52.

107. See, for example, Julia Ward Howe's *A Trip to Cuba* (Boston: Tic-

knor and Fields, 1860) and Fredrika Bremer, *The Homes of the New World: Impressions of America*, tr. Mary Howitt, Volume II (New York: Harper & Brother Publishers, 1853).

108. Martin, 44.

109. Gilman, 20.

110. "The resulting basic categories of difference reflect our preoccupation with the self and the control that the self must have over the world. Because the Other is the antithesis of the self, the definition of the Other must incorporate the basic categories by which the self is defined. . . . All of these categories reflect the cultural categories of seeing objects as a reflection or distortion of the self" (Gilman, 23).

111. Bhabha's thesis needs necessarily to be translated to a Spanish American context, for Creole thinkers could not be seen as strictly colonialist, inasmuch as they were operating within the orbit of a repressive colonial machinery that denied them cultural and political autonomy.

112. Knight, 134, 136. This would not be true of the female domestic slave, often tormented by the sexual attacks of the white master or his sons, a drama poignantly depicted in Anselmo Suárez y Romero's *Francisco* (1836).

113. I follow here Joan Scott's suggestion that women's histories dissolve existing binary oppositions and/or categories of historical thought.

114. Turnbull, 49.

115. *La Havane*, vol. 2, 122–23; *Los esclavos*, 38.

116. Gilman, 26–27.

117. "Such [works] are written and marketed to fulfill certain needs of specific groups within a given society" (Gilman, 27).

118. "In some works, tensions incident to conflicts between the 'realities' of a given culture and the author's idealized sense of the audience results in parodic distortion of the stereotypes" (Gilman, 27).

119. Gilman, 27.

120. *La Havane*, vol. 2, "Lettre XX," 160; *Los esclavos*, 71.

121. "Relata con detalles en que se mezclan lo espeluznante con lo ridículo" (Bueno, 36).

122. "The fictional world as structured by the author is the world under control, in which even the loss of control is reduced to the level of fiction directed and formed by the author" (Gilman, 27).

123. Hugh Thomas cites the episode of the slave cook from *La Havane* as proof of the "loyalty of town slaves to their masters and families" (180–81).

124. Saco, *La supresión*, 59.

125. Cf. Bhabha, 173.

126. Gilman, 23, 25.

127. José Antonio Saco, *La supresión*, 59 (emphasis added).

128. Merlin, *La Havane*, vol. 2, "Lettre XXIV," 287.

129. *La Havane*, vol. 2, "Lettre XXIX," 285.

130. *La Havane*, vol. 2, "Lettre XXIV," 281.

131. *La Havane*, vol. 2, "Lettre XXIV," 281.

132. *La Havane*, vol. 2, "Lettre XXIV," 287; punctuation slightly modified.

133. *La Havane*, vol. 2, "Lettre XXIV," 301–5.

134. *La Havane*, vol. 2, "Lettre XXIV," 306–7.

135. *La Havane*, vol. 2, "Lettre XXIV," 306.

136. La Havane, vol. 3, "Lettre XXXIII," 256.

137. *La Havane*, vol. 3, "Lettre XXXIII," 309.

138. Thomas, *Cuba*, 197–99.

139. Thomas, *Cuba*, 197.

140. *La Havane*, vol. 2, "Lettre XXIII," 260.

141. *La Havane*, vol. 2, "Lettre XXIV," 310–11.

142. *La Havane*, vol. 2, "Lettre XXIV," 22 and note 45, 309.

143. Letter from Saco to José Luis Alfonso, Paris, October 10, 1842. [Antonio Bachiller y] Morales, *Varios sobre Saco*, Ms. collection, Morales, vol. 16, nos. 1–10. National Library José Martí, Havana, Cuba. Reproduced in Domingo Figarola Caneda, *La Condesa de Merlin* (Paris: Ed. Excelsior, 1928), 119. Also quoted in Bueno, "Una escritora habanera," 33.

144. See the section "Arreglo forense" included in "Clamor," *Ideario reformista*, 17–18. However, Saco's critique does not go so far as Merlin's biting wit and irony.

145. González Echevarría, *Myth and Archive*, 59.

146. "L'ordre, qui est la représentation idéale de la puissance divine se manifestant *dans la nature*, n'a pas . . . d'autre symbole dans la société humaine, que la loi: dans tous les pays où la loi n'est pas sacrée, la société n'existe pas" (*La Havane*, vol. 2, "Lettre XXIII," 244, my emphasis).

147. *La Havane*, vol. 2, "Lettre XXIII," 243.

148. *La Havane*, vol. 2, "Lettre XXII," 242.

149. Leví Marrero, *Cuba: economía y sociedad*, vol. 14, 22. The prejudice against Merlin is clear in the next segment, where the author emphasizes, once again, Merlin's adherence to her class of origin and her oblivion to pressing social issues. Despite the fact that Leví Marrero has a point here, would a male writer have provoked such disparaging comments?

150. *La Havane*, vol. 2, "Lettre XXII," 264.

151. *La Havane*, vol. 2, "Lettre XXIII," 242.

152. *La Havane*, vol. 2, "Lettre XXIII," 261.

153. González Echevarría, 54.

154. González Echevarría, 53–54.

155. González Echevarría, 55, 69–70.

156. González Echevarría, 55, 71.

NOTES TO CHAPTER 7: CREOLE WOMEN

157. "Law and history are the two predominant modes of discourse in the colonial period. Their truthfulness is guaranteed by mediating codes of State, chiefly notarial rhetoric" (González Echevarría, 55).

158. Merlin: *La Havane*, vol. 2, "Lettre XXIII," 251.

159. Leví Marrero, *Cuba: economía y sociedad*, vol. 14, 23.

160. *La Havane*, vol. 2, "Lettre XXIII," 246–47.

161. E. Mansion, *Harper's Modern College French and English Dictionary* (New York: Charles Scribner's Sons, 1940; rev. 1967), 43.

162. *La Havane*, vol. 2, "Lettre XXIII," 248.

163. *La Havane*, vol. 2, "Lettre XXIII," 249.

164. González Echevarría, *Myth and Archive*, 70.

165. *La Havane*, vol. 2, "Lettre XXIII," 251.

166. Leví Marrero, *Cuba: economía y sociedad*, vol. 14, 20.

167. *La Havane*, vol. 2, "Lettre XXIII," 258.

168. Marrero, *Cuba: economía y sociedad*, vol. 14, 18.

169. *La Havane*, vol. 2, "Lettre XXIII," 251–52.

170. *La Havane*, vol. 2, "Lettre XXIII," 266.

171. *La Havane*, vol. 2, "Lettre XXIII," 260.

172. *La Havane*, vol. 2, "Lettre XXIII," 267–68.

173. *La Havane*, vol. 2, "Lettre XXIII," 268.

CHAPTER 7: CREOLE WOMEN

1. Merlin, "Lettre XXV," *La Havane*, vol. 2 (Paris: Librairie d'Amyot, 1844), 315–39. With the haunting subtitle of "Las mugeres de la Habana," the series appeared in the *Diario de la Habana* from Sunday to Tuesday, September 10–12, 1843, and as a single entry in the *Faro Industrial de la Habana*, Sunday, September 10, 1843. In this chapter, all quotes are from the original periodical publications and not from the French edition.

2. Carmen Vásquez makes a similar point when she states: "la Condesa de Merlin, al escribir sobre ella misma y sobre aquello que la rodeaba, dio una visión singularísima de la mujer criolla y del lugar que ésta ocupaba en la sociedad colonial que le tocó vivir" ("In writing about herself and her surroundings, Countess Merlin gave a very singular vision of Creole women and of the place she held in the colonial society in which she had to live.") "Las mujeres cubanas de la Condesa de Merlin," *Femmes des Ameriques* (Toulouse: Université de Toulouse-Mirail, 1986), 70.

3. Vásquez, 70.

4. "Mercedes Merlin, al hablar de la mujer cubana, no puede sino compararla con su equivalente europeo" ("In speaking of Cuban women, Mercedes Merlin cannot but compare her with her European double" [Vásquez, 74]).

5. Salvador Bueno, "Una escritora habanera de expresión francesa," *De*

Merlin a Carpentier: Nuevos temas y personajes de la literatura cubana (Havana: UNEAC Contemporáneos, 1977), 42. In the interest of accuracy, it must be noted that Bueno lists the date of publication as November 1843 instead of September and attributes to the polemicist the male pseudonym of "Serafín," an error that may be due to the fact that Domingo Figarola Caneda reproduced the first set of the "Cartas a Chucha" with the same errors in his *La Condesa de Merlin* (Paris: Editions Excelsior, 1928), 160–64.

6. [Félix Tanco y Bosmeniel], "Veráfilo," *Refutacion al folleto intitulado "Viage a la Habana" por la Condesa de Merlin* (Havana: Imprenta de Gobierno y Capitanía General, 1844), 59.

7. Bridget Aldaraça, "El ángel del hogar: The Cult of Domesticity in Nineteenth-Century Spain," *Theory and Practice of Feminist Literary Criticism*, eds. Gabriela Mora and Karen S. Van Hooft (Ypsilanti, Mich.: Bilingual Press, 1982), 71.

8. The writer must have had in mind "Lettre XV of *La Havane*, for he or she refers to the famous scene in which Merlin was pitilessly persecuted by mosquitoes. "La Habana y la Condesa de Merlin," *Faro Industrial de la Habana* (December 19, 1843), 1. This scene is also recalled in Reynaldo González's *Contradanzas y latigazos* (Havana: Editorial Letras Cubanas, 1983), 19–20, an analysis of *Cecilia Valdés* within the context of Cuban plantation culture.

9. Agustín de Palma translated *Mis doce primeros años* in a self-financed edition (the 1838 Philadelphia edition has no publisher listed). He explains in his introduction that his motive was primarily "that all the sons of Cuba read the literary productions of an *habanera*" (9). Interestingly enough, Palma adopts a tone of "feminine" apology for perceived faults in the translation (9). Then in 1853, the Imprenta de Antonio Ma. Davila in Havana brought out *Memorias y recuerdos de la Señora Condesa de Merlin, publicados por ella misma y traducidos del francés por A. de P.*, the Spanish version of *Souvenirs et Mémoires* (Paris: Charpenter, 1836).

However, there is also earlier evidence of at least a partial translation of this latter work by Rosa Aldama. In a letter written to José Luis Alfaro on March 4, 1837, Domingo del Monte refers rather patronizingly to the fact that "Rosita" was responsible for translating the "Fragmentos de los 'Recuerdos de una Criolla'" which appeared in the 1837 volume of *Aguinaldo Habanero* (Havana: Imprenta de D. Jose Maria Palmer, 1837), 73–84. Del Monte himself prefaced this selection with the note "Una habanera en París" (*Aguinaldo Habanero* [Havana: Imprenta de D. Jose Maria Palmer, 1837]), 69–72. There he claims that he himself corrected, although only slightly, his wife's translations. "Cartas de Domingo del Monte," *Revista de la Biblioteca Nacional* 2, nos. 3–6 (September 30–December 31, 1909): 160 and note 4. In a similar way as "Serafina" with her father, Aldama hid herself behind her husband's more established literary reputation.

10. "Cartas a Chucha. 'Las mugeres de La Habana, II,'" *Faro Industrial de la Habana* (September 24, 1843): 2.

11. "Cartas a Chucha. 'Las mugeres de La Habana, I,'" *Faro Industrial de la Habana* (September 21, 1843): 2.

12. "Cartas dirigidas por la Condesa de Merlin a Jorge Sand. Las mugeres de La Habana (I)," *Diario de la Habana* (September 12, 1843): 1.

13. "Cartas a Chucha," *Faro Industrial de la Habana* (September 21, 1843): 2.

14. "Cartas a Chucha," *Faro Industrial de la Habana* (September 24, 1843): 2. "Serafina" blames this lack of tolerance on women's inadequate education, "que nos hace mirar con mala voluntad á los que nos dicen alguna de las muchas cosas que debe mejorar la ilustración" ("that makes us view with ill will those that tell us many of the things that may enlighten and improve us") (2). Note here again the tension between her willingness to accept Merlin as "illustrious precursor" and the barriers imposed by her immediate social circle.

15. "Cartas dirigidas por la Sra. de Merlin a Jorge Sand. Las mugeres de la Habana," *Diario de la Habana* (September 10, 1843): 1. Note the lack of stylistic flow and errors in translation, justified in the following: "A pesar de algunos defectos que se notan en la traducción de este articulo escrito en francés y publicado en dos idiomas en el Correo de Ultramar creemos que será interesante á nuestros suscriptores, [sic] ver que ocupamos la atencion europea de un modo que nos honra" ("Despite some defects that are evident in the translation of this article, which was written in French and was published in two languages in the Correo de Ultramar, we think that it will be of interest to our subscribers, to see that we are catching the attention of the Europeans in a way that gives us honor") (1). For another Spanish rendition of this letter, see La Condesa de Merlin, *La Habana*, ed. Amalia E. Bacardí (Madrid: Cronocolor, 1981), 229–37.

16. Figarola Caneda, Merlin's biographer, was the first to establish this fact, followed by more contemporary critics like Nara Araújo, who asserts that "contaba entre sus amistades a toda una generación de escritores y artistas famosos, Rossini, Musset, la Sand" ("she counted among her friends a whole generation of famous writers and artists: Rossini, Musset, Sand"). See Araújo's prologue to *Mis doce primeros años* (1838; Havana: Editorial Letras Cubanas, 1984), 9.

17. George Sand, "Souvenirs de Madame Merlin," *Oeuvres Complètes. Questions d'art et de littérature* (Paris: Calmann Lévy, 1878), 53–60.

18. "Si no hay en las obras de nuestra compatriota creaciones estupendas, contrastes maravillosos, poseen la ventaja de que no dejan en el alma ni terror, ni desaliento" ("If the works of our compatriot do not reveal wonderful creations, marvelous contrasts, they at least have the advantage of marking the soul neither with terror nor disappointment" [Gertrudis Gómez de Avellaneda, prólogo, la Condesa de Merlin, *Viaje a la Habana* {Madrid: Imprenta de la Sociedad Literaria y Tipográfica, 1844}, xv]).

19. *Diario de la Habana* (September 12, 1843): 1.

20. "Cartas dirigidas por la Sra. de Merlin a Jorge Sand," *Diario de la Habana* (September 10, 1843): 1.

21. Ibid.

22. Condesa de Merlin, *Mis doce primeros años* (1838; Havana: Editorial Letras Cubanas, 1984), 78.

23. Aldaraça, 69, 80.

24. Aldaraça, 65.

25. In his prologue to the 1788 edition of *Paul et Virginie*, Saint-Pierre considers his intention to be "to join to the beauty of nature between the tropics the moral beauty of a little society," adding that "[i]t was also my purpose to exhibit a number of great truths, among them this one: that our happiness consists in living according to Nature and virtue" (Jacques Henri Bernardin de Saint-Pierre, *Paul and Virginia*, trans. John Donovan [London and Boston: Peter Owen, 1982], 37).

26. "Cartas dirigidas por la Sra. de Merlin a Jorge Sand," *Diario de la Habana* (September 10, 1843), 2.

27. "Paul and Virginia had no clocks or almanacs, no books of chronology, history or philosophy. They regulated their lives according to the cycles of Nature" (Saint-Pierre, 70).

28. Sand, 60.

29. I paraphrase here the title of Fredrika Bremer's travelogue to North America and Cuba: *The Homes of the New World; Impressions of America*, tr. Mary Howitt, 2 vols. (1853; New York: Negro Universities Press, 1968).

30. "Cartas a Chucha. 'Las mugeres de La Habana, I,'" *Faro Industrial de la Habana*, (September 21, 1843), 2."

31. Ibid.

32. Ibid.

33. Ibid.

34. Tanco, 3–4. Despite these echoes, one cannot identify the "cronista" as Tanco, given the differences in their respective tones: the first lively and entertaining; the second, bitter and vitriolic.

35. "Crónica del buen tono," *Diario de la Habana* (September 24, 1843), 2.

36. "Crónica del buen tono," 2.

37. Along with publication notices, a favorable review of Palma's translation appeared in the *Diario de la Habana* (January 30, 1839): 2.

38. "Crónica del buen tono," *Diario de la Habana* (September 24, 1843), 2.

39. "Crónica del buen tono," 2.

40. "Asi, esta sencillez primitiva de las costumbres de la Habana, sin riesgo alguno para temperamentos ardientes y para un desarrollo precoz, seria un motivo de escándalo y de desórdenes en un pais de Europa, para ciertas del norte, pálidas, irritadas y atrasadas, las cuales adelantándose al amor por una cultura forzada, pierden la virginidad del corazón antes de conocer lo que es una pasión." ("Therefore, the primitive simplicity of the customs of Havana, although no risks for those of passionate temperament and precocious devel-

opment, would be a source of scandal and disorder in a European country [and especially] for some Northern women who, pale, irritable and backward, would rush into love out of a repressed culture, and lose their virginity of the heart before knowing what true passion is" ["Cartas dirigidas por la Sra. de Merlin á Jorge Sand. Las mugeres de La Habana," *Diario de la Habana* {September 11, 1843}: 2]).

41. Ibid.

42. "Cartas a Chucha. 'Las mugeres de La Habana, II,'" *Faro Industrial de la Habana*, (September 24, 1843), 2.".

43. "Cartas dirigidas por la Sra. de Merlin á Jorge Sand," *Diario de la Habana* (September 11, 1843): 2.

44. Aldaraça, 72, 73–74.

45. "Cartas dirigidas por la Sra. de Merlin á Jorge Sand," *Diario de la Habana* (September 11, 1843): 2.

46. "Cartas a Chucha. 'Las mugeres de La Habana, II,'" 2."

47. Ibid.

48. "Cartas dirigidas por la Sra. de Merlin á Jorge Sand. Las mugeres de la Habana," *Diario de la Habana* (September 11, 1843): 2.

49. "Cartas a Chucha. 'Las mugeres de La Habana, II,'" 2.".

50. Ibid. However, "Serafina" falls into a notable contradiction when she denies the practice of intermarriage, citing the example of family and friends. This might be a way to deny that Merlin had direct knowledge of "home" affairs, keeping in tune with the attitude current at the time.

51. "Cartas dirigidas por la Sra. de Merlin a Jorge Sand," *Diario de la Habana* (September 11, 1843): 2.

52. "Cartas a Chucha. 'Las mugeres de La Habana, III,'" *Faro Industrial de la Habana* (September 28, 1843): 2.

53. "Cartas dirigidas por la Sra. Merlin á Jorge Sand," *Diario de la Habana* (September 11, 1843): 2.

54. "Cartas a Chucha. 'Las mugeres de La Habana, III,'" 2.

55. "Cartas dirigidas por la Sra. de Merlin á Jorge Sand," *Diario de la Habana* (September 11, 1843): 2.

56. "Cartas a Chucha. 'Las mugeres de La Habana, III,'" 2.

57. Ibid..

58. Ibid.

59. "Sobre la educación. Carta tercera," *La Moda ó el Recreo Semanal del Bello Sexo* (May 14, 1831): 371. For the ideologizing process of women and children during the nineteenth century, see Aldaraça, 64.

60. "Cartas dirigidas por la Sra. de Merlin á Jorge Sand," *Diario de la Habana*, (September 12, 1843): 1.

61. Ibid.

62. Ibid.

63. Ibid.

64. "Cronica del buen tono," *Diario de la Habana* (September 24, 1843), 2.

65. Ibid.

66. "Cartas dirigidas por la Sra. de Merlin á Jorge Sand," *Diario de la Habana*, (September 12, 1843): 1.

67. "Este relato del viaje de la Condesa a La Habana muestra a la mujer de la aristocracia cubana cuyo retrato aparece evidentemente idealizado" [In her travel account to Havana, the Countess shows the woman from the Cuban aristocracy whose portrait is quite frankly idealized."]. Vásquez, 77.

68. Figarola Caneda, 10.

69. Sand, 58.

70. "Cartas dirigidas por la Sra. de Merlin á Jorge Sand," *Diario de la Habana* (September 11, 1843): 2. Vásquez also comments on the contrasts between Merlin's rendition of the slave woman and the aristocrat, which, in her view, is also idealized (77), and quotes the opening sentence of the passage cited above from the second volume of *La Havane*, 1844 Paris edition, 326 (74).

71. "Cartas dirigidas por la Sra. de Merlin á Jorge Sand," *Diario de la Habana*, (September 12, 1843): 2.

72. Ibid.

73. Ibid.

74. Aldaraça, 63–71.

75. See Figarola Caneda, 45–54, for a description of the predominant role of Merlin's salon in nineteenth-century Paris.

76. "Cartas dirigidas por la Sra. de Merlin á Jorge Sand," *Diario de la Habana* (September 12, 1843): 1.

77. Ibid.

78. "Cartas a Chucha. 'Las mugeres de La Habana, III,'" 2.

79. Ibid.

80. Aldaraça, 71.

81. "Cartas a Chucha. 'Las mugeres de La Habana, III,'" 2.

82. "Cronica del buen tono," 2.

83. Ibid.

84. C. Valdés [Plácido], "A la Señora DA María de las Mercedes Santa Cruz y Montalvo, Condesa de Merlin," *El Artista*, 1 (August 13, 1848): 21.

85. Aldaraça, 84.

86. Poems commemorating either Merlin's performance at the Peñalver concert or her resounding voice include: "A la Señora Condesa de Merlin," *Diario de la Habana* (July 12 1840): 3; "Poesía," *Diario de la Habana* (July 18, 1840): 2; and "A la Señora Condesa de Merlin—Soneto," *Diario de la Habana* (July 23, 1840): 2. Others are farewell odes that pay homage to the "hija de Cuba" as she retreats to France: "El frenólogo," "Fabula—El Fenix (Imitacion de Florian), Dedicada a la Sra. Condesa de Merlin," *Noticioso y Lucero* (July 8, 1840): 2; Fran-

cisco Orgaz, "Poesía—A la Sra. Condesa de Merlin," *Diario de la Habana* (July 21, 1840): 2; and N. de F., "Despedida á la Señora Condesa de Merlin," *Diario de la Habana* (July 26, 1840): 2.

87. Serafín Ramírez, "La Condesa de Merlin," *La Habana artística. Apuntes históricos* (Havana: Imprenta del E.M. de la Capitanía General, 1891), 35–55. However, the entire text of *Lola y María* was published in the 1845 edition of the *Faro Industrial de la Habana*.

88. Ramírez, 55.

89. *Diario de la Habana* (October 1, 1843): 2.

90. Sand, 57.

CHAPTER 8: LA COMTESSE STARES BACK

1. Cintio Vitier, *Lo cubano en la poesía* (Havana: Universidad Central de Las Villas, 1958), 12.

2. Vitier, 13.

3. Vitier, 110.

4. José María Heredia, "A . . ., en el baile," *Poesías completas*, vol. 1 (Havana: Municipio de la Habana, 1940), 225, partially quoted in Vitier, 62.

5. Vitier, 110.

6. Gertrudis Gómez de Avellaneda, *Obras de la Avellaneda. Poesías líricas*, vol. 1 (Havana: Imprenta de Aurelio Miranda, 1914), 1.

7. "En medio de la naturaleza y el mundo femenino de la familia criolla, *que es también esencialmente naturaleza, irrumpe el torcedor varonil de la historia*; en medio de la edénica delicia natural, único ámbito de nuestra poesía antes de Heredia, aparecen los problemas de la conciencia" ("In the midst of nature and the feminine world of the Creole family, *which is essentially nature also, erupts male historical influence*; in the midst of Edenic delight, the only existing sphere of poetry before Heredia, the problems of conscience appear" [Vitier, 71, emphasis added]).

8. Vitier, 73, 70.

9. José Antonio Portuondo makes this allegation in "La dramática neutralidad de Gertrudis Gómez de Avellaneda," *Capítulos de literatura cubana* (Havana: Ed. Letras Cubanas, 1981), 227.

10. "[E]s de suponer que las dos cubanas notables y desterradas se hayan conocido en Madrid al año siguiente (1845), cuando la Condesa de Merlín viajó a la capital española por asuntos de negocios" ("It is to be supposed that the two notable exiled Cubans must have met in Madrid the following year [1845], when the Countess of Merlin traveled to the Spanish capital for business reasons" [Raquel Romeu, *La mujer y el esclavo en la Cuba de 1840* {Uruguay: Asociación de Literatura Femenina Hispánica, 1987}, 80]. But in her "Apuntes biográficos de la Señora Condesa de Merlin," which serves as a prologue to La

Condesa de Merlin, *Viaje a la Habana* (Madrid: Imprenta de la Sociedad Literaria y Tipográfica, 1844), Gertrudis Gómez de Avellaneda laments that she has not experienced "el placer de conocerla personalmente" ("the pleasure of personally meeting her"), xv.

11. Vitier, 70.

12. "¡Cuba! al fin te verás libre y pura/Como el aire de luz que respiras/ . . . Aúnque viles traidores le sirvan,/Del tirano es inútil la saña,/Que no en vano entre Cuba y España/Tiende inmenso sus olas el mar" ("Cuba, you shall finally see yourself free and pure / like the air of light that you breathe / . . . though vile traitors serve her/the cruelty of the tyrant is useless / for not in vain between Cuba and Spain/the ocean spreads out its immense waves" [Heredia, 225, partially quoted in Vitier, 62]).

13. Severo Sarduy, "Tu dulce nombre halagará mi oído," *Homenaje a Gertrudis Gómez de Avellaneda: Memorias del simposio en el centenario de su muerte,* ed. Rosa M. Cabrera and Gladys B. Zaldívar (Miami: Ed. Universal, 1981), 19–20.

14. La Condesa de Merlin, *Mis doce primeros años e Historia de Sor Inés* (Havana: Imprenta el Siglo XX," 1922), 91.

15. Gómez de Avellaneda, "Apuntes biográficos de la Señora Condesa de Merlin," x–xi.

16. Gertrudis Gómez de Avellaneda, "Al partir," in *Poesías líricas,* 1.

17. I am indebted to my friend Madeline Cámara for this insight.

18. Sarduy, 19–20; my emphasis.

19. "[F]ue la naturaleza tan excesivamente pródiga, que habiéndola hecho un modelo de belleza, de gracia y de virtudes; . . . la dotó además con una preciosísima voz de *soprano* . . . de timbre puro, sonoro y perfectamente igual y poderosa en todos sus registros; dándole por último el sentimiento de lo bello, el buen gusto en las artes y una imaginación vivaz; un alma sensible y apasionada, un corazón de fuego" ("Nature was so excessively prodigal that after making her a model of beauty, of grace, and of virtues . . . it also endowed her with the most beautiful soprano voice . . . of a pure, sonorous timbre, perfectly even and powerful in all the registers; in short, giving her a feeling for the beautiful, for good taste in the arts, and a lively imagination; a sensitive and passionate soul, and a fiery heart" [Serafín Ramírez, "La Condesa de Merlin," *La Habana Artística. Apuntes históricos* {Havana: Imprenta del E. M. de la Capitanía General, 1891}, 50–51]).

20. "La condesa de Merlín [*sic*], de quien pudiera decirse como del famoso Pedro Gurat, *su nombre es un elogio* . . . pudo, como el Greco, buscar por el mundo inútilmente, una rival" ("The Countess of Merlin, of whom one could say, as in the case of the famous Pedro Gurat, that her name is a tribute . . . was able, like El Greco, to look fruitlessly around the world for a rival" [Ramírez, 37]). Ramírez describes a scene between María Malinbran and Merlin when, singing a duet from *Semirámide,* the first is so overtaken by Merlin's voice that she breaks up the duet to praise her for following in her father's footsteps (52–53).

21. The original reads: "sus escritos están muy lejos de igualarse al hechizo

y originalidad de sus conversaciones" ("her writings are far from reaching the charm and originality of her conversations" [Anonymous, "La Condesa de Merlin, *Mis doce primeros años*," *La cartera cubana* 2 {January 1839}: 102]).

22. Gómez de Avellaneda, "Apuntes biográficos," xv.

23. Gómez de Avellaneda, v.

24. Gómez de Avellaneda, vii.

25. Gómez de Avellaneda, v.

26. Gómez de Avellaneda, v. This condition still holds true in the case of contemporary Cuban writers.

27. Gómez de Avellaneda, xv.

28. Gómez de Avellaneda, xv.

29. Gómez de Avellaneda, xv.

30. "[F]elicitamos al mismo tiempo á nuestra cara patria, á nuestra bella Cuba, por la gloria que le cabe en contar entre sus hijos á la señora Condesa de Merlin" ("We congratulate at the same time our dear homeland, our beautiful Cuba, for the glory due her in counting among her children the Countess of Merlin" [Gómez de Avellaneda, "Apuntes biográficos," xv–xvi]).

31. Vitier, 13.

32. Merlin, *Viaje a la Habana*, 3.

33. Merlin, 2.

34. Such has been the fate of Gómez de Avellaneda.

35. For an analysis of this complex as exemplified in Villaverde's *Cecilia Valdés*, a classic in Cuban literature, see my "Identity and Incest in *Cecilia Valdés*: Villaverde and the Origin(s) of the Text," *Cuban Studies* 24 (1994): 83–104.

36. Severo Sarduy, *De donde son los cantantes*, 2nd ed. (México: Joaquín Mortiz, 1970), 75.

37. Sarduy, 76.

38. Guillermo Cabrera Infante, "Meta-Final," in Roberto González Echevarría, *The Voice of the Masters: Writing and Authority in Modern Latin American Literature* (Austin: University of Texas Press, 1985), 144. The translation that follows is from the same source.

39. Roberto Ignacio Díaz has pointed out that Carpentier is similarly ridiculed as "Cerpentier," suggesting that the parodic effect is the same for both writers. However, I cannot help but think that there is an (un)conscious gender valorization at play here, for at the very least Alejo is granted the venerable status of a mythic serpent, long associated as a phallic symbol.

40. Roberto González Echevarría, "Commentary to Meta-End," *The Voice of the Masters*, 162.

41. González Echevarría, "Commentary to Meta-End," 162 (emphasis added).

42. "Hay que reconocerlo. Dolores ha llegado a su barroco" ("It must be acknowledged. Dolores has reached the epitome of the baroque" [Sarduy, 76]).

43. González Echevarría, "Commentary to Meta-End," 164.

44. González Echevarría, "Commentary to Meta-End," 164 (emphasis added).

45. González Echevarría, "Commentary to Meta-End," 163.

46. See, for example, Arenas's July 24, 1973, letter to Delfín Prats signed as "Dña. Mercedes Santa Cruz, Condesa de Merlin" and the editor's note in Reinaldo Arenas, *Necesidad de libertad. Mariel: Testimonios de un intelectual disidente* (Costa Rica: Kosmos Editorial, 1986), 81–82.

47. Reinaldo Arenas, *Viaje a La Habana (Novela en tres viajes)* (Miami: Ed. Universal, 1990).

48. Arenas, *Viaje a La Habana*, 145.

49. "Te reconocí al momento. Y yo estoy seguro de que tú te diste cuenta de quién yo era. . . . Yo sabía que tú eras mi padre y eso me alegraba, y tú sabías que yo era tu hijo" ("I recognized who you where right from the start. And I am sure that you also knew who I was. . . . I knew that you were my father and that made me glad, and you knew that I was your son" [Arenas, 179]).

50. Jorge Olivares, "Otra vez *Cecilia Valdés*: Arenas con(tra) Villaverde," *Hispanic Review*, 62: 2 (Spring 1994): 172, 174–75.

51. Merlin, *Viaje a la Habana*, 107–9.

52. Reinaldo Arenas, *La loma del ángel* (Miami: Mariel Press, 1987), 64. Also quoted in Olivares, 173.

53. Arenas, *La loma del ángel*, 64–65.

54. Arenas, *La loma del ángel*, 65.

55. For another reading of this scene, see Olivares, 173–74.

56. Arenas, *La loma del ángel*, 66.

57. Olivares, 180–82.

58. Olivares, 180–81.

59. Olivares, 180–82.

60. Arenas, *La loma del ángel*, 67.

61. Arenas, *La loma del ángel*, 67.

62. Arenas, *La loma del ángel*, 68.

63. Olivares, 182.

64. "Bella . . . con fama literaria (aunque hay que confesar que casi todos sus libros se los escribió Próspero Merimée") ("Beautiful, enjoying literary fame (although it must be said that almost all of her works were written by Próspero Merimée" [Reinaldo Arenas, *El color del verano* {Miami: Ed. Universal, 1991}, 257]).

65. This answers Olivares's claim that, in the ensuing ideological battle between Dolores Santa Cruz ("negra y ex-esclava)" ("a former slave and black) and Merlin ("blanca y esclavista)" ("white and pro-slavery"), the latter's exclusion was completely justified: "se expulsa, humillada, a la 'extranjera' que pretendía ser 'voz' de su patria" ("the 'foreigner' who pretended to be spokesperson for her country is thus thrown out and humiliated" ["Otra vez *Cecilia Valdés*," 182]).

Díaz claims that "[i]n *La Loma del Angel*, Reinaldo Arenas traces a parallel between Merlin's marginality and that of black slaves, which leads, in the novel,

to their violent expulsion—both of Merlin and the slaves—from Cuban society"
("Merlin's Foreign House: The Genres of *La Havane*," *Cuban Studies* 24
[1994]: 79n.16). I hold, however, that, in Arenas's rewriting, Merlin's humiliation and banishment must be seen as tied to the consistently devalued position
which all female characters occupy in his fiction, a meaning conveyed precisely
by the parodic charge of the scene.

66. González Echevarría, 163.

67. Arenas, *El color del verano*, 72.

68. Arenas, *El color del verano*, 140.

69. Arenas, El color del verano, 67, 262.

70. "Un concurrente," "Concierto del Sr. Conde de Peñalver," *Diario de
la Habana*, July 12, 1840, 2–3.

71. Arenas, *El color del verano*, 257.

72. Arenas, *El color del verano*, 257. The echoes of Merlin's early autobiographical writings are found in 252–56, which portrays the Countess as a great
seductress.

73. Arenas, *El color del verano*, 368.

74. Arenas, *El color del verano*, 368.

75. Arenas, *El color del verano*, 369.

76. Arenas, *El color del verano*, 369.

77. Arenas, *El color del verano*, 370.

78. Arenas, *El color del verano*, 371.

79. I am indebted to my friend Fernando Baqueiro for this insight.

80. I am paraphrasing here the title of Miguel Barnet's famous essay, "The
Culture that Sugar Created."

81. Arenas, *El color del verano*, 370–73.

82. Arenas, *El color del verano*, 373–77. I was a privileged witness to the fact
that Arenas himself had to resort to this strategy in his Old Havana apartment,
located right next to the Cathedral.

83. Reinaldo Arenas, *Antes que anochezca* (Barcelona: Ed. Tusquets, 1992),
273–78.

84. These were my feelings precisely when I visited the Convent in February 1996 with the Casa de las Américas tour, which made me think that Arenas's fiction is closer to reality than any verifiable account.

85. Arenas, *El color del verano*, 437.

86. Arenas, *El color del verano*, 442.

87. See Guillermo Cabrera Infante, *Vista del amanecer en el trópico* (Barcelona:
Ed. Seix Barral, 1974), 233.

88. Lourdes Gil, "Confesiones de la Condesa de Merlin o lamento de la
escritora cubana que regresa a la isla," *El cerco de las transfiguraciones* (Coral Gables:
La Torre de Papel, 1996), 49. I am indebted to my friend Lourdes Gil for kindly
sending me a copy of her book.

89. Gil, 49.

BIBLIOGRAPHY

Abbreviations

AG   Aguinaldo Habanero
CA   Cuba y América
CSEC   Cuban Studies/Estudios Cubanos
DG   Diario de Gobierno
DH   Diario de la Habana
DM   Diario de la Marina
DS   Diario de las Señoras
El Alm   El Almendares
El Art   El Artista
EA   El Album
EV   El Velorio
FIH   Faro Industrial de la Habana
GH   Gaceta de la Habana
HA   La Habana Artística
HL   La Habana Literaria
LCC   La Cartera Cubana
LP   La Presse
LT   La Tarde
NL   Noticioso y Lucero
RBC   Revista Bimestre Cubana
RBN   Revista de la Biblioteca Nacional
RRBIC   Revista y Repertorio Bimestre de la Isla de Cuba
RU   Revista Universal

Merlin's Works

Books

Mes douze premières années. Paris: Gautier-Laguionie, 1831.
Histoire de la Soeur Inés. First edition. Paris: P. Dupont et Laguionie, 1832.
Souvenirs et Mémoires de Madame la Comtesse Merlin, publiés pour elle-même. Four volumes. Paris: Charpentier, 1836.
Les loisirs d'une femme du monde. Two volumes. Paris: Librairie de L'Advocat et Comp., 1838.
Madame Malinbran. Two volumes. Bruxelles: Sociéte Typographique Belge. Ad. Wahlen et Cie., 1838.
Mis doce primeros años. Tr. Agustín de Palma. Philadelphia: 1838 (privately published).

292

Historia de la Hermana Santa Inés. Tr. Agustín de Palma. J. C. Clark, 1839.

Malinbran. Milan: Pirotta et C., 1840.

Memoirs and Letters of Madame Malinbran. Philadelphia: Carey and Hart, 1840.

Memoirs of Madame Malinbran. London: Henry Colburn, 1840.

Los esclavos en las colonias españolas. Madrid: Imprenta de Alegría y Charlain, 1841.

Lola et Maria. Paris: L. Potter, Librairie Editeur, 1843.

La Havane. Three volumes. Paris: Librairie d'Amyot, 1844.

La Havane. Three volumes. Bruxelles: Sociéte Belge de Librarie Hauman et Cie, 1844.

La Havane. Five volumes in one. Bruxelles: Sociéte Typographique Belge, 1844.

La Havane. Rare edition. La Haye: n.p., 1844.

Memoirs of Madam Malinbran, with a selection from her correspondence and notices of the musical drama in England. Second edition. London: Henry Colburn, 1844.

Viaje a la Habana. Prólogo de Gertrudis Gómez de Avellaneda. Madrid: Imprenta de la Sociedad Literaria y Tipográfica, 1844.

Les lionnes de Paris. Two volumes. Paris: Librairie d'Amyot, 1845.

Le Duc d'Athènes. Three volumes. Paris: Paul Bermain et Cie, 1852.

Memorias y recuerdos de la Señora Condesa de Merlin, publicados por ella misma y traducidos del francés por Agustín de Palma. Three volumes. Havana: A. M. Dávila, 1853.

Biographie Universelle des Musiciens et Bibliographie Generale de la Musique. Paris: 1880.

Mis doce primeros años. Tr. Agustín de Palma. Havana: Imprenta de la Unión Constitucional, 1892.

Viaje a la Habana. Havana: Biblioteca de la Unión Constitucional, 1892.

Mis doce primeros años. Havana: Imprenta el Siglo XX, 1922.

Viaje a la Habana. Havana: Librería Cervantes, 1922.

Viaje a la Habana. Havana: n.p., 1922

Memorias de la Condesa de Merlin. Tr. G. de Z. Paris: Charpentier de Paris, 1922–1923.

Boxhorn, Emilia, ed. *Correspondencia íntima de la Condesa de Merlin.* Tr. Boris Bureba. Madrid and Paris: Industrial Gráfica Reyes, 1928.

Viaje a La Habana. Prologue by Salvador Bueno. Havana: Ed. de Arte y Literatura, 1974.

La Habana. Tr. Amalia E. Bacardí. Madrid: Cronocolor, 1981.

Memorias de Sor Inés. #16. Havana.

Mis doce primeros años. Ed. Nara Araújo. Havana: Ed. Letras Cubanas, 1984.

Souvenirs et Mémoires de Madame la Comtesse Merlin. Souvenirs d'une Créole. Ed. Carmen Vásquez. Paris: Mercure de France, 1990.

JOURNAL PUBLICATIONS AND BOOK CHAPTERS

"Fragmentos de los 'Recuerdos de una Criolla.'" *AG* (Havana: Imprenta de D. Jose Maria Palmer: 1837), 73–84.

"A la vista de Cuba." *HL* 2 Number 9 (May 15, 1892): 213. (Fragment of *Viaje a la Habana.* June 6, 1840 entry).

"Les esclaves dans les colonies espagnoles." *Revue des Deux Mondes* 26 (April–June, 1841): 743–69.

"Cartas dirigidas por la Señora de Merlin a Jorge Sand: 'Las mugeres de la Habana.'" *FIH* (September 10, 1843): 2–3.

"Cartas a Chucha: 'Las Mugeres de la Habana I.'" *FIH* (September 21, 1843): 2.

"Cartas a Chucha: 'Las Mugeres de la Habana II.'" *FIH* (September 24, 1843): 2.

"Cartas a Chucha: 'Las Mugeres de la Habana III.'" *FIH* (September 28, 1843): 2.

"Cartas dirigidas por la Señora de Merlin a Jorge Sand:. 'Las mugeres de la Habana (1).'" *DH* (September 10, 1843): 1–2.

"Cartas dirigidas por la Señora de Merlin a Jorge Sand: 'Las mugeres de la Habana.'" *DH* (September 11, 1843): 2.

"Cartas dirigidas por la Señora de Merlin a Jorge Sand: 'Las mugeres de la Habana.'" *DH* (September 12, 1843): 1.

"Fragmens d'un *Voyage a la Havane* (1): Lettre XIII—A Madame Gentien de Dissay." *LP* (October 26, 1843): 1–2.

"Fragmens d'un *Voyage a la Havane* (1): Lettre XIV—A Madame Gentien de Dissay." *LP* (October 27, 1843): 1–2.

"Fragmens d'un *Voyage a la Havane* (1): Lettre XV—A Madame Gentien de Dissay." *LP* (October 28, 1843): 1–2.

"Fragmens d'un *Voyage a la Havane*: Lettre XV (Suite)." *LP* (October 29, 1843): 1–2.

"Fragmens d'un *Voyage a la Havane*: Lettre XIX—A Madame Sophie Gay." *LP* (October 31, 1843).

"Fragmens d'un *Voyage a la Havane*: Lettre XIX (Suite)." *LP* (November 1, 1843).

"Fragmens d'un *Voyage a la Havane*: Lettre XX—A Mademoiselle Marquis de Custine." *LP* (November 4, 1843).

"Fragmens d'un *Voyage a la Havane*: Lettre XX—(Suite)." *LP* (November 8, 1843).

"Fragmens d'un *Voyage a la Havane*: Lettre XXII—A Madame la Vicomtesse de Walsh." *LP* (November 9, 1843).

"Fragmens d'un *Voyage a la Havane*: Lettre XXII (Suite)." *LP* (November 10, 1843).

"Fragmens d'un *Voyage a la Havane*: Lettre XXIX (Suite)." *LP* (November 11, 1843).

"Fragmens d'un *Voyage a la Havane*: Lettre XXIX (Suite)." *LP* (November 12, 1843).

"Fragmens d'un *Voyage a la Havane*: Lettre XXIX (Suite)." *LP* (November 14, 1843).

"Fragmens d'un *Voyage a la Havane*: Lettre XXIX (Suite)." *LP* (November 15, 1843).

"Fragmens d'un *Voyage a la Havane*: Lettre XXX—A Colonel Georges Damer Dawson, Membre du parlament anglaís." *LP* (November 16, 1843).

"Lola, por la señora Condesa de Merlin, traducida por P.D.E.," *FIH* May 2, 1845: 2–3.

"Lola." *FIH* May 3, 1845: 2–3.

"Lola." *FIH* May 5, 1845: 3.
"Lola." *FIH* May 7, 1845: 3.
"Lola." *FIH* May 8, 1845: 3
"Lola." *FIH* May 9, 1845: 3.
"Lola." *FIH* May 11, 1845: 3.
"Lola." *FIH* May 13, 1845: 2–3.
"Lola." *FIH* May 15, 1845: 2–3.
"Fragmentos." In *Cuba and the Cubans*, 75–81. New York: n.p., 1850.
"*Mis doce primeros años* (Fragment): 'La mujer en Cuba.'" *El Figaro* 11 Number 6 (February 24, 1895): 69.
"*Mis doce primeros años* por la Condesa de Merlin." *CA* 6 Number 7 (January 26, 1902): 93–96.
"*Mis doce primeros años* por la Condesa de Merlin." *CA* 6 Number 8 (February 9, 1902): 109–12.
"*Mis doce primeros años* por la Condesa de Merlin." *CA* 6 Number 9 (February 16, 1902): 125–28.
"*Mis doce primeros años* por la Condesa de Merlin." *CA* 6 Number 10 (February 23, 1902): 141–44.
"*Mis doce primeros años* por la Condesa de Merlin." *CA* 6 Number 11 (March 9, 1902): 157–58.
"*Historia de Sor Inés* por la Condesa de Merlin." *CA* 6 Number 12 (March 16, 1902): 173–76.
"*Historia de Sor Inés* por la Condesa de Merlin." *CA* 6 Number 13 (March 23, 1902): 189–92.
"*Historia de Sor Inés* por la Condesa de Merlin." *CA* 6 Number 14 (March 30, 1902): 205–8.
"*Historia de Sor Inés* por la Condesa de Merlin." *CA* 6 Number 15 (April 13, 1902): 221–24.
"*Historia de Sor Inés* por la Condesa de Merlin." *CA* 6 Number 16 (April 20, 1902): 233–36.
"*Historia de Sor Inés* por la Condesa de Merlin." *CA* 6 Number 17 (April 27, 1902): 245.

Secondary Sources on Merlin

BOOKS

Bacardí Moreau, Emilio. *La Condesa de Merlin*. Santiago de Cuba: Tip. Arroyo Hermanos, 1924.
Figarola-Caneda, Domingo. *La Condesa de Merlin, María de la Merced Santa Cruz y Montalvo, Estudio bibliográfico e iconográfico, escrito en presencia de documentos inéditos y de todas las ediciones de sus obras. Su correspondencia íntima [1789–1852]*. Paris: Editions Excelsior, 1928.
Figueroa, Agustín. *La Condesa de Merlin: Musa del Romanticismo*. Madrid: Imprenta de Juan Pueyo, 1934.
Romeu, Raquel. *La mujer y el esclavo en la Cuba de 1840*. Uruguay: Asociación de Literatura Femenina Hispánica, 1987.

Tanco y Bosmeniel, Felix. *Refutación al folleto intitulado "Viage a la Habana" por la Condesa de Merlin*. Havana: Imprenta de Gobierno y Capitanía General, 1844.

ARTICLES

Monte, Domingo del. "Artículo sobre Merlin." *RRBIC* 1 Number 1 (May–June, 1831): 346–60. Reproduced in *La Habana* (October, 1859): 274–84, 303–9.
———. "Sobre *Mis doce primeros años*." *Revista Bimestre Cubana* 1: 3 (October 1831): 346–60.
———. "Una habanera en Paris." In *Aguinaldo Habanero*. Ed. Ramón de Palma and José Antonio Echeverría, 69–84. Havana: Imprenta de D. Jose Maria Palmer, 1837.
———. *Cartas a José Luis Alfonso*. Vol. II (1838–1847). Manuscript Collection #39, Colección Cubana, Biblioteca Nacional José Martí.
"*Mis doce primeros años*. Announcement." *DH* (December 25, 1838): 4.
N.R.B. "*Mis doce primeros años* por la Condesa de Merlin Obra traducida por A. de P.—e impresa en FILADELFIA con el mayor esmero." *DH* (January 30, 1839): 2.
Anonymous. "La Condesa de Merlin. *Mis doce primeros años*." *LCC* 2 (January 1839): 99–102.
Palma, Ramón de. "Memorias y recuerdos de la Condesa de Merlin." *El Album*. 2 (1839). 5–61.
"Variedades: Concierto de la Señora Condesa de Merlin." *DH* (December 21, 1839): 1.
"Variedades: 'María Malinbran Beriot.' (Fragment of *Memorias de Madam Malinbran* por la Condesa de Merlin. 2 tomos en 12.)." *DH* (May 28, 1840): 1–2.
"Puerto de la Habana." *NL* (June 10, 1840): 1.
"Noticias de la Habana." *NL* (June 17, 1840): 2.
"Tanto vales cuanto pesas." *NL* (June 24, 1840): 2.
"Noticias de la Habana." *NL* (July 3, 1840): 2.
"El frenólogo." "Poesía. Fabula—El Fénix (Imitacion de Florian) Dedicada a la Señora Condesa de Merlin." *NL* (July 8, 1840): 2.
"Novedades en Nueva York (On Merlin's Arrival in New York)." *DH* (June 17, 1840): 1–2.
"Un concurrente: La Señora Condesa de Merlin. (Concierto del Señor Conde de Peñalver—Comunicados)." *DH* (July 12, 1840): 2–3.
"Poesía: A la Señora Condesa de Merlin. Comunicados." *DH* (July 12, 1840): 3.
A. P. "Carta a Señores Editores del *Diario de Gobierno*." *DH* (July 13, 1840): 2.
M. A. A. "Justo elogio al merito de la Sra. Condesa de Merlin. (Announcement of Merlin's departure)." *DH* (July 17, 1840): 2.
"Comunicados: El concurrente. (Letter to A. P.)." *DH* (July 18, 1840): 2.
"Poesía." *DH* (July 18, 1840): 2.
Francisco Orgaz. "Comunicados: Poesía a la Señora Condesa de Merlin." *DH* (July 21, 1840): 2.
"Noticias de la Habana: Teatros." *NL* (July 21, 1840): 2.

J. de C. "Noticias: Concierto in Casa de Beneficencia." *DH* (July 22, 1840): 2.

"Poesía—A la Señorita Doña Maria de Jesus Martínez." *DH* (July 23, 1840): 2.

"A la Señora Condesa de Merlin. Soneto." *DH* (July 25, 1840): 2.

N. de F. "Comunicados: Soneto—Despedida á la Señora Condesa de Merlin." *DH* (July 26, 1840): 2

"Miscelanea." *NL* (October 16, 1840): 2.

"Miscelanea." *NL* (December 2, 1840): 2.

Alfonso, Jose Luis, Marquéz de Montelo. "Noticia sobre el estado político y administrativo de Cuba, dirijida [sic] á la Señora Condesa Merlin [sic] en Abril de 1842." Manuscript collection #9. Havana: Biblioteca Nacional Jose Martí.

"Noticia acerca de la partida para Liverpool desde Nueva York de la bailarina Fanny Essler y de su exito en EE.UU." *FIH* (August 14, 1842): 3.

"Anuncios: *Mis doce primeros años*." *FIH* (June 5, 1843): 4.

"Libros interesantes: Anuncio de venta de *Mis doce primeros años* e *Historia de Sor Inés*." *FIH* (September 17, 1843): 1.

"Cronica del buen tono." *DH* (September 24, 1843): 2.

"Cronica del buen tono: 'Las Mugeres de la Habana.'" *DH* (October 1, 1843): 2.

"La Habana y la Condesa de Merlin." *FIH* (December 19, 1843): 1.

"*Viage a la Habana* por la Señora Condesa de Merlin." *FIH* (April 10, 1844): 2.

"Obra nueva é interesante." *FIH* (April 12, 1844): 1.

"Librería de los subscritores del Faro." *FIH* (April 14, 1844): 1.

"Comunicado: José de la Luz. 'Carta a los editores.'" *FIH* (April 27, 1844): 2.

"Anuncio de librería de los subscritores del Faro." *FIH* (April 29–30, 1844): 1.

'Fair Play' [pseudonym of José de la Luz y Caballero]: "Letter to Editors—Cronica insular: (Comunicados)." *FIH* (April 30, 1844): 2.

Veráfilo. "*Viage a la Habana* por la Condesa de Merlin. Artículo I." *DH* (April 22, 1844): 2.

———. "*Viage a la Habana* por la Condesa de Merlin. Artículo II." *DH* (April 23, 1844): 2.

———. "*Viage a la Habana* por la Condesa de Merlin. Artículo III." *DH* (April 24, 1844): 2.

———. "*Viage a la Habana* por la Condesa de Merlin. Artículo IV." *DH* (April 25, 1844): 2.

———. "*Viage a la Habana* por la Condesa de Merlin. Artículo V. Los Guagiros." *DH* (April 26, 1844).

———. "*Viage a la Habana* por la Condesa de Merlin. Artículo VI. Los Guagiros." *DH* (April 27, 1844): 2.

———. "*Viage a la Habana* por la Condesa de Merlin. Artículo VII. La Vida en la Habana etc. etc..." *DH* (April 28, 1844): 2.

———. "*Viage a la Habana* por la Condesa de Merlin. Artículo VIII." *DH* (April 29, 1844): 2.

———. "*Viage a la Habana* por la Condesa de Merlin. Artículo IX. El Velorio." *DH* (April 30, 1844): 2.

———. "*Viage a la Habana* por la Condesa de Merlin. Artículo X. Velorios." *DH* (May 1, 1844): 2.

———. "*Viage a la Habana* por la Condesa de Merlin. Artículo XI. Un poco más de mondongo—Costumbres íntimas—Las Pascuas." *DH* (May 2, 1844): 2.

———. *"Viage a la Habana* por la Condesa de Merlin. Artículo XII. Continuan las Pascuas y las costumbres íntimas." *DH* (May 3, 1844): 2.

———. *"Viage a la Habana* por la Condesa de Merlin. Artículo III. Un día en la Habana..." *DH* (May 4, 1844): 2.

"Las cavernas del Monte Libano." *FIH* (May 29, 1847): 2.

Ferrer, Miguel Rodríguez. "Carta 2a." *FIH* (May 3, 1847): 2.

Valdés, G. C. (Plácido). "A la Señora DA Maria de las Mercedes Santa Cruz y Montalvo, Condesa de Merlin." *El Artista* 1 Number 1 (August 13, 1848): 20–21.

Aguero, Pedro de. "Mujeres célebres. La Condesa de Merlin." *El Alm* (July 11, 1881).

———. "Mujeres célebres. La Condesa de Merlin." *El Alm* (July 12, 1881).

———. "Mujeres célebres. La Condesa de Merlin." *El Alm* (July 14, 1881).

———. "Mujeres célebres. La Condesa de Merlin." *El Alm* (July 15, 1881).

———. "Mujeres célebres. La Condesa de Merlin." *El Alm* (July 16, 1881).

Sand, George. "Souvenirs de Madame Merlin." In *Oeuvres Complètes—Questions d'art et de littérature*, 53–60. Paris: Calmann Lévy Editeur, 1878.

Ramírez, Serafín. "La Condesa de Merlin." *La Habana artística: Apuntes históricos*, 35–55. Havana: Imprenta del E. M. de la Capitanía General, 1891.

Cyrano [Peudonym of Ramiro Eulogio Cabrera Bilbao]. "La Condesa de Merlin." *CA* 6: 7 (January 26, 1902): 99.

Gómez de Avellaneda, Gertrudis. "Apuntes biograficos de la Condesa de Merlin." *CA* 6: 11 (March 9, 1902): 158–60.

Monte, Domingo del. "Cartas de Domingo del Monte." *RBN* 2: 3–6 (September 30–December 31, 1909).

Cabrera-Bilbao, L. "La Condesa de Merlin y Cuba—Respuesta al habanero curioso y callejero." *Diario de la Marina* (June 22, 1938).

Villa Urrutia, Wenceslao Ramírez. "La Condesa de Merlin." *RBC* 27 (1931): 362–70.

de la Lastra, Joaquín. "Teresa Montalvo: Una habanera en la Corte de España." *RBC* 48: 1 (July–August, 1941): 73–88.

Souza, B., "La Condesa de Merlin, la Condesa de Montijo y Prospero Merimée." *Diario de la Marina*, September 5, 1943.

Luz y Caballero, José de la. *"El Viaje a la Habana de la Condesa de Merlin."* "El comunicante del Faro." In *Escritos literarios*. Biblioteca de Autores Cubanos, Volume II. Obras de José de la Luz y Caballero Volume VI. Havana: Ed. de la Universidad de la Habana, 1946.

Bueno, Salvador. "Una escritora cubana en francés: La Condesa de Merlin." *Bohemia* (October 30, 1964): 12–15.

———. "Un libro polémico: El *Viaje a la Habana* de la Condesa de Merlin." *Cuadernos americanos* 199: 2 (March–April 1975): 161–77.

———. "Una escritora habanera de expresión francesa." In *De Merlin a Carpentier: Nuevos temas y personajes de literatura cubana*, 9–35. Havana: UNEAC Contemporáneos, 1977.

Male, Belkis Cuza. "Viaje a la Habana: La Condesa de Merlin." *Linden Lane Magazine* 2: 1 (1983): 11–12.

Vásquez, Carmen. "Las mujeres cubanas de la Condesa de Merlin." In *Colloque International Femmes des Amériques*, 69–84. Université de Toulouse-Le Mirail / Université de Paris III. Service des Publications Université de Toulouse-Le Mirail, 1986.

Méndez Rodenas, Adriana. "Voyage to *La Havane*: La Condesa de Merlin's Pre-View of National Identity," *CSEC*. 26 (1986): 71–99.

———. "A Journey to the (Literary) Source: The Invention of Origins in Merlin's *Viaje a la Habana* (1844)." *New Literary History* 21: 3 (Spring 1990): 707–31.

———. "'Las mugeres de La Habana:' Una polémica feminista en el romanticismo hispanoamericano." *Revista de Estudios Hispánicos*, 24: 1 (January 1990): 161–84.

Díaz, Roberto Ignacio. "La habitación contigua. Extraterritorialidad y multilingüismo en la literatura hispanoamericana." Ph.D. dissertation, Harvard University, 1991.

Vásquez, Carmen. "*Histoire de la soeur Inès*, de la Condesa de Merlin, relato de una mujer crítica de su época." *La Torre*, 6: 21 (January–March 1992): 85–103.

Martin, Claire Emilie. "La Condesa de Merlin y *Mis doce primeros años*: O el contradiscurso de la subjetividad romántica." *Alba de América* 18–19: 10 (1992): 195–202.

Díaz, Roberto Ignacio. "Merlin's Foreign House: The Genres of *La Havane*." *CSEC* 24 (1994): 57–82.

Martin, Claire Emilie. "Slavery in the Spanish Colonies: The Racial Politics of The Countess of Merlin." In *Reinterpreting the Spanish American Essay: Women Writers of the 19th and 20th Centuries*, ed. Doris Meyer, 37–45. Austin: University of Texas Press, 1995.

Gil, Lourdes. "Confesiones de la Condesa de Merlin o Lamentos de la escritora cubana que regresa a la isla." In *El cerco de las transfiguraciones*, 45–50. Coral Gables: La Torre de Papel, 1996.

Díaz, Roberto Ignacio. "Paratextual Snow; or, The Threshold of Mercedes Merlin." *Colby Quarterly* 32, no. 4 (December 1996): 237–254.

Other Works Cited

Books and Pamphlets

Alexander, J. G. *Observaciones sobre la esclavitud y comercio de esclavos e Informe del Dr. Madden sobre la esclavitud en la isla de Cuba*. Barcelona: Imprenta de A. Bergnes y Co., 1841.

Anderson, Benedict. *Imagined Communities: Reflections on the Origin and Spread of Nationalism*. Rev. ed. London and New York: Verso, 1991.

Araújo, Nara, ed. *Viajeras al Caribe*. Havana: Casa de las Américas, 1983.

Arenas, Reinaldo. *Necesidad de libertad. Mariel: Testimonios de un intelectual disidente*. San José, Costa Rica: Kosmos Editorial, 1986.

———. *La loma del ángel*. Miami: Mariel Press, 1987.

————. *Viaje a La Habana (Novela en tres viajes)*. Miami: Ed. Universal, 1990.

————. *El color del verano*. Miami: Ed. Universal, 1991.

————. *Antes que anochezca*. Barcelona: Ed. Tusquets, 1992.

Bachiller y Morales, Antonio. *Tipos y costumbres de la isla de Cuba*. Havana: Miguel de Villa, 1881.

Bakhtin, M. M. *The Dialogic Imagination*. Ed. Michael Holquist; tr. Caryl Emerson and Michael Holquist. Austin: University of Texas Press, 1981.

Benítez Rojo, Antonio. *The Repeating Island: The Caribbean and the Postmodern Perspective*. Tr. James Maraniss. Durham, N.C.: Duke University Press, 1992.

Benjamin, Jessica. *The Bonds of Love: Psychoanalysis, Feminism, and the Problem of Domination*. New York: Pantheon Books, 1988.

Betancourt, José R. Victoriano, *Una feria de la Caridad en 183...* Havana: Editorial Letras Cubanas, 1978.

————. *Artículos de costumbres*. Havana: Ministerio de Educación, 1941.

Bremer, Fredrika. *The Homes of the New World: Impressions of America*. Tr. Mary Howitt. Two volumes. 1853; rpt. New York: Negro Universities Press, 1968.

Bueno, Salvador, ed. *Costumbristas cubanos del siglo XIX*. Vol. 115. Caracas: Biblioteca Ayacucho, 1985.

————. *Figuras cubanas: Breves biografías de grandes cubanos del siglo XIX*. Havana: Comisión Nacional Cubana de la UNESCO, 1964.

————. *Las ideas literarias de Domingo del Monte*. Havana: Comisión Nacional Cubana de la UNESCO, 1954.

Cabrera Infante, Guillermo. "Meta-End." In Roberto González Echevarría, *The Voice of the Masters: Writing and Authority in Modern Latin American Literature*, 137–68. Austin: Univerity of Texas Press, 1985.

————. *Vista del amanecer en el trópico*. Barcelona: Ed. Seix Barral, 1974.

Calcagno, Francisco. *Diccionario biográfico cubano*. New York: Imprenta y Librería de N. Ponce de Leon, 1878.

Carpentier, Alejo. *Guerra del tiempo*. Mexico City: Cia General de Ediciones, 1956.

————. *Tientos y diferencias*. Havana: UNEAC Contemporáneos, 1966.

Castro-Klarén, Sara, Sylvia Molloy, and Beatriz Sarlo, eds. *Women's Writing in Latin America: An Anthology*. Boulder: Westview Press, 1991.

Los cubanos pintados por sí mismos. Colección de tipos cubanos. Havana: Imprenta y Papelería de Barcina, 1852.

García, Domitila. *Album poético-fotográfico de las escritoras cubanas*. Second edition. Havana: Imprenta Militar de la Viuda de Soler y Ca., 1872.

Gilbert, Sandra M., and Susan Gubar. *The Madwoman in the Attic: The Woman Writer and the Nineteenth-Century Literary Imagination*. New Haven and London: Yale University Press, 1979.

Gilman, Sander L. *Difference and Pathology: Stereotypes of Sexuality, Race, and Madness*. Ithaca: Cornell University Press, 1985.

Gómez de Avellaneda, Gertrudis. *Obras de Avellaneda: Poesías líricas*. Havana: Imprenta de Aurelio Miranda, 1914.

González, Reynaldo. *Contradanzas y latigazos*. Havana: Ed. Letras Cubanas,

1983.

González Echevarría, Roberto. *Alejo Carpentier: The Pilgrim at Home*. Ithaca: Cornell University Press, 1977.

———. *Myth and Archive: A Theory of Latin American Narrative*. Cambridge and New York: Cambridge University Press, 1990.

González del Valle, José Zacarías. *La vida literaria en Cuba, 1836–1840*. Havana: Secretaría de Educación y Cultura, 1938.

Guerra y Sánchez, Ramiro. *Manual de historia de Cuba (económica, social y política)*. Havana: Cultural, S.A., 1938.

Guicharnaud-Tollis, Michèle. *Regards sur Cuba au XIXᵉ siècle: Témoignages européens*. Paris: Editions l'Harmattan, 1996.

Henríquez Ureña, Max. *Panorama histórico de la literatura cubana*. New York: Las Americas Publishing Company, 1963.

Heredia, José María. *Poesías completas*. Havana: Municipio de la Habana, 1940.

Herrera y Tordesillas, Antonio de. *Historia general de los hechos de los castellanos, en las islas, y tierra firme de el Mar Oceano*. Vols. I and II. Asunción del Paraguay: Ed. Guaranía, 1944–1945 (1726–1730).

Hirsch, Marianne. *The Mother/Daughter Plot: Narrative, Psychoanalysis, Feminism*. Bloomington: Indiana University Press, 1989.

Humboldt, Alexander von. *Personal Narrative of Travels to the Equinoctial Regions of the New Continent During the Years 1799–1804*. Paris: 1807.

———. *The Island of Cuba*. Tr. J. S. Thrasher. Rpt. New York: Negro Universities Press, 1969.

———. *Ensayo político sobre la isla de Cuba*. Prologue by Fernando Ortiz. First edition 1826. Havana: Publicaciones del Archivo Nacional, 1960.

Ibarra, Jorge. *Nación y cultura nacional*. Havana: Editorial Letras Cubanas, 1981.

Informe fiscal sobre Fomento de la poblacion blanca en la Isla de Cuba y Emancipacion progresiva de la esclava. Madrid: Imprenta de J. Martín Alegría, 1845.

Jaruco, Conde de San Juan de. *Historia de familias cubanas*. Volume I. Havana: Ed. Hércules, 1940.

Jensen, Larry R. *Children of Colonial Despotism: Press, Politics, and Culture in Cuba, 1790–1840*. Tampa: University of South Florida Press, 1988.

Keller, Evelyn Fox. *Reflections on Gender and Science*. New Haven: Yale University Press, 1985.

Kimball, Richard B. *Cuba, and the Cubans*. New York: S. Hueston, 1850.

Kirkpatrick, Susan. *Las románticas: Women Writers and Subjectivity in Spain, 1835–1850*. Berkeley: University of California Press, 1989.

Knight, Franklin W. *Slave Society in Cuba During the Nineteenth Century*. Madison: University of Wisconsin Press, 1970.

Lezama Lima, José. *Las eras imaginarias*. Madrid: Ed. Fundamentos, 1971.

Luis, William. *Literary Bondage: Slavery in Cuban Narrative*. Austin: University of Texas Press, 1990.

Mansion, J. E. *Harper's Modern College French and English Dictionary*. New York: Charles Scribner's Sons, 1940 (rev. 1967).

Marinello, Juan. *Americanismo y Cubanismo literarios. Ensayo en Marcos Antilla, cuentos de Cañaveral por Luis Felipe Rodríguez*. Havana: Ed. Hermes, n.d.

Marrero, Leví. *Cuba: economía y sociedad*, vols. 9, 13–14. Madrid: Ed. Playor, 1983, 1986.

Masiello, Francine. *Between Civilization and Barbarism: Women, Nation, and Literary Culture in Modern Argentina*. Lincoln and London: University of Nebraska Press, 1992.

Milan Women's Bookstore Collective. *Sexual Difference: A Theory of Social-Symbolic Practice*. Bloomington: Indiana University Press, 1990.

Miller, Alice. *The Drama of the Gifted Child*. Tr. Ruth Ward. New York: Basic Books, 1981.

Mink, Louis O. *Historical Understanding*. Ed. Brian Fay, Eugene O. Golob, and Richard T. Vann. Ithaca: Cornell University Press, 1987.

Molloy, Sylvia. *At Face Value: Autobiographical Writing in Spanish America*. Cambridge and New York: Cambridge University Press, 1991.

Monte, Domingo del. . *Biblioteca cubana. Lista cronologica de los libros inéditos e impresos que se han escrito sobre la isla de Cuba y de los que hablan de la misma desde su descrubimiento y conquista hasta nuestros días, formada en Paris en 1846*. Havana: Establecimiento Tipográfico de la Viuda de Soler, 1882.

———. *Centón epistolario de Domingo del Monte*. Ed. Domingo Figarola-Caneda. Havana: Imprenta "El Siglo XX," 1926.

Moreno Fraginals, Manuel. *El ingenio. Complejo económico social cubano del azúcar*. Three volumes. Havana: Ed. de Ciencias Sociales, 1978.

———. *The Sugar Mill: The Socioeconomic Complex of Sugar in Cuba, 1760–1860*. Tr. Cedric Belfrage. New York: Monthly Review Press, 1976.

Palma, Ramón de. *Cuentos cubanos*. Havana: Cultural, S. A. 1928.

Paquette, Robert L. *Sugar Is Made with Blood: The Conspiracy of La Escalera and the Conflict between Empires Over Slavery in Cuba*. Middletown, Conn.: Wesleyan University Press, 1988.

Paz, Octavio. *Puertas al campo*. Mexico City: UNAM, 1966.

———. *El laberinto de la soledad*. 7th ed. Mexico City: Fondo de Cultura Económica, 1969.

Pérez, Louis A., Jr. *Slaves, Sugar, and Colonial Society: Travel Accounts of Cuba, 1801–1899*. Wilmington, Del.: Scholarly Resources, 1992.

Pérez Firmat, Gustavo. *The Cuban Condition: Translation and Identity in Modern Cuban Literature*. Cambridge and New York: Cambridge University Press, 1989.

Porter, Dennis. *Haunted Journeys: Desire and Transgression in European Travel Writing*. Princeton: Princeton University Press, 1991.

Portuondo, José Antonio. *Capítulos de literatura cubana*. Havana: Ed. Letras Cubanas, 1981.

———. *Bosquejo histórico de las letras cubanas*. Havana: Ministerio de Relaciones Exteriores, 1960.

Pratt, Mary Louise. *Imperial Eyes: Travel Writing and Transculturation*. London and New York: Routledge, 1992.

Saco, José Antonio. *Mi primera pregunta: ¿La abolición de comercio de esclavos africanos arruinara o atrasara la agricultura cubana?* Madrid: Imprenta de Don Marcelo Calero, 1837.

————. *Examen analítico del informe de la comisión especial nombrada por las Cortes, sobre la esclusion de los actuales y futuros diputados de Ultramar, y sobre la necesidad de regir aquellos paises por leyes especiales.* Madrid: Oficina de D. Tomas Jordan, 1837.

————. *La supresión del trafico de esclavos africanos en la isla de Cuba. Examinada con relación a su agricultura y seguridad.* Paris: Imprenta de Panckouke, 1843.

————. *Ideario reformista.* Havana: Secretaría de Educación, 1935.

Saint-Pierre, Jacques Henri Bernardin de. *Paul and Virginia.* Tr. John Donovan. London and Boston: Peter Owen, 1982.

Santa Cruz y Mallén, Francisco Xavier de. *Historia de familias cubanas,* vol. II. Havana: Ed. Hercules, 1942.

Sarduy, Severo. *De donde son los cantantes.* 2nd. ed. México: Joaquín Mortiz, 1970.

————. *La simulación.* Caracas: Monte Avila, 1982.

Scott, Joan W. *Gender and the Politics of History.* New York: Columbia University Press, 1988.

Smith, Sidonie. *A Poetics of Women's Autobiography: Marginality and the Fictions of Self-Representation.* Bloomington: Indiana University Press, 1987.

Sommer, Doris. *Foundational Fictions: The National Romances of Latin America.* Berkeley: University of California Press, 1991.

Suárez y Romero, Anselmo. *Colección de artículos.* Havana: Consejo Nacional de Cultura, 1963.

Suchlicki, Jaime. *Historical Dictionary of Cuba.* Metuchen, N.J.: The Scarecrow Press, 1988.

Thomas, Hugh. *Cuba: The Pursuit of Freedom.* New York: Harper & Row, 1971.

Turnbull, David. *Travels in the West: Cuba; With Notices of Porto Rico and the Slave Trade.* London: Longman, Orme, Brown, Green and Longmans, 1840.

Villaverde, Cirilo. *La joven de la flecha de oro y otros relatos.* Ed. Imeldo Alvárez. Havana: Editorial Letras Cubanas, 1984.

————. *Excursión a Vuelta Abajo.* Havana: Imprenta "El Pilar" de Manuel de Armas, 1891.

————. *Excursión a Vuelta Abajo*: A. M. Eligio de la Puente, Introduction to *Dos Amores* by Cirilo Villaverde. Havana: Cultural, S. A., 1930.

————. *Cecilia Valdés; or Angel's Hill (A Novel of Cuban Customs).* Tr. Sydney G. Gest. New York: Vantage Press, 1962.

Vitier, Cintio. *Lo cubano en la poesía.* Santa Clara: Universidad Central de Las Villas, 1958.

von Hagen, Victor Wolfgang. *South America Called Them; Explorations of the Great Naturalists: La Condamine, Humboldt, Darwin, Spruce.* New York: Alfred A. Knopf, 1945.

Articles

Aldaraça, Bridget. "El ángel del hogar: The Cult of Domesticity in Nineteenth-Century Spain." In *Theory and Practice of Feminist Literary Criticism,* ed. Gabriela Mora and Karen S. Van Hooft, 62–87. Ypsilanti, Mich.: Bilingual Press/Editorial Bilingüe, 1982.

Anonymous. "El velorio." *La Cartera Cubana* 2 (January 1839): 47–51.

Anonymous. "Sobre la educación. Carta tercera." *La Moda ó el Recreo Semanal del Bello Sexo* (May 31, 1831): 370–72.

Benítez Rojo, Antonio. "Power/Sugar/Literature: Towards a Reinterpretation of Cubanness." *CSEC* 16 (1986): 9–31.

Berg, Mary. "Rereading Fiction by 19th Century Latin American Women Writers: Interpretation and Translation of the Past into the Present." In *Translating Latin America: Culture as Text*, ed. William Luis and Julio Rodríguez Luis, 127–33. Binghamton: SUNY Press, 1991.

Betancourt, José Victoriano. "Velar el mondongo." *La Cartera Cubana* (December 1838): 363–68.

Bhabha, Homi K. "Signs Taken for Wonders: Questions of Ambivalence and Authority Under a Tree Outside Delhi, May 1817." In *"Race," Writing and Difference*, ed. Henry Louis Gates, Jr., 163–84. Chicago: University of Chicago Press, 1986.

———. "DissemiNation: Time, Narrative and the Margins of the Modern Nation." In *Nation and Narration*, ed. Homi K. Bhabha, 291–322. London and New York: Routledge, 1990.

———. "Of Mimicry and Man: The Ambivalence of Colonial Discourse." In *The Location of Culture*, 85–92. London and New York: Routledge, 1994.

Bueno, Salvador. "Tema negro en las letras de Cuba hasta fines del siglo XIX." In *Orbita de José Antonio Fernández de Castro*, ed. Salvador Bueno, 156–93. Havana: UNEAC Contemporáneos, 1966.

Cixous, Hélène. "The Laugh of the Medusa." In *New French Feminisms: An Anthology*, ed. Elaine Marks and Isabelle de Courtivron, 245–64. New York: Schocken Books, 1981.

Delfino, Silvia. "Conversar, escribir: dos tramas de un secreto." In Carmen Berenguer, Eugenia Brito, Diamela Eltit, Raquel Olea, Eliana Ortega, and Nelly Richard, *Escribir en los bordes: Congreso internacional de literatura femenina latinoamericana, 1987*, 117–26. Santiago de Chile: Ed. Cuarto Propio, 1990.

Echeverría, José Antonio. "Estudios históricos: Diego Velázquez." *El Plantel* 1 (1838): 15–20.

Franco, Jean. "Un viaje poco romántico: Viajeros británicos hacia Sudamérica: 1818–1828." *Escritura* 4: 7 (1979): 129–42.

García, Enildo A. "Cartas de Domingo del Monte a Alexander H. Everett." *Revista de Literatura Cubana* 7: 13 (July–December 1989): 105–48.

González del Valle, Francisco. "Luz, Saco y del Monte ante la esclavitud negra. Cinco cartas inéditas de Félix Tanco y Bosmeniel a D. del Monte relativas a la propaganda abolicionista inglesa." *RBC* 47 (1941): 190–96.

González Echevarría, Roberto. Introduction to Alejo Carpentier, *Los pasos perdidos*. Madrid: Ed. Cátedra, 1985.

Gugelberger, Georg M. "Decolonizing the Canon: Considerations of Third World Literature." *New Literary History* 22: 3 (Summer 1991): 505–24.

J. M. de A. "Hernan Cortés." *El Plantel* 1 (1838): 158–61.

Leante, César. "*Cecilia Valdés*: Espejo de la esclavitud." In *El espacio real*, 27–42. Havana: UNEAC Contemporáneos, 1975.

Martí, José. "Nuestra America." In *Literatura hispanoamericana—una antología*, ed. David William Foster, 453–61. New York: Garland, 1994.

Méndez Rodenas, Adriana. "Identity and Incest in Cecilia Valdés: Villaverde and the Origin(s) of the Text." CSEC 24 (1994): 83–104.

Morales, [Antonio Bachiller y]. "Varios sobre Saco." Manuscript Collection, Morales #16, nos. 1–10. Havana: Biblioteca Nacional José Martí.

Naranjo Orovio, Carmen, and Miguel Angel Puig-Samper Mulero. "El legado hispano y la conciencia nacional en Cuba." *Revista de Indias* 50, no. 190 (September–December 1990): 789–808.

Olivares, Jorge. "Otra vez *Cecilia Valdés*: Arenas con(tra) Villaverde." *Hispanic Review* 62/2 (Spring 1994): 169–84.

Palma, Ramón de. "Don Francisco de Arango." *El Plantel* 1 (1838): 44–54.

———. "Introducción a *El espetón de oro* de Villaverde." *El Album* 4 (1838): 5–11.

———. "La novela." *El Album* 1 (1838): 5–35.

Pratt, Mary Louise. "Scratches on the Face of the Country, or, What Mr. Barrow Saw in the Land of the Bushmen." *Critical Inquiry* 12/1 (Autumn 1985): 119–43.

———. "Humboldt y la reinvención de América." *Nuevo Texto Crítico* I, no. 1 (1988): 35–53.

Randall, Margaret. "Appropriate(d) Discourse: Plagiarism and Decolonization." *New Literary History* 22/3 (Summer 1991): 525–41.

Sarduy, Severo. "Tu dulce nombre halagará mi oído. In *Homenaje a Gertrudis Gómez de Avellaneda: Memorias del simposio en el centenario de su muerte*, ed. Rosa M.Cabrera and Gladys B. Zaldívar. Miami: Ediciones Universal, 1981.

Slovic, Scott. "Alexander von Humboldt's Comparative Method of Landscape Description." *Publications of the Society for Literature and Science* 5: 3 (May 1990): 4–10.

Sommer, Doris. "Irresistible Romance: The Foundational Fictions of Latin America." In *Nation and Narration*, ed. Homi K. Bhabha, 71–98. London and New York: Routledge, 1990.

Suárez-Murias, Marguerite C. "Cuba Painted by the Cubans: The Nineteenth Century Journalistic Essay." In *Essays on Hispanic Literature—Ensayos de literatura hispana: A Bilingual Anthology*, 47–66. Washington, D.C.: University Press of America, 1982.

Tanco y Bosmeniel, Félix. "Escenas de la vida privada en la isla de Cuba: Petrona y Rosalía." *Cuba Contemporánea* 39, no. 156 (December 1925): 255–88.

Villaverde, Cirilo. "Amorios y contratiempos de un guajiro." *La Cartera Cubana* II (1839): 229–38.

———. "Escursion [sic] a Vuelta Abajo." *El Album* 6–8 (1838–1839): 11–46, 89–108.

INDEX

on *lejanía*, 6, 221, 223–24, 226,
245n.22; *Lo cubano en la poesía*,
217–20, 287n.7
Vives, Captain-General Dionisio,
56, 174
voice, Merlin as, 84–87, 101–2, 223,
288n.19, 288n.20

white immigration, 151, 152,
157–58, 163
women, Creole, 15–16; and children's education, 205–7; vs.

European women, 187, 281n.4;
and the feminine ideal, 200,
207–9, 286n.67, 286n.70; and
marriage, 187, 200, 202–5;
modesty of, 200–202, 284n.40;
physical and spiritual traits of,
193–95; Tanco y Bosmeniel on,
95–96, 188, 197
women's histories, 3, 5–13; the "her-
story approach" in, 8

Zambrana, Antonio, 140, 270n.63

Adriana Méndez Rodenas is associate professor of Spanish and comparative literature at the University of Iowa. She is also the author of *Severo Sarduy: el neobarroco de la transgresión*, which won the National Literary Essay Prize from the Mexican Fine Arts Institute.

GENDER AND NATIONALISM IN COLONIAL CUBA

was composed electronically using
Janson Text type faces with displays in Copperplate and Stuyvesant.
The book was printed on 60# Booktext Natural acid-free paper,
and was Smyth sewn and cased in Pearl Linen cloth
by BookCrafters.
The dust jacket was printed in three colors by
Vanderbilt University Printing Services.
Book and dust jacket designs are the work of Tom Ventress.
Published by Vanderbilt University Press
Nashville, Tennessee 37235